D1193980

Africa
in the United Nations
System

Africa
in the United Nations
System

Wellington W. Nyangoni

Rutherford ● Madison ● Teaneck
Fairleigh Dickinson University Press
London and Toronto: Associated University Presses

Associated University Presses
440 Forsgate Drive
Cranbury, NJ 08512

Associated University Presses
25 Sicilian Avenue
London WC1A 2QH, England

Associated University Presses
2133 Royal Windsor Drive
Unit 1
Mississauga, Ontario
Canada L5J 1K5

Library of Congress Cataloging in Publication Data

Nyangoni, Wellington Winter.
    Africa in the United Nations system.

    Bibliography: p.
    Includes index.
    1. United Nations–Africa. 2. Africa–Foreign
relations–1960-   . 3. Africa–Politics and govern-
ment–1960-   . 4. Organization of Africa Unity.
I. Title.
JX1977.2.A4N9 1985   341.23′6   82-71565
ISBN 0-8386-3118-5

Printed in the United States of America

Dedication

Kuna Amai vangu
Runia Rusere na Ambuya va Andamukanei Rusere.

Contents

Tables

Acknowledgments

In writing this book, I came to rely on the works of a wide range of committees, organizations, and individuals who painstakingly developed their research and offered insights on the behavior of Africans at the United Nations. The bibliography and footnotes in this book reveal some meager indication in this regard. At a more personal level, I have enjoyed the friendship of many African delegates to the United Nations, officers of the Organization of African Unity at the United Nations, and numerous international civil servants at the United Nations headquarters in New York City who helped me gain a better understanding of the intricate and complex operation of the United Nations system. Although it is impossible for me to name all of these individuals, I would like to acknowledge my colleagues at Wagner College, Staten Island, New York, and at Brandeis University, in particular, Dr. Jack S. Goldstein, the former dean of Faculty. I would like also to recognize the encouragement I received from Dr. Winston Langley of Boston State College. Every chapter in the book has benefited in some way from the comments of my cousin, Dr. Vincent Vera, and the administrative secretary of the African and Afro-American Studies, Mrs. Yvette Dudley of Brandeis University. Although I have received assistance from these many sources, the work, views, and any errors that it contains are, of course, my own responsibility.

Of the many librarians who gave me their patient help, special mention must be made of the United Nations Library, the Howard University Library, and the Goldfarb Library at Brandeis University. I wish to acknowledge the United Nations and the Organization of African Unity's permission to use their resolutions, documents, and publications in the production of this work.

Wellington Winter Nyangoni, Ph.D.
African and Afro-American Studies
   Department
Brandeis University
Waltham, Massachusetts

Introduction

Africa and the United Nations system is a study of the activities of African States within the United Nations Organization (UNO) and its numerous organs, structures, committees, and specialized agencies. By the term United Nations system, we refer to all parts of the UNO that are concerned with promoting the economic, political, social, nutritional, medical, and social goals embedded in the United Nations Charter. In the context of the UN Charter, the term *organization* is applied to the United Nations as a political, juridical, and administrative entity with its own membership. In this sense, the relationship between the United Nations and its agencies have a defined legal framework. This constitutional framework has enabled the UN General Assembly to create many agencies of the United Nations that fifty-one African states are using for the economic and social betterment of Africa.

The decision-making process of the UNO is decentralized throughout the agencies of the UN system. Functionally speaking, the UN system was set up as a kind of loose confederation of international agencies. Some of the articles of the UN Charter that outline the dejure and de facto framework of relations between the UNO and its specialized agencies are:

Article 17, paragraph 3: The General Assembly "shall examine the administrative budgets of such specialized agencies with a view to making recommendations to the agencies concerned."

Article 57, paragraph 1: "the Various specialized agencies ... shall be brought into relationship with the United Nations in accordance with the provisions of Article 63."

Article 57, paragraph 2: "Such agencies thus brought into relationship with the United Nations are hereinafter referred to as specialized agencies."

Article 58: "The Organization shall make recommendations for the coordination of the policies and activities of the specialized agencies."

Article 60: "authority for international economic and social cooperation is vested 'under the authority of the General Assembly in the Economic and Social Council'."

Article 62, paragraph 1: "enables the Economic and Social Council (ECOSOC) to make recommendations to the specialized agencies."

Article 63, paragraph 5: ECOSOC "may coordinate the activities of the specialized agencies through consultations with and recommendations to the General Assembly and to the Members of the United Nations."

By being members of the United Nations and by participating in initiating resolutions and adopting them, African states have joined the community of nations that is responsible for the present legal norms of the UN system.

Through the legal framework of the UN system, African UN member states are now involved in the peaceful settlement of international conflicts through negotiations, and in shaping new codes of international law and diplomacy. The African member states also participate in the proceedings of the International Court of Justice. Although the UN system does not have coercive powers of disciplining states that violate international legal norms of behavior, its moral influence as an international legal restraint should not be minimized. Condemnations by the General Assembly, Security Council, and UN specialized agencies of the use of force as a means to resolve conflicts among nations has, to a degree, restrained military aggression among African and non-African States. International conferences through the UN system have made it legally and morally imperative for people to talk about the laws of the seas, disposal of hazardous wastes, decolonization, apartheid, international piracy, and a host of other related issues.

Fifty-one African states, which are now an integral part of the United Nations Organization, serve in all its organs and specialized agencies. The United Nations system provides an important functional diplomatic arena for the African states. The more powerful the UNO becomes, the more African states and other nations will use it for resolving disputes and conflicts within the international community. The United Nations is, therefore, an important channel through which African states can actively participate in the conduct of international diplomacy and world politics.

Today, many people are of the opinion that the United Nations has failed to fulfill the objectives of its Charter. It has failed, people say, in its central role of keeping world peace and decolonization. The United Nations has become little more than a debating chamber, dominated by poverty-stricken, small, Third World nations, where demagogues and hotheads ferociously abuse each other, and where nothing effective gets accomplished. Others are of the opinion that whereas we have to have the United Nations, the existing organization is largely irrelevant to present needs, and is of little importance in relation to more potent factors in world politics—superpower diplomacy, the multinational corporation, and regional communities, such as the Organization of American States (OAS), the Organization of African Unity (OAU), North Atlantic Treaty Organization (NATO), European Economic Community (EEC), Warsaw Pact, and the Arab League. It is also important to note that other people merely take the United Nations for granted and do not attribute anything to it.

Although there are varied views about the United Nations, it appears that a consensus on two issues is observable. A few people have not the slightest or haziest idea of what the United Nations does or does not do. Others are opposed to the United Nations because African, Asian, Caribbean, and Latin American states constitute a majority in the General assembly. As a region, Africa has the largest number of states that are members of the United Nations. It is these additions to the

UN system of intergovernmental organizations that opponents of the less developed countries (LDCs) claim have made the United Nations less and less effective as matrixes for international cooperation, particularly in regard to problems in which substantial interests of the Organization of Economic Developed Countries (OECD) are directly or indirectly involved. Some of the OECD leaders, who are critical of the new LDCs majority in the United Nations, state that one of the main causes of the current troubles is an apparent difference of aim and purpose between the founder members of the United Nations and those of newly independent African, Asian, and Caribbean states, which have elected to join the United Nations Organization.

The admission of large numbers of new members from Africa and the rest of the Third World has led to demands that the United Nations involve itself more substantively in the process of economic development. As a result, the United Nations system has assumed new responisbilities and mandates mostly subsumed under the rubric of a New International Economic Order (NIEO). New agencies and structures have been created for carrying out new responsibilities. The proliferation of new agencies and the resort to new mechanisms for dealing with issues concerning the NIEO has created problems of coordination within the UN system and friction between the LDCs and OECD. The problems encountered deal with maintaining political neutrality among UN civil servants, the fluctuating nature of their functions, and the employment and staffing plans to fill openings in agencies of the United Nations Organization. Demands that more Africans be employed and promoted to the top echelons on the UN Civil Service run counter to the Western view of political impartiality and independence of international staffs. African states are among the UN members that feel that the secretariats of the specialized agencies should have people who are ideologically sympathetic to the political and economic aspirations of the LDCs–particularly those advocated by the NIEO.

The NIEO wants the present world economic system rearranged in such a way to make African states and other LDCs have sovereignty over their minerals and raw materials and be able to get a fair price for the sale of their products. Differences exist between the OECD and the LDCs in perceptions concerning the need for, and even the legitimacy of, the NIEO. Some view the NIEO as a threat to the free-market system, others as a temporary corrective measure, whereas others see it as a fundamental and necessary instrument for the restructuring of the entire economic system. Responsibility for undertaking appropriate measures through the United Nations Conference on Trade and Development (UNCTAD) and other agencies of the United Nations is disputed. The importance of African states to the NIEO is that they have religiously advocated for its implementation at North and South Dialogues, United Nations seminars, conferences, and meetings of the nonaligned countries.

Whereas the African states are making the UN General Assembly sensitive and responsive to their interests, these countries are also consolidating their power base by enlisting as members of the numerous UNO organs and units. The reason is that if these countries are represented in various UN bodies, their interests will always be given greatest consideration. Whereas the Organization of African Unity states is recognized as the most influential group on issues concerning decolonization, racism, and economic development within the General Assembly, these countries realize that if they are to succeed in their objectives, they have to work closely with other UN member states. The increase of African states membership into the United Nations from four (Egypt, Ethiopia, Liberia, and South Africa) in 1945 to fifty-one in 1981 is of great importance to Africa's role within the UN system. Whereas the continued increase of the membership and influence of African states enhances the status and importance of Africa within the United Nations and particularly in the General Assembly, where a simple majority is needed to pass some of the resolutions, individually, the African states remain weak. The OAU states may not always be able to get what they themselves propose, but they have the capability to block passage of a resolution to which they object. Within the Security Council, the OAU member states do not have a single member state that has the right to exercise a veto to any resolution inimical to African interests in the Security Council. What this implies is that, whereas the African states are influential in the General Assembly, they do have minimal influence in the Security Council. To this extent African states have to cooperate with permanent members of the Security Council to get a sympathetic understanding of their needs and problems. It can also equally be argued that if the OECD members of the Security Council need the LDCs or the General Assembly to take decisions favorable to their views, cooperation with the QAU states is definitely a prerequisite.

Because of the phenomenal changes it has undergone, the UNO of 1982 is in many ways a different organization from what it was in 1945. At the inauguration of the United Nations, its charter was based on the assumption that on matters directly affecting their individual interests the permanent members of the Security Council would be able to prevent UN action through the use of individual or collective vetos. The common belief of consensus among the permanent members of the Security Council has remained a dream. Cold war conflicts over East and West Germany, Congo (Zaire), Angola, Ethiopia, Somalia, the Middle East, Cuba, Vietnam, Cambodia, and Afghanistan have undermined collective UN action to resolve the conflicts peacefully. Before 1960, the United Nations was heavily influenced by the United States of America, which had the largest single bloc of votes in the General Assembly. On issues where the United States differed with the Soviet Union, the United States had support from its NATO allies and the Organization of American States (OAS). Of the fifty original members of the UNO who signed its charter, 40 per cent were members of the OAS. Because of its political, economic, military, technological, and leadership dominance of the OAS, the United States became the most influential country within the United Nations system.

Today, the numerical dominance of the OAS and Western European countries in the General Assembly has been eclipsed by the admission into that body of new African, Asian, and Caribbean states. Recognizing the changes that have occurred within the United Nations, many states want it restructured to reflect the changes brought about by the independence of many Third World nations. At the center of discussion is what kind of United Nations do the African states want. Given the fact that there are ideological, as well as other political, religious, and economic differences among the OAU states, how can they work collaboratively to effect changes in the United Nations? Are the common problems of racism, decolonization, and the declarations of the NIEO sufficient enough for the African countries to continue operating as a united front? Taking into consideration that the African oil-producing countries are getting richer and richer and those LDCs without oil are getting poorer and poorer, what is the basis available for coordinated African policies at the United Nations? The issues raised concerning African activities and influence in the UN system constitute the subject matter of this book.

Africa
in the United Nations
System

1
Africa and the Evolution of the United Nations System

Any comprehensive consideration of world politics has to take into account the activities of African states within the United Nations system. African states are now part and parcel of the United Nations system. Through the United Nations Organization, African countries have joined other member states who are interested in reducing political tensions and conflicts among states, solving international disputes through peaceful means, supporting the right to national self-determination and independence for all colonized people, fostering peaceful and fraternal relations among the nations of the world, encouraging economic cooperation between the less developed countries (LDCs) and the Organization of Economically Developed Countries (OECD) through the framework of the New International Economic Order (NIEO), and raising the standard of living of the poor peoples of the LDCs. As members of the United Nations, African states are now involved with international issues that affect all peoples of the world. By being an integral part of the United Nations system, African states share in the success and failures of the United Nations Organization. Through participation in all of the bodies, organs, and the specialized agencies of the United Nations, African states are part of the UN diplomatic and legal system.

One of the most notable aspects of the evolution of the United Nations has been the immense increase in its membership. Newly independent African states have contributed the largest number of these new members. Total membership of the UNO has jumped from 51 in 1946 to 154 in 1981. In the same period, the number of African states in the United Nations increased from 4 to 51. (See Table 1).

The results of the increase of African membership in the United Nations have been mutually beneficial. The new African, Asian, and Caribbean states, by virtue of their majority in the United Nations and their numerous concerns and preoccupations have added new business and dynamism to the entire operation of the United Nations system. The United Nations has, in turn, acted as a magnet to African states that were overly zealous to set the seal of recognition to their independence through acceptance as full-fledged members of the United Nations Organization.

19

Table 1:   List of Independent African States and the Dates on Which They Were Admitted

Country	Date of Admission to the UNO	Date of Independence
Algeria	8 October 1962	3 July 1962
Angola	1 December 1976	11 November 1975
Benin	20 September 1960	1 August 1960
Botswana	17 October 1966	30 September 1966
Burundi	18 September 1962	30 June 1962
Cameroon	20 September 1960	1 January 1960
Cape Verde	16 September 1975	5 July 1975
Central African Republic	20 September 1960	13 August 1960
Chad	20 September 1960	11 August 1960
Comoros	12 November 1975	1 January 1976
Congo	20 September 1960	15 August 1960
Djibouti	20 September 1977	27 June 1977
Egypt	24 October 1945*	1 March 1922
Equatorial Guinea	12 November 1968	12 October 1968
Ethiopia	13 November 1945*	11th Century B.C.
Gabon	20 September 1960	17 August 1960
Gambia	21 September 1965	18 February 1965
Ghana	8 March 1957	6 March 1957
Guinea	12 December 1958	2 October 1958
Guinea-Bissau	17 September 1974	24 September 1973
Ivory Coast	20 September 1960	7 August 1960
Kenya	16 December 1963	12 December 1963
Lesotho	17 October 1966	4 October 1966
Liberia	2 November 1945*	26 July 1847
Libya	14 December 1955	24 December 1951
Madagascar	20 September 1960	26 June 1960
Malawi	1 December 1964	6 July 1964
Mali	28 September 1960	22 September 1960
Mauritania	27 October 1961	28 November 1960
Mauritius	24 April 1968	12 March 1968
Morocco	12 November 1956	2 March 1956
Mozambique	16 September 1975	25 June 1975
Niger	20 September 1960	3 August 1960
Nigeria	7 October 1960	1 October 1960
Rwanda	18 September 1962	1 July 1962
Sao Tome and Principe	16 September 1975	12 July 1975
Senegal	28 September 1960	20 August 1960
Seychelles	21 September 1976	29 June 1976
Sierra Leone	27 September 1961	27 April 1961
Somalia	20 September 1960	1 July 1960
South Africa	7 November 1945*	31 May 1910
Sudan	12 November 1956	1 January 1956
Swaziland	24 September 1968	6 September 1968
Togo	20 September 1960	27 April 1960
Tunisia	12 November 1956	20 March 1956
Uganda	25 October 1962	9 October 1962
United Republic of Tanzania	14 December 1961	9 December 1961
Upper Volta	20 September 1960	5 August 1960
Zaire	20 September 1960	30 June 1960
Zambia	1 December 1964	24 October 1964
Zimbabwe	25 August 1980	18 April 1980

Source: Extracted from the United Nations Press Release: Department of Public Information, Press Sector (New York; United Nations, September 16, 1980). Information on dates of independence of some African countries were compiled by Mrs. Yvette Dudley of the African and Afro-American Studies Department, Brandeis University.
* Indicates the original members of the United Nations Organization.

Most of the African states are politically, militarily, and economically weak. Membership in the United Nations not only provides them with a forum through which they can participate in world diplomacy but also enables them to bring to the attention of other member states their problems of decolonization, racism, economic development, and the amicable resolution of international conflicts. In addition to offering them the most convenient arena to coordinate their policies, the United Nations offers the African states a podium to submit for consideration their policies and political points of view they otherwise might not be able to place effectively before the world community of nations. Furthermore, African states view the UNO and its Charter as being indispensable to the preservation of their independence and also as an instrument through which colonialism can be eliminated.

The UN Charter, which was designed to be a foundation for a global restructuring of interstate relationships, has over the years become the testament of faith and a documentary confirmation of the legitimacy of African nationalist aspirations. In addition to ensuring the preservation of international peace and security, African, Asian, and other small Third World powers view the United Nations as an organization concerned with the attainment of human rights by all mankind. For the African states (with the exception of the Republic of South Africa), the UN Charter has become a kind of documentary expression of natural law and a global bill of human rights for the underprivileged, decolonized, and economically underdeveloped. The Afro-Asian documentary reaffirmation of faith in the fundamental human rights, in the dignity and worth of human persons, and in the equal rights of men and women of nations large and small was the basis upon which the Bandung Conference (attended by African and Asian states) declared the following.

> The Asian-African Conference declared its full support of the fundamental principles of Human Rights as set forth in the Charter of the United Nations and took note of the Universal Declaration of Human Rights as a common standard of achievement for all peoples and all nations.
> The Conference declared its full support for the principles of self-determination of peoples and nations as set forth in the Charter of the United Nations and took note of the United Nations resolutions on the rights of peoples and nations to self-determination, which is a prerequisite of the full enjoyment of all fundamental Human Rights.[1]

To enhance our understanding of the activities and the behavior of African states at the United Nations, it is necessary that we give a brief discussion of how the organs of the United Nations operate.

Organs of the UN System

The name United Nations was first used by President Franklin D. Roosevelt in the Declaration by United Nations of January 1, 1942, when representatives of twenty-six nations pledged to continue their war against Germany and its allies. The UN Charter was drawn up by the representatives of fifty nations at the UN Conference that met in San Francisco from April 25 to June 26, 1945. The United Nations officially came into existence on October 24, 1945, when the UN Charter was ratified by Great Britain, the United States of America, the USSR, France, and China, and a majority of the other fifty signatories.

Article 1 of the UN Charter stated that the purposes and principles of the organization are:

1. To maintain international peace and security, and to that end: to take effective collective measures for the prevention and removal of threats to the peace, and for the suppression of acts of aggression or other breaches of the peace, and to bring about by peaceful means and in conformity with the principles of justice and international disputes or situations which might lead to a breach of the peace;

2. To develop friendly relations among nations based on respect for the principle of equal rights and self-determination of peoples, and to take other appropriate measures to strengthen universal peace;

3. To be a center for harmonizing the actions of nations in the attainment of these common ends.[2]

Pertaining to the structure of the United Nations, Article 7 of the Charter stated that:

1. These are established as the principal organs of the United Nations: a General Assembly, a Security Council, an Economic and Social Council, a Trusteeship Council, an International Court of Justice, and a Secretariat.

2. Such subsidiary organs as may be found necessary may be established in accordance with the present Charter.[3]

The United Nations General Assembly is comprised of all the member states. Each state is limited to, at most, five representatives in the General Assembly. Each country makes its own decisions as to how it chooses its own UN representatives. In the General Assembly, where African countries are among the most influential, each member state is allowed one vote. The functions of the General Assembly are:

To Consider and make recommendations on the principles of international cooperation in the maintenance of peace and security, including the principles governing disarmament and the regulation of armaments;

To Discuss any problem affecting peace and security and, except where a dispute or situation is currently being discussed by the Security Council, to make recommendations on it;

To Discuss and, with the same exception, to make recommendations on any question within the scope of the Charter or affecting the powers and functions of any organ of the United Nations;

To Initiate studies and make recommendations, promote international political cooperation, the development of international law and its codification, the realization of human rights and fundamental freedoms for all, and international collaboration in economic, social, cultural, educational and health fields;

To Receive and consider reports from the Security Council and other organs of the United Nations;

To Make recommendations from the peaceful settlement of any situation, regardless of origin, which might impair friendly relations among nations;

To Supervise, through the Trusteeship Council, the execution of the Trusteeship agreements for all areas not designed as strategic;

To Elect the non-permanent members of the Security Council, the members of the Trusteeship Council which are elected; to take part with the Security Council in the Election of Judges of the International Court of Justice; and, on the recommendation of the Security Council, to appoint the Secretary-General;

To Consider and approve the budget of the United Nations, to apportion the contributions among Members, and to examine the budgets of specialized agencies.[4]

The General Assembly normally meets once a year for about three months from September to December. In times of a crisis the period of meeting may be extended. The General Assembly begins each year with General Debate in plenary session. This is addressed by foreign ministers and occasionally by heads of states. After the UN General Assembly debates, the main committees begin to meet. Some of the chief subsidiary bodies and committees of the General Assembly are listed in Table 2.

Under the Charter of the United Nations, the General Assembly is the highest authority of the UN system. As the supreme political organ of the UN system, as the instrument that makes most of the major initiatives that are elaborated and followed up by the system's component parts, the General Assembly has always played a significant part in leading, and in a wider sense, in coordinating the policies and activities of the UN system.

The Security Council in which the African states have minimal influence is made up of five permanent members (Great Britain, the USSR, the United States, France, and China). The General Assembly also elects ten nonpermanent members into the Security Council for two-year terms. These ten members are not eligible for reelection immediately when their term of service in the Security Council elapses. Initially, the Security Council was composed of eleven numbers, but this figure was enlarged to fifteen when the UN Charter was amended in 1965. Only a permanent member of the Security Council has the right to veto any resolutions it considers inimical to its interests. According to the UN Charter, the functions of the Security Council are:

To Maintain international peace and security in accordance with the purposes and principles of the United Nations;

To Investigate any dispute or situation which might lead to international friction;

To Recommend methods of adjusting such disputes or terms of settlement;

To Formulate plans for the establishment of a system to regulate armaments;

Table 2: General Assembly: Chief Subsidiary Bodies and Committees

First Committee	General Committee	Peace Observance Commission
(Political and Security)	(25 members: president, 17 vice-presidents and committee chairman)	(14 members)
Special Political Committee		Committee on Peaceful Uses of Outer Space (28 members)
Second Committee (Economic and Financial)	Credentials Committee (9 members)	
Third Committee (Social, Humanitarian, and Cultural)		Committee on Peacekeeping (33 members)
Fourth Committee		Special Committee on Apartheid (11 members)
(Trust and Non-Self- Governing Territories)		Advisory Commission for UNRWA (9 members)
Fifth Committee		Commission for the Unification and Rehabilitation of Korea (7 members)
(Administrative and Budgetary)		
Sixth Committee (Legal)		Committee on Sanctions against Southern Rhodesia (7 members)
		Special Committee on the Implementation of the Declaration on Colonialism (24 members)
Economic and Social Council and its subsidiaries	Trusteeship Council	Scientific Advisory Committee (7 members)
	Council for Namibia	Committee on Contributions (12 members)
		Committee on Conferences (15 members)
		Advisory Committee of Administrative and Budgetary Questions (ACABQ) (14 members)

SOURCE: Evan Luard, *The United Nations: How It Works and What It Does* (London: Macmillan Co., 1979) and also cited in Martin Hill's book: *The United Nations System* (London: Cambridge University Press, 1978).

To Determine the existence of a threat to the peace or act of aggression and to recommend what action should be taken;

To Call on Members to apply economic sanctions and other measures not involving the use of force in order to prevent or stop aggression;

To Take Military Action against an aggressor;

To Recommend the admission of new Members and the terms on which states may become parties to the Statute of the International Court of Justice;

To Exercise the Trusteeship functions of the United Nations in strategic areas;

To Recommend to the General Assembly the appointment of the Secretary-General and, together with the General Assembly, to elect the judges of the International Court;

To Submit annual and special reports to the General Assembly.[5]

When the Security Council takes a decision in times of a crisis, it does so on behalf of all UN members who also agree to carry out its decisions and to undertake to make available to the council at its request armed forces and provide other assistances and facilities essential for the preservation and maintenance of international peace and security.

At the formation of the United Nations there was a general desire to avoid those mistakes that led to the failure of the League of Nations. People believed that there were four reasons that contributed to that failure. First, the League of Nations had no power of coercion: no armed force of its own that could be used to thwart aggression. Second, it lacked authority to impose collective decisions to defend a member state that was attacked. Third, it had been rendered ineffective by many centuries of hostilities among many European countries. Fourth, the absence of the USSR, United States, Germany, Japan, and Italy from the league made it unrepresentative and weak. The creation of the Security Council in the United Nations was regarded as a remedy to the enumerated problems.

Although the UNO has addressed these problems, the council remains partially representative. Since the establishment of the United Nations, its membership has trebled. What is more, there has been significant change in the representation of the United Nations as a result of the process of decolonization, which brought into its membership more than eighty additional sovereign nations. In the last three decades or so, the world has witnessed important changes in the international power structure: the emergence of nonaligned and developing nations as important actors in international affairs and the increased mutual interdependence of the OECD and LDCs. Given the changes that have occurred within the UN system, the Security Council permanent membership should reflect the diversity of the UN membership if it is to be a true representative of that international organization.

The supreme administrative and coordinating organ of the UN system is the

Secretariat headed by the secretary-general. To run the administration of the whole UN system, the secretary-general has available to him an international civil service. The UN civil servants work in multifaceted roles that are similar to those of a national civil service. Under-secretary-generals in the United Nations run whole departments and operate as assistants of the secretary-general. In addition, directors of divisions of departments and their assistants operate individual services as human rights, non-self-governing territories, social development, and various centers, institutions, sections, branches, and units into which departments are structured.

The Secretariats of the United Nations and the specialized agencies are important coordinating fixtures of the entire UN system.[6] Of signficant importance to the success of the coordination system is the role played by the United Nations Economic and Social Council (ECOSOC), which deals with economic and social activities of the UN system: Article 68 of the Charter empowers the ECOSOC to set up commissions in economic and social fields and for the promotion of human rights throughout the world, and such other commissions as may be necessary for maximizing its efficiency and functions. Presently the ECOSOC has four regional economic commissions: the Economic Commission for Europe (ECE) established in 1947, whose membership includes all European states, Canada, and the United States; the Economic Commission for Asia and the Far East (ECAFE) established in 1947, which comprises all Asian member states of the United Nations; the Economic Commission for Latin America (ECLA) established in 1948, composed of all Caribbean and Latin American states; and the Economic Commission for Africa (ECA) founded in 1958, which is entirely composed of African states. Through the activities of UNDP, UNIDO, CPC, ACAST, and CDP, the ECOSOC is deeply involved in UNCTAD conferences concerning the new economic international order.

In conclusion, the work of the secretary-general emanates from the Security Council, the General Assembly, ECOSOC, and issues arising from the office of the secretary-general and secretariats of the thirteen specialized agencies under the offices of the ACC. In addition, African states are members of and party to the overall structures and organs of the UN system. As organs of the United Nations have evolved and developed so have African members of the United Nations been integral to that development. Apart from their membership in all the agencies and bodies of the UN system, Africans are now to be found in the secretary-general's office working as international civil servants. African influences are now felt throughout the UN system.

African Influence in the United Nations

The decades of the 1950s and 1960s witnessed the admission into the United Nations Organization of many independent African states. Because of their numerical regional preponderance in the General Assembly, African states have assumed a new status within the United Nations system and the world community. These fifty-one states are extremely active in popularizing African issues in the General Assembly, the Security Council, the office of the Secretariat, the ECOSOC, and all the specialized agencies. The increased participation of African states in the activities of the United Nations system have additionally made it possible for the United Nations Organization to devote more time to the discussion and solution of African problems. One of the recent noticeable results of active participation of African states in the United Nations Organization and other international organizations is in the area of foreign intervention in African conflicts. Some of the conflicts in which foreign interventions have been minimal are The Nigerian Civil War; the Angolan Conflict; the Sudanese Civil War; and the Organization of African Unity's support for the liberation of Mozambique, Cape Verde, Guinea-Bissau, Zimbabwe, Angola, Namibia, and the Republic of South Africa.

Prior to 1960, African issues at the United Nations received very little attention within the UN system, which was dominated by the United States, and Western European colonial and capitalist interests. Cold war conflicts increased in the United Nations as the USSR-led Warsaw Pact countries challenged American hegemonic domination of the UN system. African interests in the United Nations were obviously the least of concern for Western Europe, the United States, and the Warsaw Pact countries. David Kay observed: "The United Nations has been created primarily through the efforts of states with a European or European dervied political and social culture, possessing a common history of political involvement at the international level. During its first ten years the Organization was dominated by the problems and conflicts of these same states."[7] In this respect, the founding fathers of the United Nations did not have the African continent as an important international region to consider in the preservation of international security and peace. Founding fathers viewed Africa as an appendage of Western European colonial powers. In a sense, a majority of the United Nations members generally assumed that European colonial powers were responsible for the maintenance of peace and security in Africa. Acknowledging this to have been the situation during the formative epoch of the United Nations, it is not surprising, that the Annual Report by Trygve Lie, the first United Nations general-secretary, contained only two sentences on Africa. After the admission into the UNO of more than eighteen African nations by 1960, the Annual Report of the then Secretary-General, Dag Hammarskjold, devoted 42 percent of its proceedings to African issues. Today, with fifty-one members of the United Nations being African nations, African issues of decolonization, political conflicts, economic development, and world peace and security are now commonplace within the UN system.

The presence of newly independent African and Asian and Caribbean states have brought about changes in the structured roles of the United Nations. The demands of these newly independent states have broadened the political, economic, and social horizons of the UNO. Instead of limiting itself to causes of conflict and the maintenance and preservation of international peace and security, the United Nations now concerns itself with issues ranging from decolonization to world hunger and the attainment of economic development of the LDCs. Additional changes in the United Nations Organization and its structure are coming from the nonaligned group of countries, the Group of 77, the Organization of African Unity, the Arab League, and the Organization of Oil Producing and Exporting Countries (OPEC). As a result of these changes taking place, the United Nations of 1982 is radically different from that of 1945. The United Nations of 1982 in which fifty-one African states are members and participating has dedicated itself to the attainment of freedom, equality, and independence by all colonized people throughout the world. On this basis, it can also be argued that whereas Africa has influenced the UN system in many aspects, the UN system has also contributed peace, decolonization, and economic development in Africa.

While recognizing the changes that African, Asian, and Caribbean newly independent states have brought about in the international political power structure, it is important not to overlook the fact that the nature and character of world politics in the post World War II era have been shaped by the two superpowers; the United States and the Soviet Union. The ideological hostility and competition between these nations brought about the cold war, which is still being fought in Europe, Africa, North America, South America, the Caribbean, Asia, and Australasia. The rivalry between these two superpowers has caused many countries to take sides with either the United States or the Soviet Union. The ideological differences were crystallized by the Truman Doctrine, which was promulgated in 1947. While reinforcing this view, David Horowitz quotes President Harry Truman to have stated the following:

> One way of life is based upon the will of the majority, and is distinguished by free institutions, representative government, free elections, guarantees of individual liberty, freedom of speech and religion and freedom from political repression.
> The second way of life is based upon the will of a minority forcibly imposed upon the majority. It relies upon terror and oppression, a controlled press and radio, fixed elections, and the suppression of personal freedom.[8]

The Truman Doctrine polarized and consecrated the ideological conflict between the United States and the Soviet Union. As the verbal or cold war between the two superpowers escalated and the United States adopted a policy of containing communism throughout the world, so did the Soviet Union embark on a global policy to expand communism and to extirpate capitalism.

> Probably nothing could have prevented the emergence of the "cold war." Throughout history the existence of the two powers obviously stronger than the rest has produced a polarity between them and forced the rest of the world to adapt itself as best it can to their inevitable mutual suspicion and consequent hostility. In such situations differences of ideology, whether religious, socio-economic, or political, are purely incidental, but they serve as useful cloaks for the underlying power struggle, inspiring their respective supporters and seeming to give meaning to the conflict. The "cold war" between the United States and the Soviet Union is often idealized, on both sides, as the conflict between "bourgeois" democracy and the dictatorship "of the toilers," between capitalism and communism, between religion and atheism.[9]

The ideological conflict between the USSR and the United States affected the operations of the entire UN system. Because of the conflicts, issues concerning the maintenance and preservation of international peace and security were deadlocked in the Security Council as one veto after another was cast by the USSR. The vetoes greatly reduced the effectiveness of the Security Council in dealing with explosive political issues of the world. The Soviet Union used the veto not to protect important concerns, but to prevent the passage of any resolution with which it happened to disagree. As the newly independent African, Asian, and Caribbean states became the new majority of the United Nations membership, the United States, France, and Britain have since 1970, vetoed more than the USSR. Thomas Hovet, Jr.'s, analysis of the deadlocks in the Security Council is illuminating.

> That international peace and security would depend on the degree of unanimity of the permanent members of the Security Council was an essential concept of the 1945 Conference. But the effectiveness of the Security Council system was dead-locked by the rift in relations between the United States and the Soviet Union and the Cold War. Because of their failure to agree, the military arrangements conceived in Article 43 could not be implemented. Without big power unanimity on maintaining the entire system of collective security in the Charter would be shattered, unless alternatives could be found.[10]

To circumvent the Soviet Union's vetoes in the Security Council, some changes were gradually made by the ruling majority Western countries. Various measures were introduced to expand the roles and functions of the General Assembly where the veto could not be applied. An important outcome of delegating power to the Assembly led to the adoption in 1950 of the Uniting for Peace Resolution. This resolution recommended the creation of committees that could be used in the pacific settlement of disputes and in framing possible collective operations. The first test of this came during the Suez Canal Crisis of 1956, when the Security Council became deadlocked over that crisis. The General Assembly under the provisions called for in the Uniting for Peace Resolution met and granted the Office of the Secretary-General responsibilities for negotiating and organizing the United Nations Emergency Force (UNEF). The creation of UNEF fulfilled the objectives of Article 43 of the UN Charter, which calls for the creation of a military force to enforce, if necessary, the decisions of the Security Council.

While some of the Security Countil's powers were being delegated to the General Assembly, the council also took measures to improve its operation. Gradually, it came to be accepted that an abstention did not automatically constitute a veto. The implication of this act is that the concurring vote of all the permanent members required under Article 27(3) of the Charter did not have to be interpreted as an affirmative vote by each member. As time went on, the tradition of consensus emerged by which a statement of the chairman summarizing the views of the council members was taken to represent the sense of the meeting. In this way, deadlocks were avoided as voting was not necessary.

Similar to what it had done to the General Assembly, the Security Council also delegated some of its powers to the secretary-general. Researchers G. E. Taylor and B. Cashman have noted that:

> In the effort to maintain peace and security, then it could be argued that the General Assembly and the Secretary-General had assumed much of the role of the Security Council.
> This is not to imply that the Security Council is not being used in its original capacity. There still is a tendency to take crucial issues first to the Council to see whether it can act. But there is always a readiness to transfer the issue to the Assembly if the Council can not act.[11]

The Office of the Secretary-General is now actively involved in the pacific settlement of international as well as domestic political conflicts. The demands of UNEF also mean that the secretary-general has to share responsibilities with the General Assembly. These responsibilities are not granted to the secretary-general by the UN Charter. Although the Charter prohibits the United Nations Organization from intervening in "matters which are essentially within the domestic jurisdiction of any state," the United Nations' organs and specialized agencies have acted in many instances to the contrary.

The devolution of some of the power by the Security Council to the General Assembly and to the Office of the Secretary-General makes African, Asian, Caribbean, and Latin American states increase their participatory roles in the maintenance and preservation of international peace as was the UNEF in Lebanon, Sinai, Syria, and Zaire. The total UN membership is 154, and since resolutions of the General Assembly on important questions require a two-thirds majority, African states if they voted as a block, could almost muster a blocking third by themselves. Through their memberships in all organs, committees, and specialized agencies, African states are maximizing their presence in the entire UN system. It can be argued that not only has the role of maintaining peace and security been thrust on the General Assembly but also on the nations of Africa who have such considerable voting power in the General Assembly and its committees and the specialized agencies. The nonaligned, Third World Nations have an absolute majority in the assembly and can control all its procedural matters. This power gives the Africans and their Third World allies the opportunity to block Assembly action on issues that may be antithetical to their interests. In addition, the increase in African membership will inevitably have the effect of expanding the collective strength of small-power opinion and diplomacy in the UN system.

A major area targeted for influence by African states and other LDCs is the international civil service of the United Nations system. African states have periodically denounced the international civil service as being unrepresentative and unreflective of the diversity of the membership of the United Nations. Western Europe has provided the organization with the largest number of staff. In 1978, 639 or 23 percent of the entire United Nations civil service was from Western Europe. North America and the Caribbean nations had 621 staff members. Of this figure, the United States alone had 516 or 20 percent of the entire civil service staff. Thirty-eight percent of the civil service staff list English as their mother language.[12] Membership in the United Nations Organization, financial contribution to its budget, and the overall size of the population determine the employment of the United Nations civil service staff; the dominating factor is financial contribution to the UNO. In 1977, the "desirable rate of employment for the U.S.A."[13] was from 386 to 522, whereas that of Togo was 2 to 7. African states and other United Nations members resent the fact that national quotas are based on the size of a country's fiscal contributions to the UNO.

In 1960, Afro-Asian states made the General Assembly review the procedure under which the quotas in the civil service staff were determined solely on the basis of financial contribution. On the basis of this review, the General Assembly further urged the secretary-general "to intensify his effort to implement the General

Assembly resolutions on the question of the geographical distribution of the staff of the Secretariat."[14] Additional pressure was applied on the secretary-general to maintain wide geographical representation in the Secretariat. In 1962, the General Assembly further noted that the "principle of an equitable geographical distribution in the composition of the Secretariat does not conflict with the paramount considerations of employment of staff, namely, the necessity of securing the highest standards of efficiency, competence and integrity."[15] The assembly also stated that "significant imbalances in the geographical distribution of the staff of the Secretariat continue to exist" and recommended that in the recruitment of staff "due regard shall be paid to as serving as wide a geographical distribution as possible."[16] The activities of African states to make the Secretariat accept its position finally bore fruit in 1976. In that year the General Assembly finally adopted a proposal presented by the secretary-general which recommended some revisions to the method of calculating "desirable ranges" of posts of member states.[17] General Assembly Resolution 31/26 of 1976 further provided that the "allowance of posts for the factor of membership" would be increased from one to six and from two to seven for each member state.

African states are convinced that the staff hired by the UN civil service should be of top quality and be distributed in such a way as to reflect the diverse interests of the member states. According to the Algerian representative,

> ...Personnel questions were becoming increasingly important, since personnel costs accounted for more than two-thirds of the Organization's budget. Some high-level posts seemed to be reserved for nationals from a certain category of countries; since these posts were of vital importance to developing countries, it was essential that the principle of rotation of posts be observed. The issue had political implications, and the Secretariat should submit proposals for corrective measures at the next session.[18]

In addition, most of the African member states have within the last decade reiterated that the Secretariats of international nongovernmental organizations should not be composed of impartial, value-neutral civil servants. Rather the African states want the appointees to the Secretariats to be people who are ideologically sympathetic to the goals and aspirations of the LDCs. Such sentiments were the moving forces that contributed, to a great degree, to the creation of UNCTAD, UNIDO, and the New International Economic Order.[19] These pressures by the African member states have brought about the recent increase in the number of African civil servants on the staff of the Secretariat, ECOSOC, and all the specialized agencies. Many African states feel that new UN civil servants from Africa, now part of the UN bureaucracy, will act as their spokes-persons.

Because African states operate as a bloc within the UN system, they have been able to procure numerous benefits from the UNO. The African Group, which is an organ of the OAU at the United Nations, is responsible for coordinating some of the diplomatic strategies of the African member states. It holds discussions among African member states on numerous issues the OAU wants accomplished. The OAU requires African member states to coordinate their efforts in implementing its heads of governments or ministerial council decisions. Since many of the OAU heads of state decisions are generally directives, the African member states delegations have little option for digression.

Bloc politics in the General Assembly enables African member states to create helpful alliances or solidarity relations with other members or blocs. Caucusing groups form an integral part of bloc politics.[20] The caucusing sessions are also important for acquiring and transmitting information, to mend alliances, to plan programs and strategies, and also for back-door diplomacy. Bloc politics and caucusing groups also give African member states the political stature in the United Nations, which as individual, small, and vulnerable minipowers they would otherwise never acquire. The success of the African Group as a caucusing group should be attributed to the OAU as a collective body. As a recognized legal, regional body at the United Nations headquarters in New York, the OAU office is funded by its parent body based in Addis Ababa, Ethiopia. Through the efforts of the African member states and other caucusing groups, the General Assembly adopted, by acclamation, a resolution on cooperation with it as a regional body.[21]

The African Group incorporation with all African member states makes it one of the largest and most active caucusing groups in the United Nations. The caucusing blocs that were operative at the United Nations as of 1980 are shown as Tables 3, 4. *A. The African Group.*   (The names of these countries are listed in Table 1.) The country in the chair rotates on a monthly basis, following alphabetical order. Because of its apartheid policies, the Republic of South Africa is excluded from membership. However, African liberation movements such as ANC, PAC, and SWAPO are allowed to join discussions of the African Group at the discretion of the Secretariat of the OAU.

Table 3: The Asian Group as of 1980

Afghanistan	Japan	Qatar
Bahrain	Jordan	Samoa
Bangladesh	Kuwait	Saudi Arabia
Bhutan	Lao People's	Singapore
Burma	Democratic Republic	Solomon Islands
China	Lebanon	Sri Lanka
Cyprus	Malaysia	Syrian Arab Republic
Democratic Kampuchea	Maldives	Thailand
Democratic Yemen	Mongolia	Turkey
Fiji	Nepal	United Arab Emirates
India	Oman	Vietnam
Indonesia	Pakistan	Yemen
Iran	Papua New Guinea	
Iraq	Philippines	

The country in the chair rotates on a monthly basis, following alphabetical order. Japan belongs to this group merely for election purposes; it participates in the Western European and Other States Groups for the purpose of the discussion of some policy issues. Israel belongs to this regional grouping but it has been rejected and ostracized.

Table 4: The Caribbean and Latin American Group, 1980

Argentina	Guyana
Bahamas	Haiti
Barbados	Honduras
Bolivia	Jamaica
Brazil	Mexico
Chile	Nicaragua
Colombia	Panama
Costa Rica	Paraguay
Cuba	Peru
Dominica	Saint Lucia
Dominican Republic	Surinam
Ecuador	Trinidad and Tobago
El Salvador	Uruguay
Grenada	Venezuela
Guatemala	

The country in the chair rotates on a monthly basis, following alphabetical order.

Table 5: The Western European and Other States Group, 1980

Federal Republic of Germany	*Observers:*
Australia	Monaco
Austria	Switzerland
Belgium	Vatican
Canada	Norway
Denmark	New Zealand
Spain	Pays-Bas
Finland	Portugal
France	Royaume-Uni
Greece	Sweden
Ireland	Turkey
Iceland	
Italy	
Luxembourg	
Malta	

The country in the chair rotates on a monthly basis, following alphabetical order in French. The participation of the United States is decided on a case-by-case basis. Japan participates for the purpose of the discussion of some policies concerning the OECD.

Table 6: The Arab Group, 1980

Algeria	Libyan Arab Republic	Saudi Arabia
Bahrain	Mauritania	Somalia
Democratic Yemen	Morocco	Sudan
Djibouti	Oman	Syrian Arab Republic
Iraq	Palestine Liberation	Tunisia
Jordan	Organization	United Arab Emirates
Kuwait	Qatar	Yemen
Lebanon		

The country in the chair rotates on a monthly basis, following alphabetical order in Arabic. The League of Arab States may also participate in this group.

Table 7: The Eastern European Group, 1980

Albania	Poland
Bulgaria	Romania
Byelorussian SSR	Ukrainian SSR
Czechoslovakia	USSR
German Democratic Republic	Yugoslavia
Hungary	

The country in the chair rotates on a monthly basis, following alphabetical order. Albania does not participate in this group. Yugoslavia participates only for election purposes.

Table 8: The Permanent Members of the Security Council, 1980

China	Union of Soviet Socialist Republics
France	United States of America
United Kingdom of Great Britain and Northern Ireland	

Although the African Group is considered the largest caucusing bloc in the United Nations General Assembly, within the entire UN system it is a part of the Group of 77, which is made up of 122 United Nations member states as follows:

Table 9: Members of the Group of 77, as of 1980

Afghanistan	Grenada	Papua New Guinea
Algeria	Guatemala	Paraguay
Angola	Guinea	Peru
Argentina	Guinea-Bissau	Philippines
Bahamas	Guyana	Qatar
Bahrain	Haiti	Republic of Korea
Bangladesh	Honduras	Romania
Barbados	India	Rwanda
Benin	Indonesia	Saint Lucia
Bhutan	Iran	Samoa
Bolivia	Iraq	São Tomé and Principe
Botswana	Ivory Coast	Saudi Arabia
Brazil	Jamaica	Senegal
Burma	Jordan	Seychelles
Burundi	Kenya	Sierra Leone
Cape Verde	Kuwait	Singapore
Central African Republic	Lao People's Democratic	Solomon Islands
Chad	Republic	Somalia
Chile	Lebanon	Saint Vincent and the Grenadines
Colombia	Lesotho	Sudan
Comoros	Liberia	Surinam
Congo	Libyan Arab Republic	Swaziland
Costa Rica	Madagascar	Syrian Arab Republic
Cuba	Malawi	Thailand
Cyprus	Malaysia	Togo
Democratic Kampuchea	Maldives	Tonga
Democratic People's	Mali	Trinidad and Tobago
Republic of Korea	Malta	Tunisia
Democratic Yemen	Mauritania	Uganda
Djibouti	Mauritius	United Arab Emirates
Dominica	Mexico	United Republic of Cameron
Dominican Republic	Morocco	United Republic of Tanzania
Ecuador	Mozambique	Upper Volta
Egypt	Nepal	Uruguay
El Salvador	Nicaragua	Venezuela
Equatorial Guinea	Niger	Vietnam
Ethiopia	Nigeria	Yemen
Fiji	Oman	Yugoslavia
Gabon	Pakistan	Zaire
Gambia	Palestine Liberation Organization	Zambia
Ghana	Panama	Zimbabwe

SOURCE: Compiled by the author.

The purposes and objectives of the Group of 77 were summarized at its Fourth Ministerial Meeting in Arusha, Tanzania, in February 1979, by President (Mwalimu) Julius K. Nyerere in the following words:

> What we have in common is that we are all, in relation to the developed world, dependent–not interdependent–nations. Each of our economies has developed as a by-product and a subsidiary of development in the industrialized North, and it is externally oriented. We are not the prime movers of our own destiny. We are ashamed to admit it, but economically we are dependencies–semi-colonies at best–not sovereign States.[22]

The African Group operates as an integral Group of 77 at UNCTAD Conferences. The Group of 77 has become the principal organ of the Third World through which concrete plans for the implementations and actualization of ideas and objectives of the NIEO are negotiated within the UN system.

Caucusing groups are now a regular and structured process of conducting business at the United Nations and some of its specialized agencies. The raison d'être of these groups is to influence and manipulate the decisions of the organization to conform with those of their caucusing group. The effectiveness of any caucusing group on a particular issue depends on the degree of cohesion among the group's members. The more cohesive the group members are, the better organized and the more effective they will be in trying to implement their goals. By organizing themselves into larger groups they become more influential and effective in reaching their desired goals. Since African states have the largest representation of any continent in the United Nations, their caucusing group plays an extremely important function in the informal diplomacy that takes place in the corridors of the United Nations.

The roots of the success of the African Group and its cohesiveness are embedded in Africa's colonial domination, imperialism, racism, and under-development. In recognition of the gigantic and insurmountable post-independence problems of economic development, protection of national sovereignty, acceleration of decolonization, and racism, and their desire to contribute to the preservation of peace and the pacific settlement of international conflicts, eight independent African States (Ethiopia, Egypt, Ghana, Liberia, Libya, Morocco, Sudan, and Tunisia) held a heads of state meeting in Accra, Ghana.[23] The African Conference of Independent African States (ACIAS) decided that it was in the interests of African states to coordinate their policies as a group at the United Nations. The heads of state adopted the following resolution.

The Setting up of a Permanent Machinery after the Conference

The Conference of Independent African States,
Firmly convinced that a machinery for consultation and cooperation is essential,
1. Decides to constitute the Permanent Representatives of the Participating Governments at the United Nations as the informal permanent machinery,
(a) for coordinating all matters of common concern to the African States,

(b) for examining and making recommendations on concrete practical steps which may be taken to implement the decisions of this and similar future conferences, and
(c) for making preparatory arrangements for future conferences of Independent African States;
2.   Agrees that meetings of Foreign Ministers, other Ministers or experts be convened from time to time as and when necessary to study and deal with particular problems of common concern to the African States;
3.   Agrees that the Conference of the Independent African States should be held at least once every two years.[24]

The establishment of the African Group at the United Nations by African heads of states was a landmark decision in African international relations. A new era of African cooperation in the conduct of international politics and diplomacy at the United Nations was consummated. The influence of the African caucusing group began to be felt within the United Nation's General Assembly and the Secretariat in 1960. In that year, forty-three African and Asian member states were responsible for sponsoring the adoption of the Declaration on Decolonization. The General Assembly adopted this Declaration on Decolonization of December 14, 1960, as Resolution 1514: Declaration on the Granting of Independence to Colonial Countries and Peoples by eighty-nine votes to zero, with nine abstentions. The countries that abstained were Australia, Belgium, the Dominican Republic, France, Portugal, Spain, Union of South Africa, United Kingdom, and the United States.[25] The passage of Resolution 1514 was indeed an epochal achievement for the African-Asian caucusing group.

The activation of United Nations and world opinion in the passage of General Assembly Resolution 1514 reaffirmed the African and other newly independent states that the United Nations supported their goals on decolonization. Resolution 1514 did not free any colony in Africa, its greatest contribution was to international morality. For the first time in its history, the United Nations had adopted a resolution recognizing that "all peoples have the right to self-determination; by virtue of that right they freely determine their political status and freely pursue their economic, social and cultural development."[26] The other international morality imperative in Resolution 1514 is its call on all states to "observe faithfully and strictly the provisions of the charter of the United Nations, the Declaration of Human Rights and the Declaration on Decolonization on the basis of equality, the respect for the sovereign rights of all peoples and their territorial integrity."[27]

In 1960, the African Group at the United Nations successfully maximized their influence when they obviated superpower confrontation over the Congolese civil war that erupted immediately following the attainment by the Congo (now known as Zaire) of its independence from Belgium. The mutiny of the Congolese national army *force publique,* and the general collapse of law and order in large segments of the country coupled with an attempt for secession of the Katanga Province by Moise Tsombe, created a major crisis into which the Soviet Union and the United States might have become ensnared militarily. By quickly invoking Article 99 of the UN Charter that states that, the Secretary-General may bring to the attention of the Security Council any matter which in his opinion may threaten the maintenance of international peace and security, the UN secretary-general set up the United Nations operation in the Congo (UNOC) and thereafter dispatched soldiers to the Congo. In setting up UNOC, the Secretary-General, Dag Hammarskjold, stated that he chose African nations to serve in the Congo first because he wanted to see the spirit of African solidarity manifested in the administration of the United Nations.

The Congolese civil war drove a wedge into the unity and cohesiveness of the African Group at the United Nations. Attempts by conservative and revolutionary African states to find an acceptable formula to resolve the crisis further divided them, and in the course of time resulted in the formation of the Casablanca, Brazzaville, and Monrovia caucusing blocs. Without overlooking the unfortunate divisions and conflicts among the African states, we can say that the United Nations succeeded in avoiding the danger of a confrontation between the superpowers that was comparable in potential to the Korean crisis.

After numerous discussions among the African states, their three caucusing groups were disbanded. The African states formed the Organization of African Unity in 1963, which sponsors the African Group at the United Nations. This group has been highly sucessful in putting African views across in the General Assembly, the Security Council, ECOSOC, and the specialized agencies. The African Group has been among the most active caucusing blocs in demanding the creation of additional United Nations agencies and committees to implement numerous tasks that have been recommended by the General Assembly. Continued proliferation of United Nations agencies and committees will obviously mean that member states should contribute more money for the projects they want the United Nations to operate. Proliferation of UN agencies and funded nongovermental organizations (NGOs) have been criticized by the OECD on the grounds that they contribute more money for the upkeep of the entire UN system. Not only are the OECD and other developing countries contributing more money to the budget of the United Nations, they also make voluntary contributions to many of the proliferated UN nongovernmental organizations. African states and other LDCs not only contribute less money in terms of volume but also benefit most in terms of programs that have been established in the countries by ECOSOC and other specialized agencies coordinated by the ACC.

Despite the fact that the actual volume of financial contributions of over 80 percent of African states are assessed at less than .04 percent of their Gross National Product (GNP), their influence in the General Assembly and the entire UN system is definitely overwhelming. As a result of pressure from the Third World countries and some European member states, the General Assembly, the International Court of Justice, the specialized agencies, and the NGOs now support decolonization and regard the policies of apartheid in the Republic of South Africa as immoral and a crime against international law. In addition, the influence of African states in the United Nations has legitimized the role of African liberation movements in Angola, Cape Verde, Guinea-Bissau, Mozambique, Namibia, Rhodesia, and the Republic of South Africa. Not only have African states influenced the United Nations to legitimize the revolutionary activities of the African liberation movements in the white-dominated states in Africa but the United Nations and its organs have also recognized these political parties and are providing them with humanitarian financial support.

In summary, the African member states are an integral part of the UN system. By initiating, adopting, and implementing General Assembly, Security Council, ECOSOC, and specialized agencies resolutions and declarations, African states are now involved in shaping international law, world and United Nations diplomacy; reducing international political tension and conflicts, maintaining and preserving international peace and security, peacefully settling international disputes, fostering peaceful and fraternal relations among the nations of the world, encouraging cooperation between the LDCs and the OECD through the framework of the New International Economic Order, and supporting those struggling for decolonization and national liberation.

As members, African states involve themselves in the business of the United Nations that affects the economic, political, technological, and social well-being of mankind. Membership in the United Nations makes African states legally bound to the resolutions and declarations they initiate, adopt, and implement. This legal relationship transfers some aspects of their sovereignty to the United Nations Organization. Politically the United Nations General Assembly and other organs have provided African states with forums to express their ideas and frameworks in which to conduct their diplomacy.

From our analysis of the operation of the United Nations and the caucusing groups, no single country or group of states can assume effectively the leadership of the Third World or the Group of 77, without successfully courting the friendship of the African Group or the Organization of African Unity. The weight of the African vote in the General Assembly and other international organizations in which they are members is ironically a diplomatic advantage of the Balkanization of Africa into a multiplicity of ministates. Other than being an important source of influence, multiplicity has made immense contributions to the democratization of the General Assembly and the specialized agencies along with organs that constitute the UN system.

2
The United Nations and Decolonization in Africa

More than eighty nations whose people were formerly under colonial domination have joined the United Nations since it was formed in 1945. Forty-eight of these former colonies are independent African states. Because of the colonial subjugation of Africa by Western European powers at the time of the founding of the United Nations, African political and economic interests were not priority issues. Most of the founders of the United Nations expected that the issues about African political and economic independence would be the responsibility of the European colonial powers. Furthermore, Western European countries, the United States, and their allies did not think that the political status of Africa in world affairs would become a significant factor in the ability of the UN system to maintain international peace and security. Since Africa, at that time, was colonized, economically underdeveloped, and militarily weak, it was generally accepted among Western nations that the interests of Africans were not important in the preservation of international peace and security.

When the United Nations was founded, over 90 percent of the African continent was under European colonial and imperialistic subjugation. As a result, Africa had virtually no influence in the genesis of this remarkable organization. People who founded the United Nations Organization were mostly Europeans who wanted to prevent the recurrences of the hazards of World War I and II. Prevention of war in Europe and North America was a major reason for the creation of the United Nations. As African countries attained their independence and joined the United Nations, the character of that international organization gradually began to change.

Africa's influence in the UN system gradually began to be felt as more African states joined that organization. Thirty percent of the UN membership is made up of African independent states. One of the objectives of African countries that are members of the United Nations is to solicit support and aid of the UN system in their struggle to liquidate colonialism. It is this objective of the African states to use the UN system and all its member states to help in the termination of colonialism. This chapter discusses the involvement of the UN system in the decolonization process in

Namibia (South West Africa), former Portuguese colonial dependencies, the former British colony of Rhodesia (Zimbabwe), and the Republic of South Africa.

The United Nations and South West Africa (Namibia)

From 1884 until World War I, South West Africa (now officially called Namibia) was a colony of Germany. In 1915, the then Union of South Africa captured South West Africa and occupied it. At the end of World War I, the Allied powers had to make a decision on the fate of the former German colonies. After much discussion, the Allied powers resolved that the new League of Nations would be "a sacred trust of civilization" and would provide for the well-being of the subject peoples. Article 22 of the League of Nations covenant stated:

> To those colonies and territories which as a consequence of the late war have ceased to be under the sovereignty of the States which formerly governed them, and which are inhabited by peoples not yet able to stand by themselves under the strenuous conditions of the modern world, there should be applied the principle that the well-being and development of such peoples form a sacred trust of civilization, and that securities for the performance of this trust should be embodied in this Covenant.[1]

In its Charter, the League of Nations declared that the tutelage of the former German colonial subjects was to be exercised on its behalf by the Mandatories. Having done this, the league proceeded to set up a Permanent Mandates Commission to advise its own council on matters pertaining to the administration of the Mandates.

> In the case of South West Africa, the United Kingdom had wanted the former German colony to be incorporated into the neighboring Union of South Africa, which at the time was part of the British Commonwealth. Instead, the League in 1920 conferred the Mandate over South West Africa "upon his Britannic Majesty, to be exercised on his behalf by the Union of South Africa." The Territory was placed under a "C" Mandate, which permitted South Africa to administer it as an integral part of the Union. Under the Mandate, it was stated that South Africa could apply to the Territory its own laws, but that it "shall promote to the utmost the material and moral well-being and social progress of the inhabitants of the Territory."[2]

Up to the beginning of World War II, South Africa had submitted the required annual reports for examination by the Permanent Mandates Commission (PMC). In compliance with the PMC's requirements, South Africa answered questions concerning the various aspects of its administration of South West Africa. The PMC (made up of experts from member states) condemned South Africa's race laws and also made it clear that the League of Nations mandate did not permit annexation of that territory by South Africa. From the outset, South Africa placed the interests of the white minority above those of the African inhabitants. White immigration from the Union of South Africa was vigorously promoted, and limited self-government was conferred on the white population. Throughout the league period, South Africa was more concerned with maintaining harmonious relations between the German and white South African settlers than with promoting better relations between whites and Africans. For example, in 1922, an African protest occurred against forced labor at Bondelswarts. The South African government reacted to this incident by dropping bombs on the protesters, killing many of them including innocent African women and children. While the PMC was condemning the Bondelswarts incident and the forced labor policies of South Africa, it issued the following statement:

> The Commission deplores the unfortunate relations which the report discloses between the white population and a large proportion of the natives of the mandated territory. It trusts that the administration will resist the influence of these deplorable relations which are largely the heritage of past events in South West Africa and which are so much opposed to the essential principles of Article 22 of the Covenant. It hopes that future reports will be able to disclose better relations between the two races.[3]

The Charter of the United Nations came into operation on October 24, 1945. In April 1946, the League of Nations, which was for all intents and purposes already moribund, voluntarily dissolved. At its last meeting, the Assembly of the League of Nations adopted the following resolution, which was supported and approved by the government of the Union of South Africa.

> The Assembly.

> Recalling that Article 22 of the Covenant applies to certain territories placed under the mandate the principle that the well-being and development of people not yet able to stand alone in the strenuous conditions of the modern worlds form a sacred trust of civilization:

> 1. Expresses its satisfaction with the manner in which the organs of the League have performed the functions entrusted to them with respect to the mandates system and in particular pays tribute to the work accomplished by the Mandates Commission:

> 2. Recalls the role of the League in assisting Iraq to progress from the status under as "A" mandate to a condition of complete independence welcomes the termination of the mandated status of Syria, the Lebanon and Transjordan, which have, since the last session of the Assembly become independent members of the world community;

> 3. Recognizes that, on the termination of the League's existence, its functions with respect to the mandated territories will come to an end, but notes that Chapters XI, XII and XIII of the Charter of the United Nations embody principles corresponding to those declared in Article 22 of the Covenant of the League;

> 4. Takes note of the expressed intentions of the members of the League now administering territories under the mandate to continue to administer them for the well-being and development of the peoples concerned in accordance with the obligations contained in the respective mandates until other arrangements have been agreed between the United Nations and the respective mandatory powers.[4]

After the San Francisco Conference, which resulted in the formation of the United Nations, machinery was created to make necessary steps for the United Nations to take over the assets, functions, and activities of the moribund League of Nations. On February 12, 1946, the United Nations General Assembly resolved that:

> The General Assembly will itself examine, or will submit to the appropriate organ of the United Nations, any request from the parties that the United Nations should resume the exercise of functions or powers entrusted to the League of Nations by treaties, international conventions, agreements and other instruments having a political character.[5]

A detailed catalogue of arrangements for the transfer to the United Nations of the League of Nations assets is reported in the Board of Liquidation and in Volume One of the United Nations Treaty Series. In its report, the Board of Liquidation noted that:

> The mandate system inaugurated by the League has thus been brought to a close, but the board is glad to be able to report that the experience gained by the Secretariat in this matter has not been lost, the United Nations having taken over, with the small remaining staff, the mandate sections archives, which could afford valuable guidance to those concerned with the administration of the Trusteeship system set up by the charter of that organization.[6]

South Africa has never agreed to the fact that the League of Nations power was legally transferred to the United Nations. South Africa's contention is that it continues to administer South West Africa in the spirit of the League of Nations mandate and that its obligation to the league did not carry over to the United Nations Organization. According to a statement by a South African representative attending a UN meeting:

> (a) For twenty-five years, the Union of South Africa has governed and administered the Territory as an integral part of its own Territory and has promoted to the utmost the material and moral well-being and the social progress of the habitants.
>
> It has applied many of its laws to the Territory and has faithfully performed its obligations under the mandate.
>
> (b) It is geographically and strategically a part of the Union of South Africa, and in World War I a rebellion in the Union was fomented from it, and an attack launched against the Union.
>
> (c) It is in large measure economically dependent upon the Union whose railways serve it and from which it draws the great bulk of its supplies.
>
> (d) Its dependent Native peoples spring from the same ethnological stem as the great mass of the native peoples of the Union.
>
> (e) Two-thirds of the European population are of Union origin and are Union Nationals, and the remaining one-third are enemy Nationals.
>
> (f) The Territory has its own legislative assembly granted to it by the Union Parliament, and this Assembly has submitted a request for incorporation of the Territory as part of the Union.

(g) The Union has introduced a progressive policy of Native administration, including a system of local government through Native councils giving the Natives a voice in the management of their own affairs; and under Union administration Native Reserves have reached a high state of economic development.

(h) In view of contiguity and similarity in composition of the Native peoples of South West Africa the Native policy followed in South West Africa must always be aligned with that of the Union, three-fifths of the population of which is Native.

(i) There is no prospect of the Territory ever existing as a separate State, and the ultimate objective of the mandatory principle is therefore impossible of achievement.

(j) The delegation of the Union of South Africa therefore claims that the mandate should be terminated and that the Territory should be incorporated as part of the Union of South Africa.

(k) As territorial questions are however reserved for handling at the later Peace Conference, where the Union of South Africa intends to raise this matter, it is here only mentioned for the information of the Conference in connection with the mandates question.[7]

South Africa did not want South West Africa to be placed under United Nations control. South Africa strongly objected to the objectives set forth in Article 76 of the UN Charter.

a. to further international peace and security;

b. to promote the political, economic, social and educational advancement of the inhabitants of the Trust Territories, and their progressive development towards self-government or independence as may be appropriate to the particular circumstances of each Territory and its peoples and the freely expressed wishes of the peoples concerned, and as may be provided by the terms of each Trusteeship agreement;

c. to encourage respect for human rights and for fundamental freedoms for all without distinction as to race, sex, language, or religion, and to encourage recognition of the interdependence of the peoples of the world; and

d. to ensure equal treatment in social, economic, and commercial matters for all Members of the United Nations and their nationals, and also equal treatment for the latter in the administration of justice, without prejudice to the attainment of the foregoing objectives . . .[8]

Since South Africa was interested in annexing South West Africa, it did not agree to the placement of South West Africa under a UN Trusteeship system. At the first session of the United Nations General Assembly in 1946,

. . .South Africa proposed the incorporation of the Territory into the Union, and asked the Assembly to approve this step. The majority of the people, South Africa contended, favored incorporation. The Europeans had expressed this wish through their Legislative Assembly, and two-thirds of Africans were alleged to have supported the proposal in their own "Referendum" (Details on the conduct of "Referendum" by the South African-Appointed Native Commissioners were not given, and the Government refused to allow observers to enter the Territory).

The Assembly declared that it was unable to accede to South West Africa's incorporation into the Union. The African inhabitants had not yet secured political autonomy or reached a stage of political development enabling them to express a considered opinion on such an important question, it said. Instead, the Assembly recommended that the Territory be placed under the International Trusteeship System. In this first resolution on South Africa, "by presenting this matter to the United Nations, recognized the interest and concern of the Organization in the matter of the future status of Territories now held under Mandate.[9]

While the proposal for incorporation was under discussion in the UN General Assembly, the then South African Prime Minister, General Smuts, said that his country could not be forced to agree to place South West Africa under the Trusteeship System. Following this, Smuts proceeded to inform the United Nations that, if the incorporation proposals were rejected, his country would keep on administering the territory as an integral part of the Union of South Africa. Ignoring South African wishes, the General Assembly adopted resolution 65 (1).

Having considered the statements of the delegation of the Union of South Africa regarding the question of incorporating the mandated territory of South West Africa in the Union:

Noting with satisfaction that the Union of South Africa, by presenting this matter to the United Nations, recognizes the interest and concern of the United Nations in the matter of the future status of territories now held under mandate;

Recalling that the Charter of the United Nations provides in Articles 77 and 79 that the trusteeship system shall apply to territories now under mandate as may be subsequently agreed;

Referring to the resolution of the General Assembly of 9 February, 1946, inviting the placing of mandated territories under trusteeship;

Desiring that agreement between the United Nations and the Union of South Africa may hereafter be reached regarding the future status of the mandated territory of South West Africa;

Assured by the delegation of the Union of South Africa that, pending such agreement, the Union Government will continue to administer the territory as heretofore in the spirit of the principles laid down in the mandate;

Considering that the African inhabitants of South West Africa have not yet secured political autonomy or reached a stage of political development enabling them to express a considered opinion which the Assembly could recognize on such an important question as incorporation of their territory;

The General Assembly, therefore,
Is unable to accede to the incorporation of the territory of South West Africa in the Union of South Africa; and

Recommends that the mandated territory of South West Africa be placed under the international trusteeship system and invites the Government of the Union of South Africa to propose for the consideration of the General Assembly a trustee-ship agreement for the aforesaid territory.[10]

Apparently disappointed by the General Assembly's rejection of the incorpora-tion proposal, the South African government proceeded in 1947 to inform the United Nations General Assembly and the Security Council that it had decided:

... not to proceed with the incorporation plan—but that it was under no obligation to place the Territory under the Trusteeship System. It would continue to adminis-ter South West Africa "in the spirit of the Mandate," South Africa said, and would submit reports on its administration for the information of the United Nations.

The Assembly took note of South Africa's decision, but firmly maintained its recommendation that the Territory be placed under the Trusteeship System. It authorized the Trusteeship Council to examine the report submitted by South Africa on its administration of South West Africa for the year 1946, and to submit its observations.[11]

In 1948, the General Assembly discussed and criticized South Africa's administra-tion of South West Africa to the Security Council on the following matters:

(1) Africans are barred from political activity and have no say in deciding or formulating laws that govern and shape their destinies:

(2) The Trusteeship Council noted that it was convinced of the desirability of the increased political participation by the Africans in the government of SWA;

(3) The Council also abhorred South Africa's discriminatory laws; and

(4) The prohibition of Africans from voting and seeking both electoral and appointive political office.

In 1948 the National party (NP) was elected to office in South Africa on the platform of apartheid. On July 11, 1949, the apartheid government of South Africa informed the United Nations that it would discontinue its usual reports to the United Nations.

It will be recalled, however, that the Union Government have at no time recognized any legal obligations on their part to supply information on South West Africa to the United Nations, but in a spirit of goodwill, co-operation and helpful-ness offered to provide the United Nations with reports on the administration of South West Africa, with the clear stipulation that this would be done on a voluntary basis, for purposes of information only and on the distinct understanding that the United Nations has no supervisory jurisdiction in South West Africa. In this spirit a report was submitted in 1947, and in 1948, detailed replies were furnished to a subsequent questionnaire formulated by the Trusteeship Council. It was emphasized at the time that the forwarding of information on policy should not be regarded as creating a precedent, or construed as a commitment for the future or as implying any measure of accountability to the United Nations on the part of the Union Government. The Union Government also expressed their confidence that the Trusteeship Council would approach its task in an entirely objective manner and examine the report in the same spirit of goodwill, cooperation and helpfulness as had motivated the Union in making the information available.

These hopes have not been realized. Instead, the submission of information has provided an opportunity to utilize the Trusteeship Council and the Trusteeship Committee as a forum for unjustified criticism and censure of the Union Government's administration, not only in South West Africa but in the Union as well. Inferences and deductions have been drawn from the information submitted which are quite inconsistent with facts and realities. The misunderstandings and accusations to which the United Nations discussions of this subject have given rise have had repercussions both in the Union and in South West Africa, with deleterious effects on the maintenance of the harmonious relations which have hitherto existed and are so essential to successful administration. Furthermore, the very act of submitting a report has created in the minds of a number of Members of the United Nations an impression that the Trusteeship Council is competent to make recommendations on matters of internal administration of South West Africa and has fostered other misconceptions regarding the status of this Territory.

In these circumstances the Union Government can no longer see that any real benefit is to be derived from the submission of special reports on South West Africa to the United Nations, and have regretfully come to the conclusion that in the interests of efficient administration no further reports should be forwarded. In coming to this decision the Union Government are in no way motivated by a desire to withhold from the world factual and other information regarding South West Africa, published in accordance with the customary practice of democratic nations, and information of this nature previously embodied in annual reports to the League of Nations or the United Nations will continue to be made available to the general public in the form of statistics, departmental reports, reports by the Administrator to the South West African Legislature, blue books, and other governmental publications.[12]

In the same year, the South African government introduced the controversial South West Africa Affairs Amendment Act 23 of 1949, whose prime objective was to bring South West Africa closer to the Union of South Africa. The Act gives South West Africa six representatives in the Union of South Africa's House of Assembly. Four of these representatives will be elected and two will be nominated by the governor general. One of these appointed senators was to represent Africans, Coloreds, and Asians. The South West Africa Legislative Assembly was to consist of eighteen members elected by European registered voters of the territory. "A member of the House of Assembly to be elected under the Act must: (a) Be qualified to be registered as a voter for the election of members of the House of Assembly in one of the provinces, or in the Territory; (b) The obligations of the Union Government vis-à-vis the Africans, which derive from the mandate and are embodied in the original Act, thus remain in full force."[13]

The South West Africa Affairs Amendment Act was enacted to annex South West Africa into the Union of South Africa. Not only was South West Africa to be a part of the Union, but the Africans of South West Africa were to be stripped of their political rights like those of the nonwhites of the Union. Although the racist South African government denied that the provision of the South West Africa Affairs Amendment Act constituted an act of annexure, it definitely envisaged a relationship which was closer to annexation. While arguing for passage of this Act in the South African Parliament, Prime Minister Malan of South Africa stated:

We will continue to refuse to place South West Africa under the Trusteeship Council. Then the question arose what we had to do in such circumstances. Should the same thing be repeated which we experienced in regard to the future of South West Africa, namely, when, at three annual meetings at least, I think, of UNO year after year the future of South West Africa was a subject for discussion? If that were to be repeated year after year, there would never be any peace or certainty for the future in connection with this matter. Therefore a course had to be adopted in order to try to bring the matter to a conclusion in some way or another. There is as far as I can see–to me at least it was very evident–only one way to do so and that way is: Place South West Africa in a position where it will be invulnerable against that type of propaganda and incitement. Knit South West Africa and the Union together in such a manner, knit them together constitutionally in such a way that the two areas will in future be inseparably bound together. In order to achieve this, let us make use of the unquestionable right which South Africa possesses, the right which South Africa also possessed when the mandate was still in existence and the principal in regard to the mandate had not yet disappeared, and bring about a position of closer affiliation of the two territories, the Union and South West Africa, even if, at least, for the present, we do not go as far as the ultimate limit of incorporating South West Africa in the Union. Even if we do not go to that limit of incorporating South West Africa into our country, we can still knit South West Africa and the Union so closely together constitutionally that they can never again be separated. In consequence of this Bill South West Africa would cease to be a territory administered from outside, a territory with an overload, and a territory which, being outside the Union and having an overload might easily at least in the opinion of some people be transferred from one overload to another. For that reason I felt that we should first of all grant South West Africa self-government as far as its internal matters are concerned, which will mean much more freedom; the second concession we give, externally, is that every measure and every Act which is passed and which is also to be applied to South West Africa, will be passed by South West Africa in participation with the whole Union, or as I expressed it before–do not only make South West Africa a mandated country–if we can still use the term "mandate"–but make South West Africa, together with the Union as a whole, a co-mandatory of its own territory. [14]

The decision of the South African government to refuse to submit records to the United Nations General Assembly was not well received by the General Assembly. Thus, by 1949, a deadlock had been reached on the status of South West Africa and apartheid South Africa's obligations toward the United Nations. Having been frustrated by South Africa's recalcitrance to submit its annual reports to the United Nations, the General Assembly decided to seek clarity on the legal status of South West Africa by asking for an advisory opinion from the International Court of Justice (ICJ). After an exhaustive discussion, the General Assembly adopted Resolution 338 (IV), which stated:

1. *Decides* to submit the following questions to the International Court of Justice with a request for an advisory opinion which shall be transmitted to the General Assembly before its fifth regular session, if possible:

What is the international status of the Territory of South West Africa and what are the international obligations of the Union of South Africa arising therefrom, in particular:

(a) Does the Union of South Africa continue to have international obligations under the Mandate for South West Africa and, if so what are those obligations?

(b) Are the provisions of Chapter XII of the Charter applicable and, if so, in what manner, to the Territory of South West Africa?

(c) Has the Union of South Africa the competence to modify the international status of the Territory of South West Africa, or, in the event of a negative reply, where does competence rest to determine and modify the international status of the Territory?

2. *Requests* the Secretary-General to transmit the present resolution to the International Court of Justice, in accordance with Article 65 of the Statute of the Court, accompanied by all documents likely to throw light upon the question.

The Secretary-General shall include among their documents, the text of Article 22 of the Covenant of the League of Nations; the text of the Mandate for German South West Africa, confirmed by the Council of the League on 17 December 1920; relevant documentation concerning the objectives and the functions of the Mandates System; the text of the resolution adopted by the League of Nations on the question of Mandates on 18 April 1946; the text of Articles 77 and 80 of the Charter and data on the discussion of these Articles in the San Francisco Conference and the official records, including the annexes, of the consideration of the question of South West Africa at the fourth session of the General Assembly.

Forty countries voted in favor of the resolutions, seven against, and four abstained. Written statements were submitted to the ICJ by Egypt, the United States, India, and Poland. On July 11, 1950, the ICJ handed down its advisory opinion replying to the assembly's questions. The major findings of the court were:

–South Africa continued to have the international obligations contained in the League Covenant and the Mandate;
–The functions of supervision over the administration of the Territory by South Africa should be exercised by the United Nations, to which annual reports and petitions from the inhabitants were to be submitted;
–South Africa continued to have the obligation to promote to the utmost the material and moral well-being and social progress of the inhabitants as a sacred trust of civilization;
–The Charter did not impose on South Africa the legal obligation to place South West Africa under the Trusteeship system, although it provided the means by which the Territory might be brought under the system;
–South Africa acting alone was not competent to modify the international status of the Territory; such action required the consent of the United Nations.

The Assembly accepted this opinion and urged South Africa to give effect to it. Reiterating its recommendation on Trusteeship for South West Africa, the Assembly established a five-member Ad Hoc Committee to confer with South Africa on measures for implementing the Court's opinion. The Committee was authorized to examine reports and petitions concerning South West Africa.[15]

Although South Africa did not regard the court's opinion as binding on it, the General Assembly proceeded in urging the South African government to take necessary steps to give effect to the court's advisory opinion. On this issue the Ad Hoc Committee on South West Africa held discussions with the South African government on the cooperation and the resolution of the South West African problem. In 1951,

> . . .Negotiations were held with South African representatives, but the Ad Hoc Committee was unable to report any agreement. South Africa proposed that it would resume some of its international instrument with France, the United Kingdom and the United States–the three remaining members of the Principal Allied and Associated Powers of the first World War which awarded the Mandate. But South Africa would be directly responsible to the three Powers rather than to the United Nations. The Proposal was unacceptable to the Committee, since it did not implement opinion of the court.

> A counter-proposal was made by the Committee; a special commission on South West Africa would be established to undertake the functions and responsibilities of the former permanent Mandates Commission, especially the examination of annual reports and petitions concerning the Territory. But South Africa rejected this proposal; it would not compromise on the issue of accountability to the United Nations.[16]

In 1952, the General Assembly again urged South Africa to resume negotiations with the Ad Hoc Committee for possible agreement providing for the implementation of the 1950 court's advisory opinion. The General Assembly also stated that the United Nations would not recognize as valid any unilateral acts taken by South Africa to alter the international status of South West Africa. Despite the General Assembly's continued presentations to South Africa to change its attitude over the 1950 Advisory Opinion, the South Africa government remained adamant to its original position. By 1954 the Ad Hoc Committee on South West Africa reported to the General Assembly that it had been unable to reach an agreement in resolving and reconciling the differing positions between South Africa and the United Nations over the international status of South West Africa.

From 1954 to 1955, the United Nations and the Ad Hoc Committee continued to make presentations and sent invitations to:

> South Africa to negotiate on the future of the Territory, South Africa declined, stating that it would not consider proposals which did not suit its basic requirements. Since the United Nations had rejected its proposal of an arrangement with France, the United Kingdom, and the United States, that offer now had lapsed, the Union declared.

> The Committee on South West Africa, in reports endorsed by the Assembly, said the administration of the Territory by South Africa–particularly in regard to apartheid legislation–was not in conformity with the Mandate.

> In an advisory opinion requested by the Assembly, the International Court of Justice stated over South African objections that the Assembly was correct in treating decisions concerning South West Africa as "important questions" requiring a two-thirds majority vote. (The Council of the League of Nations, in contrast, required unanimous votes for its decisions).[17]

As usual, South Africa refused to comply with the United Nations' recommendations and also those of the 1955 International Court of Justice opinions. In 1956, South Africa remained consistent in its recalcitrance to negotiate with the committee. Complicating the already fragile relationship between the two antagonists was South Africa's deliberate refusal to comply with United Nations requests to submit reports on its administration of South West Africa to the committee. Further, South Africa went on to apply its apartheid laws against the wishes of the South West Africans. As a result of these actions,

> The Assembly asked the Committee to study what legal action was open to United Nations Members, or to former Members of the League, to ensure that South Africa fulfilled its obligations.

> The International Court of Justice, meanwhile, added another advisory opinion to the others underlining United Nations authority in regard to South West Africa. It stated that the Committee on South West Africa's oral hearings of petitioners were admissible, as a necessary means to enable the United Nations to perform its supervisory duties effectively. Scores of witnesses appeared before United Nation bodies in the following years to give their views on conditions in the Territory; some did so at considerable personal risk.[18]

In 1957, the General Assembly established a Good Offices Committee made up of Brazil, Great Britain, and the United States as yet another attempt to induce South Africa to negotiate for an agreement on the issue of South West Africa's international status. By 1959, the Good Offices Committee had also failed to reach an agreement with South Africa.

In the late 1950s, the wave of independence had gained momentum throughout Africa. With the attainment of independence by more than eighteen countries in 1960, Africans were no longer silent participants in the conduct of either international diplomacy or in the decision-making process at the United Nations. After forming the African Group at the United Nations, the African states began to exert pressure on the Committee on South West Africa to demand immediate changes in that colony's administration. The African Group also accused South Africa of violating the Mandate, and the UN Charter on the following counts: Application and implementation of the iniquitous apartheid system; failure to safeguard, protect, and promote the rights of the Africans in Namibia; usurpation of the Namibians' basic human rights and fundamental freedoms; and continued arrogance and failure to recognize and to submit its reports on the administration of South West Africa to the United Nations. In addition to the outlined criticism, the African states also called on all colonial powers to grant their colonial subjects freedom and independence.

African freedom fighters and members of the United Nations felt that Western countries and the United Nations had not sufficiently pressured South Africa to cooperate with the United Nations in its administration of Namibia. With the support of all independent African states, on November 4, 1960,

> ---Ethiopia and Liberia instituted proceedings in the International Court of Justice at the Hague against South Africa in regard to its administration of SWA and its failure to live up to its international obligations as the administering mandatory power.

The two former league Members asked the Court to require South Africa to carry out its obligations and cease violations of the Mandate; to end apartheid, they argued, was inherently inconsistent with the obligation to promote the well-being and social progress of the inhabitants. Furthermore, they said, South Africa had impeded opportunities for self-determination and had attempted to change the terms of the Mandate without the consent of the United Nations. The Union Government was charged with limiting the franchise to Europeans, refusing equal access to education, suppressing rights and liberties of Africans, segregating residential areas by law according to race, excluding Africans from many occupations, and restricting movement through the pass system. [19]

Between 1960 and 1966, African countries were very active in trying to convince the non-African countries at the United Nations to support the struggle for African majority rule in Namibia. As a way of exerting pressure on South Africa to cooperate and accede to African demands, the Special Committee of twenty-four studied the foreign economic interests of foreign corporations and governments. This committee concluded that foreign companies and multinational corporations share the responsibilities for the suffering of the already oppressed, exploited, and dehumanized Africans. These conclusions also noted that the policy of apartheid enables foreign companies and settler Europeans to reap huge profits while Africans continue to be exploited and impoverished. In the end, the committee recommended that the General Assembly call on all countries whose nations owned and operated business companies in Namibia to divest their investments from that colony.

On the international scene, African nationalism became a reality. African nationalism manifested itself in the passage of the General Assembly Resolution 1514 (XV), the declaration on the granting of independence to colonial countries and peoples that definitely affects South West Africa. In South West Africa, African nationalism found expression in the formation of two African liberation movements: The South West African Peoples Organization (SWAPO) and the South West African National Union (SWANU). These two liberation movements made contact with other African governments and nationalist movements and thereby came to influence policy decision making within the United Nations system. The objectives of liquidating colonialism propounded by SWAPO and SWANU were warmly received by Third World countries at the United Nations. The aims of SWAPO are to establish a free, democratic government in South West Africa founded upon the will and participation of all the people of the country, and to cooperate to the fullest extent with all Africans to rid the continent of all forms of foreign domination and to rebuild it according to the desires of the African peoples; the unification of all people of South West Africa into a cohesive, representative, national political organization, irrespective of their race, ethnic origin, religion, or creed; and the reconstruction of the economic, educational, and social foundations that will support and maintain the real African independence which the African people desire for themselves. SWANU's objectives were to unify and rally the people of South West Africa into one national front, to organize the common people, workers and peasants, of South West Africa and lead them in the struggle for national independence and self-determination; and to work with allied movements in Africa for the propagation and promotion of the concept of Pan-Africanism and unity among the people of Africa.

In addition to these goals, SWAPO and SWANU urged the termination of the South African mandate over South West Africa. Prior to this, SWAPO and SWANU had appealed to African countries to use their influence within the United Nations and the international community to end South Africa's domination of Namibia. Their efforts bore fruit when, in 1961, the General Assembly adopted Resolution 1596 (XV). This resolution condemned apartheid, labeled the situation in South West Africa a potential threat to international peace and security, and requested the UN Committee on South West Africa to visit that country with or without permission from the government of South Africa. While denouncing the policies of apartheid, the General Assembly requested the committee on South West Africa to submit to its next session a report on the implementation of Resolution 1568 (XV). The Republic of South Africa reacted negatively to the UN secretary-general and the committee on South West Africa's request to visit Namibia. As a result, the committee confined its visit to some African countries other than Namibia. Petitions to the visiting UN committee were presented in Cairo, Accra, and Dar es Salaam by many South West Africans. All the petitions were overwhelmingly condemnatory of the South Africa's racist and repressive rule over the African people of Namibia. In a statement to the UN committee hearing in Dar es Salaam, SWAPO requested the General Assembly to:

Terminate the Mandate for South West Africa immediately, and to entrust the temporary administration of the country to a United Nations Commission composed of African States with a view to arranging for free general elections in the country immediately in order to make possible the conditions necessary for South West Africa to accede:

1. To self-governement now, through the establishment of a democratic African Government based on the principle of one man, one vote, irrespective of tribe, race, religion, education, sex, property, or colour;

2. To gain independence not later than 1963;

3. To facilitate the work of the Administration Commission of African States;

4. To protect the lives of all inhabitants of the Country;

5. To free all political detainees and imprisoned leaders and members of SWAPO and other groups;

6. To disarm all South African military and paramilitary personnel and to arrange for their immediate repatriation to South Africa;

7. To disarm all organized and individual civilian elements;

8. To assist in the restoration of peace and security; and

9. To maintain law and order.

The organization asked that action for the implementation of these objectives commence immediately, and if necessary with the use of force as a last resort.[20]

While agreeing to the position held by SWAPO, SWANU took the view that there could never be peace in Namibia until white power domination was removed.

After talking to many African governments and reviewing many petitions from Namibians, the committee came to the conclusion that in view of the unfitness of the South African government to govern Namibia in the best interest of the African majority, the General Assembly should undertake to study the ways and means by which to terminate South Africa's administration over Namibia. In accordance with its findings, the UN Committee on South West Africa recommended the following:

(a) With reference to paragraph 4 (a) of General Assembly resolution 1568 (XV)–the conditions for restoring a climate of peace and security:

1.   Urgent consideration by the Security Council and all other organs, sub-organs of Member States of the United Nations of all such measures of courses of action as may be required to ensure the effective implementation of the recommendations made in this report or of any other decisions made by the United Nations on the question of South West Africa;

2.   The immediate institution of a United Nations presence in South West Africa;

3.   Removal of the present Administration from the Territory of South West Africa, with effective and simultaneous transfer of power to the United Nations or to the indigenous inhabitants of the Territory;

4.   United Nations assistance to the indigenous inhabitants, either through the Committee on South West Africa or through a United Nations Special Committee of Assistance to South West Africa;

5.   Training and organization of an indigenous police force by the United Nations, withdrawal of firearms from all Europeans and prohibition of the possession of arms by all civilians, withdrawal of South African military forces, abolition of all discriminatory laws and regulations, and cessation of all organized immigration of Europeans, especially South Africans, to the Mandated Territory.

6.   Attainment of independence by South West Africa through a Constitutional Convention, a popular referendum on the constitution adopted by the Convention, the election of representatives of the people on the basis of universal adult suffrage, the establishment of an independent government–all with the assistance of the Committee on South West Africa or the suggested United Nations Special Committee of Assistance to South West Africa.: Africa.[21]

Apartheid South Africa condemned this report and offered to invite three past presidents of the UN General Assembly to visit South West Africa with the specific objective of ascertaining whether the political and social climate in that territory constituted a threat to international peace and security. The General Assembly opposed this request. Having done that, the Assembly dissolved the Committee on South West Africa and established a Special Committee on South West Africa to prepare for the independence of the territory. After that, the General Assembly adopted Resolution 1702 (XVI). Some parts of this Resolution noted:

1. *Solemnly proclaims* the inalienable right of the people of South West Africa to independence and national sovereignty;

2. Decides to establish a United Nations Special Committee for South West Africa, consisting of representatives of seven Member States nominated by the President of the General Assembly, whose task will be to achieve, in consultation with the Mandatory Power, the following objectives:

   (a) A visit to the Territory of South West Africa before 1 May 1962.
   (b) The evacuation from the Territory of all military forces of the Republic of South Africa;
   (c) The release of all political prisoners without distinction as to party or race;
   (d) The repeal of all laws or regulations confining the indigenous inhabitants in reserves and denying them all freedom of movement, expressions and association, and all other laws and regulations which establish and maintain the intolerable system of apartheid;
   (e) Preparations for general elections to the Legislative Assembly, based on universal adult suffrage, to be held as soon as possible under the supervision and control of the United Nations;
   (f) Advice and assistance to the Government resulting from the general elections, with a view to preparing the Territory for full independence;
   (g) Co-ordination of the economic and social assistance with which the specialized agencies will provide the people in order to promote their moral and material welfare;
   (h) The return to the Territory of indigenous inhabitants without risk of imprisonment, detention or punishment of any kind because of their political activities in or outside the Territory;

3. *Requests* the Special Committee to discharge the tasks which were assigned to the Committee on South West Africa by the General Assembly in sub-paragraphs (a), (b) and (c) of paragraph 12 of its Resolution 749 A (VIII) of 28 November 1953;

4. *Urges* the Government of South Africa to cooperate fully with the Special Committee and with the United Nations in the execution of the provisions of the present resolution;

5. *Decides* to call the attention of the Security Council to the present Resolution, in the light of paragraph 7 of Resolution 1596 (XV) in which the General Assembly drew the attention of the Council to the situation in respect of South West Africa, which, if allowed to continue, would in the Assembly's view endanger international peace and security;

6. *Request* to all Member States:

   (a) To do everything in their power to help the Special Committee to accomplish its task;
   (b) To refrain, should the occasion arise, from any act likely to delay or prevent the application of the present resolution;

7. *Requests* the Special Committee to keep the Security Council, the Secretary-General and the Special Committee on the application of the Declaration on the granting of independence to colonial countries and peoples informed of its activities and of any difficulties which it may encounter;

8. *Requests* the Special Committee to study any measures likely to facilitate the execution of the other recommendations of the Committee on South West Africa, and to report to the General Assembly at its seventeenth session;

9. *Decides* to maintain the question of South West Africa on its agenda as a question demanding urgent and constant attention;

10. *Invites* the Secretary-General to facilitate the application of the present resolution.[22]

In 1962 the Republic of South Africa adopted a divide-and-rule policy in the United Nations with respect to the Namibian question. South Africa invited some members of the committee whom it considered to be sympathetic to the apartheid policies of the Republic of South Africa (RSA). After much criticism from the OAU countries in the United Nations, the UN representatives invited to South Africa repudiated the statements they had previously made that they had not observed any situation that was likely to threaten international peace and security in Namibia.

Prior to these developments, on October 4, 1960, Ethiopia and Liberia had instituted legal proceedings against South Africa in a case concerning the continued existence of the mandate for South West Africa and the duties and performance of South Africa as a mandatory power, charging that South Africa had violated its obligations under the mandate. In its judgment, the ICJ delivered on July 18, 1966, that:

> The Court, it decided, could not rule on the substance of the case because Ethiopia and Liberia had not established any legal right or interest in the matter.

> Although many observers had believed this question had been disposed of by the Court in the 1962 judgment–in which it affirmed the applicability of Article 7 of the Mandate, providing for legal action by the League Members–the Court now declared that the League Covenant made no provision for individual League Members to institute actions in regard to the administration of a Mandate. The Mandatories, it said, were to be "agents of the League" and not of the individual countries in the League; and the interest of individual states in regard to the Mandates could be exercised only through the appropriate organs of the international body. Therefore, Ethiopia and Liberia were not entitled to the pronouncements they had asked of the Court, even if the various allegations of Mandate violations had been established. The "moral ideal" must not be confused with the legal rules, the Court declared.

> As in the 1962 decision, the Court was divided. The composition of the Court had changed since 1962: one judge had died and another was unable to take part due to illness. Both had supported the earlier Court decisions upholding the United Nations position. With seven judges in favor and seven against, the President of the Court, Sir Percy Spender of Australia, had used his second "casting vote" to break the tie with a 8-7 judgment.[23]

African states and their allies were stunned and appalled by the ICJ's judgment. According to the *Times*, as quoted by Richard Gibson:

> Voting for the majority decision was the President of the Court, Sir Percy Spender (Australia), who also gave the casting vote that broke the tie among the

fourteen judges on the Court. Also voting for the decisions were the judges from Italy, Britain, Greece, France, South Africa and Poland. Mr. B. Winiarsky, the Polish judge, later retired in the West rather than return home. The dissenting votes came from the United States, USSR, Japan, Nationalist China, Mexico, Senegal and Nigeria.[24]

The United Nations were caught off balance by the negative decision of the ICJ. As a response to this unexpected decision, the Fifth Committee of the General Assembly refused to approve an additional budgetary appropriation for the court. Later, when new elections were held, the African states at the United Nations together with their Third World allies made sure that no racist white judges from the British Commonwealth of Nations would be elected to fill the vacancies that occurred within the ICJ.

Two weeks after the ICJ's judgment, thirty-five African countries requested that the Namibian problem be considered as a General Assembly priority issue of action during the Assembly's 1966 session. While expressing grave concern over the ICJ's decision, the Special Committee of 24 recommended the termination of South Africa's rights as the mandatory power on the grounds that the court's ruling did not invalidate earlier advisory opinions. (At the time, there was a general feeling among many African states that the ICJ's ruling, particularly those of the president of the court and Judge Winiarsky, was based primarily on racial, rather than legal, reasons.) Some of the judges of the ICJ who were labeled racists by the African states were Percy Spender, Spiropoulos, Gerald Fitzmaurice, Morelli, Gross, and Van Wyk. On October 27, 1966, the General Assembly adopted Resolution 2145 (XXI) terminating the mandate for South West Africa by 114 votes to 2 (the Republic of South Africa and Portugal), with 3 abstentions (Britain, France, and Malawi). Resolution 2145 (XXI) states:

Emphasizing that the problem of South West Africa is an issue falling within the terms of General Assembly Resolution 1514 (XV);

Considering that all the efforts of the United Nations to induce the Government of South Africa to fulfill its obligations in respect of the administration of the Mandated Territory and ensure the well-being and security of the indigenous inhabitants have been of no avail;

Mindful of the obligations of the United Nations towards the people of South West Africa;

Noting with deep concern the explosive situation which exists in the southern region of Africa;

Affirming its right to take appropriate action in the matter, including the right to revert to itself the administration of the Mandated Territory:

1. *Reaffirms* that the provisions of General Assembly Resolution 1514 (XV) are fully applicable to the people of the Mandated Territory of South West Africa and that, therefore, the people of South West Africa have the inalienable right to self-determination, freedom and independence in accordance with the Charter of the United Nations:

2. *Reaffirms* further that South West Africa is a territory having international status and that it shall maintain this status until it achieves independence:

3. *Declares* that South Africa has failed to fulfill its obligations in respect of the administration of the Mandated Territory and to ensure the moral and material well-being and security of the indigenous inhabitants of South West Africa and has, in fact, disavowed the Mandate:

4. *Decides* that the Mandate conferred upon His Britannic Majesty ·to be exercised on his behalf by the Government of the Union of South Africa is therefore terminated, that South Africa has no other right to administer the Territory and that henceforth South West Africa comes under the direct responsibility of the United Nations:

5. *Resolves* that in these circumstances the United Nations must discharge those responsibilities with respect to South West Africa:

6. *Establishes* an Ad Hoc Committee for South West Africa–composed of fourteen Member States to be designated by the President of the General Assembly–to recommend practical means by which South West Africa should be administered, so as to enable the people of the Territory to exercise the right of self-determination and to achieve independence, and to report to the General Assembly at a special session as soon as possible and in any event not later than April, 1967;

7. *Calls upon* the Government of South Africa forthwith to refrain and desist from any action, constituional, administrative, political or otherwise which will in any manner whatsoever alter or tend to alter the present international status of South West Africa;

8. *Calls the attention* of the Security Council to the present resolution;

9. *Requests* all States to extend their whole-hearted cooperation and to render assistance in the implementation of the present resolution;

10. *Requests* the Secretary-General to provide all the assistance necessary to implement the present resolution and to enable the Ad Hoc Committee for South West Africa to perform its duties.[25]

Prime Minister Vorster of South Africa ignored Resolution 2145 (XXI) on the grounds that the General Assembly had no legal authority to terminate South Africa's mandate over South West Africa.

Having terminated South Africa's mandate over South West Africa, the General Assembly created a United Nations Council for South West Africa made up of eleven members from Guyana, Nigeria, Chile, India, Colombia, Indonesia, Turkey, Pakistan, Egypt, Zambia, and Yugoslavia. After this, the assembly requested the council to proceed to South West Africa to take over the administration of its government and to declare the independence of Namibia at about June 1968. In addition, the General Assembly requested the Security Council to take appropriate measures that would enable the Council on Namibia to carry out its responsibilities. In Resolution 2248 (S-V) on May 19, 1967, the General Assembly declared:

II

1. *Decides* to establish a United Nations Council for South Africa (hereinafter referred to as the Council) comprising eleven Member States to be elected during the present session and to entrust to it the following powers and functions, to be discharged in the Territory:

   (a) To administer South West Africa until independence, with the maximum possible participation of the people of the Territory;

   (b) To promulgate such laws, decrees and administrative regulations as are necessary for the administration of the Territory until a legistlative assembly is established following elections conducted on the basis of universal adult suffrage;

   (c) To take as an immediate task all the necessary measures, in consultation with the people of the Territory, for the establishment of a constituent assembly to draw up a constitution on the basis of which elections will be held for the establishment of a legislative assembly and a responsible government;

   (d) To transfer all powers to the people of the Territory upon the declaration of independence;

2. *Decides* that in the exercise of its powers and in the discharge of its functions the Council shall be responsible to the General Assembly;

3. *Decides* that the Council shall entrust such executive and administrative tasks as it deems necessary to a United Nations Commissioner for South West Africa (hereinafter referred to as the Commissioner), who shall be appointed during the present session by the General Assembly on the nomination of the Secretary-General;

4. *Decides* that in the performance of his tasks the Commissioner shall be responsible to the Council;

III

1. *Decides* that:

   (a) The administration of South West Africa under the United Nations shall be financed from the revenues collected in the Territory;

   (b) Expenses directly related to the operation of the Council and the Office of the Commissioner–the travel and subsistence expenses of members of the Council, the remuneration of the Commissioner and his staff and the cost of ancillary facilities–be met from the regular budget of the United Nations;

2. *Requests* the specialised agencies and the appropriate organs of the United Nations to render to South West Africa technical and financial assistance through a coordinated emergency programme to meet the exigencies of the situation;

IV

1. *Decides* that the Council shall be based in South West Africa;

2. *Requests* the Council to enter immediately into contact with the authorities of South Africa in order to lay down procedures, in accordance with General Assembly Resolution 2145 (XXI) and the present resolution, for the transfer of the administration of the Territory with the least possible upheaval;

3. *Further requests* the Council to proceed to South West Africa with a view to:

   (a) Taking over the administration of the Territory;

   (b) Ensuring the withdrawal of South African police and military forces;

   (c) Ensuring the withdrawal of South African personnel and their replacement by personnel operating under the authority of the Council;

   (d) Ensuring that in the utilization and recruitment of personnel preference be given to the indigenous people;

4. *Calls upon* the Government of South Africa to comply without delay with the terms of Resolution 2145 (XXI) and the present resolution and to facilitate the transfer of the administration of the Territory of South West Africa to the Council;

5. *Requests* the Security Council to take all appropriate measures to enable the United Nations Council for South West Africa to discharge the functions and responsibilities entrusted to it by the General Assembly;

6. *Requests* all States to extend their wholehearted cooperation and to render assistance to the Council in the implementation of its task;

V

Requests the Council to report to the General Assembly at intervals not exceeding three months on its administration of the Territory and to submit a special report to the Assembly at its twenty-second session concerning the implementation of the present resolution;

VI

Decides that South West Africa shall become independent on a date to be fixed in accordance with the wishes of the people and that the Council shall do all in its power to enable independence to be attained by June 1968.[26]

Resolution 2248 (S-V) establishing an eleven-member United Nations Council on South West Africa was adopted by eighty-five votes to two, with thirty abstentions. The nations that abstained from voting were predominantly Western. A legal council and an acting commissioner for Namibia were appointed. The council met in August of the same year and sent a letter requesting South Africa to indicate what steps it had taken to hasten the transfer of the administration of South West Africa to the United National Council for South West Africa. Taking advantage of the objections of the

Western nations to the General Assembly Resolution 2248 (S-V), the Republic of South Africa proceeded to deny the United Nations Council entry permit into South West Africa. When the General Assembly convened in December 1967, the council reported that it had been unable to discharge any of its functions because of the continued illegal occupation of South West Africa by South Africa.

In April 1968, the Council for Namibia tried to enter into South West Africa but was unsuccessful. While in Zambia and Tanzania, the council met with several Namibians and obtained their views on problems facing the South West Africans. Having concluded these hearings, the council renamed South West Africa as Namibia, and the General Assembly officially endorsed the new name. Following this, the council also reported to the General Assembly that the Republic of South Africa had intensified its defiance of all United Nations decisions on Namibia and had sought to consolidate its illegal control over the territory. The most serious step in that direction, the council reported, was the implementation of the separate development policies that were designed to destroy the territorial integrity of Namibia and to facilitate its illegal annexation.[27]

In 1969 the South African government decided to implement the Odendaal recommendations. These recommendations were the result of the Odendaal Commission appointed in 1962 by the South African government. Its task was to find ways of improving the welfare of the people of Namibia. In 1964 the Odendaal Commission issued findings and recommendations that became the cornerstone of South African policy in Namibia. The report proposed that 40 percent of Namibia be divided into eleven separate self-governing homelands or "Bantustans"; 43 percent of the land was to be reserved for whites. South Africa was to take over direct control of the remaining area, including the diamond zones, which were to become another South African province. With these recommendations as basis for policy formulation, South Africa decided to balkanize and officially annex Namibia under the pretext of reorganizing the country into self-governing homelands. To justify its actions, South Africa enacted the South West Africa Affairs Act, no. 25, of 1969. The act drastically altered the then existing relationship between Namibia and the Republic of South Africa by transferring to the government and parliament of the Republic jurisdiction over twenty-five broad categories of subjects that until then were within the province of the local White Legislative Council. The local White Council was granted authority and power akin to the other four provinces of the Republic of South Africa. This change was followed by extensive action to bring the laws of Namibia into line with the apartheid laws of the Republic of South Africa. There is no doubt that by enacting the South West Africa Act no. 25, South Africa had intended to annex Namibia.

The Council for Namibia, the Special Committee of 24, SWAPO, and the Independent African States reacted to the South West Africa Affairs Act as a law of annexure of Namibia. Infuriated by the enactment of the South West Africa Act no. 25, the Security Council of the United Nations met and passed Resolution 269 on October 4, 1969.

Recalling its Resolution 264 (1969) of 20 March 1969.

Taking note of the report of the Secretary-General contained in document S/9204,

Mindful of its responsibility to take necessary action to secure strict compliance with the obligations entered into by States Members of the United Nations under the provisions of Article 25 of the Charter of the United Nations,

Mindful also of its responsibilities under Article 6 of the United Nations,
1. *Reaffirms* its Resolution 264 (1969);
2. *Condemns* the Government of South Africa for its refusal to comply with Resolution 264 (1969) and for its persistent defiance of the authority of the United Nations;
3. *Decides* that the continued occupation of the territory of Namibia by the South African authorities constitutes an aggressive encroachment on the authority of the United Nations, a violation of the territorial integrity and a denial of the political sovereignty of the people of Namibia;
4. *Recognizes* the legitimacy of the struggle of the people of Namibia against the illegal presence of the South African authorities in the territory;
5. *Calls upon* the Government of South Africa to withdraw its administration from the territory immediately and in any case before 4 October 1969;
6. *Decides* that in the event of failure on the part of the South African Government to comply with the provisions of the preceding paragraph of the present resolution, the Security Council will meet immediately to determine upon effective measures in accordance with the appropriate provisions of the relevant chapters of the United Nations Charter;
7. *Calls upon* all States to refrain from all dealings with the Government of South Africa purporting to act on behalf of the territory of Namibia;
8. *Requests* all States to increase their moral and material assistance to the people of Namibia in their struggle against foreign occupation;
9. *Requests* the Secretary-General to follow closely the implementation of the present resolution and to report to the Security Council as soon as possible;
10. *Decides* to remain actively seized of the matter.[28]

The Republic of South Africa replied to this action by stating that it would not comply with the Security Council Resolution 269. South Africa objected to the legal basis for the adoption of the General Assembly Resolution 2145 (XXI) and the procedure with which the Security Council had adopted Resolution 269. South Africa further argued that Resolution 2145 (XXI) was invalid on the basis that the United Nations did not inherit the supervisory powers of the moribund League of Nations, and even if that were the case, South Africa argued that the stated resolution did not have the right to terminate unilaterally its administration over Namibia. South Africa further contended that the resolution was not properly passed because of the abstention of many Western nations. On the basis of the reasons stated, South Africa refused to comply with the Security Council Resolution 269. On January 30, 1970, the Security Council passed Resolution 276. While condemning South Africa's refusal to abide by Resolution 276, the Security Council also called for all states with economic and other interests in Namibia to refrain from any dealings with the Republic of South Africa. Annoyed and frustrated by South Africa's continued unwillingness to adopt its Resolutions, the Security Council passed Resolution 283 of 1970.

1. *Requests* all States to refrain from any relations–diplomatic, consular or otherwise–with South Africa implying recognition of the authority of the South African Government over the territory of Namibia;

2. *Calls upon* all States maintaining diplomatic or consular relations with South Africa to issue a formal declaration to the Government of South Africa to the effect that they do not recognize any authority of South Africa with regard to Namibia and that they consider South Africa's continued presence in Namibia illegal;

3. *Calls upon* all States maintaining such relations to terminate existing diplomatic and consular representation as far as they extend to Namibia and to withdraw any diplomatic or consular mission or representative residing in the territory;

4. *Calls upon* all States to ensure that companies and other commercial and industrial enterprises owned by, or under direct control of the State, cease all dealings with respect to commercial or industrial enterprises or concessions in Namibia;

5. *Calls upon* all States to withhold from their nationals or companies of their nationality not under direct government control, government loans, credit guarantees and other forms of financial support that would be used to facilitate trade or commerce with Namibia;

6. *Calls upon* all States to ensure that companies and other commercial enterprises owned by the State or under direct control of the State cease all further investment activities including concessions in Namibia;

7. *Calls upon* all States to discourage their nationals or companies of their nationality not under direct governmental control from investing or obtaining concessions in Namibia, and to this end withhold protection of such investment against claims of a future lawful government in Namibia;

8. *Requests* all States to undertake without delay a detailed study and review of all bilateral treaties between themselves and South Africa in so far as these treaties contain provisions by which they apply to the territory of Namibia;

9. *Requests* the Secretary-General of the United Nations to undertake without delay a detailed study and review of all multilateral treaties to which South Africa is a party, and which either by direct reference or on the basis of relevant provisions of international law might be considered to apply to the territory of Namibia;

10. *Requests* the United National Council for Namibia to make available to the Security Council the results of its study and proposals with regard to the issuance of passports and visas for Namibians and to undertake a study and make proposals with regard to special passport and visa regulations to be adopted by States concerning travel of their citizens to Namibia;

11. *Calls upon* all States to discourage the promotion of tourism and emigration to Namibia;

12. *Requests* the General Assembly at its twenty-fifth session to set up a United Nations Fund for Namibia to provide assistance to Namibians who have suffered from persecution and to finance a comprehensive education and training programme for Namibians with particular regard to their future administrative responsibilities of the territory;

13. *Requests* all States to report to the Secretary-General on measures they have taken in order to give effect to the provisions set forth in the present resolution;

14. *Decides* to re-establish, in accordance with Rule 28 of the provisional rules of procedure, the Ad Hoc Sub-Committee on Namibia and request the Ad Hoc Sub-Committee to study further effective recommendations on ways and means by which the relevant resolutions of the Council can be effectively implemented in accordance with the appropriate provisions of the Charter, in the light of the flagrant refusal of South Africa to withdraw from Namibia;

15. *Requests* the Ad Hoc Sub-Committee to study the replies submitted by Governments to the Secretary-General in pursuance of operative paragraph 13 of the present resolution and to report to the Council as appropriate;
16. *Requests* the Secretary-General to give every assistance to the Ad Hoc Sub-Committee in the performance of its tasks;
17. *Decides* to remain actively seized of this matter.[29]

Some aspects of Resolution 283 calling for all states to ensure that companies and other commercial and industrial enterprises owned by, or under direct control of their nationals, cease all dealings with respect to commercial and industrial enterprises in Namibia were never implemented by almost all the sponsors of the resolution. For details of the foreign companies that operate in Namibia, see Table 10.

Table 10: Subsidiaries or Associates of Companies Registered in (A) United States of America, (B) Great Britain and Northern Ireland, (C) France, (D) Canada, (E) Federal Republic of Germany, and (F) South Africa

A. *Subsidiaries or Associates of Companies Registered in the United States of America*

Parent Company	Related Company in Namibia	Activites
American Metal Climax Inc. (AMAX)	Tsumeb Corporation, Ltd.	Mining copper, lead, and zinc
Standard Oil Company of California (operating through Chevron Oil)	Chevron/Regent Consortium	Prospecting for petroleum
Regent Petroleum	Chevron/Regent Consortium	Prospecting for petroleum

B. *Subsidiaries or Associates of Companies Registered in the United Kingdom of Great Britain and Northern Ireland*

Consolidated Gold Fields Ltd.	Gold Fields of South Africa, Ltd.	Prospecting for uranium
Rio Tinto Zinc Corporation Ltd. (RTZ)	Rossing Uranium Ltd.	Mining copper, lead, and zinc
Selection Trust, Ltd.	Tsumeb Corporation, Ltd.	Mining copper, lead, and zinc

C. *Subsidiaries or Associates of Companies Registered in France*

Société nationale des petroles d'Aquitaine	Consortium with DeBeers Consolidated Mines, Ltd.	Prospecting for petroleum
Total-Compagnie miniere et nucleaire (CMN)	Rossing Uranium, Ltd.	Mining uranium

D. *Subsidiaries of Associates of Companies Registered in Canada*

Brilund Mines, Ltd.	Etosha Petroleum (Pty.), Ltd.	Petroleum exploration
Falconbridge Nickel Mines, Ltd.	Oamites Mining Company (Pty.), Ltd.	Mining copper

E. *Subsidiaries of Associates of Companies Registered in the Federal Republic of Germany*

Metallgesellschaft, AG*	South West Africa Lithium Company	Mining Lithium
	Kiln Products, Ltd.	Produces zinc oxide from concentrates
Ohlthaver group	Khan Mine (Pty.), Ltd.	Mining copper

F. Subsidiaries or Associates of Companies Registered in South Africa

Anglo-American Corp. of South Africa, Ltd.	Consolidated Diamond Mines of South West Africa, Ltd., (CDM) (through Anglo-American's holding in DeBeers Consolidated Mines, Ltd.)	Diamond mining (jewelry and industrial)
Kiln Products, Ltd.	SWACO	Mining lead and vanadium
Anglo-Transvaal Consolidated Investment Company, Ltd. (ANGLOVAAL)	African Triangle Mining, Prospecting and Development Company (Pty.), Ltd.	Prospecting for copper
DeBeers Consolidated Mines, Ltd.	CDM	Diamond mining (jeweler and industrial)
	Consortium with Société nationale des petroles d'Aquitaine	Prospecting for petroleum
	Marine Diamond Corporation	Offshore diamond mining
	Tidal Diamonds (SWA) (Pty.), Ltd.	Prospecting for diamonds
Desert Finds (Pty.), Ltd.		Prospecting for uranium
DiGamma Mining Company		Prospecting for uranium
Federale Mynbou (Bpk.) of South Africa	Klein Aub Copper Cómpany	Mining copper
Fedmar Ltd.	Otjihase Mining Company (Pty.), Ltd.	Opening new copper and zinc mine
General Mining and Finance Corporation, Ltd.	Klein Aub Copper Company	Mining copper
	FEDSWA Prospekteerders (Edms,) (Bpk.)	Prospecting for copper
Gold Fields of South Africa Ltd.		Prospecting for uranium
Iron and Steel Corporation of South Africa (ISCOR)	Uis Tin Mine	Mining tin
Johannesburg Consolidated Investment Company, Ltd. (JCI)	B & O Mineral Exploration Company (Pty.), Ltd.	Prospecting for copper
Marine Pro	Otjihase Mining Company (Pty.), Ltd.	Copper and zinc mine
Marine Products, Ltd.	Klein Aub Copper Company	Mining copper
Minerts Development (Pty.), Ltd.	Otjihase Mining Company (Pty.), Ltd.	Opening new copper and zinc mine
O'kiep Copper Company, Ltd.	Tsumeb Corporation, Ltd.	Mining copper, lead, and zinc
Southern Oil Exploration Corporation (Pty.), Ltd. (SOEKOR)	Southern Oil Exploration Corporation (South West Africa) (Pty.), Ltd. (SWAKOR)	Prospecting for petroleum in partnership with various international oil companies which are mentioned individually in the present table

SOURCE: *Decolonization: Issue on Namibia:* A publication of the United Nations Department of Political Affairs, Trusteeship and Decolonization no. 9 (New York: United Nations, December 1977); 66-69, *Metallgesellschaft is owned by the Klockner and Company/Duisberg Mannheim Gesellschaft group.

Having informed the Security Council that it would not abide by the Security Council Resolution 283, South Africa appealed to the Western nations with economic interests in the Republic of South Africa and Namibia to ignore African pressures within the UN system. African states and their allies wanted the United Nations to impose economic sanctions against the Republic of South Africa because of its continued occupation of Namibia. Convinced beyond doubt that South Africa was not going to abide by the Security Council Resolution 283, the Security Council passed Resolution 284, which requested the ICJ for an advisory opinion on the legal consequences of the continued presence of South Africa in Namibia.

The Security Council debate on the ICJ's ruling was opened on September 27, 1971, by President Moktar Ould Daddah of Mauritania, then president of the OAU, who called on the Western countries to support mandatory economic and military sanctions against South Africa under Chapter VII of the United Nations. While President Dadda appealed to the Council to adopt strong punitory measures against South Africa, he also denounced the apartheid draconic laws of that state. The Security Council ended its debate by adopting the ICJ's Advisory Opinion of October 20, 1971, as Security Council Resolution 301, by thirteen votes to none with two abstentions. Parts of Resolution 301 read as follows:

1. *Reaffirms* that the Territory of Namibia is the direct responsibility of the United Nations and that this responsibility includes the obligation to support and promote the rights of the people of Namibia in accordance with General Assembly resolution 1514 (XV);

2. *Reaffirms* the national unity and territorial integrity of Namibia;

3. *Condemns* all moves by the Government of South Africa designed to destroy that unity and territorial integrity, such as the establishment of Bantustans;

4. *Declares* that South Africa's continued illegal presence in Namibia constitutes an internationally wrongful act and a breach of international obligations and that South Africa remains accountable to the international community for any violations of its international obligations or the rights of the people of the Territory of Namibia;

5. *Takes note* with appreciation of the advisory opinion of the International Court of Justice of 21 June, 1971;

6. *Agrees with* the Court's opinion expressed in paragraph 133 of the advisory opinion;

   (1)   that, the continued presence of South Africa in Namibia being illegal, South Africa is under obligation to withdraw its administration from Namibia immediately and thus put an end to its occupation of the Territory;

   (2)   that States Members of the United Nations are under obligation or recognize the illegality of South Africa's presence in Namibia and the invalidity of its acts on behalf of or concerning Namibia, and to refrain from any acts and in particular any dealing with the Government of South Africa implying recognition of the legality of or lending support or assistance to, such presence and administration;

   (3)   that it is incumbent upon States which are not Members of the United Nations to give assistance, within the scope of subparagraph (2) above, in the action which has been taken by the United Nations with regard to Namibia.

7. *Declares* that all matters affecting the rights of the people of Namibia are of immediate concern to all Members of the United Nations and as a result of the latter should take this into account in their dealings with the Government of South Africa, in particular in any dealings implying recognition of the legality of or lending support or assistance to such illegal presence and administration;

8. *Calls once again* on South Africa to withdraw from the Territory of Namibia;

9. *Declares* that any further refusal of the South African Government to withdraw from Namibia could create conditions detrimental to the maintenance of peace and security in the region;

10. *Reaffirms* the provisions of resolution 283 (1970), in particular paragraphs 1 to 8 and 11;

11. *Calls upon* all States in discharge of their responsibilities towards the people of Namibia and subject to the exceptions set forth in paragraphs 122 and 125 of the advisory opinion of 21 June 1971;

(a) To abstain from entering into treaty relations with South Africa in all cases in which the Government of South Africa purports to act on beahlf of or concerning Namibia;

(b) To abstain from involving or applying those treaties or provisions of treaties concluded by South Africa on behalf of or concerning Namibia which involve active intergovernmental cooperation;

(c) To review their bilateral treaties with South Africa in order to ensure that they are not inconsistent with paragraphs 5 and 6 above;

(d) To abstain from sending diplomatic or special missions to South Africa that includes the Territory of Namibia in their jurisdiction;

(e) To abstain from sending consular agents to Namibia and withdraw any such agents already there;

(f) To abstain from entering into economic and other forms of relationship or dealings with South Africa on behalf of or concerning Namibia which may entrench its authority over the Territory;

12. Declares that franchises, rights, titles or contracts relaing to Namibia granted to individuals or companies by South Africa after the adoption of General Assembly resolution 2145 (XXI) are not subject to protection or espousal by their States against claims of a future lawful Government of Namibia;

13. *Requests* the Ad Hoc Sub-Committee on Namibia to continue to carry out the tasks entrusted to it by paragraph 14 and 15 of resolution 283 (1970) and, in particular, taking into account the need to provide for the effective protection of Namibian interests at the international level, to study appropriate measures for the fulfillment of the responisbility of the United Nations towards Namibia;

14. *Requests* the Ad Hoc Sub-Committee on Namibia to review all treaties and agreements which are contrary to the provisions of the present resolution in order to ascertain whether States have entered into agreements which recognize South Africa's authority over Namibia, and to report periodically thereon;

15. *Calls upon* all States to support and promote the rights of the people of Namibia and to this end to implement fully the provisions of the present resolution;

16. *Requests* the Secretary-General to report periodically on the implementation of the provisions of the present resolution.[30]

This ruling was basically a victory for the Namibians, the African states, and all those who were fighting against apartheid and colonialism. As a result of the ruling, international opinion against South Africa mounted in Western Europe, Eastern Europe, Asia, South America, the Caribbean, North America, Australia, and the Pacific Islands. Inside Namibia, the advisory opinion and the Security Council's acceptance of it were big moral boosts to those seeking to overthrow South African colonial domination.

At its meeting in Addis Ababa in February 1972, the Security Council condemned South Africa's continued brutal treatment of Africans and its illegal occupation of Namibia. Despite its condemnatory speeches against South Africa, the Security Council in the spring of 1972 directed the secretary-general to initiate contact with

South Africa so that he could consult with the people of Namibia. By 1973, the Council of Namibia, SWAPO, the OAU, and the General Assembly had come to the conclusion that these contacts being made were not going to lead to a change of position by South Africa.

Apartheid South Africa reacted to the ICJ's ruling of 1971 by declaring it unacceptable to the people of South Africa and their government. While ignoring the Security Council's warnings of its illegal continued occupation of Namibia, South Africa proceeded to expand and create new Bantustans in Namibia from 1971 to 1973. In addition, South Africa increased its repressions and arrests of the Namibian political opponents. On March 7, 1973, the apartheid South African government police raided the African township at Katutura outside Windhoek, where Africans had gathered to demonstrate against Vorster's proposed Advisory Council for South West Africa. In addition to beating many demonstrators, the police also arrested 118 innocent Africans. Another second incident at Katutura took place on August 12, 1973. A rally attended by about 2,000 people calling for an end to the illegal South African domination of Namibia was held. After the rally, the South African police arrested three hundred Africans and charged them with making inflammatory statements that contravened the Sabotage Act. In addition to these acts, the racist government of South Africa has maintained a system of flogging and of detaining political prisoners. Thousands of Africans have been detained and are languishing in South African jails. Reacting to the repressive measures that were being perpetrated against the Namibian people by South Africa, nonaligned countries at the United Nations pressured the Security Council to take strong action against South Africa. As a result, the Security Council adopted Resolution 366 of 17 December 1974, which noted the following:

1. Condemned the continued illegal occupation of the Territory of Namibia by South Africa;
2. Condemned the illegal and arbitrary application by South Africa of racially discriminatory and repressive laws and practices in Namibia;
3. Demanded that South Africa make a solemn declaration that it will comply with the resolutions and decisions of the United Nations and the advisory opinion of the International Court of Justice of 21 June 1971 in regard to Namibia and that it recognizes the territorial integrity and unity of Namibia as a nation;
4. Demanded that South Africa take the necessary steps to effect the withdrawal of its illegal administration maintained in Namibia and transfer power to the people of Namibia with the assistance of the United Nations;
5. Demanded further that South Africa, pending the transfer of powers provided for in the preceding paragraph:
   (a) Release all Namibian political prisoners, including those imprisoned or detained in connection with offences under so-called internal security laws, whether such Namibians have been charged or tried or are held without charge and whether held in Namibia or South Africa;
   (b) Comply fully in spirit and in practice with the provisions of the Universal Declaration of Human Rights;
   (c) Abolish the application in Namibia of all racially discriminatory and politically repressive laws and practices, particularly bantustans and homelands;
   (d) Accord unconditionally to all Namibians currently in exile for political reasons full facilities for return to their country without risk of arrest, detention, intimidation or imprisonment.

6. Decided to remain seized of the matter and to meet on or before 30 May 1975 for the purpose of reviewing South Africa's compliance with the terms of this resolution and, in the event of noncompliance by South Africa, for the purpose of considering the appropriate measures to be taken under the Charter.[31]

Apparently frustrated by South Africa's stubborn refusal to implement this Security Council Resolution requiring South Africa to take necessary steps to effect its withdrawal from Namibia, or its intention to do so, the Council for Namibia decided to send various missions to Europe, Africa, and Latin America to hold fraternal discussions with many government and nongovernmental organizations in order to popularize the Namibian predicament. The mission to Latin America was led by Ambassador Roberto de Rosenwerg-Diaz of Mexico, and included representatives of India, Pakistan, and Senegal. The mission visited Peru, Venezuela, and Brazil. While in Peru, the delegation discussed the question of bilateral treaties between Peru and South Africa extending into Namibia; the existence of an extradition treaty dated January 26, 1904, between Peru and South Africa that was extended to Namibia on January 16, 1928; and, the general issue of solidarity with the people of Namibia in their struggle for independence. At the end of the mission's visit, the government of Peru in a press statement declared that its position on the question of Namibia was consistent with the humanistic and independent character of its revolution, which is against all forms of colonialism and discrimination.[32] From Peru, the mission visited Brazil and was informed of Brazil's unequivocal support for the right of the Namibians to self-determination and independence. The government of Venezuela reiterated to the mission its nonrecognition of any form of authority of South Africa over Namibia.

The Council of Namibia scheduled other visits to Africa. Between August and September 1976, the president of the Council of Namibia (Ambassador Dunstan Kamana of Zambia), led a Council mission to Angola, Botswana, and Zambia. The delegation included an ambassador of Botswana and representatives from Guyana, Yugoslavia, Liberia, Nigeria, Botswana, Zambia, and SWAPO. After extensive consultations with the government of Botswana, a joint communiqué that was issued stated in part, that the government of Botswana and the mission of the UN Council for Namibia were of the view that the struggle of Namibia for majority rule and independence under the leadership of SWAPO has reached a crucial stage. In the light of recent developments, the government of Botswana and the UN Council for Namibia will support all UN efforts to strengthen the role of the United Nations in the governance of Namibia.

Additional consultations were held with the government of Zambia on September 6, 1976. President Kenneth Kaunda received members of the UN Mission and reaffirmed his support for the liberation of Namibia. In a communiqué issued at the end of the discussions, the government of Zambia and the UN Council for Namibia expressed their conviction that the immediate and unconstitutional withdrawal by South Africa of all its military and police forces and its administration from Namibia constituted the only political solution for Namibia which will enable its citizens to attain independence in accordance with the General Assembly Resolution 2145 (XXI) of 1966.

The last country the committee visited was Angola, where the committee held several discussions with the officials of the Angolan government. Part of their communiqué noted that the government of Angola and the mission of the United Nations Council for Namibia endorsed the relevant resolutions of the OAU with respect to Namibia and supported all necessary measures to strengthen cooperation between the United Nations and the OAU in accordance with the resolutions of the General Assembly, particularly those provisions in support of self-determination and independence.

Aware of the fact that many Namibians will need to have the requisite know-how to administer their country after independence, the United Nations decided to establish an institute in Zambia with the hope of moving it into Namibia after the termination of the illegal occupation of their country by South Africa. The basic purposes and objectives of the institute were to enable Namibians, under the aegis of the United Nations Council for Namibia, to undertake research training, planning, and other related activities concerning the struggle for freedom and the establishment of an independent State of Namibia.[33] Many Namibians are now being trained by the institute to occupy responsible jobs in the civil service of the future free Republic of Namibia.

While the United Nations Council for Namibia and African countries were busy trying to influence the international community to support the antiapartheid forces in Namibia, South Africa was conducting the Turnhalle Conferences aimed at granting sham independence to Namibia.

> The proposals of the so-called constitutional conference do not even approach any of the requirements of genuine self-determination and independence laid down by the United Nations. These proposals make no mention of the elimination of apartheid legislation. They merely seek to perpetuate the homelands (bantustans) policies with all their deleterious effects on the integrity and unity of the Namibian people. They are also silent about free elections under United Nations supervision and control. They totally ignore SWAPO, which has been recognized by the OAU and the United Nations as the authentic representative of the Namibian people. There is no undertaking to release political prisoners or to allow the return of political exiles . . . . The reference to "unity" is couched in ambiguous terms without specifically recognizing the territorial integrity of Namibia as a unitary State. The references to the rejection of any attempt to solve the problem of Namibia by force are, to say the least, paradoxical in the light of the institutionalized brutality under the Repression of Terrorism Act and other rules and regulations, which give a free reign to the most blatant and ruthless violation of all principles of human rights and freedoms as proclaimed by the Charter of the United Nations and the Universal Declaration of Human Rights.[34]

Confronted with mounting international pressure and faced with further geopolitical and strategic problems as a result of the decolonization of Angola and Mozambique, South Africa sought to reduce international condemnation of its presence in Namibia by holding a constitutional conference to decide the future political status of Namibia. The conference was held in Turnhalle, a former German school located in Windhoek, Namibia, from September 1975 to March 1977. The Namibian Conference was attended by representatives from eight African ethnic groups, local whites, Coloreds, and Basters. The Bushmen and other smaller groups were represented by the South African government. African nationalist political organizations were disqualified from participating in the conference. As a result, the Ovambos, Kavangos Rehoboth Basters, and East Caprivians were represented by government-appointed representatives.

In September 1975, the Turnhalle Conference issued a declaration of intent expressing the objectives of the conference. Subsequently, on August 18, 1976, the constitutional committee of the conference reaffirmed the declaration of intent and proceeded to issue a statement specifying certain areas where agreement had been reached. According to the statement, an interim government was to take over the administration of the territory as soon as a constitutional foundation and other solutions to the status of the Walvis Bay and boundary lines were agreed upon. The interim government was to be responsible for handling the transfer of government functions and for establishing the independence government. The date set for independence was December 31, 1978.

South Africa definitely wanted the Turnhalle Conference not only to be accepted in Namibia but throughout the Western world. To this end, South Africa embarked on a campaign to sell the Turnhalle Conference abroad as the most practical way by which Namibia could be granted independence. In the course of the deliberations, Chief Clemens Kapuuo, a leader of the Hereros and a protégé of South Africa and one of those participating in the Turnhalle Conference made two attempts to address the United Nations General Assembly. Kapuuo failed to address the United Nations on both accounts because of the opposition of the nonaligned members of the United Nations. While in the United States, Chief Kapuuo engaged a marketing firm, Psychographic Communications, Ltd. (Psycom), run by Jack Summers to sell him and the Turnhalle Conference to the American people. According to the *New York Times,* Mr. Summers prepared an expensive press kit for Chief Kapuuo. When Chief Kapuuo was in New York in September 1977, he met Elizabeth Tayor and publisher, Dorothy Schiff and columnist James Wechsler of the *New York Post.* The chief was also introduced to such people as Muhammed Ali, Henry Ford, Senator Edward Brooke of Massachusetts, and Senator Jacob Javits of New York. In the United Kingdom, his public relations officer there was the late James Endicott who published a pro-Turnhalle magazine for Kapuuo called *Namibia Bulletin.*

In addition to Kapuuo's activities in the United Kingdom and the United States, the government of South Africa created the Pro-South West Africa Foundation in Windhoek, Namibia. The foundation was managed by the South Africa Foundation whose scandalous activities led to the resignation of John Vorster as president of South Africa. Prominent South African personalities associated with the Pro-South West Africa Foundation were Connie Mulder, Professor Marais, and Mr. Rhoode. The chairman of the foundation is Kurt Dahlmann, editor of the German-language newspaper *Allgemeine Zeitung.* The basic aim of the foundation is to convince African moderate states, Americans, the British, and other Western European people to support the Turnhalle Conference.

From the outset, the Organization of African Unity (OAU) and the United Nations denounced the Turnhalle Constitutional Conference as a maneuver by South Africa to balkanize the territory, perpetuate white minority rule, and maintain control over Namibia in perpetuity. The OAU and the United Nations have also denounced the exclusion from the Turnhalle Conference of representatives of the South West African Peoples Organization (SWAPO) and others opposed to the Odendaal recommendations. To dramatize their opposition to the Turnhalle Conference and their support for African majority rule in Namibia, the OAU and the United Nations held a joint International Conference in Maputo, Mozambique, from May 16 to May 21, in 1977. Five hundred delegates from the United Nations member countries and African Liberation movements from Namibia, Zimbabwe (Rhodesia), and South Africa participated in the deliberations. The conference strongly condemned the Turnhalle tribal talks as a South African strategy to perpetuate its colonial and racist policies in Namibia. Also denounced were South African attempts to annex the Namibia Caprivi Strip and the Walvis Bay areas. The delegates at the Maputo Conference appealed to South Africa to end its illegal occupation of Namibia, and also adopted a program of action for the liberation of Namibia:

(a) categorically reject and denounce all manoeuvres such as tribal talks by which the South African may seek to impose its will upon the Namibian people;

(b) decisively reject all attempts by South Africa to dismember the territory of Namibia and especially the design to annex Walvis Bay;

(c) refrain from according any recognition to or cooperating with any authority or regime which South Africa may install in Namibia;

(d) enact the necessary legislation consistent with Decree No. 1 on the Protection of the Natural Resources of Namibia of the United Nations Council for Namibia;

(f) implement the arms embargo against South Africa without any exceptions or reservations.

The Conference calls upon the United Nations Security Council to impose, under Chapter VII of the Charter, a mandatory arms embargo against South Africa as an important step to ensure South Africa's compliance with the United Nations resolutions and decisions on Namibia.[35]

The exertion of pressure on the United States, Canada, the Western European countries, and the United Nations by the OAU and its allies has been responsible for making South Africa agree to grant Namibia its independence. The Western group comprised of Great Britain, Canada, France, West Germany, and the United States has held several discussions with the New South African Foreign Minister, Roelof Botha, on the Namibian independence issue. Also participating in some of the discussions in New York was the president of the South West Africa Peoples Organization, Sam Nujoma. At these conferences, Sam Nujoma has repeatedly called on South Africa to accept and abide by the stipulations of the Security Council Resolution 385. This resolution notes:

Strongly deploring the militarization of Namibia by the illegal occupation regime of South Africa.

1. Condemns the continued illegal occupation of the Territory of Namibia by South Africa;

2. Condemns the illegal and arbitrary application by South Africa of racially discriminatory and repressive laws and practices in Namibia;

3. Condemns the South African military build-up in Namibia and any utilization of the Territory as a base for attacks on neighbouring countries;

4. Demands that South Africa put an end forthwith to its policy of bantustans and the so-called homelands aimed at violating the national unity and the territorial integrity of Namibia;

5. Further condemns all attempts by South Africa's failure to comply with the terms of Security Council resolution 366 (1964) of 17 December 1974;

6. Further condemns all attempts by South Africa calculated to evade the clear demand of the United Nations for the holding of free elections under United Nations supervision and control in Namibia;

7. Declares that in order that the people of Namibia be enabled to freely determine their own future, it is imperative that free elections under the supervision and control of the United Nations be held for the whole of Namibia as one political entity.

8. Further declares that in determining the date, timetable and modalities for the elections in accordance with paragraph 7·above, there shall be adequate time to be decided upon by the Security Council for the purposes of enabling the United Nations to establish the necessary machinery within Namibia to supervise and control such elections, as well as to enable the people of Namibia to organize politically for the purpose of such elections.

9. Demands that South Africa urgently make a solemn declaration accepting the foregoing provisions for the holding of free elections in Namibia under United Nations supervision and control, undertaking to comply with the resolutions and decisions of the United Nations and with the advisory opinion of the International Court of Justice of 21 June 1971 in regard to Namibia, and recognizing the territorial integrity and unity of Namibia as a nation.

10. Reiterates its demand that South Africa take the necessary steps to effect the withdrawal, in accordance with resolutions 264 (1969), and 269 (1969), and 366 (1974), of its illegal administration maintained in Namibia and to transfer power to the people of Namibia with the assistance of the United Nations.

11. Demands again that South Africa, pending the transfer of powers provided for in the preceding paragraph:

(a) Comply fully in spirit and in practice with the provisions of the Universal Declaration of Human Rights.

(b) Release all Namibian political prisoners, including all those imprisoned or detained in connection with offences under so-called internal security laws, whether such Namibians have been charged or tried or are held without charge and whether held in Namibia or South Africa.

(c) Abolish the application in Namibia of all racially discriminatory and politically repressive laws and practices, particularly bantustans and homelands.

(d) Accord unconditionally to all Namibians currently in exile for political reasons full facilities for return to their country without risk of arrest, detention, intimidation or imprisonment.

12. Decides to remain seized of the matter and to meet on or before 31 August 1976 for the purpose of reviewing South Africa's compliance with the terms of this resolution and in the event of non-compliance by South Africa, for the purpose of considering the appropriate measures to be taken under the Charter.[36]

The principal issues in the discussions between the five Western countries and SWAPO on one hand, and South Africa on the other, center around the continued presence of South African troops in Namibia and South Africa's intention to annex the Walvis Bay after Namibia acquires its independence. When Namibia wins its independence, South Africa wants to keep more than three thousand of its troops in the country along the Angolan border. The OAU, the General Assembly, SWAPO, and the representatives of the five Western countries all want South Africa to pull its soldiers out of Namibia after it acquires its independence. Realizing the uncompromising position adopted by the United Nations and the African and Western countries, South Africa softened her position on the presence of its troops in Namibia.

> The South African standpoint with regard to her military presence in South West Africa can not be considered either rigid or dogmatic. In the past South Africa has stated time and again that she will be prepared to decrease her troops in accordance with the diminishing threat to life and property in the area . . . and even then only if and when the residents of South West Africa request her to do so. However, as long as terrorism is continued, the armed forces are to remain in the country to protect the people. South Africa dare not risk delivering these people into the hands of SWAPO.

> It must also be kept in mind that South West Africa is to become independent in a little less than a year and that the RSA is quite prepared to withdraw her troops from the territory should the government of the new state so wish.[37]

With respect to South Africa's claims to own the Walvis Bay, the United Nations General Assembly, on November 4, 1977, condemned South Africa for its decision to annex Walvis Bay and it urged the Security Council to apply sanctions against South Africa. Walvis Bay is an integral part of Namibia and should continue to belong to Namibia after it gains its independence. Walvis Bay is also the only viable port on the coastline of Namibia and will play a crucial role in the economic development of that country after independence. South Africa has no juridical right to ownership or settlement of any part or section of Namibia as was stated by the Security Council Resolution 385.

By the end of 1977, the United Nations summarized the following events to have taken place in its efforts to resolve the Namibian question:

1.   The setting aside of the Turnhalle formula and the holding of territory-wide elections for a constituent assembly which would draft the constitution for an independent Namibia. South Africa has reportedly agreed to elections on the basis of universal adult suffrage with the participation of all political groups including SWAPO.

2.   The administration of the Territory in the transitional period. In June, South Africa announced that it would appoint an Administrator-General to govern the Territory until independence. It was also reported that the United Nations Secretary-General would appoint a Special Representative. The responsibilities of these two officials and their relationship to each other have not been clarified.

3.   The United Nations role in the constituent elections. This is still under discussion but is reported that South Africa would accept a United Nations presence in the Territory both before and during the electoral process.

4.   The return of all Namibian exiles and refugees and the release of Namibian detainees and political prisoners. South Africa has reportedly agreed, in principle, to the return of exiles but on the other hand claims to have no political prisoners in its gaols. As a result it has been suggested that disputes as to the status of Namibian exiles and prisoners would be decided by a commission of jurists composed of four members: two South Africans and two others appointed by the Secretary-General. The Commission would be presided over by one of the two non-South African jurists who would have a chairman's casting vote.

5.   The withdrawal of South African troops from the Territory. This apparently remains the main stumbling point with South Africa reportedly refusing to agree to their withdrawal before the elections.

In conversations held up to the end of September 1977 between the Western contact group and the leadership of SWAPO, SWAPO reportedly took the following position:

1.   It would agree to the principle of free elections but would insist that they be held under the "supervision and control" of the United Nations in accordance with numerous Security Council and General Assembly resolutions.
2.   It has expressed doubts concerning the concept of an Administrator-General appointed by South Africa as legitimising South Africa's illegal presence in the Territory.
3.   The return of the exiles and the release of Namibian political prisoners should be unconditional. Provision should also be made to allow the returnees sufficient time to establish themselves in the Territory prior to the elections.
4.   The South African armed forces should totally withdraw prior to the elections and should be replaced by a United Nations force to maintain law and order during the elections. SWAPO considers that the Namibian people will not have freedom to decide their own future as long as South African troops remain in the territory.[38]

While the Western contact group was busy negotiating with South Africa in connection with the Namibian question, the United Nations Council on Namibia was also holding series of conferences in many African sovereign states during the first five months of 1978. The Council on Namibia made the following recommendations:

1.   In all three countries visited, it was recommended that, at its extraordinary plenary meetings in Lusaka, the Council should reiterate its full and unconditional support for SWAPO in order to dispel any equivocation with regard to the representation of SWAPO in its capacity as the sole and authentic representative of the Namibian people.
2.   The President of Gabon, in his capacity as current Chairman of the OAU, recommended that all African States should be represented at the forthcoming ninth special session of the General Assembly at a very high level and announced that a letter to this effect would be sent to all African Heads of State.
3.   The Algerian Government recommended that Namibia, represented by the Council, should be admitted to full membership in all international organizations and conferences, including the General Assembly.
4.   The Nigerian Government recommended that, if any solution to the Namibian problem were to be devised involving a period of interim administration which had a United Nations character, the Council should be associated with that interim administration.
5.   The Nigerian Government also recommended that the Council should prepare for the eventuality that the Security Council might determine the existence of a threat to international peace and security in Namibia and thus assume jurisdiction over the Namibian question.
6.   In all three countries, it was recommended that, in view of the critical stage now reached, the Council should make full use of the extraordinary plenary meetings in Lusaka to ensure that a clear direction is given to the future policies of the Council.[39]

The Namibian question is now being actively discussed throughout the independent African states, in various organs and agencies of the UN system, and at many Third World nonaligned conferences. African states are using as many international forums as they can get to bring into the open the plight of the Namibians. Because of the pressures that are being exerted within the world community, South Africa has now been forced reluctantly to accept the inevitability of the independence of Namibia.

In addition to African states, Western countries (particularly the contact group) have been active in exerting pressure on South Africa to comply with the General Assembly, the Council on Namibia, and the OAU requests for majority rule in Namibia. Having ignored all of these requests, South Africa was in the process of setting up a puppet government in Namibia when, in April 1977, the five Western contact group (United States, Great Britain, France, West Germany, and Canada) intervened and demanded that the Turnhalle Conference be abandoned and free elections be held according to the specifications of UN Resolution 385. Although the precise contents of the discussions were not officially disclosed, the first demarche in Cape Town was reported to have attained these results:

–The Turnhalle conference would be disbanded and not installed as an interim government;
–South Africa would hold elections on the basis of universal adult suffrage and allow the participation of all political groups including SWAPO;
–South Africa would appoint an Administrator General until independence. United Nations supervision and control would be established through a Special Representative appointed by the UN Secretary-General and UN monitors. The Special Representative would not have executive power but would operate through agreement with the Administrator General;
–Disputes over the status of political prisoners and exiles would be resolved by a four-man judicial commission consisting of two jurists appointed by South Africa and two appointed by the International Commission of Jurists;
–The South African Administrator General would repeal discriminatory, restrictive or repressive legislation;
–The date of independence would remain 31 December 1978;
–"Law and order" would remain the responsibility of South Africa, which would be allowed to maintain troops in Namibia.[40]

However, while the Western contact group was trying to find an acceptable compromise formula, South Africa took precautionary measures to entrench its allies in Namibia. On September 1, 1977, the South African government appointed Marthinius Steyn (a judge from the Transvaal) as administrator general. At the same time, Walvis Bay was removed from Namibian jurisdiction and placed under the government of the Cape Province. The contact group remained unsatisfied by South Africa's policies on Namibia. After extensive negotiations, the Western Proposals for Settlement were agreed upon on March 30, 1978. Some of the main points of the Western Proposals for Settlement are:

1. That the government of the RSA should accept the Security Council Resolution 385 as the basis upon which it is to be granted independence;

2. A resolution will be required in the Security Council requesting the Secretary-General to appoint a United Nations Special Representative whose central task will be to make sure that conditions are established which will allow free and fair elections and an impartial electoral process. The Special Representative will be assisted by a United Nations Transition Assistance Group.

3. The prupose of the electoral process is to elect representatives to a Namibian Constituent Assembly which will draw up and adopt the Constitution for an independent and sovereign Namibia. Authority would then be assumed during 1978 by the Government of Namibia.

4. In carrying out his responsibilities, the Special Representative will work together with the official appointed by South Africa (the Administrator-General) to ensure the orderly transition to independence. This working arrangement shall in no way constitute recognition of the legality of the South African presence in and administration of Namibia.

5. In accordance with Security Council resolution 385 (1976), free elections will be held, for the whole of Namibia as one political entity, to enable the people of Namibia to freely and fairly determine their own future. The elections will be under the supervision and control of the United Nations in that, as a condition to the conduct of the electoral process, the elections themselves, and the certification of their results, the United Nations Special Representative will have to satisfy himself at each stage as to the fairness and appropriateness of all measures affecting the political process at all levels of administration before such measurers take effect. The Special Representative will have at his disposal a substantial civilian section of the United Nations, Transition Assistance Group, sufficient to carry out his duties satisfactorily. He will report to the Secretary-General of the United Nations, keeping him informed and making such recommendations as he considers necessary with respect to the discharge of his responsibilities. The Secretary-General will in turn report to the Security Council.

6. Elections will be held to select a Constituent Assembly which will adopt a Constitution for an independent Namibia. The Constitution will determine the organization and powers of all levels of government. Every adult Namibian will be eligible, without discrimination or fear of intimidation from any source, to vote, campaign and stand for election to the Constituent Assembly. Voting will be by secret ballot, with provisions made for those who cannot read or write. The date for the beginning of the electoral campaign, the date of elections, the electoral system, the preparation of voters rolls, and other aspects of electoral procedures will be promptly decided upon so as to give all political parties and interested persons, without regard to their political views, a full and fair opportunity to organize and participate in the electoral process. Full freedom of speech, assembly, movement and press shall be guaranteed. The official electoral campaign shall commence only after the United Nations Special Representative has satisfied himself as to the fairness and appropriateness of the electoral procedures.

7. To ensure that the elections are held fairly and freely, the United Nations Special Representative will have to be satisfied that the following requirements are fulfilled:

    (a)   Prior to the beginning of the electoral campaign, the Administrator General will repeal all remaining discriminatory or restrictive laws, regulations, or administrative measures which might abridge or inhibit that objective.

    (b)   The Administrator General shall make arrangements for the release, prior to the beginning of the electoral campaign, of all Namibian political prisoners or political detainees held by the South African authorities so that they can participate fully and freely in that process, without risk of arrest, detention, intimidation or imprisonment. Any disputes concerning the release of political prisoners or political detainees shall be resolved to the satisfaction of the Special Representative acting on the independent advice of a jurist of international standing who shall be designated by the Secretary-General to be legal adviser to the Special Representative.

(c) All Namibian refugees or Namibians detained or otherwise outside the territory of Namibia will be permitted to return peacefully and participate fully and freely in the electoral process without risk of arrest, detention, intimidation or imprisonment. Suitable entry points will be designated for these purposes.

(d) The Special Representative with the assistance of the United Nations High Commissioner for Refugees and other appropriate international bodies will ensure that Namibians remaining outside of Namibia are given a free and voluntary choice whether to return. Provision will be made to attest to the voluntary nature of decisions made by Namibians who elect not to return to Namibia.

8. A comprehensive cessation of all hostile acts shall be observed by all parties in order to ensure that the electoral process will be free from interference and intimidation. The provisions for the implementation of the cessation of all hostile acts, military arrangements concerning the United Nations Transition Assistance Group, the withdrawal of South African forces, and arrangements with respect to other organized forces in Namibia, and SWAPO follow:

(a) A cessation of all hostile acts by all parties and the restriction of South African and SWAPO armed forces to base.

(b) Thereafter a phased withdrawal from Namibia of all but 1,500 South African troops within 12 weeks and prior to the official start of the political campaign. The remaining South African force would be restricted to Grootfontein or Oshivello or both and would be withdrawn after the certification of the election.

(c) The demobilization of the citizen forces, commandos, and ethnic forces, and the dismantling of their command structures.

(d) Provision will be made for SWAPO personnel outside of the territory to return peacefully to Namibia through designated entry points to participate freely in the political process.

(e) A military section of the United Nations Transition Assistance Group to make sure that the provisions of the agreed solution will be observed by all parties. In establishing the military section of UNTAG, the Secretary-General will keep in mind functional and logistical requirements. The Five Governments, as members of the Security Council, will support the Secretary-General's judgment in his discharge of this responsibility. The Secretary-General will, in the normal manner, include in his consultations all those concerned with the implementation of the agreement. The Special Representative will be required to satisfy himself as to the implementation of all these arrangements and will keep the Secretary-General informed of developments in this regard.

9. Primary responsibility for maintaining law and order in Namibia during the transition period shall rest with the existing police forces. The Administrator General to the satisfaction of the United Nations Special Representative shall ensure the good conduct of the police forces and shall take the necessary action to ensure their suitability for continued employment during the transition period. The Special Representative shall make arrangements when appropriate for United Nations personnel to accompany the police forces in the discharge of their duties. The police forces would be limited to the carrying of small arms in the normal performance of their duties.[41]

10.   Immediately following the certification of election results, the Constituent
Assembly was to meet, draw up and adopt a Constitution for an independent
government of Namibia.

For the Western Proposals for Settlement to succeed, the neighboring countries
were requested by the Security Council to ensure to the best of their abilities that the
provisions of the transitional arrangements and the outcome of the election be
respected. Additionally, these countries were requested to afford the necessary
facilities to the UN special representative and to all United Nations personnel to
carry out their assigned functions and to facilitate such measures as may be desirable
for ensuring tranquility in the border areas.

Under intensive pressure from the contact group, Prime Minister Vorster
announced on April 25, 1978, that the government of South Africa had accepted the
Western contact group's Proposal for Namibian Independence with reservations
concerning the status of Walvis Bay. SWAPO intimated that it would officially
accept the Western Proposals for Independence on May 4, 1978, in New York when
a meeting was to be held between it and the contact group. Determined to prevent
SWAPO from attending the May 4 meeting at the United Nations in New York,
South Africa invaded and bombed a SWAPO refugee camp and a school at Kassinga,
South Angola. About one thousand people including children and women were
killed. Although SWAPO postponed the meeting at the United Nations to deal with
the crisis emanating from the South African attacks of its refugee camp, President
Sam Nujoma proceeded to say that SWAPO would hold negotiations at a later date.
South African claims that its preemptive strikes were on SWAPO guerrilla camps in
southern Angola have been refuted by many journalists who visited the camp, the
Angolan government, officials of the World Health Organization, and the United
Nations High Commission for refugees. Following these strikes against SWAPO,
South Africa arrested twenty prominent SWAPO leaders and hundreds of its cadres
inside Namibia. Having weakened SWAPO's power base in the country, the South
African government began to arrange for a general election in the territory. Before
the elections, SWAPO President Nujoma informed the contact group at a meeting
on July 11 and 12, in Luanda, Angola, that SWAPO had accepted the Western plan.

As provided in the Western Proposals for Namibian independence, the Security
Council with pressure from African states and other nonaligned countries at the
United Nations passed Resolution 431. The text of the resolution reads:

Recalling its resolution 385 (1976) of 30 January 1976, taking note of the proposal
for a settlement of the Namibian situation contained in document S/12636 of 10
April 1978.

   1.   *Requests* the Secretary-General to appoint a Special Representative for
Namibia in order to ensure the early independence of Namibia through free
elections under the supervision and control of the United Nations.

   2.   *Further requests* the Secretary-General to submit at the earliest possible
date a report containing his recommendations for the implementation of the
proposal in accordance with Security Council resolution 385 (1976);

   3.   *Urges* all concerned to exert their best efforts towards the achievement of
independence by Namibia at the earliest possible date.[42]

The then United Nations Secretary-General Kurt Waldheim appointed the former Finnish ambassador to Tanzania, Martti Ahtisaari as the United Nations commissioner for Namibia. At the request of SWAPO and the General Assembly, the Security Council further adopted Resolution 432 (1978), which states that Walvis Bay is an integral part of Namibia.

Immediately following his appointment, Ambassador Ahtisaari visited Namibia for two and a half weeks in August 1978. On the basis of his recommendations, Secretary-General Waldheim submitted a report on the implementation of the Western plan for Namibia. On general guidelines, the report noted the following:

1. The implementation of the proposal in paragraph 2 of Resolution 431 (1978) will require the establishment of a United Nations Transition component and a military component. Because of the unique character of the operation and the need for close cooperation between them, both components will be under the over-all direction of the Special Representative of the Secretary-General.

2. The Special Representative will report to me, keeping me informed and making such recommendations as he considers necessary with respect to the discharge of his responsibilities. The Secretary-General, in accordance with the mandate entrusted to him by the Security Council, will keep the Council fully informed of developments relating to the implementation of the proposal and to the functioning of UNTAG. All matters which might affect the nature or the continued effective functioning of UNTAG will be referred to the Council for its decision.

3. The deployment of both components of UNTAG must take into account the specific geographic, demographic, economic and social conditions prevailing in Namibia. These include, in particular, the vast distances and varied nature of topography and vegetation; the broad ranges of climatic conditions; the scarcity of water; the population distribution and existing communication network; the distribution and concentration of ethnic groups; and the lack of an adequate infrastructure in the north, such as roads and other communications and facilities. All these factors, when analysed, make it evident that sizeable resources, both military and civilian, will be required to provide the close monitoring called for in document S/12636.

4. In performing its functions, UNTAG will act with complete impartiality. In order that the proposal may be effectively implemented, it is expected that the Administrator-General and all other officials from within the Territory will exhibit the same impartiality.

5. For UNTAG to carry out all its tasks effectively, three essential conditions must be met. First, it must, at all times, have the full support and backing of the Security Council. Second, it must operate with the full cooperation of all the parties concerned, particularly with regard to the comprehensive cessation of all hostile acts. Third, it must be able to operate as a combined United Nations operation, of which the military component will constitute an integrated, efficient formation within the wider framework of UNTAG.

6. To monitor the cessation of hostilities effectively, to maintain surveillance of the Territory's vast borders and to monitor the restriction to base of the armed forces of the parties concerned, the cooperation and support of the neighboring countries will be necessary. Such cooperation will be most important, particularly during the early stages.

7. Implementation of the proposal, and thus the work of UNTAG, will have to proceed in succesive stages. These stages, which are detailed in the annex to Document S/12636, can be grouped as follows:

    (a) Cessation of all hostile acts by all parties and the withdrawal, restriction or demobilization of the various armed forces;

    (b)   Conduct of free and fair elections to the Constituent Assembly, for which the pre-conditions include the repeal of discriminatory or restrictive laws, regulations or administrative measures, the release of political prisoners and detainees and voluntary return of exiles, an adequate period for electoral campaigning;

    (c)   The formulation and adoption of a constitution for Namibia by the Constituent Assembly;

    (d)   The entry into force of the constitution and the consequent achievement of independence of Namibia.

8.   The length of time required for these stages is directly related to the complexity of the tasks to be performed and to the overriding consideration that certain steps are necessary before it can be said that elections have been held under free and fair conditions. It will be recalled that the proposal envisaged a series of successive stages, spaced so as to provide a sufficient lapse of time before the holding of the elections. This should permit, among other things, the release of political prisoners and detainees, the return and registration of all Namibians outside the Territory who may wish to participate in the electoral process, the deployment of United Nations military and civilian personnel and electoral campaigning by all parties in an atmosphere of tranquility. The time-table set out in the proposal called for the lapse of approximately seven months from the date of the approval of the present report by the Security Council to the holding of the elections.

9.   In his discussions with the Special Representative, the Administrator-General said that the South African authorities, having previously established 31 December 1978 as the date of independence, felt that they were committed thereto and that, consequently, the elections should take place as scheduled, regardless of the fact that it would necessitate substantially reducing the time-table necessary for completion of the preparatory plans. A majority of the political parties was of the opinion, however, that it was essential to maintain the orderly phasing of the preparatory stages and to allow sufficient time for electoral campaigning in order to ensure free and fair elections. Further, it was pointed out that the actual date of independence would fall within the competence of the Constituent Assembly.

10.   It will be recalled, however, that at the time the proposal was first formulated, the date of 31 December 1978 was consistent with completion of these steps. The delay in reaching agreement among the parties now makes completion by this date impossible. It is therefore recommended that the transitional period begin on the date of approval of the present report by the Security Council and proceed in accordance with the steps outlined in Document S/12636. Using the same time-table that earlier provided the 31 December 1978 date, an approximate date for elections would be approximately seven months from the date of the approval of the present report.

11.   Estimates of the periods of time required for completion of stages (a) and (b) of paragraph 14 above are included in the annex to Document S/12636. In view of the fact that the periods required for stages (c) and (d) of paragraph 14 would be determined by the Constituent Assembly, it is expected that the duration of UNTAG would be one year, depending on the date of independence to be decided by the Constituent Assembly.

12.   UNTAG will have to enjoy the freedom of movement and communication and other facilities that are necessary for the performance of its tasks. For this purpose UNTAG and its personnel must necessarily have all the relevant privileges and immunities provided for by the Convention on the Privileges and Immunities of the United Nations, as well as those especially required for the proposed operation.

To make the Western Plan for Namibia operative, Secretary-General Waldheim recommended the establishment of the military wing of UNTAG.

The military component of UNTAG will not use force except in self-defense. Self-defense will include resistance of attempts to prevent it from discharging its duties under the mandate of the Security Council. UNTAG will proceed on the assumption that all parties concerned will cooperate with it and take all the necessary steps for compliance with the decisions of the Security Council. The functions of the military component of UNTAG are:

(a) Monitoring the cessation of hostile acts by all parties, the restriction of South African and SWAPO armed forces to base, the phased withdrawal of all except the specified number of South African forces and the restriction of the remainder to specified locations;

(b) Prevention of Infiltration as well as surveillance of the borders of the Territory;

(c) Monitoring the demobilization of citizen forces, commandos and ethnic forces, and the dismantling of their command structure;

(d) Assisting and supporting the civilian component of UNTAG in the discharge of its tasks.

The military component of UNTAG will be commanded by the Secretary-General under the authority of the Security Council. The command in the field will be exercised by a Commander appointed by the Secretary-General with the consent of the Security Council. The Commander will report through the Special Representative to the Secretary-General on matters concerning the functioning of the military component of UNTAG. The military component will be comprised of contingents provided by member countries upon the request of the Secretary-General. The contingents will be selected in consultation with the Security Council and with the parties concerned, bearing in mind the accepted principle of equitable geographical representation.

To augment its military component, UNTAG recommended the establishment of a civilian police force whose function would be to assist the special representative in implementing the objectives of the Western plan. The tasks of the civilian police would consist, in particular, of the following:

1. Supervising and controlling all aspects of the electoral process, considering the fairness and appropriateness of the electoral procedures, monitoring the balloting and the counting of votes, or order to ensure that all procedures are strictly complied with, and receiving and investigating complaints of fraud or challenges relating to the electoral process;

2. Advising the Special Representative as to the repeal of discriminatory or restrictive laws, regulations or administrative measures which may abridge or inhibit the objective of free and fair elections.

3. Ensuring the absence of, or investigating complaints of, intimidation, coercion or restrictions on freedom of speech, movement or peaceful political assembly which may impede the objective of free and fair elections;

4. Assisting in the arrangements for the release of all Namibian political prisoners or detainees and for the peaceful, voluntary return of Namibian refugees or Namibians detained or otherwise outside the Territory;

5. Assisting in any arrangements which may be proposed by the Special Representative to the Administrator-General and implemented by the Administrator-General to the Special Representative's satisfaction intended to inform and instruct the electorate as to the significance of the election and the procedures for voting.

In his report, Secretary-General Waldheim hoped that some of these officials would be provided from among existing United Nations staff and that some of them would be persons, appointed especially for serving as monitors. According to the secretary-general, the costs of UNTAG should be considered expenses of the United Nations to be borne by the member states in accordance with Article 7, paragraph 2, of the Charter.[43]

The South African government objected to many aspects of the secretary-general's report. In a letter to the contact group, Foreign Minister P. Botha argues that:

–The proposed UN military force of 7,500 was, he maintained, several times larger than that originally proposed by the "contact group". Together with the reduction of the South African troops from an estimated 30,000 to 1,500 (less than half the number South Africa had previously accepted), this would mean that the United Nations would be virtually taking over as the peace-keeper in Namibia, whereas, he argued, it had initially been agreed that South Africa should be responsible for "law and order";

–To accord the UN Police Officers executive powers would, Mr. Botha asserted, be going beyond the Western proposals which only specified that the United Nations should monitor the South Africa police;

–Finally, Mr. Botha was convinced that it was "imperative" that the elections take place before the date set by the Turnhalle Conference for independence–31 December 1978. Keeping to this date should, he believed, override the need for a seven month preparation for polling.[44]

SWAPO, the Security Council, the General Assembly, the contact group, and the African states accepted the Waldheim Report. In addition to the secretary's report, Sam Nujoma requested that a voter's registration be carried throughout Namibia. Immediately following this request, SWAPO informed the contact group that it was prepared for a cease-fire agreement with South Africa so that elections could take place in April 1979. Meanwhile, Kurt Waldheim continued his efforts to reach a compromise with South Africa. After accepting South African criticisms on the role of the United Nations police, and agreeing to restrict their role to that of monitors, Waldheim later assured South Africa that the proposed number of United Nations troops would be a ceiling which would not be reached or exceeded unless there were breaches to the cease-fire agreement. By agreeing to this compromise, both Vorster and Waldheim had by implication confirmed the peacekeeping role of the UN forces in Namibia.

Although the South African government had agreed to the Western proposals for the independence of Namibia, it had no intention whatsoever to implement them. On September 20, 1978, (the day on which Prime Minister Vorster resigned), the government of South Africa announced that it was unprepared to accept an extended and amended "provisions of the plan which was described to us as being final and definite," and that an election would take place before the end of the year with or without United Nations supervision. It has been speculated that this shift in policy seems to be largely associated with the rise to power of former Defense Minister (now Prime Minister) P. W. Botha. Earlier in 1978, at the National Party Congress, Botha had defiantly stated that he had no intention of letting the Marxists come closer to the "other side of the Orange River." His uncompromising position has been responsible for South Africa's unwillingness to implement the Western plan.

Meanwhile, at the United Nations, the Waldheim Report with a clarifying statement was adopted by the Security Council on September 28 1978, in Resolution 435. The statement reads:

> According to Security Council Document S/12636, primary responsibility for maintaining law and order in Namibia during the transition period shall rest with the existing police.
> However, the Special Representative is also given explicit responsibilities:
> (a) To satisfy him that the Administrator-General ensures the good conduct of the police force;
> (b) To satisfy himself that the Administrator-General takes the necessary action to ensure the suitability of the police for continued employment during the transition period;
> (c) To make arrangements when appropriate for United Nations personnel to accompany the police forces in the discharge of their duties.
> It was therefore necessary to have designated personnel at the disposal of the Special Representative to ensure that their monitoring responsibilities would be satisfactorily performed. Moreover, I concluded that, for reasons of safety and effectiveness, these tasks would best be performed by civilian personnel who are professionally qualified. Concern has also been expressed as to whether the number of United Nations personnel to monitor the police is appropriate to the tasks they are expected to perform. I will of course keep this question under continuous review.

> A number of considerations have been raised regarding the timing of elections and the date of independence for Namibia. As indicated in my report, a majority of the political parties is of the opinion that it is essential to maintain the orderly phases of the preparatory stages and to allow sufficient time for electoral campaigning in order to ensure free and fair elections. Surely, the objective is not simply the holding of elections by a certain date, but the holding of elections which are manifestly free and fair.

> It is essential that all aspects of the electoral process be beyond reproach and, equally important, that this be apparent. Various parties have expressed concern over the process of registration for elections, and a number of complaints about the existing registration have been brought to my notice. The proposal makes clear that at each stage of the entire electoral process the Special Representative must satisfy himself as to the fairness and appropriateness of all measures affecting the political process at all levels of administration before such measures take effect.

> Clearly, therefore, the Special Representative on arrival in the territory will look afresh at all the processes and measures, including the registration of voters, in order to satisfy himself that these are fair and appropriate. Accordingly, the Special Representative will review the registration process and I can assure all parties that no registration process will receive the approval of the Special Representative until he is fully satisfied as to its fairness.

> In accordance with paragraph 10 of Document S/12636, the Special Representative will take steps to guarantee against the possibility of intimidation or interference with the electoral process from whatever quarter.

> In conclusion, Mr. President, I should like to emphasize once again that the

implementation of my report will depend on the cooperation and understanding of all the parties concerned, and of course, of all members of the Security Council. In this connection, I am glad to note that the five Western governments have given me full assurances of their continued good offices to facilitate the implementation of the Report. To this end, my Special Representative will also conduct such further consultations as are deemed necessary.[45]

A further Security Council Resolution, 439, demanded that South Africa cancel its unilateral elections in Namibia and threatened the imposition of sanctions on South Africa if it proceeded with the elections. Security Council Resolution 439 of 1978 reads:

> *Recalling* its Resolutions 385 (1976), 431 (1978) 432 (1978) and 435 (1978);
> *Having considered* the report submitted by the Secretary-General pursuant to paragraph 7 of Resolution 435 (1978) (S/12903),
> *Taking note* of the relevant communications addressed to the Secretary-General and the President of the Security Council (S/12900 and S/12902);
> *Having heard* and considered the statement by the President of the United Nations Council for Namibia;
> *Taking note also* of the communication dated 23 October 1978, from the President of the South West Africa People's Organization (SWAPO) addressed to the Secretary-General (S/12913);
> *Reaffirming* the legal responsibility of the United Nations over Namibia and its continued commitment to the implementation of Security Council resolution 385 (1976), in particular, the holding of free elections in Namibia under United Nations supervision and control;
> *Reiterating* the view that any unilateral measure taken by the illegal administration in Namibia in relation to the electoral process, including unilateral registration of voters or transfer of power, in contravention of the above-mentioned resolutions of the Security Council and this resolution is null and void;
> *Gravely concerned* at the decision of the Government of South Africa to proceed with unilateral elections in Namibia in clear contravention of Security Council resolutions 385 (1976) and 435 (1978);
> 1. *Condemns* the decision of the South African Government to proceed unilaterally with the holding of elections in the Territory from 4 to 8 December, 1978, in contravention of Security Council Resolutions 385 (1976) and 435 (1978);
> 2. *Considers* that this decision constitutes a clear defiance of the United Nations and, in particular, the authority of the Security Council;
> 3. *Declares* those elections and their results null and void and that no recognition will be accorded either by the United Nations or any Member States to any representatives or organ established by that process;
> 4. *Calls upon* South Africa immediately to cancel the elections it has planned in Namibia in December 1978;
> 5. *Demands once again* that South Africa cooperate with the Security Council and the Secretary-General in the implementation of its Resolutions 385 (1976), 431 (1978), and 435 (1978);
> 6. *Warns* South Africa that its failure to do so would compel the Security Council to meet forthwith to initiate appropriate actions under the Charter of the United Nations including Chapter VII thereof, so as to ensure South Africa's compliance with the aforementioned resolutions;
> 7. *Calls* on the Secretary-General to report on the progress of the implementation of this resolution by 25 November 1978.[46]

The fear of sanctions that was being advocated by some of the Security Council members made South Africa reverse its position, which included a dialogue with the contact group as a basis for a mutually agreed Namibian settlement. In response to South Africa's volte face, the representatives from the contact group countries went to South Africa for discussions with Prime Minister Botha. Within three days (October 18, 1979) of their arrival in South Africa, Prime Minister Botha announced that his country would proceed with the planned December 1978 Namibian elections as an internal process to elect leaders, but that the West would not be expected to recognize them. Botha went on to say that the elected leaders of the Namibian government together with the government of South Africa would jointly find a solution that would be acceptable for international recognition. Finally, Botha recommended that Judge Marthinius Steyn and Mr. M. Ahtisaari meet in the future to discuss the Security Council Resolution 435.

African states and the General Assembly denounced South Africa's intention of holding elections in Namibia. African states reacted to Botha's policies on Namibia by stating that the elections he had scheduled for Namibia were a way of circumventing the Western plan which they had endorsed. It was also speculated that once the elections were held and a new government set up in Namibia, South Africa's major problem would be in finding one or two countries that would recognize the new regime in Namibia. Recognition of the regime would free South Africa from having to deal with the United Nations, African states, and the contact states. Because of the criticisms by SWAPO, nonaligned states, and the African Group at the United Nations, the contact countries were forced to oppose the South African elections in Namibia.

The South African intransigence to a settlement in Namibia can be looked at as a humiliating defeat for American and Western European diplomacy at the United Nations. The contact group made up of people of European origin was expected to convince South Africa to agree to Namibian independence through negotiations. Negotiations had been the approach that the contact group had emphasized as a realistic method for seeking a rapprochement with South Africa. South African unwillingness to accept the Western plan was definitely a major diplomatic setback for the contact group and the United Nations efforts to settle the Namibian independence issue through negotiation. Although the contact group had reiterated that it would not recognize South African-sponsored elections in Namibia, its failure to tell South Africa that it would oppose any form of elections without UN approval was construed by that state as a license to proceed with its own elections. The lack of condemnation by the contact group on the elections in Namibia was regarded by South Africa as a support for its concept for "elected leaders" who would try (jointly with South Africa) to find an internationally accepted settlement solution to the Namibian conflict. Meanwhile, African states meeting at the United Nations made it unequivocally clear that they were opposed to a meeting between Judge Steyn and Mr. Ahtisaari. It is in this confused, gloomy situation that South Africa held elections in Namibia from December 4 to December 8, 1979.

At the demand of African, Asian, Caribbean, and Latin American states, the Security Council met to discuss the internal elections in Namibia. During the debate, the council heard statements by ten members: Bolivia, China, Czechoslovakia,

Gabon, India, Kuwait, Mauritius, Nigeria, USSR, and Venezuela. At its invitation, the Security Council heard statements by representatives of Bangladesh, Burundi, Cuba, Egypt, Ghana, Guyana, Mozambique, Saudi Arabia, Somalia, and SWAPO. While criticizing the internal elections, the representative from Mauritius, Radha Krishna Rampul, said that the five Western members had informed the Security Council that their recent trip to Pretoria had resulted in a compromise plan which made it possible for elections to be held in Namibia under United Nations supervision in the spring of 1979. It was admitted that nothing would be done to prevent South Africa from holding its so-called elections in Namibia before December 4, 1978. According to the joint statement of the five council members and the South African government, those elections would be "an internal process to elect leaders." The Western powers also suggested that South Africa might be able to persuade the newly elected Namibian leaders to hold further elections under United Nations supervision. There was no effort to try to provide credible reasons for believing that it might do so. The matter was mentioned in the apparent hope that someone would persuade the Security Council to go along with the idea. In view of the foregoing, how could the five Western members of the council say that the Pretoria meetings had brought about a compromise?

The immediate problem before the Security Council was that South Africa stood in defiance of Security Council resolutions on Namibia. There could be no elections in Namibia under United Nations supervision and control after an "internal settlement." The purpose of an "internal settlement" was to entrench an administration that would allow the continuation of South Africa's occupation. Such an administration would oppose free and open elections, and particularly one under United Nations supervision and control. A free election would mean the end of South Africa's power in Namibia.

Before deciding on what exactly the Security Council should do, the situation should be considered in the wider context of an expanding war in southern Africa. South Africa had made a choice about Namibia in a situation in which it felt increasingly threatened. The liberation struggles had over the past decade intensified throughout southern Africa. With the independence of Mozambique, Angola, and Zimbabwe, the liberation struggles had been brought to the borders of South Africa. These developments had caused South Africa to reject the plan of the secretary-general for elections in Namibia under United Nations supervision and control. Confronted with an intensifying offensive against apartheid on all sides, South Africa feared to surrender control over any territory on its borders that it had the remotest chance of holding. Those strategic considerations were the decisive factor in South African calculations about Namibia. South Africa had been playing for time; it never intended to accept the terms of Resolution 385 (1976).

Pretoria knew that serious consequences might follow if it obstructed the United Nations directives over the question of Namibia. It therefore sought to promote a solution that appeared to satisfy the conditions posed in Resolution 385 (1976), but which, in fact, ensured it a very good chance of maintaining control of Namibia after a brief transitional period. It can also be argued that it was the so-called Western proposals on Namibia, which opened the possibility of conducting a fraudulent election in Namibia under United Nations auspices. That possibility, buried in the ambiguities of language, attracted South Africa to those proposals. In fairness to the Western proposals, it should be noted that they called for free elections in Namibia under the direction and control of the United Nations. However, the elections were to be held before South Africa withdrew from the territory altogether.

The proposals failed to conform to the terms of Resolution 385 (1976) in letter and in spirit. The combination of continuing South African control and a weak United Nations presence opened the way for a subversion of United Nations efforts to ensure true independence for the Namibian people. The report of the secretary-general issued at the end of August 1978 reflected general agreement on the need to take precautions.

The report had caused considerable alarm in South Africa because it had fore-closed the possibility of any easy manipulation of the electoral process and of a United Nations stamp of approval for the results of a "fixed" election. If the United Nations presence was to be as strong as that indicated in the report, then South Africa had little chance of carrying out its plan to a successful conclusion. The increased risk of losing control had caused the apartheid South African regime, in an apparent reversal of policy, to reject the idea of cooperation with the United Nations and to decide upon an "internal settlement." The Security Council was back where it had started in July, 1976, when its demands for South Africa's withdrawal from Namibia had been formulated. The Western representatives had failed to deliver its client. The Western powers had been seeking to arrange what they called "peaceful solu-tions" in Namibia and Zimbabwe. It was no secret that it was part of their strategy to "stabilize" the area, to ensure some kind of majority rule, but majority rule with "economic" stability. The situation in southern Africa presented the West with its "gravest crisis" because it was no longer possible to avoid choosing between Western interests in a "stable" southern Africa and respect for human rights and democracy.[47]

Gwendolyn Konie of Zambia, president of the UN Council for Namibia, stated that the impressive efforts of the secretary-general and his special representative had met with the fanatical intransigence of the Pretoria regime. That intransigence, masked behind extremes of devious maneuvering, had led to one of the most extraordinary statements of political mystification. Commenting on the same issue, the representative of Algeria emphatically stated that the debate in the Security Council must strengthen and confirm the prime responsibility of the United Nations to achieve the decolonization of Namibia by implementation of the internationally acceptable plan, in accordance with Resolution 385 (1976), taken as a whole, and Resolutions 431 (1978), 432 (1978), and 435 (1978), subsequently adopted by the Security Council. Under these conditions, Algeria had hoped that the council would not fail to face up to its obligations at a time when the situation created by South Africa, in defiance of the African continent, the United Nations, and the five Western countries constituted a threat to international peace and security.

The Algerian diplomat categorically rejected the results of the electoral mas-querade decided upon by Pretoria and refused to grant any legitimacy to a small group of "puppets," the product of rigged elections, traitors to their people who were manipulated by the racist Pretoria regime. The concerns of South Africa were not so much to promote or to prepare a democratic tradition in Namibia, but rather to perpetuate and consolidate its economic and strategic advantages there and, above all, to perpetuate the policy of apartheid.[48]

Concerning the foreign journalists South Africa had invited to report on the internal elections, the chairmen of three United Nations bodies dealing with southern Africa issued a joint statement on November 28 calling upon representatives of the press to turn down invitations extended to them by South Africa to observe the internal elections in Namibia, which were being held in defiance of recent Security Council decisions. To report on the bogus arrangements that South Africa intended to promote in December as a bona fide electoral process, they said, was to do a disservice to the United Nations efforts to obtain the withdrawal of the illegal South African administration from Namibia and to dismantle the system of apartheid and other racist practices which South Africa had instituted in Namibia.

The chairman of the Special Committee on Decolonization, Salim A. Salim (Tanzania), the chairman of the Special Committee against Apartheid, Leslie Harriman (Nigeria), and the president of the UN Council for Namibia, Gwendolyn Konie (Zambia), said they had been informed that South Africa had extended invitations to selected politicians, journalists, and other individuals, mainly from Western countries, to observe what the South African government had called "elections" in Namibia which was under illegal occupation by South Africa.

While clearly recognizing and respecting the freedom of the representatives of the media to perform their responsibilities as they saw fit, the three United Nations spokesmen shared the view that the representatives of the press had a great responsibility in upholding the Security Council decisions and should, therefore, refrain from endorsing such a South African maneuver, the purpose of which was to legitimize the appointment of racists and other supporters of apartheid under the pretense that they were the chosen representatives of the Namibian people.

In a statement on November 24, 1978, Mr. Harriman, the chairman of the Special Committee against Apartheid, said that the sham "elections" in Namibia were being conducted by the illegitimate racist regime of South Africa which had continued its illegal occupation of Namibia. The elections in Namibia had been denounced by the national liberation movement, SWAPO, and all the churches of Namibia. The elections were a nefarious exercise to install a puppet regime composed of tribal chiefs and some white settlers whose claim to Namibian nationality was in question. They were not only an affront to the United Nations and the international community but part of a racist conspiracy against the people of Namibia.[49]

Recognizing the overwhelming opposition by the African and Third World states to the position taken by the contact group and by South Africa, the South African Foreign Minister Pik Botha informed Dr. Waldheim in November 1978, that the elections assembly elected in Namibia would not be granted self-government or independence. Botha also tried to persuade President Carter of the United States to accept the position that South Africa had adopted on Namibia. Instead, President Carter condemned South African racial policies.

Disregarding the opposition of African states, SWAPO, and the United Nations, South Africa went ahead with its election plans in Namibia. On the announcement of his victory in the Namibian December elections, Dick Mudge of the Democratic Turnhalle Alliance (DTA), whose aim was to implement the Turnhalle proposals, stated that the Alliance had nothing against free and fair elections under United Nations supervision. However, he expressed reservations about the conditions under which such elections would take place. The reservations were made public on December 22, 1978, when Prime Minister Botha addressed members of the Turnhalle Constituent Assembly.

–The United Nations, the DTA maintained, should withdraw its recognition of SWAPO as the sole legitimate representative of the Namibian people;
–The UN elections should take place before July with a ceasefire by mid-January;
–If there were any breach of the ceasefire, there should be no reduction in the number of South African troops;
–Even if there were no reduction in the level of South African troops, the election date should remain fixed;
–The UN military force should be less than the proposed 7,500 troops since the DTA felt that the presence of UN troops would afford SWAPO a psycholigical advantage.[50]

Aware that the DTA reservations on the UN role in Namibia were going to alienate South Africa further from the United Nations and the rest of the international community, Prime Minister Botha refused to endorse them. Instead, the prime minister called for a meeting between Judge Steyn and Mr. Ahtisaari. Although, Foreign Minister Botha carefully distanced South Africa from the reservations of the DTA, he stated that Namibian elections should take place before September 30, 1979. Like his prime minister, the foreign minister invited the UN representative for Namibia, Mr. M. Ahtisaari, to visit South Africa and Namibia to finalize arrangements for the independence elections of that territory.

The African states and the United Nations General Assembly were critical of the actions South Africa was taking on Namibia. Convinced that South Africa was not willing to implement the Western proposals for settlement, the General Assembly requested the Security Council and the contact group to take action that would rectify the situation. With intense pressure from the African states to initiate a program of economic sanctions against South Africa, the contact group's foreign ministers met in London to decide on what actions they should take against South Africa. The United States favored the impositions of sanctions against South Africa. On December 23, 1978, news broke out in London that with heavy pressure from the United States, the British government had started discussions on the possibility of imposing sactions against South Africa. If sanctions were employed against South Africa, it was to cover banking, insurance, and engineering, and the chemical products and shipbuilding industries. Interestingly, oil, which is important for the operation of the South African economic and political system, was excluded from the sanctions list.

While Mr. Ahtisaari was predicting the deployment of a United Nations military force in Namibia, and also declaring that he would not renegotiate the size of this force, South Africa informed the secretary-general that it would not withdraw its troops from Namibia unless there was a complete cease-fire. By February 20, 1979, South Africa had modified its position by stating that it would tolerate a minimal level of violence during its phase out operation because of the problems involved with removing land mines planted in many parts of northern Namibia and the Caprivi Strip. In its desire to contain the movement of SWAPO freedom fighters in exile, South Africa suggested that these thirty thousand people be restricted to detention camps, which South Africa called reception centers, for a limited period.

Many differences have emerged between South Africa on one hand, and on the other SWAPO, African states, and the United Nations. SWAPO objected to the placement of its returning freedom fighters into South African detention camps for a limited period. Another difference between SWAPO and South Africa arose over the monitoring of its existing bases. SWAPO had suggested that it be allowed five bases in Namibia for two thousand, five hundred freedom fighters. South Africa unequivocally rejected SWAPO's request on the grounds that SWAPO did not have bases inside Namibia and that the presence of these freedom fighters would give SWAPO undue advantage over the other nationalist groups during the elections. Because of these conflicts, Dr. Waldheim issued a report concerning the implementation of Security Council Resolutions 435 and 439 (1978) on the question of Namibia. The report follows:

REPORT OF THE SECRETARY-GENERAL CONCERNING THE IMPLEMENTATION OF SECURITY COUNCIL RESOLUTIONS 435 (1978) AND 439 (1978) ON THE QUESTION OF NAMIBIA

11.   According to the settlement proposal, coincidental with a cessation of all hostile acts, the South African Defense Forces (SADF) and SWAPO armed forces will be restricted to base. This would involve the restriction to base of all SADF forces within Namibia and their subsequent phased withdrawal as outlined in the Proposal. Any SWAPO armed forces in Namibia at the time of the cease-fire will likewise be restricted to base at designated locations inside Namibia to be specified by the Special Representative after necessary consultation. The monitored move of these SWAPO armed forces to base cannot be considered as a tactical move in terms of the cease-fire.

12.   All SWAPO armed forces in neighboring countries will, on the commencement of the cease-fire, be restricted to base in these countries. While the Proposal makes no specific provision for the monitoring by UNTAG of SWAPO bases in neighboring countries, nevertheless, however, paragraph 12 of the Proposal states that: "Neighboring countries shall be requested to ensure to the best of their abilities that the provisions of the transitional arrangements, and the outcome of the election, are respected. They shall also be requested to afford the necessary facilities to the United Nations Special Representative and all United Nations personnel to carry out their assigned functions and to facilitate such measures as may be desirable for ensuring tranquility in the border areas."

13.   I attach special importance to the repeated assurances which I have received from the neighboring States to the effect that they will ensure to the best of their abilities that the provisions of the settlement are adhered to. In this connection, in order to facilitate further this cooperation, I have sought the agreement of the Governments of Angola, Botswana and Zambia for the establishment of UNTAG offices in their countries to cooperate with them in the implementation of the relevant provisions of the Proposal.

C. Cease-fire Arrangements:

14. The Settlement Proposal calls for "a comprehensive cessation of all hostile acts." As previously indicated by me (see S/12869 and S/12938) it is my intention to propose a procedure for the commencement of the cease-fire. Thereafter, the various steps indicated in the Proposal for a settlement, as reflected in Resolution 435 (1978), would take place. I intend to send identical letters to South Africa and SWAPO proposing a specific hour and date for the cease-fire to begin. In that letter I would also request both parties to inform me in writing of their agreement to abide by the terms of the cease-fire. I would require that they advise me of their agreement by a specific date which would be ten days before the beginning of the cease-fire. This period is necessary for both parties to have adequate time to inform their troops of the exact date and time for the commencement of the cease-fire and for UNTAG to deploy. The text of the proposed letter is attached as an annex to this report.

D. Composition of the Military Component:

15. Aside from the outstanding issues concerning the implementation of the settlement Proposal mentioned above, the question of the composition of the military component of UNTAG remains to be finalized. In the course of my consultations with the parties, I have communicated to them a list of possible troop-contributing countries which, in the circumstances, I consider can best meet the requirements of UNTAG. Before the commencement of the United Nations operation in Namibia, I shall submit to the Security Council, in accordance with established practice, the proposed composition of the military component. In drawing up the list of contributing countries, I shall take into due account the views of the parties while seeking to balance those factors I consider essential in the case, such as the principle of equitable geographical representation, the willingness of the troop contributing countries to participate and, in the case of logistics, the capacity to perform the required tasks.

E. Agreement on the Status of UNTAG:

16. A draft agreement on the status of UNTAG was first presented to the South African authorities in August, 1978. Agreement has now been reached with those authorities in respect to most of its provisions. As stated in my report of 29 August 1978 (S/12827) UNTAG and its personnel must necessarily have all the relevant privileges and immunities provided for by the Convention on the Privileges and Immunities of the United Nations, as well as those especially required for the proposed operation.

Concluding Remarks

17. The settlement Proposal requires that all its provisions be completed to the satisfaction of the Special Representative. In agreeing to the implementation of Security Council Resolution 435 (1978), the parties have agreed to abide by those provisions. The United Nations has the responsibility of assessing the implementation of the various military provisions of the Proposal. Similarly, the Special Representative is to be satisfied about the various provisions regarding the creation of conditions for and the conduct of elections. There is no basis for unilateral determinations or for unilateral actions by any party. At the same time, it is recognized that the effective implementation of the Proposal is dependent upon the continued cooperation of the parties. Should the implementation of the Proposal be jeopardized as a result of failure of any party to carry out its provisions, I would bring the matter immediately to the attention of the Security Council.

18.   I have already communicated to the Government of South Africa and SWAPO the basic elements of the proposals contained in this report. In the light of the above proposals, and if the cooperation of the parties concerned is forthcoming, I intend to designate the date of 15 March 1979 for the commencement of the emplacement of UNTAG and the entry into force of the cease-fire. The letter on the cease-fire will be transmitted accordingly. In the interim, I appeal to all parties to exercise restraint and to refrain from actions which might jeopardize the settlement.

19.   I should like to draw attention to paragraph 11 of my report of 29 August 1978 (S/12827) in which I stated that "it is expected that the duration of UNTAG would be for one year, depending on the date of independence to be decided by the Constituent Assembly."

ANNEX

CEASE-FIRE LETTER TO BE SENT BY THE SECRETARY-GENERAL TO BOTH THE SOUTH AFRICAN GOVERNMENT AND SWAPO

"In accordance with the Proposal for a Settlement of the Namibian situation as approved by Security Council Resolution 435 (1978), I propose that a cease-fire take place beginning at 0000 hours on 15 March, 1979. At that time comprehensive cessation of all hostile acts is to take effect.

I request you to assure me in writing no later than 5 March, 1979, that you have accepted the terms of the cease-fire and that you have taken all necessary measures to cease all warlike acts and operations. These include tactical moves, cross-border movements and all acts of violence and intimidation in, or having effect in Namibia."

The Security Council adopted the Report of the secretary-general and its Annex as Resolution A/13120 on February 20, 1979.

For the UN plan to work, the African frontline states gave an assurance that they would supervise the strict observance of the cease-fire agreement. South Africa rejected these UN compromises labeling them deviations. On March 6, 1979, Prime Minister Botha informed the UN secretary-general that officials of the United Nations would no longer be admitted into Namibia after March 15. Determined to be uncompromising and to show its military might to sympathizers of SWAPO, South Africa launched a series of military incursions into southern Angola and Zambia. It justified its invasion of these countries by claiming that it was attacking SWAPO guerrilla bases and not civilians.

Anticipating a Conservative party victory in the British elections and the likely changes in British policy toward southern Africa, the South African government decided to remain uncooperative with the United Nations. Meanwhile, in Namibia, Dick Mudge of the DTA announced that his party was going to form an interim government in May. A week later, Prime Minister Botha accused the American Embassy in South Africa of spying and expelled three American diplomats. A major figure in the negotiations over Namibia, an American top black diplomat, Donald McHenry (later to be US ambassador to the United Nations) was publicly denounced by Botha and labeled an enemy of South Africa. In 1980, South Africa stalled its attempts to reach a solution with the United Nations because of the Lancaster Peace Talks on Zimbabwean independence and the presidential and congressional elections in the United States.

In sum, African states have played crucial roles in both the General Assembly, the Security Council, the Council for Namibia, and in the Committee of 24 on Namibian issues. These countries have untiringly striven to maintain the momentum against South Africa's continued illegal occupation of Namibia. Their activities in seeking the attention of the world community to the plight of the oppressed Namibians were responsible in making the United Nations pass numerous resolutions condemning South African occupation of that territory. Today, the world community is constantly urging South Africa to terminate apartheid and grant majority rule to the Namibians. Although African countries are not militarily powerful, their moral campaign against colonialism and imperialism in Namibia has won them allies from North and South America, the Caribbean, Western and Eastern Europe, Asia, Australia, and many of the Pacific Islands. Because of the crusade against the apartheid policies of South Africa by these African countries, the world community is now actively calling for the independence of Namibia. Through pressure from the Western countries, the OAU, and the United Nations, South Africa agreed to grant independence to Namibia.

The United Nations and Portuguese Colonialism

Portuguese colonialism in Africa was based on the principle of political unity of the metropolis and the overseas provinces. Throughout the 1950s, 1960s, and early 1970s, the United Nations, pressured by its African members, was actively involved in trying to find ways and means of liquidating Portuguese colonialism in Africa. While Portugal resisted the United Nations and African states' interference in the colonial administration of her African dependencies, it enacted laws that curtailed the economic and political mobility of Africans. The Colonial Act of 1933 as reenacted in 1954 delineated this sociopolitical mobility in the following manner: A person shall be considered an *indigena,*

> . . . if he is a member of the Negro race or a descendant of a member of that race, and was born, or habitually resides in the province, but does not yet possess the level of education of the personal and social habits which are a condition for the unrestricted application for the public and private law pertaining to Portuguese citizens.[51]

Africans could change their status and procure Portuguese citizenship or the assimilation status if the following conditions were satisfied: That an African was engaged in any employment or trade from which he derived sufficient income to support his household; that he could speak Portuguese fluently and correctly; that the African should act and behave as if he were a Portuguese person; and that he should be willing and available to serve in the Portuguese army at any time the Portuguese government requested his services. The *indigena* status had an implication that the occupant of that status was an uncivilized person or a barbarian. The Portuguese African colonial population was also divided into two categories: the *civilizado* (civilized) and the *não-civilizado* (noncivilized). All Europeans, Asians, and mestizos (people of mixed origin) were granted automatic citizenship. Africans had to qualify as *civilizados*. Up to the inception of the Portuguese coup d'etat of 1974, about one-tenth of the entire African population was able to qualify as *assimilados* and *civilizados*. Those within the *indigena* status were subjected to unrestricted conscripted labor services, and in most cases, these people could not hold title to land. Under these conditions, the status of the African *indigena* resembled that of the enslaved.

During its epoch of colonial domination in Africa, the Portuguese government claimed that its African territorial possessions were integral provinces of the State of Portugal. The Constitution of Portugal outlined the following as its territorial possessions:

1. In Europe: the mainland and the archipelagos of Madeira and the Azores.
2. In West Africa: the Cape Verde archipelago, Guinea, Sao Tome and Principe and their dependencies, São Joao Baptista de Ajuda, Cabinda and Angola.
3. In East Africa: Mozambique.
4. In Asia: Macao and its dependencies.
5. In Oceania: Timor and its dependencies. [52]

Until 1974 Portugal did not recognize the right to self-determination and independence for its colonial peoples.

Prior to the African Nationalist's efforts to seek active support for their struggle for national liberation, Africans in Portuguese colonies formed various political parties. Some of the parties were Union of Angolan People (UPA); The People's Movement for the Liberation of Angola (MPLA); Frente Nacional de Libertacao de Angola (FNLA), which later established a government-in-exile known as Gouvernement Revolutionnaire de l'Angola en exile (GRAE); the National Democratic Union of Mozambique (UDENAMO); the Mozambique African National Union (MANU); Frente de Libertacao de Mocambique (FRELIMO); and the Comité Revolutionnaire de Mocambique (COREMO); the Partido Africano da Independencia de Guine e Cabo Verde (PAIGC); and the Comité de Libertacao de São Tomé e Principe (CLSTP). All these political parties arrogated to themselves the responsibilities of leading the Africans in Portuguese colonial dependencies to independence.

Having been unable to convince the colonial Portuguese government to agree to the inevitable attainment of independence by its colonial subjects, African leaders began to look for support for the fulfillment of their goals within the international community. In 1952, over five hundred Angolans addressed a petition to the United Nations that charged the Portuguese government with maltreatment and oppression of its African subjects. These Angolan nationalists requested the United Nations to take steps to terminate Portuguese colonialism in Africa. The United Nations reacted to these charges only after Portugal joined the United Nations in 1955.

United Nations involvement began on February 24, 1956, when, in accordance with previous practice, the Secretary-General addressed a letter to 16 new members, including Portugal. As was customary, the Secretary-General inquired whether these states had any territories which did not fully govern themselves, since Chapter XI of the Charter obliges member states to accept a series of obligations towards territories administered by them.

By denying that it did not have such territories, and that the overseas provinces it administered were really integral provinces of metropolitan Portugal, the Portuguese government went on to say that the Portuguese Constitution guaranteed equality to all its people regardless of race or status. At the end of 1960, the General Assembly resolved that the territories under "Portuguese administration were non-self governing within the meaning of Chapter XI of the Charter and that Portugal was obliged to transmit information on them to the United Nations." The General Assembly also passed Resolution 1514 (XV) concerning the declaration on the granting of independence to colonial countries and peoples. The Resolution notes:

The General Assembly

Mindful of the determination proclaimed by the peoples of the world in the Charter of the United Nations to reaffirm faith in fundamental human rights, in the dignity and worth of the human person, in the equal rights of men and women and of nations large and small and to promote social progress and better standards of life in larger freedom,
Conscious of the need for the creation of conditions of stability and well-being and peaceful and friendly relations based on respect for the principles of equal rights and self-determination of all peoples, and of universal respect for, and observance of human rights and fundamental freedoms for all without distinction as to race, sex, language or religion,
Recognizing the passionate yearning for freedom in all dependent peoples and the decisive role of such peoples in the attainment of their independence,
Aware of the increasing conflicts resulting from the denial of or impediments in the way of the freedom of such peoples, which constitute a serious threat to world peace,
Considering the important role of the United Nations in assisting the movement for independence in trust and non-self-governing territories,
Recognizing that the peoples of the world ardently desire the end of colonialism in all its manifestations,
Convinced that the continued existence of colonialism prevents the development of international economic co-operation, impedes the social, cultural and economic development of dependent peoples and social, cultural and economic development of dependent peoples and militates against the United Nations ideal of universal peace,
Affirming that peoples may, for their own ends, freely dispose of their natural wealth and resources without prejudice to any obligations arising out of international economic cooperation, based upon the principle of mutual benefit, and international law,
Believing that the process of liberation is irresistible and irreversible and that, in order to avoid serious crisis, an end must be put to colonialism and all practices of segregation and discrimination associated therewith,
Welcoming the emergence in recent years of a large number of dependent territories into freedom and independence, and recognizing the increasingly powerful trends towards freedom in such territories which have not yet attained independence,
Convinced that all peoples have an inalienable right to complete freedom, the exercise of their sovereignty and the integrity of their national territory,
Solemnly proclaims the necessity of bringing to a speedy and unconditional end to colonialism in all its forms and manifestations;

and to this end

Declares that:

1. The subjection of peoples to alien subjugation, domination and exploitation constitutes a denial of fundamental human rights, is contrary to the Charter of the United Nations and is an impediment to the promotion of world peace and cooperation.

2. All peoples have the right to self-determination; by virtue of that right they freely determine their political status and freely pursue their economic, social and cultural development.

3. Inadequacy of political, economic, social or educational preparedness should never serve as a pretext for delaying independence.

4. All armed action or repressive measures of all kinds directed against dependent peoples shall cease in order to enable them to exercise peacefully and freely their right to complete independence, and the integrity of their national territory shall be respected.

5. Immediate steps shall be taken, in trust and non-self-governing territories or all other territories which have not yet attained independence, to transfer all powers to peoples of those territories, without any conditions or reservations, in accordance with their freely expressed will and desire, without any distinction as to race, creed or colour, in order to enable them to enjoy complete independence and freedom.

6. Any attempt aimed at the partial or total disruption of the national unity and the territorial integrity of a country is incompatible with the purposes and principles of the Charter of the United Nations.

7. All states shall observe faithfully and strictly the provisions of the Charter of the United Nations, the Universal Declaration of Human Rights and the present Declaration on the basis of equality, non-interference in the internal affairs of all states and respect for the sovereign rights of all peoples and their territorial integrity.[53]

The 1514 Resolution, as it was properly called at the United Nations, was one of the greatest achievements of the anticolonial forces in the United Nations. It was sponsored by forty-three African and Asian countries, and was adopted by eighty-nine votes to zero, with nine abstentions. The nine countries that abstained were Australia, Belgium, the Dominican Republic, France, Portugal, Spain, the Union of South Africa, the United Kingdom, and the United States. Resolution 1514 of 1960 was important because it became a legal framework upon which the UN General Assembly could lean to secure Portugal's acceptance and recognition of the right of the people in its territories to determine their destinies.

With the achievement of independence by many African countries in 1960, intensified campaigns for national liberation by African political parties began in all the former Portuguese-dominated African territories. As the struggle for national liberation continued to gather momentum, so did Portugal tighten its colonial, repressive grips on its subjects. Massive arrests and cold-blooded murders against innocent African peasants and workers were committed by the Portuguese government. Having learned of the massacres and atrocities perpetrated against the Africans, on February 20, 1961, Liberia with the support of the Afro-Asian UN members requested an immediate Security Council meeting to discuss and take immediate action against the further deterioration of human rights.

At the Security Council meeting convened between March 10 and March 15, 1961, the Portuguese government held the view that the Liberian request to discuss the Portuguese colonial crisis in Angola was a contravention of the United Nations Charter's provision which deals with the noninterference of member states in the domestic matters within the jurisdiction of other UN members. This recalcitrant position of Portugal was criticized by many Afro-Asian states.

These views of Portugal were critized in the Security Council debate. African and Asian delegations vehemently denied that Angola was an integral part of Portugal. The representative of Ceylon, for example, said the African people of Angola were not Portuguese by an economic, cultural, ethnological or linguistic identity. He said that even if there was racial equality, which all evidence denied, the imposed rule of one people by another was not acceptable. He stated that "no amendments of the Portuguese Constitution can alter the facts of history, geography, anthropology, economics and, above all, of common sense. Arbitrary legislation or edicts cannot hold back the tide of history."

The United Arab Republic, Congo (Brazzaville) and Ghana were among those that pointed out that the Portuguese Government had arbitrarily and unilaterally decided Angola was an integral part of Portugal without consulting the Angolan people to determine if they agreed with this integration. Portugal's "juridical fiction" that the territories were provinces, they said, should not impede Council consideration of the question. It was also pointed out by a number of states, that the General Assembly had already decided by Resolution 1542 (XV) that the territories were "non-self governing territories" and not integral parts of Portugal. Many delegations believed that the situation in Angola could be construed as a threat to international peace (and therefore warrant Security Council consideration under Article 34 of the Charter) since the Portuguese authorities' contravention of the Declaration on ending colonialism was causing tension between African States and Portugal. It was also argued that a situation endangering world peace did not necessarily have to be a dispute between Member States.[54]

The resolution submitted to the Security Council by Egypt, Ceylon, and Liberia condemning Portuguese atrocities in Angola was rejected as it was unable to obtain the necessary majority votes: Five voted for it, none against, and six abstained.

Immediately following the Security Council deliberations, the Angolan African Nationalists began to deploy their revolutionary cadres into armed confrontation against the Portuguese military and police forces. Because of this conflict, African and Asian states brought the matter up for discussion within the General Assembly. Although Portugal was opposed to having its colonial problems discussed in the Security Council and the General Assembly, the Afro-Asian concerted pressure later made the General Assembly adopt Resolution 1603 (XV) that called for Portugal to introduce needed reforms which would solve its colonial problems. Portugal ignored all these UN resolutions and proceeded to increase its suppression of Africans with military equipment it received from its allies in the North Atlantic Treaty Organization.

As the war continued to spread all over Guinea Bissau, Angola, and Mozambique, and as the international climate became increasingly more hostile, there were calls for far-reaching reforms. The most important of these reforms was the repeal of the native statute. As a result of this repeal, Angolans, Mozambicans, and Guineans became Portuguese *civilizados*. Africans were granted the right to vote and could also be elected into the Portuguese National Assembly and to various territorial municipal councils. Also abolished were discriminatory labor laws which allowed for the *indigena* to be compelled to work against his or her will. All these reforms did not recognize the Africans' right to self-determination and independence. Consequently, the African freedom fighters from MPLA, FRELIMO, and PAIGC escalated the theaters of war against Portuguese colonialism. Now spearheading UN efforts on decolonization, the Special Committee of 24 (with its support from the Afro-Asian countries) issued many reports on the deplorable conditions of the African life in the Portuguese colonies and concluded that the so-called reforms did not recognize the principle of the right to self-determination of the colonial subjects. Convincingly persuaded to this position, the Committee of 24 traveled to Africa to hear petitions from African freedom fighters on the struggle for national liberation in Portuguese African-dominated territories. In general, the African freedom fighters informed the committee of their legitimate and necessary struggle for national liberation. The committee's reports were also critical of the Portuguese government's inhumane maltreatment of Africans.

From 1965 onward, the United Nations started to take actions aimed at isolating Portugal by denying it military and economic assistance. Some of the actions taken were

(a)   to break off diplomatic and consular relations with Portugal;
(b)   to close all their ports to all vessels flying the Portuguese flag or in the service of Portugal;
(c)   to prohibit their ships from entering ports in Portugal and its colonial territories;
(d)   to refuse landing and transit facilities to all aircraft belonging to or in the service of the government of Portugal and to companies registered under the laws of Portugal; and
(e)   to boycott all trade with Portugal.[55]

While the African states claimed victory for the passage of this resolution, many NATO members continued to sell military hardware to the Portuguese government. This insensitive disregard for the Africans' struggle for national liberation were heavily critized by African, Asian, Caribbean, and South American countries. These countries were convinced that without NATO and US military supplies, Portugal would not be able to execute its colonial wars in Africa. Disappointed by this continued flow of aid to Portugal, African states and their supporters pressed the General Assembly to impose economic sanctions against Portugal by appealing to the International Monetary Fund to refrain from granting Portugal any financial, technical, or economic assistance. In addition, the General Assembly called for a halt to the systematic influx of European foreign immigrants into the Portuguese colonies. These new immigrants were being brought primarily to augment the settler white minority population that was supporting the continuation of Portuguese imperialism and colonialism.

Throughout the 1960s, the General Assembly, the Afro-Asian states and the Organization of African Unity became increasingly concerned with reports of growing economic collaboration between Portugal, Rhodesia, and South Africa. The Committee of 24 cited that Mozambique served as a reservoir of unskilled labor for

South African and Rhodesian mines and farms. Vital to racist Rhodesian and South African economics were the Mozambican ports of Beria and Lourenço Marques.

From the information which the subcommittee obtained from its members, from African countries which submitted petitions and from the working papers of the Secretariat for the Mining Industry and Land Ownership in Angola and Mozambique, it is evident that the new Portuguese colonial policy (in sharp contrast to the traditional Portuguese colonial policy) has encouraged foreign investments which in turn support and strengthen the Portuguese venture in this area.

It is significant that Portugal's policy of increasing the volume of foreign investment in the areas under its administration coincides exactly with the start of the national liberation movements in Africa. The aim of this deliberate policy was, as experience has shown, to gain financial, material and other support from the foreign interests, which should then help Portugal in future exploitation of the natural and human resources in repression of the growing political aspirations of the population in the area administered by Portugal (Angola, Guinea-Bissau, Mozambique).[56]

As the war raged throughout its colonies, the Portuguese international trade began to expand rapidly with South Africa, Rhodesia, and the western European countries. In order to consolidate the control of its African colonies in southern Africa, Portugal signed the Cabora Bassa and the Cunene Projects contracts with South Africa. Income from these agreements was to be used to finance Portugal's colonial wars. In 1968, the then Portuguese dictator, Antonio Salazar, granted the commission to construct and finance the Cabora Bassa Project to the Zambezi Consorico Hidroelectrico (ZAMCO), which was to be controlled and directed by the Anglo-American Corporation of South Africa. After Salazar's death, his successor (Marcello Caetano) actively encouraged ZAMCO to operate the project. ZAMCO is composed of the following companies:

Germany
AED–Allgemeine Elektrizitats–Gesellschaft
AED–Telefunken (Berlin-Frankfurt)
B.B.C.–Brown, Boveri & Cie AG (Mannheim)
HOCHTIEF–Hochtief A. G. (Essen)
Siemens–Aktiengesellschaft (Berlin-Munich)
Voith–J. M. Voith Gmbh (Maschinenfabrik, Heidenheim) (machine manufacture)

Switzerland
B.B.C.–Brown, Boveri and Cie AG (Basel)

France
ALSTHOM–Société Génerale de Constructions Electriques et Mecaniques Alsthom (Paris) (CGEE has most of the shares)
C.C.I.–Compagnie de Constructions Internationales (Paris)
COGELEX–CGEE–Compagnie Génerale de d'Enterprises Electriques (Paris)
ENTERPRISE FOUGEROLLE-LIMOUSIN

Italy
SOCIETA ANONIMA ELETTRIFICAZIONE, S.P.A. (S.A.E.) (since withdrawn)

South Africa
A.A.C.–Anglo-American Corporation of South Africa, (Johannesburg)
L.T.A.–Limited (Johannesburg)
Shaft Sinkers (Proprietary Ltd.) (Johannesburg)

Portugal
SOREFAME–Sociedades Reunidas de Fabricacoes Metallicas
S.A.R.L. (subsidiary of the French Alsthom-Neyrpic)[57]

The Cunene Project in southern Angola comprised the construction of several dams, power plants, canals, and pipelines. Water and electricity from the Cunene Project were to be shared between Angola and Namibia. The signatories to this contract were the Portuguese government, the South African Ambassador to Portugal, A. J. Viljoen, and Dr. Sieg Kuschke, president of the South African Industrial Development Corporation (IDC).[58] The South African Authority responsible for the Cunene Project was the South West African Water and Electricity Commission (SWAWEC), which delegated its responsibilities to the following:

1. The Department of Water Affairs, Windhoek/Pretoria, deals with water affairs;
2. The Electricity Supply Commission (ESCOM), Johannesburg, deals with questions of electrical energy; ESCOM is also responsible for current distribution in the Cabora Bassa project.
3. The Industrial Development Corporation (IDC), Johannesburg, is responsible for coordination and finance.[59]

As African states began to close their airports to South African airlines, the Portuguese government opened its African colonial airports to the South Africans.

Like South Africa, economic relations between Rhodesia and Portugal expanded rapidly after 1963. In 1964, an oil pipeline running from Beira to Feruka in Umtali was completed. After the Rhodesian Unilateral Declaration of Independence (UDI) the pipeline was used to break United Nations economic sanctions against Rhodesia. With pressure from African states in April 1966, the United Nations Security Council called on Portugal to refrain from using the pipeline to supply oil to Rhodesia. Having refused to comply with the United Nations General Assembly and Security Council resolutions in support of the Africans right to self-determination and that on economic sanctions against Rhodesia, the World Health Assembly, the executive arm of the UN World Health Organization, suspended the right of Portugal to participate in regional activities that dealt with Africa.

Annoyed by the Portuguese intransigence in terminating its colonialism in Africa, African states at the United Nations adopted many tactics aimed at isolating Portugal diplomatically from the world community. Portugal was criticized at every General Assembly meeting and other UN conferences. Demands for economic boycotts against Portugal and its expulsion from the United Nations became some of the major objectives of the African states. African states were successful in their objective to gain General Assembly recognition of the fact that foreign investments in the Portuguese colonies of Angola, Guinea-Bissau, Cape Verde, and Mozambique would solidify the forces of oppression. In December 1970, the General Assembly recognized the wishes of the African States, FRELIMO, MPLA, FLNA, and the PAIGC by adopting a resolution that condemned the foreign business involvement and expansion in the Cunene and Cabora Bassa projects as a plot to perpetuate Portuguese colonialism in Angola and Mozambique. The General Assembly adopted another resolution in 1971, which requested member states to terminate their involvement in economic projects likely to strengthen the Portuguese government's stranglehold over Angola, Guinea-Bissau, Cape Verde, and Mozambique.

In addition to other activities, the African states together with the rest of the nonaligned states and supporters of decolonization in Africa held seminars through the auspices of the UN organs and nongovernmental organizations on humanitarianism and colonialism in southern Africa. Some of the general ideas developed by the UN Secretariat at the Oslo Conference in 1973 are:

A. Inside the territories controlled by colonial minority regimes;
 1. Legal assistance to persons persecuted under repressive and discriminatory legislation;
 2. Assistance, including assistance for education and training to families of political prisoners, restrictees, banned persons, ex-prisoners and students expelled from schools for political activities;
 3. Grants for emigration of persecuted persons in exceptional cases;
 4. Scholarship and other education assistance to victims of racial discrimination;
 5. Grants to education institutions which cater to such persons, including correspondence colleges;
 6. Appropriate assistance to groups opposed to colonialism and racial discrimination, especially for specific welfare projects;
 7. Research grants for institutions and individuals;

B. Inside liberated areas;
 1. Supplies for educational materials, medical equipment and supplies, foodstuffs, seeds, agricultural implements, supplies of telecommunication equipment, radios, trucks, etc;
 2. Technical assistance inside the territory.

C. Outside the territories;
 1. Assistance to refugees, resettlement, employment, legal protection;
 2. Scholarships and facilities for education and training at various levels for the indigenous inhabitants;
 3. Subventions to institutions providing places for students from the territories;
 4. Assistance to institutions associated with the liberation movements for education, health, and other activities;
 5. Provision of hospitals, schools, print shops, and other facilities of the liberation movements;
 6. Printing and supply of textbooks, technical assistance to the liberation movements including supply of doctors and teachers;
 7. Other assistance to the liberation movements such as grants for travel to conferences, printing and distribution of publications, provision of facilities and grants for offices of liberation movement, and treatment of the wounded.[60]

The adoption of this comprehensive humanitarian program for the colonized people of Cape Verde, Angola, Guinea-Bissau, Mozambique, South Africa, Zimbabwe, and Namibia was hailed as a success for the African group and their supporters within the UN system.

In addition to the humanitarian program, the African representatives at the United Nations backed by their Third World supporters began to campaign for more United Nations political and military aid to PAICG, FRELIMO, MPLA, FLNA, and UNITA. Meanwhile, guerrilla war escalated in the Portuguese colonies. As the intensity and severity of this guerrilla war increased, so did the cost of waging the colonial war rise. Apparently frustrated by its inability to finance the war and to defeat the African freedom fighters, Portugal adopted the strategy of hot pursuit. Numerous Portuguese armed incursions were reported in Guinea, Zaire, Zambia, and Senegal. As a result of these Portuguese invasions, the United Nations General Assembly (after its own investigations) condemned Portugal's violation of the territorial integrity of African states.

Of these military incursions, those into Guinea received the greatest international attention. In response to these Portuguese military provocations, President Sekou Toure of Guinea sent his troops to the Guinea-Bissau border and instructed them to repel any Portuguese attacks on Guinea. President Toure also openly gave military hardware to the PAIGC. He viewed the PAIGC struggle for national liberation as being inseparably intertwined with the overall struggle against capitalism, imperialism, and neocolonialism. To him, the struggles for freedom and independence have their ultimate objectives as the establishment of an egalitarian society where the means of production, distribution, and exchange are owned and controlled by the African peasants and workers.

Apparently frustrated by its incapacity to prosecute a successful guerrilla war against the PAIGC freedom fighters, Premier Caetano of Portugal began to actively seek help from the Western European capitalist countries including the United States. While drumming support for his fragile administration, Caetano justified the reasons for continuing colonialism in Angola, Guinea-Bissau, Cape Verde, and Mozambique in this manner:

> It seems that in this area terrorism is finding a much larger and more effective support, especially from the Soviet Union. It is certain that a concerted and accelerated effort is being made there for which neither arms nor other aid are being spared. And the reason for this special interest is no secret: Those responsible do not conceal the fact that Guinea serves as a point of departure for an attack on the Cape Verde Islands, which are in a key position as regards the connection between the North and South Atlantic . . . .
> . . .The freedom and independence of the countries of West Europe is not only decided in Europe itself, but equally so in Africa. That is why we must defend Guinea. Certainly it is in our interest, but also in the interest of West Europe and even of America.[61]

What, therefore, was the impact of this Portuguese deliberate misrepresentation on the nature of the PAIGC struggle for national liberation? To answer this question, it is important to briefly review the Western European countries and the United States policies toward Africa. These policies in Africa were to stop the outbreak of socialist revolutions, to eliminate all socialist-oriented governments, to preserve and expand the boundaries of capitalism, and to weaken and destabilize all possible areas of Russian influence. This view is amply supported by a "top secret document" prepared by the magazine *Africasia* under the chairmanship of the deputy, Sir Frederick Bennett for the British Conservative Commonwealth and Overseas Council and submitted by Patrick Orr, a member of the committee. A summary of these views on the significance of the Portuguese African colonial empire are:

We suggest this policy in order to avoid events which would be regarded by history as tragedies:
1. The Cape Route
Due to the closure of the Suez Canal, control of the Cape Route countries is necessary to safe transportation along this route is assured.
General Points:
(a) The increased economic and strategic importance of this route due to the closure of the Suez Canal.
(b) For the Western Allies, the Suez Canal has become practically useless because large cargo ships, oil tankers are too big for it.
(c) A large percentage of NATO trade takes place along the Cape Route.
(d) The route leads to South Africa, one of Great Britain's most important trading partners.
(e) Oil transportations from the Near East to Europe and North America go along the Cape Route.
(f) Because it gives access to Asia, Australia and New Zealand, the route is of strategic value.
Threats to British Interests:
(a) Armed attacks (not necessarily wars) could occur upon the South African coast and inland, without any immediate retaliation being implied, as in the NATO areas.
(b) Because the route is particularly vulnerable as a non-NATO area, wars, for example, inspired and supported by communists and directed against Angola, Mozambique, Port Guinea, South Africa could threaten its safety. The Russians and perhaps even the Chinese could easily station warships in Zanzibar or Cape Verde. This last possibility could be realized if the communist inspired opposition in Portuguese Guinea is successful.
Suggested Necessary Measures:
(a) In the political sphere, the first step will be the reinstatement of contact with South Africa on the basis of common interest, improvements and trade between the two countries and the selling of arms to South Africa. At the same time, the ending of sanctions against Rhodesia.
Otherwise, the danger exists that South Africa which is politically isolated, will thereby be forced to become neutral. This would mean the loss of the Simonstown fleet base.
(b) Support of the African States, which maintain a positive attitude towards Portugal, South Africa and Rhodesia.
(c) Renewal of the Simonstown Agreement.
(d) Joint South African and British naval exercises.
(e) Use could be made of the British-Portuguese alliance in order to reach a defense agreement in the Southern Atlantic. In this context, particular thought must be given to the harbours of Beira (Mozambique), Libito (Angola) and also the harbours of Cape Verde.
(f) The furthering of an alliance between Britain, South Africa, Brazil, and Argentina.

General Conclusions:
There is nothing to indicate that Portugal cannot keep its colonies of Mozambique and Angola forever. Neither can one conclude that the present political situation in Portugal will change. British diplomats in these states, with instructions suitable of their status should work in this way.
–In the future Britain should not condemn Portugal in the Safety Committee for having defended herself against armed attacks.
–Portugal is very weak in the naval sphere. Bearing in mind the significance of the Cape Verde Islands, England should give up her present attitude towards her Portuguese allies and support Portugal, particularly in the region of San Vicente.

III. The prevention of economic independence in African Countries.
With the political strategy of the imperialist powers as a background, one can assume the existence of a great deal of scheming in West Africa, among other places in the Republic of Guinea. The governments of the Cape Route countries must be kept under control. This is achieved by their economic dependence. If these countries were to attempt to achieve economic, and therefore political independence, then the imperialist powers would try to overthrow their governments.[62]

The political strategy outlined supported the preservation of the Portuguese colonial status quo. At that time, Great Britain and the United States openly announced their distaste of Portuguese colonialism, the Rhodesian UDI, and South African apartheid. These countries publicly declared their preference for peaceful decolonization and the attainment of African majority rule. While the United States supported the peaceful resolution of the African struggles for national liberation, its policies were formulated within the context of the following:

–The strategic importance of southern Africa, particularly with the closing of the Suez Canal following the 1967 Middle East war and the increased Soviet naval activies in the Indian Ocean;
–The US need to use overflight and landing facilities for military aircraft heading to and from Indochina;
–Significant investment and balance of trade advantages to both Britain and the US in South Africa;
–South Africa's status as the major gold supplier in the capitalist world and its importance in guaranteeing the useful operation of the two-tier gold price system.[63]

Having won the presidential election in 1968, the Republican administration under President Richard M. Nixon, decided to review American policy toward southern Africa. Its secret National Security Council Study Memorandum (NSSM) Number 39, prepared by the National Security Council in 1969, under the direction of Dr. Henry Kissinger, defined US objectives and priorities in southern Africa as follows:

–To improve the US standing in black Africa and internationally on the racial issue;
–To minimize the likelihood of escalation of violence in the area and risk of US involvement;
–To minimize the opportunities for the USSR and communist China to exploit the racial issue in the region for propaganda advantage and to gain political influence with black governments and liberation movements;

–To encourage moderation of the current rigid racial and colonial policies of the white regimes;

–To protect economic, scientific and strategic interests and opportunities in the region, including the orderly marketing of South Africa's gold production.[64]

Although the United States was against racism, apartheid, and the oppressive nature of Portuguese, Rhodesian, and South African white domination, it also opposed Afro-Asian attempts at passing strong UN resolutions entailing the use of force to overthrow these colonial regimes. Although the United States admitted that it did not have vital security interests in southern Africa, it also viewed the region as being logistically important for its defense system. In the final analysis, the United States adopted *option* two of its NSSM 39, which states:

Premise
The whites are here to stay and the only way that constructive change can come about is through them. There is no hope for the blacks to gain the political rights they seek through violence, which will only lead to chaos and increased opportunities for the communists. We can, by selective realization of our stance toward the white regimes, encourage some modification of their current racial and colonial policies and (a total of about 5-million dollars annually in technical assistance to the black states) help to draw the two groups together and exert some influence on both for peaceful change. Our tangible interests form a basis for our contacts in the region, and these can be maintained at an acceptable political cost.

General Posture
We would maintain public opposition to racial repression but relax political isolation and economic restrictions on the white states. We should begin by modest indications of this relaxation, broadening the scope of our relations and contacts gradually and to some degree in response to tangible–albeit small and gradual moderation of white policies. Without openly taking a position undermining the United Kingdom on Rhodesia, we would be more flexible in our attitude toward the Smith regime. We would take present Portuguese policies as suggesting further changes in the Portuguese territories. At the same time, we would take diplomatic steps to convince the black states of the area that their current liberation and majority rule aspirations in the south are not attainable by violence and that their only hope for a peaceful and prosperous future lies in closer relations with white-dominated states. We would emphasize our belief that closer relations will help to bring change in the white states. We would give increased and more flexible economic aid to black states of the area to focus their attention on their internal development and to give them a motive to cooperate in reducing tensions. We would encourage economic assistance from South Africa to the developing black nations.[65]

The United States policy was definitely sympathetic to the white racists, despite its claims to the contrary. The United States, Portuguese, British, French, and South African opposition to revolutions, communism, and armed struggle were similar. Although the United States supplied military hardware to Portugal, it vigorously opposed the supply of military weapons to African nationalists who were engaged in wars to overthrow colonialism. However, military equipment given by the United States to the Portuguese government was used in the wars against FRELIMO, PAIGC, and MPLA. For its colonial wars in Angola, Guinea Bissau, and Mozambique, Portugal required an increasing number of sophisticated weapons that it did not produce because of economic and technological limitations. Portugal was, therefore, dependent on the United States and other NATO members for the supply of the much needed military hardware. Without this source of weapons, the Portuguese government would not have been able to wage its colonial wars.

Before the eruption of the wars in its colonial dependencies, Portugal had a small external national debt. With the intensification of the struggle for national liberation in its African colonies, Portugal's external debt rose from 8,600 million escudos in 1969 to 48,828 million escudos in 1972. In addition to the spiraling of its national debt, Portugal had increasing problems with its balance of trade deficit. In 1972, Portugal's imports were valued at 60,700 million escudos and exports at 35 million escudos.[66] While exploiting the resources of Angola, Cape Verde, Mozambique, and Guinea-Bissau to finance the balance of trade deficit and its national debt, Portugal also obtained financial aid from the United States, Great Britain, and France.

During the hearings before the Subcommittee on Africa of the United States Committee on Foreign Affairs, House of Representatives, the following information showing US support for Portugal was revealed: US aid to Portugal from 1946 to 1972 amounted to $571.8 million, of which $334 million were for military assistance; export-import bank loans for the fiscal year 1972 amounted to $46 million; in 1974, US development aid to Portugal was $7.9 million; and in 1972, President Nixon announced a $435 million aid package to Premier Caetano's government as a part of an agreement for the United States to use bases in the Azores.

Like the United States, other Western countries have heavily invested in the escudo zone. Of the 1.8 million escudos invested in this zone in 1969 by Western countries, 60 percent went to Portuguese colonial dependencies. The extent of their financial support for Portugal is vividly illustrated in Table 11, which shows that 98.5 percent of the investments in the Portuguese colonies in 1969 came from five countries.

Table 11: Foreign Investments in Portugal, 1969

Belgium	775,000,000 escudos
United States	158,193,000 escudos
South Africa	105,910,000 escudos
Great Britain	53,010,000 escudos
Federal Republic of Germany	19,400,000 escudos

The order is different for the investments in Portugal:

Federal Republic of Germany	139,173,000 escudos
United States	109,736,000 escudos
Great Britain	83,935,000 escudos
Spain	67,038,000 escudos
France	47,596,000 escudos

SOURCE: J. Angola Martins, *L'intensificazione dello Struttamento Imperialistics nel Settore Minerario* (Conferenza internazionale di solidarità con i popoli delle colonie portughesi, Roma 1970) pp V-VII.

More economic and financial aid in support of Portugal in its colonial wars continued through to the Portuguese coup d'etat of 1974. Meanwhile, at the United Nations, African countries continued their untiring efforts of ending the Portuguese murders of Africans in its colonies. One such horrible incident was the Wiriyamu Massacre of 1973 in which thousands of innocent men, women, and children were bombed and shot by the Portuguese army in Mozambique on suspicion of harboring FRELIMO freedom fighters. On receiving detailed reports of these Portuguese murders, the OAU instructed the African group at the United Nations to take appropriate action against Portugal. Although the Portuguese denied that the Wiriyamu Massacre had occurred, the reports submitted by the African group eventually persuaded the Security Council to set up a special committee to investigate the Wiriyamu allegations. In its report, the UN special committee concluded that Portuguese troops had indeed killed many innocent African peasants and children. Based on this report, the General Assembly adopted a resoltuion that condemned the Wiriyamu Massacre and called on Portugal to grant independence to its colonial dependencies in Africa.

While African UN member states backed by most of the nonaligned countries were demanding that Western European countries, the United States, Canada, Brazil, Argentina, Iran, and Middle Eastern oil-producing countries impose an economic and military boycott on Portugal because of its recalcitrance in terminating colonialism in Africa, the United Nations declared and affirmed that African liberation movements in Angola, Guinea-Bissau, and Mozambique were the true authentic representatives of their peoples. To demonstrate its support for African liberation, the General Assembly appealed to the "Governments and the peoples of the world to hold annually, a week of Solidarity with the Colonial people of Southern Africa, Guinea (Bissau) and Cape Verde fighting for Freedom, Independence and Equal Rights and proposed that the week of 25 May should be known as Africa Liberation Day."[67]

Support from the African group, PAIGC, FRELIMO, MPLA, FLNA, and UNITA provided the Special Committee on Decolonization with information about the Portuguese colonial administration in Angola, Cape Verde, Guinea-Bissau, and Mozambique. These reports generally detailed Portuguese brutal and oppressive treatment of Africans and the continued denial of the majority the right to self-determination. While presenting their 1973 reports to the committee, the representatives of these liberation movements strongly condemned the Portuguese-controlled and managed Mozambican election for its legislative assembly. FRELIMO argued that the election had nothing to do with the attainment of African majority rule. The African Group, MPLA, PAIGC, and the committee on decolonization also held the same views as FRELIMO. These views were:

1. The Mozambican people do not want autonomy from Lisbon. They want independence–that is, recognition of their personality as an African people and the possibility of governing themselves, of choosing their own leaders and of establishing the political, economic, and social system that best serves their interests.[68]

With increased support from the OAU, the General Assembly, and numerous international nongovernmental organizations, guerrilla warfare in the Portuguese colonies intensified throughout 1973. It was this support that encouraged the PAIGC to unilaterally declare its independence from Portugal. The OAU's Liberation Committee actually encouraged the PAIGC's declaration of independence and promised to increase its fiscal and military aid. Additionally, the African group took upon itself the responsibility of securing an early recognition from the United Nations General Assembly, which, in a resolution adopted on November 2, 1973, by ninety-three votes to seven, with thirty abstentions, welcomed the accession to independence of the people of Guinea-Bissau.

The assembly's action followed a request, made on October 12, 1973, by fifty-six member states of the United Nations, for inclusion in the agenda of the assembly's current session of an item entitled "Illegal occupation by Portuguese military forces of certain sectors of the Republic of Guinea-Bissau and acts of aggression committed by them against the people of the Republic." The proposal, adopted by fifty-six nations, was made following the receipt by the Assembly's Fourth Committee of a cabled message dated September 27 from Aristides Pereira, secretary-general of the Partido Africano da Independencia da Guinee Cabo Verde (PAIGC). After receiving the full text of the UDI Proclamation and the Constitution of the Republic of Guinea-Bissau, the General Assembly adopted the following resolution on November 2, 1973.

> *Recognizing* the inalienable right of all peoples to self-determination and independence in accordance with the principles of the Charter of the United Nations and the Declaration on the Granting of Independence to Colonial Countries and Peoples,
> *Deeply concerned* at the explosive situation resulting from the continued illegal occupation by the armed forces of Portugal of certain sectors of the Republic of Guinea-Bissau,
> *Mindful* that all States should, in conformity wth Article 2, paragraph 4, of the Charter, refrain in their international relations from the threat or use of force against the territorial integrity or national independence of any State or from taking any action inconsistent with the principles and purposes of the Charter.
> *Noting with satisfaction* that the State of Guinea-Bissau assumes the sacred duty to expel the forces of aggression of Portuguese colonialism from that part of the territory of Guinea-Bissau which they still occupy and to intensify the struggle in the Cape Verde Islands which form an integral and inalienable part of the national territory of the people of Guinea-Bissau and Cape Verde,
> *Aware* of the urgent need of the people of the newly established State of Guinea-Bissau for all possible international assistance in its national reconstruction programmes,
> 1. *Welcomes* the recent accession to independence of the people of Guinea-Bissau thereby creating the sovereign State of the Republic of Guinea-Bissau;
> 2. *Strongly condemns* the policies of the Government of Portugal in perpetuating its illegal occupation of certain sectors of the Republic of Guinea-Bissau and the repeated acts of aggression committed by its armed forces against the people of Guinea-Bissau and Cape Verde;
> 3. *Demands* that the Government of Portugal desist forthwith from further violation of the sovereignty and territorial integrity of the Republic of Guinea-Bissau and from all acts of aggression against the people of Guinea-Bissau and Cape Verde by immediately withdrawing its armed forces from those territories;
> 4. *Draws the attention* of the Security Council, in conformity with Article II,

paragraph 3, of the Charter of the United Nations, to the critical situation resulting from the illegal presence of Portugal in Guinea-Bissau and to the urgent need for taking, as a matter of priority, all effective steps to restore the territorial integrity of the Republic;

5. *Invites* all Member States, the specialized agencies and other organizations within the United Nations system to render all necessary assistance to the Government of Guinea-Bissau in its national reconstruction and development programmes;

6. *Decides* to keep the situation under continuous review.[69]

Despite its setback in Guinea and the Cape Verde, the Portuguese government remained stubborn to its objective of holding on to its territorial possessions of Angola and Mozambique. Having lost the Cape Verde and Guinea, the Portuguese government removed its troops from the UDI states to Angola and Mozambique. However, with increasing OAU military aid to freedom fighters in Angola and Mozambique and mounting adverse international opinion, political and economic restlessness raged throughout Portugal. Portuguese soldiers in Angola and Mozambique came to the conclusion that they would never win protracted guerrilla wars against MPLA, UNITA, FLNA, and FRELIMO. As a result, the political and military morale of the Portuguese army was at its lowest ebb at the beginning of 1974. Because of these factors, hundreds of soldiers began to defect to the African nationalists and called on Portugal to grant independence to Angola and Mozambique. As divisions and conflicts increased among the Portuguese military and civilians, the Portuguese army toppled the government of Premier Caetano in 1974.

Following the coup in Portugal and a change in government in April 1974, the chairman of the Committee on Decolonization, in conjunction with the chairman of the Special Committee Against Apartheid and the president of the United Nations Council for Namibia, issued a joint statement on May 9, 1974 to the Portuguese government reiterating that it should abide by the United Nations declarations which support that all colonial peoples have a right to freedom, self-determination, and independence. In response to this:

Portugal, in a note herbale to the Secretary-General on 3 August, pledged to cooperate fully with the United Nations in the decolonization of its African territories and announced its readiness to recognize the Republic of Guinea-Bissau as an indepentent State, to arrange for the immediate transfer of its administration and to support the Republic's application for membership in the United Nations. Portugal also stated that it was prepared to cooperate closely with the United Nations in speeding decolonization in the Cape Verde Islands, that it would take immediate steps to enter into negotiations with the Mozambique Liberation Front (FRELIMO) in order to speed independence for that territory and that it intended to make early contacts with the liberation movements in Angola with a view to formal negotiations.

The President of Portugal, in an address to the General Assembly in October, pledged his Government's full compliance with the Charter and fulfillment of all its international obligations, and stated that Portugal had embarked upon an "irreversible and definite" process of decolonization in its territories.

The Assembly welcomed the acceptance by the new Government of Portugal of the principle of self-determination and noted with satisfaction that Mozambique would accede to independence on 12 July 1975, and that provisional governments would be established in Angola and Cape Verde with a view to the attainment by those territories during 1975 of the goals set forth in the Charter and the Declaration on Decolonization.[70]

All these former African-Portuguese colonial dependencies are independent states that are active members of the United Nations and the Organization of African Unity. Although it can be argued that the activities of African states within the UN system are not directly responsible for the attainment of African independence in the former Portuguese colonies of Angola, Cape Verde, Guinea-Bissau, and Mozambique, it can be stated that their activities within the UN system were diplomatic. The African group constantly brought the issue of Portuguese colonialism in Africa for discussion within the Security Council, the General Assembly, and other appropriate organs and agencies of the UN system. They appealed to UN member states to impose economic and military embargoes against Portugal. The African states can be credited with influencing a majority of the UN members and the world community to condemn publicly the Portuguese colonial policies. Even Portugal's traditional friends in NATO were constantly embarrassed by their association with it.

The greatest achievement of the African countries lies in the OAU's economic, military, and political support for the liberation of Portuguese colonies. While the OAU supplied military hardware to freedom fighters in the Portuguese colonies, it also mounted diplomatic attacks against Portugal within the world community. At gatherings like those of the nonaligned states, Afro-Asian conferences, the Arab League, Third World conferences, numerous nongovernmental organizations, and others, the OAU states individually or collectively condemned Portuguese colonialism and atrocities in Africa. Embassies of the member states of the OAU also influenced their host countries to take African anticolonial objectives very seriously. The anti-Portuguese activities of the African states within the international system strongly influenced the General Assembly and other appropriate organs of the UN system in their handling of the issues concerning the decolonization of the Portuguese colonies of Angola, Cape Verde, Guinea-Bissau, and Mozambique.

Zimbabwe in the UN System

The Rhodesian (Zimbabwean) colonial problem is another issue the United Nations has spent considerable time trying to resolve. In 1961, Southern Rhodesia adopted a new constitution that granted 4.5 million Africans fifteen legislative seats and two hundred and fifty thousand whites fifty seats. Africans overwhelmingly rejected this constitution and called on Great Britain to suspend it and convene a new constitutional conference. Great Britain then suggested to the African leaders of the National Democratic party (NDP) to help in making the 1961 Constitution work. The duke of Devonshire, the undersecretary of State for Commonwealth Relations, told the NDP team, comprised of Joshua Nkomo, Enoch Dumbutshena, and Morton Malianga, that Africans could never be given political and economic power because the complex industrial organization in Rhodesia would never be in the hands of the untrained and less experienced people. Convinced beyond reason that the British interests in Rhodesia were overly weighted in favor of the whites, Africans decided to appeal to the United Nations, which seemed the most hopeful channel. Early in 1961, Nkomo had first decided to put the case of Rhodesia at the United Nations, mainly as a way of bringing leverage on Great Britain. He appeared as a petitioner before the committee set up to implement the declaration in the UN Charter on the granting of independence to all colonial countries and all territories that are not self-governing.[71] Britain protested to the United Nations about Nkomo's petition before that organization. He had appeared as a petitioner against Britain's handling of African opposition to the 1961 Constitution. Britain's objections were based on the following reasons: (1) Rhodesia had been self-governing since 1923; (2) Rhodesia was responsible for its internal affairs and did not have to report to Britain about its administration; and, (3) the world organization had no right to discuss any issues involving Southern Rhodesia's internal affairs. Despite the protestations of Britain, on December 14, 1961, the United Nations committee resolved that Southern Rhodesia was not a self-governing territory within the context of Chapter II of the Charter; therefore, the United Nations Organization could discuss the internal affairs of Southern Rhodesia. It should be recalled that African countries at the United Nations had attacked and denounced Britain's stand on the 1961 Constitution. The most vocal of these were Ivory Coast, Ghana, Sierra Leone, Tanganyika, Guinea, Nigeria, and Liberia.

From March to May 1962, the special committee considered the question of Rhodesia, hearing statements by the petitioners Nkomo (ZAPU), Paul Mushonga (Zimbabwe National party), and Garfield Todd, former prime minister of Rhodesia. It also set up a Subcommittee on Rhodesia, which was to remain in touch with the British government and to discuss future action. Consisting of India, Mali, Tanganyika, Tunisia, and Venezuela, with C. S. Jha of India as chair-person, the subcommittee visited London in April 1962 at the invitation of the British government. In its report, the subcommittee said that the 1961 Constitution needed revision, since it did not provide adequately for African representation; and proposed that Britain be asked to convene another conference to draw up a new constitution.[72]

On the basis of this resolution, Zimbabwean nationalists had found sympathy at the United Nations, and Britain was pressured from many angles to reconvene a Rhodesian constitutional conference. ZAPU and PASU sent more petitioners to the United Nations who were enthusiastically received by many Afro-Asian UN representatives. On behalf of the Afro-Asian states, Togo submitted a draft resolution calling (1) for the release of African nationalists, and (2) for the lifting of the ban on ZAPU. Finally, it asked Britain to inform the General Assembly on the implementation of this resolution. By eighty-three votes to two, with eleven abstentions, the assembly adopted it on October 12, 1962, as Resolution 1755 (XVIII).

From 1953 to 1963, Southern Rhodesia, Northern Rhodesia (Zambia), and Nyasaland (Malawi) were united by Britain into a federation dominated by whites. When the federation dissolved on December 31, 1963, Nyasaland and Northern Rhodesia were to be granted independence as Malawi and Zambia, respectively. With the independence of Malawi and Zambia, the Rhodesia Front government of

Prime Minister Ian D. Smith initiated discussions for the independence of Rhodesia with the prime minister of Britain, Harold Wilson. British policy on Rhodesia was based on the principle that there would be no independence without majority rule, and that there should be a gradual termination of segregation and racial discrimination. Ian Smith's Rhodesia Front (RF) government refused to go along with the six principles that Prime Minister Wilson had outlined as satisfying Britain's conditions for granting independence to Rhodesia:

(1)   The principle and intention of unimpeded progress to majority rule, already enshrined in the 1961 Constitution, would have to be maintained and guaranteed;

(2)   There would also have to be guarantees against retrogressive amendment of the Constitution;

(3)   There would have to be immediate improvement in the political status of the African population;

(4)   There would have to be progress towards ending racial discrimination;

(5)   The British Government would need to be satisfied that any basis proposed for independence was acceptable to the people of Rhodesia as a whole; and

(6)   It would be necessary to ensure, that, regardless of race, there was no oppression of majority by minority or minority by majority.

Throughout 1965, African states tried to exert pressure on Britain to find a peaceful solution that would lead to African majority rule in Rhodesia. From the dissolution of the Federation of Northern Rhodesia, Southern Rhodesia, and Nyasaland, it was generally felt by African countries that Ian Smith would one day make a unilateral declaration of independence in Rhodesia. Putting political pressure on Britain was considered and regarded as one of the most efficient mechanisms of stopping such an eventuality. As reports on preparations for a Rhodesian declaration of independence began to spread throughout Africa and the UNO, Zimbabwe African Peoples Union (ZAPU), and ZANU increased their pressures on African states to convince Britain to use force to quell the white rebellion. Zimbabwean nationalists also appealed to African states to use their influence and offices at the United Nations in soliciting support in their condemnation of Rhodesian independence. It was hoped that by constantly raising the Rhodesian issue within the General Assembly, the Security Council, and other UN organs and agencies, Britain would be influenced by the United Nations and the rest of the world community to use force or other drastic means to terminate white domination of Zimbabwe. Zimbabwean nationalists' pressures on the OAU and other United Nation member states resulted in the Security Council's adoption of a resolution on May 5, 1965.

The Security Council requested the United Kingdom and all Member States not to accept a unilateral declaration of independence by Southern Rhodesia. It also asked the United Kingdom to take all necessary action to prevent such a declaration and to carry out the measures previously requested by the General Assembly so that the earliest possible date might be set for independence under a democratic system of government.[73]

Following the Security Council meeting, African members of the British

Commonwealth countries began to mobilize other members of the organization to exert pressure on Britain to take a strong stand on the use of force to prevent a Rhodesian declaration of independence. During the London Commonwealth Conference in June 1965, President Nkrumah of Ghana speaking on behalf of African states (except Malawi) put forward a six-point plan.

(1) Britain must convene a constitutional conference of all parties and groups in Rhodesia.
(2) Britain must tell Ian Smith to release political prisoners.
(3) Smith should be given a specific time in which to carry out these instructions.
(4) Failing that, Britain should suspend the Rhodesian constitution.
(5) An interim and representative government should be appointed, charged with the repeal of all repressive legislation.
(6) A general election should be held on a franchise based on one man one vote.[74]

While supporting this plan, President Julius Nyerere of Tanzania went on to rebuke Britain for failing to use military force in Rhodesia, contrasting its inaction with earlier British intervention in Cyprus, Kenya, Aden, and British Guiana. President Nyerere also dismissed the purported difficulties of a military operation in a landlocked country like Rhodesia which is three hundred miles from the nearest sea and sheltered therefrom by almost uniformly friendly territory. He also stated that action was needed now. Rhodesian independence from Britain if allowed to happen, would confirm the case for a swift military retribution. Negotiations were useless, and indeed dangerous. Nyerere added that they were negotiating with the wrong people; Smith would never accept one-man one-vote. It was not enough to talk of guarantees of unimpeded progress to majority rule. He concluded by saying that independence should come only after the introduction of universal adult suffrage. President Nkrumah's plan and President Nyerere's insightful comments were supported by a majority of African, Caribbean, and Asian Commonwealth countries.

Aware of these demands for use of force, Britain opted to impose economic sanctions against Rhodesia if it were to proceed with its plans for independence. While emphasizing the grave consequences of economic sanctions, Harold Wilson noted that Britain found

  ... it necessary to declare what serious consequences would flow from such an act ....

  −A mere declaration of independence would have no constitutional effect .... A declaration of independence would be an open act of defiance and rebellion and it would be treasonable to take steps to give effect to it ....
  −No Commonwealth Government would be able to recognize a unilateral declaration.
  −Commonwealth membership would be out of the question, with all the related economic consequences.
  −The British Government would be bound to sever relations with those responsible for such a declaration.

–There would be no relations with the Crown. Southern Rhodesians would cease to be British subjects.
–The economic effects would be disastrous to the prosperity and prospects of the people of Southern Rhodesia. All financial and trade relations between Britain and Southern Rhodesia would be jeopardized. Any further aid or any further access to the London market would be out of the question . . . .

In short, an illegal declaration of independence in Southern Rhodesia would bring to an end relationships between her and Britain, would cut Rhodesia off from the rest of the Commonwealth, from most foreign governments and international organizations, would inflict disastrous economic damage upon her, and would leave her isolated and virtually friendless in a largely hostile continent.[75]

African countries were disappointed by these proposals, which they regarded weak and inadequate. Frustrated by British actions they regarded racist and supportive of the white racist Rhodesians, the OAU at its summit meeting in Accra, Ghana, adopted Resolution AHG 26 II.

The Assembly of Heads of State and Government meeting in its Second Ordinary Session in Accra, Ghana, from 21 to 25 October 1965.

Deeply concerned at the gravity of the situation in Southern Rhodesia,
Considering that the situation constitutes a serious threat to world peace,
Noting:
(a)   The statement of the Government of the United Kingdom of Great Britain and Northern Ireland that it will regard any Unilateral Declaration of Independence by the European minority in Southern Rhodesia as illegal and amounting to an act of rebellion and treason punishable solely by the imposition of economic sanctions and nonrecognition,
(b)   The recent United Nations resolution passed with an overwhelming majority calling on the United Kingdom Government to take all posssible steps to prevent a Unilateral Declaration of Indpendence and pledging support for any future measures that the United Nations might decide upon in this matter,
1.   *Deplores* the refusal of the United Kingdom Government to meet with the firmness and resolution the threat of a Unilateral Declaration of Independence by a European minority government;
2.   *Deplores* the refusal of the United Kingdom Government to state categorically that it will not grant independence to Rhodesia except on a basis of a majority government;
3.   *Calls upon* the United Nations to regard any such Unilateral Declaration of Independence as constituting a threat to international peace, and to take any steps that such a situation requires in accordance with the Charter and to help to establish a majority government in Southern Rhodesia;
4.   *Requests* the United Kingdom Government, the administering power having sole responsibility for the present situation:
(a)   To suspend the 1961 Constitution of Southern Rhodesia forwith and to take all necessary steps including the use of armed force to resume the administration of the territory;
(b)   To release the leaders of the Nationalist movements Joshua Nkomo, Ndabaningi Sithole, and other political prisoners;
(c)   To hold a constitutional conference with the participation of the representatives of the entire population of Southern Rhodesia with a view to adopting a new Constitution guaranteeing universal adult suffrage (one

man, one vote), free elections and independence;
5.   *Calls upon* all governments and all international organizations to withhold recognition of a European minority government in the event of a unilateral declaration of independence, and to apply all necessary sanctions;
6.   *Resolves* in the event of failure on the part of the United Kingdom to take the measures set forth in operative paragraph 2 (a):
   (a)   To reconsider all political, economic, diplomatic and financial relations between African countries and the United Kingdom Government in the event of this Government's granting or tolerating Southern Rhodesian independence under a minority government;
   (b)   To use all possible means including force to oppose a unilateral declaration of independence;
   (c)   To give immediate assistance to the people of Zimbabwe with a view to establishing a majority government in the country;
7.   *Empowers* the African Group at the United Nations to ensure that the request sent to the United Nations and the Security Council receives due consideration.[76]

With this charge from the OAU Assembly of Heads of State and Government, the African group at the United Nations, Zimbabwean Liberation movements, and their sympathizers at the United Nations began to argue that a unilateral declaration of independence by Rhodesia be considered a United Nations Security Council matter because it was likely to threaten international peace and security. Britain began to adopt the position that, as the colonial power adminitering Rhodesia, it had the final say in what happens in its colony of Rhodesia. Central to British policy on Rhodesia were the objectives to secure universal acknowledgment of British responsibility for Rhodesia, to retain at all times the initiative in the United Nations regarding any action taken against Rhodesia, and to discourage the use of force against Rhodesia.

On Thursday, November 11, 1965, Rhodesian Prime Minister, Ian Smith declared Rhodesian independence from Britain. Britain reacted to this declaration by imposing economic sanctions on Rhodesia. While the debate on sanctions was taking place on November 11, 1965, in the House of Commons, the British foreign secretary was dispatched to the United Nations in New York. As expected, Prime Minister Wilson stated:

We intend to inform the United Nations of our responsibilities and of the measures which we are taking, and we shall ask for the support of other countries in those economic measures. He stated further that he believed the problem will be to avert excessive action by the United Nations. As for the economic sanctions, I think that it will be right for us to concentrate on trying to get other nations to follow our lead rather than seeing them get too far ahead of us.[77]

The sanctions Britain imposed on Rhodesia on November 11, 1965, outlined some of the following:

1.   The British high commissioner was withdrawn and the Southern Rhodesia high commissioner in London was asked to leave.
2.   Export of arms, including spare parts, were stopped.
3.   All British aid ceased.
4.   Rhodesia was removed from the sterling area.
5.   Export of United Kingdom capital to Rhodesia was prohibited.

6. Rhodesia's access to the London capital market was halted.
7. United Kingdom Export Credits Guarantee Department stopped further coverage for exports to Rhodesia.
8. Rhodesia was suspended from the Commonwealth Preference Area and her goods no longer received preferential treatment on entering the United Kingdom.
9. United Kingdom banned purchase of Rhodesian sugar and tobacco–stopping a net total of 71 percent (by value) of Rhodesian exports to Britain.
10. United Kingdom no longer recognized passports issued or renewed by the illegal regime.[78]

African countries condemned British sanctions against Rhodesia as inadequate means of toppling the regime of Ian Smith. At the United Nations, the African states led most of the Third World countries in putting pressure on the Security Council to take a decision against Rhodesian independence. As a result, the Security Council passed Resolution (S/RES/216) of November 12, 1965, which condemned the illegal regime of Ian Smith and called on all states neither to recognize nor to do anthing likely to assist in the successful implementation of the Rhodesian declaration. Third World dissatisfaction with Security Council Resolution 216 made the Security Council adopt another resolution on November 20, 1965. This resolution (S/RES/217) noted the gravity of the situation caused by Rhodesian independence and determined that its prolonged existence would definitely constitute a threat to international peace and security. In addition, Resolution S/RES/217 called on Britain to use its power to end the rebellion and urged the OAU states to cooperate in the successful implementation of this resolution. Resolution S/RES/217 further requested all states not to supply Rhodesia with oil, petroleum products, or arms and to do their utmost in order to break off economic relations with Southern Rhodesia. Only France abstained, on the grounds that Rhodesia was a purely British responsibility. All other members of the Security Council voted in favor of the Security Council Resolution 217.

On November 17, 1965, following African and other Third World pressure at the United Nations, which had led to the adoption of the Security Council Resolutions 216 and 217, British Foreign Secretary Michael Stewart told the Security Council that Britain was ready to envisage the possibility of wider economic measures against Rhodesia including an embargo on oil. The British Commonwealth African states were hardly impressed by Foreign Secretary Stewart's outline of British sanctions programs that led to the adoption of Security Council Resolutions 216 and 217.

While supporting the Security Council Resolution 217, African states resented Stewart's call for African cooperation in implementing UN sanctions against Rhodesia. African states never believed that sanctions would topple the Smith regime in Salisbury. The OAU states felt that by cooperating or implementing the sanctions resolutions (which they believed would never work) they would by that very act, be abandoning their obligations in helping Africa free itself from British as well as French, Portuguese, and Spanish colonialism and imperialism. To make sure that Britain and other Western countries understand the OAU's seriousness of toppling the new Rhodesian regime, the OAU Council of Ministers held a meeting in Addis Ababa from May 3 to December 5, 1965. The Council adopted the following three resolutions:

Having considered the illegal declaration of independence by the European settler minority government in Southern Rhodesia and after reviewing the present activities designed to bring about majority rule in that country,

Decides,

1. That all Member states of the OAU should bring into immediate effect a complete blockage against Southern Rhodesia while it is still under the illegal government of a European settler minority and especially that the following measures should be taken;

(a)   All economic relations, including trade and payment transactions, with Southern Rhodesia should be stopped forthwith and especially that country should be denied sterling area facilities in respect of Commonwealth trade;

(b)   All accounts of Southern Rhodesia in Africa's Banks should be blocked;

(c)   All travel documents issued or renewed by that illegal government should be treated as invalid;

(d)   All means of transportation, including aircraft to or from Southern Rhodesia must be denied all servicing and other facilities including the rights to overfly;

(e)   All OAU Member States should cut off all communication channels including telegraph, telephone, teleprinter or radio-telephone with Southern Rhodesia;

2. That if the United Kingdom does not crush the rebellion and restore law and order, and thereby prepare the way for majority rule in Southern Rhodesia by 15 December 1965, the Member States of the OAU shall sever diplomatic relations on that date with the United Kingdom;

3. To call on all friends of Africa to give all assistance and support to measures designed to bring an end to the illegal government of the European settler minority;

4. To call on all the countries of the world to deny Southern Rhodesia under the present illegal government, all oil and fuel facilities;

5. That all African States and other friendly States should use radio and other information media at their disposal to serve the cause of the Africans in Southern Rhodesia;

6. That all Member States of the OAU should inform the Administrative Secretary-General of the measures taken to implement the above decisions and also transmit to the General Secretariat of the OAU copies of the legislation or instructions issued in this connection;

7. That the African Group at the United Nations should take action to ensure that the relevant operative paragraphs in this resolution, especially operative paragraph 4, are adopted by the appropriate organs of the United Nations.

Resolution, ECM Res. 15 (VI)

The Council of Ministers meeting in Addis Ababa in its Sixth Extraordinary Session from 3 to 5 December, 1965,

Having examined critically the grave situation which exists in Southern Rhodesia after the Unilateral Declaration of Independence by the racist minority regime, with the connivance of the British Government,

1. *Requests* the Committee of Five to invite military advisers from Member States in order to study and plan the use of force to assist the people of Zimbabwe;

2. *Requests* all Member States to render through the Committee of Five all means of assistance to the people of Zimbabwe in their national struggle against alien rule;

3. *Requests* the Committee of Five to call upon Member States to make military or other contributions to meet any emergency that may rise in Member States which are neighbors of Southern Rhodesia without prejudice to the right of

Member States to appeal directly to any African brother State to ensure such assistance;

4. *Requests* the Committee of Five to explore what military or other contributions can be made by Member States to meet any emergency which may arise if any Member State of OAU which is a neighbor of Southern Rhodesia is in danger of being attacked;

5. *Urgently appeals* to all Member States to facilitate by all means the mission entrusted to the Committee of Five.

Resolution ECM Res. 16 (VI)

The Council of Ministers meeting in Addis Ababa in its Sixth Extraordinary Session from 3 to 5 December, 1965,

Having studied sufficiently the grave situation which exists in Southern Rhodesia after the Unilateral Declaration of Independence by the racist minority regime;

Instructs the African Group at the United Nations to request the execution of Resolution No. S/Res. 217 (1965) of 22 November, 1965 on Southern Rhodesia;

Invites the Foreign Ministers of Algeria, Senegal and Zambia to continue their efforts before the Security Council on the Southern Rhodesian issue.[79]

Britain ignored the three OAU resolutions thinking that African countries would not fulfill them. To the astonishment of Britain, on December 15, 1969, thirteen African countries, including two commonwealth countries, broke off their diplomatic relations with it. On December 16, 1965, the very date that the OAU deadline expired, the British Prime Minister, Harold Wilson, addressed the United Nations General Assembly.

The next morning, as I spoke, some twenty African delegates walked out. There is no denying that it hurt; I was a passionate believer in the independent Commonwealth. I had gone to great lengths, and risked not only political unpopularity, but even parliamentary defeat in our total opposition to the policies of the Rhodesian Front. But all one could do was to be good-tempered about it. At the end of my scripted speech I made an appeal to the African delegates, in absentia, "when they are able to listen": "Today we see some of our friends, passionate to intervene and unable to do so, directing their understandable anger not against Rhodesia but against Britain. All right, I understand that. But the British Government is not going to be deflected from the course that we are convinced is right, in which I believe the whole British people are behind us . . . ."[80]

While accusing Prime Minister Wilson and the British government of racism, one hundred delegates from the OAU states walked out of the UN General Assembly in protest over its policies on Rhodesia. After this humiliation, the British government informed the UN Security Council and the General Assembly that its sanctions order was to come into operation on December 17, 1965. Sanctions imposed included:

1. Several Rhodesian minerals (including copper, chrome, and asbestos) and foodstuffs (including maize and beef) were boycotted thus stopping a net total of 95 percent (by value) of Rhodesian exports to Britain.

2. The payments of dividents, interest, and pensions to Rhodesian citizens were put into blocked accounts in London.

3. The Board of Governors of the Reserve Bank of Rhodesia were dismissed

and replaced by a British board in London, thus British assumed legal control over all Rhodesian funds outside Rhodesia. The United States, the Republic of South Africa and Switzerland blocked the Rhodesian Reserve Bank's accounts held in their respective countries.[81]

It should, however, be noted that the 1965 British Sanctions Order followed the Security Council Resolutions passed on October 20, 1965. Although Article 1 of the Order closely resembled Article 5 of Resolution 217, some important differences are worth noting:

(1) Except under the authority of a license granted by the Minister, no person shall–
    (a) supply or deliver or agree to supply or deliver to or to the order of a person in Southern Rhodesia any petroleum which is not in that country;
    (b) supply or deliver or agree to supply or deliver such petroleum to any person knowing or having reasonable cause to believe that it will be supplied or delivered to or to the order of a person in Southern Rhodesia;
    (c) do any act calculated to promote the supply or delivery of petroleum in contravention of the foregoing provisions of this paragraph.
(2) Any person who contravenes the foregoing provisions of this Article shall be guilty of an offence against this Order and, in the case of a person who–
    (a) is a body incorporated under the law of the United Kingdom; or
    (b) is a citizen of the United Kingdom and Colonies or a British protected person and is ordinarily resident in the United Kingdom, shall be guilty of an offence wherever the contravention takes place.[82]

Despite their protests over the inadequacies of the Security Council Resolution 217 and the British Sanctions Order of 1965, the OAU set up a Sanctions Committee consisting of representatives from Egypt, Kenya, Nigeria, Tanzania, and Zambia. In addition, the OAU requested African and other Third World members of the British Commonwealth to continue exerting pressure on Britain to end the Smith rebellion in Rhodesia. It was these Third World states that were members of the commonwealth whose efforts and influence made it possible for the convening of an emergency two-day Commonwealth Conference in Lagos, Nigeria, to discuss the Rhodesian crisis. The Commonwealth Conference held from January 11 to 12, 1966, was marked by deep divisions between Britain and the African states. Presidents Kaunda and Nyerere boycotted the conference and those who attended it still wanted Britain to use force to end the Rhodesian rebellion. On the other hand, Britain continued to insist that the Rhodesian rebellion would be "over in a matter of weeks rather than months." Although the Third World members of the Commonwealth did not subscribe to the view that the problem would be over in a matter of weeks, they did agree to set up a sanctions committee under the aegis of the Commonwealth secretariat. This commitee pressured Britain to actively patrol the Mozambique channel with the hope of stopping the violations of United Nations sanctions against Rhodesia. On April 19, 1966, the Security Council passed Resolution S/RES/221, which declared that the Rhodesian crisis was a threat to world peace and international security. Resolution 221 called on all states not to supply oil to the Mozambiquean port of Beira, knowing that it would be illegally delivered to Rhodesia. No mention was made of ships that stopped in Lourenço Marques or in the Republic of South Africa with oil destined for Rhodesia. African states wanted a British naval blockage applied to both Lourenço Marques and all the ports in the Republic of South Africa. When Britain refused to accede to these demands, Mali, Bulgaria, and the Soviet Union abstained from voting because they insisted that the naval blockage should apply to all South African ports as well as Lourenço Marques. Although the Malagasy Republic provided Britain with both naval and air facilities to patrol the Mozambiquean channel, Britain remained adamant in its refusal to stop vessels carrying oil destined for Rhodesia through Lourenço Marques.

As usual, African states were disappointed by the British government's refusal to extend its blockade over Lourenço Marques. This setback did not dampen the hopes of African states to convince Britain to use its power to topple the racist regime of Ian Smith. African Commonwealth countries reemployed their old techniques of exerting pressure on Britain to use force to remove the Smith government from office. This pressure was felt by Harold Wilson during the September 1966 Commonwealth Conference. In order to appease the Third World members of the Commonwealth, Wilson issued an ultimatum to the Rhodesian government to end its rebellion before the end of 1966. If his demands were not met, Wilson threatened to adopt more drastic measures against Rhodesia. The ultimatum did not impress the Africans; they did not believe that Wilson would employ any sterner measures than he had previously done. A majority of the Third World countries felt that Wilson was trying to buy time for Rhodesia to strengthen its military might against Zimbabweans.

Immediately following the London Commonwealth Conference, the OAU held its annual meeting in Addis Ababa, Ethiopia, from October 31, to November 4, 1966. While accusing Britain of bad faith, hypocrisy, and racism, the OAU council of ministers adopted Resolution CM/RES. 79 (VII) which noted the following:

HAVING REVIEWED events in Southern Rhodesia covering a period of nearly one year and the illegal seizure of independence by British racist, minority settlers in that country.

HAVING OBSERVED the hypocritical attitude and vacillation of the British Government towards the rebel regime in Southern Rhodesia.

CONVINCED that the programme of sanctions against the British colony of Southern Rhodesia as conceived and directed by the British Government will not and cannot bring down the illegal regime at Salisbury.

MORE CONVINCED than ever that the Southern Rhodesia independence crisis constitutes a threat to international peace and security.

(1) *Bitterly and unreservedly* condemns the current talks the British Government and the rebel, settler regime in Southern Rhodesia as a conspiracy aimed at recognizing the independence seized illegally by the rebel settlers;
(2) *Calls upon* all Member States of the OAU and all other States to continue to refuse recognition to the present government of Southern Rhodesia and to refuse recognition to any independent regime which the present talks between Britain

and the Southern Rhodesian rebels may bring about unless such a government is based on majority rule;

(3) *Strongly condemns* Britain for her refusal to crush the Southern Rhodesian rebel regime and repeats its demands to the United Kingdom Government to bring about the immediate downfall of that regime by any means including the use of force;

(4) *Reiterates* the terms of paragraph 4 of the Resolution of 5 March 1966, and accordingly recommends to the OAU and to all friendly governments, to give material and financial aid to the Zimbabwe people who are actually fighting inside Zimbabwe;

(5) *Condemns* those States especially those of Portugal and South Africa which render support to the rebel regime in Southern Rhodesia;

(6) *Invites* member countries in consultation with each other to take measures against those persons, companies and institutions in their own countries which, in pursuance of colonialist interests continue to have dealings with or business under, the illegal regime in Southern Rhodesia;

(7) *Calls upon* all member countries and all countries which wish to see human dignity and freedom in Africa and throughout the world to support a programme of mandatory and comprehensive sanctions against Southern Rhodesia under Chapter VII of the Charter of UN;

(8) *Repeats* its call upon all member countries to contribute to a Special Southern Rhodesia Liberation Fund to enable all Zimbabwe Nationalists to intensify the fighting against the rebels;

(9) *Calls upon* Member States to give practical implementation to paragraph 3 of the Resolution of 5 March 1966 which states:

"Decides to establish a 'Committee of Solidarity for Zambia' composed of five Members whose task shall be to seek appropriate measurers of technical economic assistance by Member States to Zambia."

So as to enable Zambia not only to withstand the effects of UDI, but also to help all Zimbabwe Freedom Fighters more effectively;

(10) *Reiterates* its call upon all Member States of the OAU and UN who have not taken any notice, to implement the United Nations Security Council Resolution of 20 November, 1965, and to intensify their efforts for the adoption of other more effective measures, including the release of all Zimbabwe leaders from the Nazi-type concentration camps of Southern Rhodesia;

(11) *Expresses* its appreciation here to the Foreign Ministers of Algeria, Senegal and Zambia and all African delegations at the United Nations for their efforts to move the Security Council to consider the Southern Rhodesian situation under Chapter VII of the United Nations Charter; and requests the Ministers to continue with their efforts in the Security Council and submit reports to the Council of Ministers;

(12) *Pays tribute* to the sons of Zimbabwe who have died in battle with the racist settler regime's usurper forces.[83]

Ian Smith ignored both the British ultimatum and the OAU Resolution CM 79 (VII). Most African states had long believed that Britain was not really anxious to topple the Smith government. Their criticisms of the British handling of the Rhodesian problem was the reason why the committee of 24 on decolonization had met and demanded a meeting of the Security Council. As a result of these African demands at the United Nations, the Security Council on December 16, 1966, passed Resolution 232 which;

Imposed selective sanctions against Southern Rhodesia, acting under Chapter VII of the Charter (which is concerned with measures in cases of threats to the peace, breaches of the peace and acts of aggression). It banned imports of Southern Rhodesian asbestos, iron ore, chrome, pig-iron, sugar, tobacco, copper, meat and meat products, and hides, skins and leather, and also banned the export to Southern Rhodesia of arms, amunition, military aircraft and vehicles, as well as equipment and materials for the manufacture and maintenance of arms and ammunition.[84]

The passage of Resolution 232, which for the first time involved United Nations mandatory sanctions as a means of solving a crisis, was of great significance to African nationalists. Whereas Resolution 232 could be criticized for its weakness in the sense that it did not ban oil as one of the items that was to be supplied to Rhodesia, its significance rested on the fact that this was the first time that the United Nations had imposed an economic sanction to any country on an issue that dealt with African decolonization. When this resolution came into effect, eleven members of the Security Council approved it, four abstained: the USSR, Bulgaria, and Mali, because, as the ambassador of Mali, Mr Keita, put it, the resolution had been stripped of its teeth, and France because the Rhodesian problem fell within the domestic jurisdiction of Britain. The two African Commonwealth countries on the Security Council, Uganda and Nigeria, voted for the resolution with little enthusiasm. Whereas the rest of the Afro-Asian countries recognized the inadequacy of this resolution, they also wanted some form of measure which would not have led to a British veto in the Security Council.

South Africa, France, and Portugal expressed their displeasure of having to comply with the UN sanctions against Rhodesia on the grounds that this was a problem that had to be resolved by Britain. As pressure to enforce the sanctions against Rhodesia mounted, Portugal proceeded to request the United Nations to provide her with some form of compensation for the economic benefits its colony of Mozambique would have accrued if the sanctions had not been applied against Rhodesia. In 1966, Portugal requested $US 27.4 million and $US 15 million in 1967, as compensatory aid. Other countries (Belgium, Brazil, Argentina, South Africa, Italy, Japan, Spain, Switzerland, Portugal, France, and others) did not comply with the first UN resolution on sanctions. Because of the ineffectiveness of this resolution as a result of noncompliance by many countries, the United Nations was forced to reconvene another Security Council meeting on Rhodesia. The Rhodesian execution of five African nationalists for political reasons in March 1968 made the African states request for an early meeting of the Security Council. When the council convened, it adopted Resolution 253 of May 29, 1968, which made it:

> ... mandatory on all UN Member States, the imposition of an embargo on all trade with Rhodesia (with certain minor exceptions such as medical and educational supplies), on all shipment in their vessels and aircraft of goods to or from Rhodesia, and on the provision of funds for investment and other purposes. Member States were also required to prevent entry into their territories of persons travelling on Rhodesian passports (save on exceptional humanitarian grounds) and persons believed to be aiding the illegal regime, to prevent their aircraft companies from operating to and from Rhodesia and to discourage emigration to Rhodesia.[85]

Resolution 253 further called on all members of the United Nations and its appropriate agencies to report to the secretary-general on measures they had taken to implement the terms of the resolution.

Security Council Resolution 253 was enacted by the British House of Commons as the (United Nations Sanctions) Order 1968 (S.I. 1968/885) "the 1968 Sanctions Order" which became effective on June 14, 1968. This order was approved by the House of Commons, but not by the House of Lords. A further order was therefore necessary. The Southern Rhodesian (United Nations Sanctions) (No. 2) Order 1968 (S.I. 1968/1020) "the Sanctions Order," which became effective on July 3, 1968, was duly approved by both Houses of Parliament. Article 5 of the Sanctions Order provides the following:

(1)   Except under the authority of a license granted by the Minister, no person shall;

(a) supply or deliver or agree to supply or deliver to or to the order of any person in Southern Rhodesia any goods that are not in that country;

(b) supply or deliver or agree to supply or deliver any such goods to any person, knowing or having reasonable cause to believe that they will be supplied or delivered to or to the order of a person in Southern Rhodesia or that they will be used for the purposes of any business carried on in or operated from Southern Rhodesia; or

(c) do any act calculated to promote the supply or delivery of any goods in contravention of the foregoing provisions of this paragraph.

(2)   Any person who contravenes the foregoing provisions of this Article shall be guilty of an offence against this Order and, in the case of a person who–

(a) is a citizen of the United Kingdom and Colonies or a British subject without citizenship or a British protected person; or

(b) is a citizen of Southern Rhodesia; or

(c) is a body incorporated or constituted under the law of the United Kingdom or the law of any other country or place to which the Southern Rhodesia Act 1965 extends, shall be guilty of an offence wherever the contravention takes place.

2.3 Article 6 of the Sanctions Order is in these terms:

(1)   Except under the authority of a license granted by the Minister, no person shall import any goods into Southern Rhodesia.

(2)   Except under such authority as aforesaid, no citizen of Southern Rhodesia or person in Southern Rhodesia shall;

(a) accept delivery outside Southern Rhodesia of any goods which he intends to import or has reason to believe that another person intends to import into Southern Rhodesia; or

(b) make or carry out any contract providing for such importation or delivery.

(3)   Any person who contravenes the foregoing provisions of this Article shall be guilty of an offence against this Order.

2.4 Article 16(2) of the Sanctions Order provides that:

Where any body corporate is guilty of an offence against this Order and that offence is proved to have been committed with the consent or connivance of or to be attributable to any neglect on the part of, and director, manager, secretary, or other similar officer of the body corporate or any person who was purporting to act in any such capacity, he, as well as the body corporate, shall be guilty of that offence and shall be liable to be proceeded against and punished accordingly.

2.5 Article 15 and Schedule 1 of the Sanctions Order confer power to facilitate the obtaining of evidence and information "for the purpose of securing compliance with or detecting evasion of this Order." Article 1 of the Sanctions Order revokes the 1968 Sanctions Order but Article 19 (1) sets out transitional provisions the effect of which is (so far as relevant for present purposes) that Article 15 and Schedule 1 are to be treated as the 1968 Sanctions Order and that the revocation is not to affect any liability in respect of or any offence against the Orders revoked.

The terms of the 1968 Sanction Order

2.6 The 1969 Sanctions Order contained in Articles 4 and 5 provisions identical to Articles 5 and 6 of the Sanctions Order set out above. It revoked a number of earlier Sanctions Orders, including the Southern Rhodesia (Petroleum) Order 1965 (S. I. 1965/2140) "the 1965 Sanctions Order" but contained transitional provisions and provisions concerning the liability of Directors and company officers to the same effect as those in the Sanctions Order summarized above.[86]

Both the Security Council Resolution 253 and the British Sanctions Order of 1968, called for economic aid to Zambia to help it alleviate its economic problems brought about by the sanctions imposed on Rhodesia. Both resolutions set up a committee to gather information on UN member implementation of the sanction resolutions. On September 4, 1968, the UN Council Committee felt that there were sources of information about sanctions breaking that could be identified. The committee later invited individuals and organizations to provide the following information:

(a)   Trade, or the promotion of trade, with Southern Rhodesia, including carriage of goods;
(b)   Financial or investment transactions with Southern Rhodesia;
(c)   Foreign travel by Southern Rhodesians;
(d)   Transport to or from Southern Rhodesia;
(e)   Encouragement of emigration or tourism to Southern Rhodesia;
(f)   The maintenance of any relations or any representation, official or unofficial, with Southern Rhodesia.[87]

The members of this committee were Australia, Austria, Kenya, USSR, Peru, Panama, United States, Yugoslavia, Indonesia, China, India, Sudan, Great Britain, Guinea, and France. According to the committee, these countries did not comply fully with the UN sanctions against Rhodesia during the period 1965-1971: Belgium, France, Federal Republic of Germany, Italy, Netherlands, United Kingdom, Denmark, Norway, Luxembourg, Portugal, Switzerland, Greece, Cyprus, Australia, Zambia, Zaire, Malawi, Gabon, Japan, Ivory Coast, Canada, Botswana, Republic of South Africa, Fiji, and Liberia.

Immediately following the Rhodesian rebellion, British Prime Minister Harold Wilson said that Rhodesia was the greatest moral issue which the British government has had to face in the postwar era. On November 16, 1965, the British Parliament enacted the Southern Rhodesia Act of 1965, declaring that Southern Rhodesia continued to be a part of Her Majesty's dominions and giving power by Order in Council to impose economic and other sanctions against Southern Rhodesia. Initially, it was hoped that sanctions would be adequate means for toppling the new Rhodesian government, but the British sanctions and the United Nations resolutions against Rhodesia were never effective. As a result, the Rhodesian white minority was able to defy the British and United Nations' sanctions for fourteen years. Why was it possible for a small, landlocked country like Rhodesia to be able to defy the international community? Who is to be blamed for the failure of the economic sanctions imposed on Rhodesia?

The British government and the oil companies were blamed for the failure of the sanctions. According to a British politician, David Steel, "Those who shipped in oil were not hostile powers. They were British companies, backed by the British Foreign Office, with the connivance of British Cabinet Ministers and the knowledge of the Prime Minister . . . . The sanctions-busters were our own leaders."[88] The British government secretly collaborated with British Petroleum (BP) and Shell Oil from 1965 to 1977 in busting both its own sanctions and those of the United Nations Security Council.

The story of how petroleum has been delivered to Rhodesia since the Smith regime declared independence illustrates two significant aspects of the operations of the oil companies in southern Africa. First and foremost, the oil companies are naturally concerned with maximizing profits and they have shown little interest in encouraging African self-determination and independence. Second, the Republic of South Africa, through a series of laws and regulations, has restricted the activities of the oil conglomerates and forced them to serve the interests of Rhodesian and South African whites.

Petroleum is vital to the survival of the Rhodesian economy. After the Smith government declared Rhodesian independence from Britain, the British government and the United Nations imposed sanctions on Rhodesia. When the pipeline from the Mozambican port of Beira to Umtali, which is owned by the London and Rhodesian Mining and Land Company (Lonrho) was closed, supplies of crude oil for the Feruka Refinery were cut off. The Feruka Refinery, with a capacity of twenty thousand barrels of oil a day, is also owned by the Central African Refineries (Pvt.) Limited (CAPREF), a company incorporated in Rhodesia in 1963 in order to construct and operate the refinery. The ownership of CAPREF is divided into the following companies:

The Shell Petroleum Company Limited 20.75%
The British Petroleum Company Limited 20.75%
Mobil Petroleum Company, Inc. 17.75%
Caltex U.K. Limited 15.75%
Total Rhodesia (Pvt.) Limited 05.00%
American Independent Oil Company 15.00%
Kuwait National Petroleum Company . . . . .05.00%[89]

Despite the oil embargo, these oil companies continued to supply Rhodesia with oil. According to Martin Bailey, the flow of petroleum from South Africa to Rhodesia started as a trickle of gifts organized by various friends of Rhodesia throughout the Republic of South Africa. These voluntary groups would hire oil tankers or trucks, fill them with oil, and drive them up to Rhodesia across Beit Bridge.[90] Elaborating on this subject, the Bingham Report noted:

Many contemporary estimates were made of the quantities of products crossing Beit Bridge by road in the early months of 1966. The British Embassy, as already mentioned, made its own observations; so also did certain newspapers, and the results were published; reports and estimates were made by the marketing companies in South Africa; and further information reached the Ministry of Power in London from other sources. The results, not being based on a full and continuing census, vary widely, but we think that estimates can be made which are probably of the right order of magnitude. In January, leakage of oil products to Rhodesia by this route had scarcely begun to attract attention and reports are scanty. This leads us to think that until towards the end of the month the quantities involved are likely to have been small. This is what we would have expected, since stocks within the country at the date of the 1965 Sanctions Order were sufficient for about two months (see Chapter IV, paragraph 4.22) and only towards the end of January would the problem of procurement have become a pressing one. Over the course of February 1966, we think that quantities averaged about 35,000 gallons per day. During March and April, it appears that the volume rose to an average daily rate of 50-60,000 gallons. In May, when Mr. Walker personally counted oil trucks travelling to and from Rhodesia on a visit made for that purpose to the Transvaal and over the Rhodesian border, the average daily volume was estimated to have risen 80-100,000 gallons.

After May, few reliable estimates are to be found, but there was general agreement that the volume of road traffic fell rapidly away. This method of supply was then effectively superseded by supply routes by rail through Mozambique which were more efficient, less costly and less conspicuous. Those routes, with which Chapters VII and VIII are largely concerned, carried much larger quantities and, unlike the Beit Bridge road route, enabled Rhodesia to obtain supplies sufficient to meet its reduced demand under rationing. But the Beit Bridge road route filled a very important gap before the rail route was organized. The quantities carried were not adequate for Rhodesia's needs: at 60,000 gallons per day, they amounted to 6-7,000 tons per month compared with Rhodesia's requirement under rationing of about 25,000 tons per month. But they made a significant contribution at a crucial time.

Brief mention should be made of another small contributory source of supply to Rhodesia in these early days. In January 1966, the Mozambiquan authorities opened a duty free petrol station at Machipanda, on the Mozambique side of the Rhodesian border, close to Umtali. Established for the purpose of encouraging tourism in Mozambique, this petrol station not surprisingly attracted a large number of Rhodesian customers who crossed the border in order to fill up their cars. According to Mr. Jardim, sales amounted to some 300 tons per month.[91]

Through 1966, Shell and BP continued to supply oil to Rhodesia via South Africa and Mozambique. According to the Bingham Report, railway tank cars were loaded with refined oil in Lourenço Marques destined to South Africa. Shortly after they had crossed the South African border at Komatipoort, the tank cars were immediately turned back the way they had come. From Mozambique they were rerouted to Rhodesia as if they had originated from South Africa. The reason for developing this system of supplying oil to Rhodesia was aimed at making it difficult for those trying to uncover those countries that were violating the sanctions.

In respect of Caltex Oil Rhodesia more direct information is available. This company, instructed by the Rhodesian Government to procure oil supplies, borrowed a District Manager from the Johannesburg office of Caltex Oil South Africa who knew the Transvaal intimately and, speaking Afrikaans, was able to tap every possible source of supply in the Transvaal area. He established a system whereby supplies could be routed to Mopane, a point on the railway and near the Rhodesian border. He also arranged that a service station at Kruispad, also in the Transvaal, should be run by a Rhodesian contractor: this service station could be served by the railway line, and from it the contractor arranged supplies into Rhodesia by road for the Caltex Depots. The understanding within Caltex Oil Rhodesia was that the Shell and BP marketing companies in Rhodesia had some similar system for obtaining supplies.

But the traffic did not depend solely on the efforts of wellwishers, nor on those of contractors exploiting the commercial opportunities which the situation offered, not on the efforts of the Rhodesian marketing companies themselves. As early as the 14th of February, 1966, Walker was cabling de Bruyne:

"The Smith Government has formed a holding company called GENTA to which a number of oil companies' employees in Rhodesia have been seconded. This company has dispatched lorries across border and seems to be carrying out a systematic search for products. By buying in small quanities from a number of points they are able to accumulate considerable quantities without focusing attention on abnormal offtake at any one point."

Later, on the 2nd of June, 1966, Walker wrote to de Bruyne in London:

"The major part of Rhodesia's supplies comes from third parties, customers of the oil companies who re-sell to GENTA. The procedure is quite simple. The oil company dispatches an order to its customer, who takes delivery into his own tanks. The GENTA agent–usually a Transport Contractor–then picks it up and pays the 'customer.' The GENTA agent is paid for the transport service he renders."

Later, GENTA organized the traffic more efficiently. A GENTA depot was built at Messina, a rail point just south of Beit Bridge, and commercial consumers in the Transvaal ordered one or more wagons of POL surplus to their real requirements and re-consigned there by rail to the Messina depot. There GENTA arranged for transfer to road tankers which took the oil to Rhodesia, in early days to Bulawayo and later to the rail depot at Rutenga, where the regime built new storage tanks which were completed in the last quarter of 1966.[92]

GENTA, Shell, and BP collaborated their oil transaction in South Africa with a subsidiary of Mobil South Africa. The oil had first been brought into Rhodesia by road or rail via Mozambique and until March 1976, when the FRELIMO government halted it.

African states at the United Nations had traditionally held the view that Britain, the oil companies, France, the United States, Italy, and Belgium were responsible for the failure of the Security Council sanctions against Rhodesia. African Nationalists in Zimbabwe constantly informed the OAU countries about the sanctions breaking by these European companies and by multinational corporations. Non-Africans also joined in exposing the illegal British and multinational economic relations with Rhodesia.

The primary source of such accusations at this time was Portugal. In February 1967, the Portuguese Minister for Foreign Affiairs, Dr. Nogueira, told the British Ambassador that the Portuguese Government possessed damaging evidence about trading with Rhodesia on the part of major Western commercial powers and that it might be unwelcome to Britain if this evidence was released. In early May, the Portuguese Minister was even more explicit: the Portuguese had positive proof that during the first three months of 1967, 85 percent of Rhodesia's requirements were being supplied by British and American companies, mainly Shell. At a meeting at the Quai d'Orsay on the 7th of June 1967, the French passed on to HMG information received from the Portuguese Government, again purporting to show Shell as the major participant in the rail traffic from Lourenço Marques to Rhodesia. Following a written parliamentary answer by Mr. George Thompson (as he then was), the Minister of State at the Foreign Office, on the 5th of June 1967, in which he said that it was not possible to identify vessels which delivered to Lourenço Marques the oil which ultimately found its way to Rhodesia, the Portuguese Ministry of Foreign Affairs issued figures showing the number of tankers calling at Lourenço Marques, with the intention of showing that British companies were involved in the trade and Portuguese companies were not. In September 1967, Dr. Nogueira repeated his allegation of complicity by British oil companies to President Kaunda's personal representative and repeated the 85 percent allegation recorded above.

Zambia itself was a source of accusations. In May, President Kaunda suggested that HMG were deliberately permitting the carriage of oil to Lourenço Marques because it feared a confrontation with South Africa if any further attempt were made to block the supply of oil to Rhodesia.

Further accusations were made by Mr. R.W. Rowland of Lonrho Limited. At a meeting at the Commonwealth Relations Office on the 22nd of May 1967, he said that just about 60 percent of the total supplies reaching Rhodesia through Lourenço Marques were being supplied by Shell or B.P. and that he was absolutely certain of his ground.

In a letter written the following day, Mr. Rowland repeated: "My information is that a very significant part of the oil coming to Lourenço Marques is British controlled oil." An article in the Guardian of the 2nd June 1967 asserted that "the British oil companies, Shell and B.P., are supplying a big proportion of Rhodesia's needs through Lourenço Marques, from which it travels to Rhodesia by rail."[93]

In 1976 Tiny Rowland, the chief executive of Lonrho intensified his campaign against Shell and BP for their violations of the oil sanctions. Rowland launched a crusade against the oil companies because he held them responsible for encouraging the British government to set up an investigation into the activities of Lonrho in breaking sanctions. When the investigative report on Lonrho was released, it contained a section on Lonrho activities in South Africa and Rhodesia in which accusations of sanctions breaking were leveled against Rowland and two other directors of Lonrho. According to Martin Bailey, by 1962, Rowland had come to the conclusion that the financial viability of Lonrho depends on increasing its investments in independent African states north of Rhodesia. By 1970, over 50 percent of Lonrho investments was in Black-ruled African states. Aware that revelations of sanctions violations by Lonrho would hurt its financial interests in African states, Rowland launched a counterattack, claiming that his company's activities were quite minor compared with the sanctions breaking by BP and Shell. Angry about the bad treatment he had received from the British Department of Trade, Rowland wrote a letter complaining that what was not given publicity was the untrammeled and constant off-loading of refined petroleum products destined for Rhodesia. Rowland's most astonishing claim was that over 50 percent of these petroleum products were imported into Rhodesia by Shell and BP. In 1974, Rowland also claimed that Shell and BP had assured Ian Smith that they would continue to supply oil to Rhodesia if he were to go ahead with his breakaway regime. Rowland began to distribute this information to the antiapartheid movement, newspapers, and African governments. African governments in turn distributed this information to the OAU and to the appropriate organs of the United Nations system.

After receiving this information, Ghana, Nigeria, and Zambia began to issue threats that they would nationalize British companies involved with breaking UN sanctions against Rhodesia. On December 20, 1976, and in early January 1977, a Ghanaian judge, Hayfrou-Benjamin, sent letters to Shell, BP, Mobil, Caltex, and Total on behalf of Zimbabwean nationalist organizations stating that overwhelming evidence existed on the conspiracy to maintain the Smith government in power. The judge then threatened to institute a legal proceeding against the oil companies if they continued their violations of the British and Security Council Resolutions on Rhodesia. According to Martin Bailey,

> The strongest call for a tightening of oil sanctions came from Zambia, Rhodesia's northern neighbor, which had suffered enormously from UDI. The Zambian Government strongly opposed the Smith regime, and at the time of UDI President Kaunda had called on Britain to use force to topple the rebel regime. Sanctions, the Zambians predicted, would prove ineffective. But in spite of this, the Zambians went ahead and cut economic links with their neighbors, at tremendous cost to themselves. The United Nations has estimated that the additional costs incurred by Zambians as a result of UDI have now exceeded £500 million.
>
> In December 1976, President Kaunda was given a copy of The Oil Conspiracy Report, and was furious to discover that his earlier suspicions that the international oil companies were fueling Rhodesia had, indeed, been correct. The escalating war in Rhodesia, he therefore believed, was partly the responsibility of the oil companies; so, too, were the eleven years of UDI which had caused such enormous financial hardship to his own country.
>
> Kaunda spoke out publicly against the involvement of the oil companies on 29 January 1977. He opened the Liberation Committee of the Organization of African Unity by accusing the oil companies of responsibility "for the deaths of thousands in Zimbabwe (Rhodesia) and for Smith's attacks against independent African states." They could no longer "run with the hare and hunt with the hounds."
>
> Two days later, Kaunda had his first opportunity to express his anger to a Western emissary. Ivor Richard, Britain's UN Representative and Chairman of the abortive Geneva Conference, was in Lusaka for discussions over Rhodesia. He was invited to the State House for the evening. But, to Richard's astonishment, he was greeted by a very angry President, full of rage at Britain's hypocrisy over Rhodesia in general, and over oil supplies in particular.
>
> One Zambian Minister later commented that the President had "drenched" the unfortunate Richard. Half an hour later, the stunned British engoy emerged from the State House, having virtually been thrown out of the President's office. With him he clutched a letter which Kaunda had asked him to pass on to the British Prime Minister.[94]

British Prime Minister James Callaghan replied to President Kaunda's accusations on February 11, 1977. In his response, Callaghan noted:

I am shocked and astonished that you should not only say, but apparently believe that I have been cheating you for years, both as Chancellor of the Exchequer and as Foreign Secretary over the matter of oil sanctions, on the grounds that I must have known what "Shell had been doing." On the contrary, during my two years as Foreign and Commonwealth Secretary I went to great pains to see that sanctions were maintained and indeed tightened up . . . .

You raised with Ivor Richard the question of our personal relations from now on, I will not go into that here because I find it too painful, having been a faithful friend of yours and of African independence for thirty years or more. Deeply, though, I regret the break in our personal relations, what is perhaps even more important is that our two countries should understand one another and, Kenneth, you must understand, if I have evidence about sanctions-breaking, then that evidence will be followed up and, if it is possible to bring the culprits to book, then that will happen . . . .[95]

Despite denials by the British prime minister that British companies were not breaking the Security Council sanctions against Rhodesia, President Kaunda of Zambia requested his government to take the following action:

The Zambian Ministry of Legal Affairs quickly began to assemble evidence that the oil companies had sustained the rebel regime, and by 23 March 1977, the first draft of Zambia's Statement of Claim had been completed. One week later, Kaunda was quoted in an interview in *The Times* as saying that his government planned to take the oil companies to court over sanctions-busting. But the paper's Southern African correspondent apparently did not understant the significance of the remark, since two sentences about the case were buried in a longer article.

Four days later, *The Observer* announced that Zambia was "actively considering" legal action against five Western companies for "oiling Rhodesia's war machine" in defiance of U.N. sanctions. The newspaper added that "a spokesman for Shell International in London yesterday denied that the company was in any way evading sanctions." The following day, one oil company executive complained that there was "a growing and carefully orchestrated campaign against us by certain African leaders."

By the Spring of 1977, the British government and the oil companies were under increasing pressure to take action over allegations of sanctions-busting. My report on Shell and BP in South Africa, published on 1 March, had led to public discussion on the issue. But, at this time the pressures from Lonrho, the Rhodesian nationalists, and the Zambian government had been almost entirely behind the scenes. Nevertheless, the British government realized that it was probably only a matter of weeks before the different accusations came together and the issue could well blow up as a major political scandal.[96]

Also wanting to expose the British coverup in the sanctions violations was Jardin, a Portuguese friend of the former Portuguese dictator Marcello Caetano. Jardin wanted Brtian to take full responsibility for sanctions, violations, rather than Premier Caetano of Portugal. Because of the accusations by African states, African liberation movements, and numerous international non-governmental organizations (anti-apartheid groups), Lonrho, and Jardin, the British government set up an inquiry to conduct an investigation into these allegations on April 8, 1977. The charge to the committee stated:

(a) of establishing the facts concerning the operations whereby supplies of petroleum and petroleum products have reached Rhodesia since 17th December 1965;

(b) of establishing the extent, if any, to which persons and companies within the scope of the Sanctions Orders have played any part in such operations;

(c) of obtaining evidence and information for the purpose of securing compliance with or detecting evasion of the Southern Rhodesia (United Nations Sanctions) (No.2) Order 1968 ("The Sanctions Order"); and offences against the Sanctions Order which may be disclosed.[97]

At the end of the inquiry, overwhelming evidence compiled showed that the oil companies, the British Department of Trade, the Foreign Office, and Whitehall had acquiesced in the violations of oil sanctions against Rhodesia. The African states, the nongovernmental organizations, Lonrho, researchers Martin Bailey and Bernard Rivers, African liberation movements, the antiapartheid movements, the British Harlesmere group, Front for the Liberation of Mozambique and the Independence of Mozambique, and finally, the activities of the United Nations Committee on Rhodesia Sanctions were all involved in the exposure of British complicity in the violations of the sanctions orders and resolutions against Rhodesia. (For more details on the subject, consult the Bingham Report on the supply of Petroleum and Petroleum Products to Rhodesia and Martin Bailey's book, *Oilgate: The Sanctions Scandal.*)

In addition to oil, other United Nations sanctions against Rhodesia were not universally applied. Western bloc countries including the United States, Canada, and New Zealand have permitted their citizens either to migrate or tour Rhodesia (see Table 12).

Table 12:   U.N. Security Council Records on Rhodesian Immigrants, January-June 1978.

	Immigrants	Emigrants	Net Migration
1971	14.743	5,336	9,407
1972	13,966	5,141	8,825
1973	9,433	7,751	1,682
1974	9,649	9,069	580
1975	12,425	10,497	1,928
1976	7,782	14,854	-7,072
1977	5,730	16,638	-10,908
1978 (January to June)	2,817	6,493	3,676

Source: UN Security Council Official Records, Special Supplement, no. 2, vol. 1,2,3,4 (1978): 103.

Violations of the 1966 and 1968 UN resolutions were particularly pronounced in the area of tourism. Many of the tourists who visited Rhodesia were from the capitalist states of the Western world. The trend in the Rhodesian tourist industry is reproduced in Table 13.

While foreign tourists were visiting in Rhodesia, the Rhodesian government officials were welcome in Malawi, Ivory Coast, Zaire, Zambia, Gabon, West Germany, Greece, Switzerland, South Africa, Portugal, Britain, France, Australia, Belgium, Italy, Norway, Denmark, Holland, Sweden, Malta, and the United States.

Table 13: Rhodesia—Visitors from Abroad

	In Transit	On Business	For Education	On Holiday	Total
1965	103,816	25,194	5,643	208,725	343,378
1974	12,498	22,878	7,758	229,570	272,704
1975	14,668	20,368	5,257	244,404	284,697
1976	7,615	16,909	4,907	140,423	169,854
1977	1,748	14,522	2,194	103,515	121,979

SOURCE: UN Security Council Official Records, Special Supplement, no. 2, vol. 1,2,3,4 (1978): 103.

Although the Security Council Resolution 253 prohibited the entry into UN member states of individuals or persons residing in Rhodesia who had furthered the objectives of the illegal Smith government, the United States allowed the Rhodesian information service to operate in Washington, D.C. The United States also ignored the UN Security Council Resolution 409, which states that all UN member states shall prohibit the use or transfer of any funds in their territorial designations by the Rhodesian government for the purposes of operating an office or an agency of the Rhodesian regime. According to Resolution 409, the Rhodesian information service was not to receive funds for operation from Rhodesia or voluntary groups from any member state of the United Nations.

In the United States, as reported by the Congressional Record, Senators Jesse Helmes (R-North Carolina) and James McClure (R-Idaho) took strong exception to the Security Council Resolution 409 and its enforcement in the United States because they felt that it infringed upon the Frist Amendment of the US Constitution's guarantee of freedom of speech. According to Harry Strack:

> As a legal entity and law-abiding agency, the RIO is entitled to the protection of the U.S. Constitution. Senator Dick Clark (D-Iowa) argued that it was not a question simply of denying freedom of speech, but rather a question of abiding by the Security Council decision for which the United States voted. Senator Clark, however, did join Senator Clifford Case (D-New Jersey) in sponsoring a "sense of the Congress" resolution declaring that any foreign country should be allowed to maintain an information office in the United States. The resolution was adopted on a voice vote. Kenneth Towsey told the author on January 30, 1978, that as of that day, "in a practical sense, the activities of my office have not been affected by S/RES/409." The RIO was still being funded via the "free accounts."

> The operations of the Rhodesian offices raised fundamental legal questions in both Australia and the United States. The issue was whether the respective governments possessed the constitutional authority to fully implement the provisions and intent of some sections of the U.N. sanctions resolution. Another area where this problem arises, for example, is in the area of tourism; the U.S. government does not have the legal authority to prevent U.S. citizens who choose to visit Rhodesia from doing so.

> A broader question arises in this context. The U.N. Participation Act of 1945 legally commits the United States to give effect to the resolutions passed by the U.N. Security Council. A fundamental principle of the United Nations is that when the Security Council passes binding resolutions, the member states cannot pick and choose which resolutions or parts of resolutions they will obey. The question

arises as to what happens in the event that the Security Council passes a resolution which violates the U.S. Constitution–the president not having ordered it to be vetoed.[98]

In 1978 the United States representative reported to the Security Council and the UN Committee on Rhodesian Sanctions that his country had granted visas to Ian Smith and some of his colleagues to visit the United States. The committee also heard from the representative of the OAU to the United States who admonished the wisdom of the admission of Smith and his cohorts into the United States. In view of the seriousness of the issue, the United States, and the OAU at the United Nations submitted their statements outlining their respective positions:

(1) *Statement of the United States of America Issuance of a Visa to Ian Smith*

We have been involved jointly with the United Kingdom in a major initiative to settle the Rhodesian conflict.

Our involvement in this effort has been predicted from the outset on our commitment to democratic majority-ruled governments in southern Africa. That commitment has not changed.

However, the situation has become increasingly dangerous in Rhodesia itself. As conditions worsen, so too do the prospects for resolving the conflict in a way that will bring peace and security to the people of Zimbabwe, and to the region.

Over the past 18 months we have spared no effort to try to bring the parties together. To our great regret, those efforts have thus far proven unsuccessful.

The situation is such that we cannot afford merely to let events take their course. We must, if anything, redouble our efforts.

Nor can we afford to miss any opportunity no matter how remote it may seem, to impress upon the parties the need for negotiation and compromise as the only alternative to an increasingly brutal war.

Last April, Secretaries Owen and Vance visited Dar-es-Salaam and Salisbury in an effort to reconcile the differences between the parties. Their visit to Salisbury underscored our determination to maintain a dialogue with all parties in an effort to bring about a settlement.

As you know, Ian Smith and the other members of the Salisbury Council have sought permission to visit the United States in response to an invitation issued by 27 members of the United States Senate.

We have weighed that request with utmost care, having in mind our responsibilities as a member of the United Nations and to our desire to see an end to the Rhodesian conflict.

In the interest of making every effort to conclude a Rhodesian settlement, we have decided, as an exceptional matter, to grant Smith and other Executive Council members permission to visit the U.S.

We intend to use this unique opportunity to continue the discussions with Smith and his colleagues to convince them of the necessity of moving toward a genuine transfer to majority rule.

We continue to regard the Anglo-American proposals as the basis for such a settlement.

We believe that this transfer of power can only take place by means of a negotiated settlement calling for free and fair internationally-supervised elections through which the will of the people of Zimbabwe can be expressed.

We will continue to comply with Security Council sanctions until the negotiation process leads to the formation of a legal, internationally recognized government in that country.[99]

Countering the US statement, the OAU at the United Nations, issued a lengthy statement which noted the following:

(2) *Statement of the African Group*

The African Group at the United Nations has learned with dismay, and is profoundly concerned, at the decision of the United States to allow entry to the head of the illegal racist regime in Southern Rhodesia, Ian Smith. The Group is constrained to remind the United States Administration that its decision is contrary to the United Nations Charter and is in direct violation of the letter and spirit of the United Nations Security Council resolutions, particularly Resolution 253 (1968) and 423 (1978). In the view of the African Group, this development casts serious doubts on the Administration's much vaunted new policies towards our continent. It would also appear to be intended to give credibility to Smith's claim to have evolved an international settlement, a claim which has not only been rejected, but also condemned as a colossal fraud by the Security Council in paragraph 2 of Resolution 423 (1978), which states: *Declares* as illegal and unacceptable any internal settlement under the auspices of the illegal regime and calls upon all States not to accord any recognition to such settlement." Article 2, paragraph 5, of the United Nations Charter states that all Members shall give the United Nations every assistance in any action it takes in accordance with the present Charter, and shall refrain from giving assistance to any state against which the United Nations is taking preventive or enforcement action." While the African Group recognizes the principle of sovereignty of States, it however, wishes to remind the United States Administration that this principle shall not prejudice the application of enforcement measurers under Chapter 7, as stated in paragraph 7, Article 2, of the United Nations Charter. The African Group also recalls especially operative paragraph 5(b) of Security Council Resolution 253 (1968) which calls on states to "Take all possible measures to prevent the entry into their territories of persons whom they have reason to believe to be ordinarily resident in Southern Rhodesia and whom they have reason to believe to have furthered or encouraged, or to be likely to further or encourage, the unlawful actions of the illegal regime in Southern Rhodesia or any activities which are calculated to evade any measure decided upon in this resolution or resolution 232 (1966) of 16 December 1966."

Ian Smith is the personification of illegality in Southern Rhodesia. The United States Government voted positively for this resolution and is therefore bound by its terms. The decision of the United States Administration, if implemented, would merely serve to provide solace to Smith's regime and certainly undermine further the efforts of the international community to isolate that illegal regime. The basic factor of seizure of power by Smith and a handful of white supporters from the British Crown to pre-empt independence and self-determination for the 6-million Africans continues to be the problem. This, no nation should circumvent by any manoeuvres. It is evident that the rebel leader would naturally interpret the gesture as proof of acceptability of his illegal regime and a weakening of the international community's commitment against it. Furthermore, the gesture would also serve to encourage the rebel leader to intensify his persistent acts of aggression against the independent African States of Mozambique, Zambia and Botswana . . . . Such a gesture to the rebel leader can only serve to embolden the illegal regime in its recalcitrance and continued defiance of the will of the international community . . .to persist in his treasonable acts against the Administering Power and further encourage him in his policies of repression and careless brutality against the people of Zimbabwe. In spite of this retrogressive step, the African Group would like to believe that the United States Administration is still interested in exploring the possibility of a negotiated solution to the Zimbabwe question. The African group recalls also that the United States Administration is one of the co-authors of the Anglo-American proposals for settlement of the problems of Zimbabwe. It is logical to expect that the United States Administration would scrupulously avoid any acts which would further aggravate an already depressing situation or place its own settlement proposals in jeopardy. Africa expects the United States Administration, which has made pronouncements to the effect that their respect for human rights constitute one of the cornerstones of its foreign policy, to reason its decision bearing in mind the morality inherent in the burning issues facing mankind today in southern Africa, as well as the legal and binding obligation it had to discharge under the Charter as a permanent member of the Security Council. The African Group also appeals to all states to deny transit facilities to the rebel Ian Smith and his collaborators. The African Group draws the attention of the United Nations Security Council and the United Nations General Assembly to this act which violates the relevant United Nations resolutions and urges these bodies to take urgent and appropriate action. For its part, the African Group expresses its total and unflinching support for the Patriotic Front.[100]

Subsequently, the Security Council convened on October 10, 1978, to consider the OAU's request to the United States to revoke its decision on Ian Smith and his delegation's visit to the United States. The Security Council adopted Resolution 437, which noted that the decision of the United States to allow Ian Smith and the officials of his regime to enter the United States was in contravention of Security Council Resolution 253 of 1968 and of the obligations under Article 25 of the United Nations Charter. The resolution also called upon the United States to observe scrupulously the appropriate provisions of the United Nations Security Council sanctions resolutions on Rhodesia.

Another case of American noncompliance with the Security Council resolutions on Rhodesian sanctions was involved with what is generally known as the Byrd Amendment of 1972. Under this act, the Treasury Department on January 25, 1972, authorized imports of Rhodesian chromium, ferrochrome, and other minerals that were considered strategic and critical to American national interests. Although Britain and African states at the United Nations condemned the Byrd Amendment, the US government continued to violate the Security Council resolutions. Some of these violations are revealed in Table 14.

Table 14: United States Imports from Rhodesia, 1972-1977 (US$ in thousands)

Commodity	1972	1973	1974	1975	1976	1977*
Asbestos, crude and fiber	99	423	1,011	1,271	2,307	2,368
Chrome ores	2,751	1,483	2,531	7,181	1,399	0
Miscellaneous ores	20	0	373	73	574	406
Ferrochrome, low carbon	1,114	1,871	2,258	5,369	8,098	7,496
Ferrochrome, high carbon	1,548	7,904	6,520	33,160	15,131	16,109
Miscellaneous Ferroalloys	2,246	2,936	1,053	1,631	6,323	5,132
Copper, unwrought	0	62	0	0	217	0
Nickel, unwrought	4,521	10,977	5,629	9,880	11,773	17,459
Miscellaneous	57	14	40	38	6	133
TOTAL	12,356	25,670	19,415	59,603	45,828	49,103

SOURCE: U.S. Bureau of the Census, U.S. General Imports Report FT 135, December 1973, 1974, 1975, 1976; and August 1977. Value cited excludes all freight and insurance charges incurred in shipping.

Table 15: Rhodesian Trade with Selected Countries, 1965-1975 (US$m.)

	1965	1966	1967	1968	1969	1970	1971	1972	1973	1974	1975
Exports to:											
South African Customs Union	41.0	60.0	80.0	80.0	85.0	95.0	105.0	130.0	200.0	250.0	302.0
Switzerland	5.7	4.2	3.9	3.5	3.6	4.2	4.5	4.6	7.7	7.4	7.3
Malawi	20.8	17.3	14.7	12.6	12.5	18.6	16.1	21.2	21.3	24.1	29.5
Zambia	99.5	64.9	45.1	31.6	30.5	30.5	28.9	29.6	16.2	12.0	nil
West Germany	35.1	30.5	16.0	13.3	1.1	0.6	0.5	0.4	0.5	0.5	0.7
Australia	3.3	0.8	nil	nil	nil	nil	nil	nil	nil	nil	nil
Imports from:											
South African Customs Union	78.0	110.0	135.0	150.0	155.0	180.0	215.0	182.0	220.0	230.0	270.0
Switzerland	1.6	1.9	1.9	2.5	1.5	2.0	2.9	3.2	3.8	4.5	2.8
Malawi	4.4	3.0	2.7	2.9	3.8	5.0	5.3	5.8	7.2	8.4	8.5
Zambia	15.3	7.0	2.9	1.3	0.6	0.5	0.7	0.5	1.5	0.5	0.8
West Germany	10.9	11.2	12.3	12.9	1.2	1.2	1.6	2.0	2.2	2.6	2.5
Australia	4.5	4.1	5.7	5.9	3.5	4.9	4.8	4.1	nil	nil	nil

SOURCE: UN Security Council, Official Records of the Security Council, Thirty-second Year, Special Supplement no. 2 (12265), Annex VI.

Although African states were extremely vocal in their criticisms of the U.S. violations of the UN sanctions on Rhodesia, only Kenya and Nigeria made verbal protests to the United States against its adoption of the Byrd Amendment.

Like the United States, other countries have violated UN sanctions against Rhodesia-Zimbabwe. Tables 15 and 16 show some of the international economic activities in violation of the UN sanctions.

Table 16: Summary of Rhodesian International Trade, 1966-1975 (US$m.)

	1966	1967	1968	1969	1970	1971	1972	1973	1974	1976
Total Domestic Exports	238	238	234	297	346	379	474	625	600	64
To countries reporting to the U.N.	181	96	68	48	50	48	72	68	60	93
To South African Customs Union	60	80	80	85	95	105	130	200	250	302
To World markets via indirect trade	-3	62	86	164	201	226	272	357	290	245
Indirect trade as a	-	26	37	55	58	60	57	57	48	38
Excess of reported imports of 23 countries over reported exports of South Africa, Mozambique, Zambia, and Malawi	236	102	122	195	317	243	298	398	333	261
Total Imports		262	290	278	329	395	404	480	515	588
From countries reporting to the U.N.	110	63	44	15	16	18	18	18	20	18
From South African Customs Union		135	150	155	180	215	182	220	230	270
Unaccounted trade	47	64	96	108	133	162	204	242	265	300
Unaccounted trade as a percentage of total	20	24	33	39	40	41	50	50	51	51

SOURCE: UN Security Council, Official Records of the Security Council, Thirty-second Year, Special Supplement no. 2 (12265), Annex VI, 1976.

Some of the sanctions violations were in the area of foreign investment. One Rhodesian company that attracted active international investment for expansion was the Rhodesian Iron and Steel Company (RISCO) of Queque. RISCO had drawn up plans in 1972 for external financing of a scheme to expand production from 410,000 tons to about one million tons per year. The scheme was estimated to cost R$63.5 million, of which R$42.5 million was to be derived from external borrowing. Business representatives from thirteen organizations located in West Germany, Bermuda, South Africa, Austria, Switzerland, and Rhodesia met in Paris in 1972 to make the arrangements. The European-American Finance (EAF), a banking corporation with headquarters in Bermuda, was to lend money to a Swiss trading company, HGZ, which in turn would transfer the money to another Swiss firm, Femetco. Femetco was to lend the money to a South African company that was to transfer the money to RISCO. HGZ would buy the steel from RISCO and resell it to two West German Steel manufacturers, taking a commission in the process. The West German firms guaranteed the loan.

Additional sanctions violations involved communications and transportation. France, Greece, Turkey, Liberia, Canada, the United States, Panama, Australia, Zambia, Mozambique, Malawi, Peru, Zaire, Botswana, Gabon, Argentina, Lesotho, Portugal, Swaziland, South Africa, Italy, Federal Republic of Germany, Switzerland, Belgium, Netherlands, Sweden, Denmark, United Kingdom, Austria, Jordan, Cape Verde, Seychelles, Ghana, Nigeria, Israel, Ivory Coast, Cameroon, Mauritius, Cyprus, India, Malaysia, Philippines, Iran (before the fall of the Shah), Comoro Islands, United Arab Emirates, Oman, Bulgaria, Lebanon, Yugoslavia, Iraq, Spain, Egypt, and the Republic of the Congo have at one time or another violated United Nations sanctions on Rhodesia.

Despite these blatant evasions, the Rhodesian sanctions were not without effect. Rebel Rhodesia was forced to lower the price of its exports and to buy imports at higher prices. Inflationary pressures took a heavy toll on the Rhodesian economy. Within the white employment sector, the illegal government required private firms to maintain their payrolls even when production had decreased. The Smith government also enlarged the public service by employing more people who could not be employed within the private sectors of the economy. The net result of the deterioration of the economic conditions in Rhodesia led local investment capital to be diverted to real estate which financed the boom in the local contruction industry rather than in industries that would have stimulated real investment and capital growth. Adding to these problems were rumblings of discontent from the business groups, the churches, and former prime ministers of the defunct Federation of the Rhodesias and Nyasaland, Lord Malvern and Sir Roy Welensky. Among other reasons, rebel Prime Minister Ian Smith held two conferences with the prime minister of Britain in 1966 and another in 1968 to resolve the Rhodesian crisis. No agreement was concluded. In 1969, Rhodesia adopted a republican constitution that described the following as the composition of the legislature:

A. Fifty shall be European members duly elected thereto by the Europeans enrolled on the rolls of European voters for fifty European Roll constituencies.
B. Sixteen shall be African members, of whom—
    I. Eight are duly elected thereto, four by the Africans enrolled on the rolls of African voters for four African Roll Constituencies in Mashonaland and four by the Africans enrolled on the rolls of African voters for four African Roll Constituencies in Matebeleland.
    II. Eight are duly elected thereto, one by each of four electoral colleges in Mashonaland and four electoral colleges in Matebeleland, each electoral college comprising such Chiefs, headmen and elected councilors of the African Councils in the Tribal Trust Lands in Mashonaland and Matebeleland, respectively, as may be prescribed in the Electoral Law.[101]

The new Constitution became the infrastructure of the 1971 Anglo-Rhodesian Accord that later became the basis for the Pearce Commission. Zimbabweans under the resolute leadership of Bishop Abel Muzorewa now president of the United African National Council (UANC) overwhelmingly rejected this Anglo-Rhodesian

Accord which was aimed at entrenching the domination by white settlers over the African majority.

Meanwhile, African delegates at the United Nations unswervingly continued to raise the Rhodesian crisis for discussion within the General Assembly and other organs of the UN system. Their efforts and pressure from others were responsible for the Security Council's passing a resolution that condemned the illegal proclamation of republican status by Rhodesia. While the Security Council requested the international community to refrain from recognizing the Rhodesian government, the General Assembly declared illegal all measures and acts taken by the Salisbury regime, and condemned the British government for its failure to topple the Smith government and transfer political power from minority to majority rule. The General Assembly rejected the Anglo-Rhodesian proposals for settlement previously agreed upon by Britain and the Rhodesian government on the basis that they constituted a flagrant violation of the Zimbabweans right to self-determination, freedom, and independence. In conformity with these ideas, the General Assembly reiterated that a settlement which did not conform strictly to the principle of no independence before majority rule would not be acceptable to the United Nations.

As the escalation of Zimbabwean guerrilla warfare began to affect the stability of the settler government, Prime Minister Ian Smith became increasingly desperate. This desperation drove him to bomb innocent Zambian peasants under the pretext of striking guerrilla hideouts and bases. Most of the Zimbabwean guerrillas were operating from Zambia. Being unable to strike back because of its military weakness, Zambia, with the support of the Africa Group, requested an urgent meeting of the Security Council in January 1973, to consider the Rhodesian acts of aggression against it. Before the meeting, the Zambian government announced that the Rhodesian army, which had been reinforced by South African soldiers, had been deployed along the Zambezi River in preparation for further invasions against its territorial confines.

Convening at Zambia's request, the Security Council resolved and condemned all acts of provocation, harassment, blackmail, threats of economic blockage, and military attacks against Zambia by Rhodesia in collusion with South Africa. The Security Council dispatched a special ad hoc committee to Zambia to carry out an on sight investigation and to assess the situation in the area, as well as the needs of Zambia in procuring alternative systems of road, rail, air, and sea communications for the normal operations. In its report to the Security Council, the committee noted that tension had increased in the area following the Rhodesian bombing of innocent civilians and that the continuing deployment of Rhodesian and South African soldiers along the Zambian border with Rhodesia was the immediate factor in the heightening of tensions. Although the report continued to be critical of the Smith regime, it also pointed out that;

> ... as a result of the closure of the border by the Smith regime, Zambia's economy would be affected by shortages of imports, depletion of stocks and higher costs, and it concluded that only adequate and timely assistance would enable Zambia to develop its economy in a normal fashion.

The Security Council appealed to all States and requested all organs of the United Nations System to give immediate technical, financial and material assistance to Zambia so that it could maintain its normal flow of traffic and enhance its capacity to implement fully the mandatory sanctions policy against Southern Rhodesia.[102]

Despite these warnings from the Security Council, the General Assembly, and the Organization of African Unity, Rhodesia continued to conduct limited military incursions into Zambia.

With the collapse of the Caetano government of Portugal, the new Portuguese military government renounced the policy of colonialism. These changes had far-reaching impact on southern African politics. Since Mozambique and Angola were being granted their independence, Rhodesia and South Africa were for the first time in history to share common borders with Marxist revolutionary countries. Also significant is that these revolutionary states actively supported the Zimbabwean, South African, and Namibian struggles for national liberation. What was also destabilizing to the racist minority-dominated Rhodesian government was the increased availability of sophisticated military hardware to South African black freedom fighters in Zambia, Angola, and Mozambique.

The collapse of Portugal's government on April 25, 1974, crucially affected the balance of power in southern Africa. Sandwiched between Mozambique and Zambia, Rhodesia became the most vulnerable white-dominated country to Zimbabwean revolutionary guerrillas. Afraid that Zimbabwean revolutionary socialists might escalate their war against Ian Smith, former Prime Minister Vorster of South Africa decided to take steps to contain the situation. Vorster immediately resumed dialogues with President Hastings Kamuzu Banda of Malawi, and President Felix Houphouet-Boigny of the Ivory Coast, which had been previously initiated in 1970. Immediately following the Portuguese coup in 1974, former South African Foreign Minister, Hilgard Muller, undertook a series of secret diplomatic moves with the Ivorian government. Muller was helped in his diplomatic contacts by the French government, whose close, growing economic, political, and military involvement with apartheid South Africa gave it a special interest in promoting a détente through their black Francophone contacts. On September 12, 1974, Muller disclosed to the South African Parliament that he had met with two African presidents whose farsightedness (he claimed) had paved the way for dialogue and détente. Muller's contacts resulted in Prime Minister Vorster's secret visit to a number of African countries at the end of September. Further secret talks were held with Presidents Leopold Senghor of Senegal, Houphouet-Boigny of Ivory Coast, Albert-Bernard Bongo of Gabon, Seretse Khama of Botswana, Kenneth Kaunda of Zambia, William Tolbert of Liberia, and Banda of Malawi.

By the beginning of October 1974, the Republic of South Africa had begun to persuade Rhodesian Prime Minister Ian Smith that time had come to negotiate for a peaceful settlement with the Zimbabwean nationalists. Meanwhile, President Kaunda of Zambia had managed to persuade Presidents Nyerere, Khama, (Sese Seko) Mobutu, and Samora Machel to agree to a dialogue with South Africa and Rhodesia. Although President Nyerere agreed with the idea of dialogue, he had many reservations, which he made public while addressing the twenty-fourth session of the OAU's Liberation Committee in Dar-es-Salaam on January 8, 1975.

Independence for Rhodesia, Nyerere said, could be only on the basis of majority rule; but if Prime Minister Smith wished to retreat from its independence to the status quo ante of being a British colony he could achieve the transition period to majority rule, which he seemed to favor. Nyerere elaborated that these thoughts had been stated over and over again. First, independence would be achieved for Rhodesia on the basis of majority rule. Second, this objective would be achieved around the conference table. Third, if the whites rejected the conference table or came to the conference table only to sabotage the achievement of independence on the basis of majority rule, Africa would intensify the armed struggle. This intensified war would be waged either until independence had been achieved on the basis of majority rule, or until Africa's enemies were willing to talk realistically. In the initial stages of the dialogue and détente exercises in southern Africa, Zimbabwean nationalist organizations were not consulted. It was not until October 1974, that the Frontline states started to talk to the Front for the Liberation of Zimbabwe (FROLIZI), the African National Council (ANC), the Zimbabwe African National Union (ZANU), and the Zimbabwe African Peoples Union (ZAPU). According to the president of FROLIZI, James Chikerema, the frontline states informed him that they had been engaged in discussions with South Africa about majority rule in Rhodesia. Prior to this, Zambian Foreign Minister Vernon Mwaanga had met with the then British Foreign and Commonwalth secretary, James Callaghan. Mwaanga proposed the formation of a committee of four countries (Britain, Botswana, Zambia, and Tanzania) to review the Rhodesian crisis and to ascertain whether there was any basis for new discussions to break the stalemate. Callaghan agreed to Mwaanga's request. Subsequent discussions between Zambia (on behalf of the Frontline states) and South Africa resulted in the release of the jailed Zimbabwean ZANU and ZAPU leaders.

After their release, the Zimbabwean leaders were flown to Lusaka, Zambia, in a South African airplane for talks with Frontline presidents. With considerable pressure from the presidents of the Frontline states, FROLIZI, ANC, ZANU, and ZAPU agreed on December 6, 1974, to dissolve and merge into the ANC. The new African National Council with an enlarged executive appointed Bishop Abel Muzorewa as its president. The terms of the ANC communiqué of December 7, 1974, stated:

> Recognizing the paramount need for unity in Zimbabwe liberation struggles, the Executive Committees of ZAPU, ZANU, FROLIZI and ANC have met in Lusaka to discuss the aims, objectives, and methods to be pursued. Full agreement was reached on the following points:
>
> 1. We have agreed to unite under one organization with immediate effect. We have agreed further, that this organization shall be the African National Council.
> 2. We shall be working for the independence of our country. We assume that on this demand for independence there is no difference among Rhodesians of all races. But there has until now been a difference on the kind of independence which Zimbabwe must have. The Rhodesian Front has, in the past, sought independence on the basis of minority rule. We reject that. The independence we have always sought, and the independence we still seek, is independence on the basis of majority rule.

3. For the purpose of achieving that objective, we have always been ready to enter into negotiations with others concerned. Now that some of us have been released from detention, we believe the time is ripe for us to repeat this offer. Without preconditions on both sides, we are ready to enter into immediate and meaningful negotiations with the leaders of the Rhodesian Front, and the British Government in Britain, on the steps to be taken to achieve independence on the basis of majority rule.
4. As a demonstration of our sincerity, all Freedom Fighters will be instructed; as soon as a date for negotiations has been fixed, to suspend fighting.
5. We are not racialists. We accept the right of white Rhodesians to live in Rhodesia and share the same rights and obligations of citizenship as their fellow Rhodesians of the majority community, without any discrimination on grounds of race, colour or creed.
6. We call upon all Rhodesians, and all who reside in Rhodesia, to remain calm, maintain peace and to go about their normal business, while these matters are being considered, and while any negotiations are proceeding.
7. We call upon all Zimbabweans, wherever they are, to remain united behind the demand for independence on the basis of majority rule, and to give full support to the African National Council.
8. We appeal to all our friends in Africa and abroad to continue their support for our struggle until independence is achieved on the basis of majority rule.[103]

Although many OAU countries were not convinced of the wisdom of the dialogue and détente with South Africa and Rhodesia, these OAU states did not completely discourage some of its members from holding discussions with the two white governments. At the 1975 OAU meeting in Dar-es-Salaam, President Tolbert of Liberia declared his support for détente. The most powerful speech in favor of détente and dialogue with South Africa over Rhodesia was made by the Ivory Coast. The Ivorian foreign minister, Arsene Assouane Usher, said during the course of his address:

My dear colleagues, the Ivory Coast has come to this special session because she is for dialogue between African States. We have found, not without incurring the displeasure of some of our colleagues, that dialogue which formerly was considered to be "sterile" now flourishes everywhere and has become a full-bodied reality. Certainly, our Organization can still pass anti-dialogue resolutions and the farce will continue. Heaven forbid that this does not become a tragedy for Africa as has been the case in other parts of the world. Under no circumstances will the Ivory Coast participate in the farce. Clairvoyance, although difficult to explain, is a well established phenomenon, but my country determines its policies by taking account of what we perceive after having taken the trouble to listen to others. At this reunion, we are once again running the risk of presenting a bad image to African and international opinion if we do not guard against our usual pitfalls.... We regard the argument that Vorster is a two-headed monster—one head a saint with whom one can discuss Rhodesia and the other a demon with whom one cannot conduct dialogue on apartheid—as venomous and full of irony. We have even been told that one does not have dialogue with enemies.[104]

The Ivorian foreign minister concluded by proposing that the OAU pursue objectives which would show that whatever disagreements existed between the Ivory Coast and other African states were over means and not ends. They agreed on the following:

1. The independence of Zimbabwe through the application of majority rule.
2. The independence of Namibia and its territorial integrity.
3. Abolition of apartheid and of racial discrimination in South Africa, and
4. Recognition of equal rights for all citizens.
5. Pressure of all kinds on South Africa to bring about a change in that country.
6. Material, political and diplomatic aid from African countries to the nationalists in their struggle.
7. Lasting unity of the independent States of Africa with the nationalists.

With the increase in support of détente among OAU moderate states, President Kaunda and the Frontline states continued their discussions with South Africa and Rhodesia in Lusaka and Pretoria. The Zimbabwean leaders of the new ANC were completely excluded from participating in these negotiations. The ANC leaders objected to the principle of having President Kaunda enter into agreements with Ian Smith and John Vorster without consulting them. Kaunda had agreed with the two white prime ministers to what is now referred as the Pretoria Agreement of August 9, 1975. With Kaunda's insistence, the agreement was later endorsed by Botswana, Mozambique, and Tanzania. The Pretoria Agreement on Rhodesia, 9 August, 1975, reads:

(a) The Rhodesian Government through its Ministerial representatives and the ANC through their appointed representatives will meet not later than 25 August on the Victoria Falls Bridge in coaches to be supplied by the South African Government for a formal conference without any preconditions.
(b) The object of the formal meeting is to give the parties the opportunity to publicly express their genuine desire to negotiate an acceptable settlement.
(c) After this, the conference was to adjourn to enable the parties to discuss proposals for a settlement in committee or committees within Rhodesia.
(d) Thereafter, the parties to meet again in formal conference anywhere decided upon to ratify the committee proposals which have been agreed upon.
(e) The South African government and the governments of Botswana, Mozambique, Tanzania and Zambia, respectively, hereby express their willingness to ensure that this agreement is implemented by the two parties involved. [105]

The ANC strongly objected to clause C of the Pretoria Agreement on having a conference to discuss the issue of majority rule inside Rhodesia. Although Ian Smith gave his assurance that there would be no new detentions while the conference was in progress, he did not overrule further arrests of the African nationalists if the conference failed. Many of the nationalists, like James Chikerema, George Nyandoro, Jason Moyo, George Silundika, and others had been sentenced to death for political crimes against the Rhodesian government. Smith had been vehement in his opposition to granting them immunity. With pressure from Kaunda and John Vorster, Smith agreed not to arrest the Zimbabwean nationalists.

The conference was held on August 26, 1975, in a train located across the Victoria Falls. Present at the Victoria Conference were Ian Smith and his Rhodesian Front government team, Bishop Abel Muzorewa's ANC delegation including Ndabaningi Sithole and Joshua Nkomo, and Kenneth Kaunda and John Vorster representing their respective governments. At this meeting, Bishop Muzorewa stated that the only genuine settlement for the majority of the people of his country is the one that shall be based on the transfer of power from the minority to the majority people of the country, that is, majority rule now. Ian Smith reacted by calling the position of the ANC unacceptable and labeling it a flagrant violation of the Pretoria Accord. Because of this development, the meeting was adjourned for a few hours. When the meeting resumed later that afternoon, the ANC produced the following document as its basis for further participation in the Victoria Conference.

(1)   The Prime Minister and other Cabinet Ministers of the Rhodesian Government and the President and other representatives of the ANC met at Victoria Falls on 25 August 1975.

(2)   Both parties took this opportunity of expressing their genuine desire to negotiate a constitutional settlement.

(3)   Both parties publicly expressed their commitment to work out immediately a constitutional settlement which will be acceptable to all the people of our country.

(4)   In pursuance of this objective, the secretary to the Cabinet and the Secretary-General of the ANC were instructed to arrange, within seven days, a plenary meeting in Salisbury of nominated representatives chosen respectively by the Government of Rhodesia and the ANC. At this meeting, detailed discussions of all aspects of the constitutional issue will commence and, where appropriate, subcommittees will be established to consider and report to the plenary meeting on particular aspects.

(5)   The ANC representatives presently in exile shall have the following immunities:

Immunity from enforcement in any way or degree in whole or in part of an existing sentence, order or direction.

Immunity from arrest, prosecution, detention or restriction or any other process whatsoever for any act or omission in or outside Rhodesia before commencement of the next meeting or conference.

Any person nominated by the ANC to attend in any capacity whatsoever any meetings in Rhodesia in connection with the conference or any committee or subcommittee thereof shall have full diplomatic immunity as though they were a diplomatic agent, including, without prejudice, to the generality of such immunity, full right of entry to and exit from Rhodesia without travel documents and full freedom of movement in Rhodesia, but so that the Government of Rhodesia shall not declare such person to be a non-personagrata except after consultation with the Governments of the Republic of South Africa and Zambia.

Subject to the confidentiality of the discussions as agreed below every such person referred to in Clause 3 above shall have freedom of expression at all meetings, formal or informal, concerning the business of the conference and any committees or sub-committees, including freedom from observation, harassment or recording.

(6)   Because of the urgent need to end the present uncertainty it was agreed that every effort should be made to expedite the proceedings. Accordingly. 31 October 1979 was set as the target date for completion of this stage.

(7)   When agreement has been reached on the form and content of the constitutional settlement, a final constitutional conference will be arranged at a mutually agreed venue, which shall be outside Rhodesia. The purpose of this conference will be to ratify formally the terms of the constitutional document giving effect to the agreement reached.

(8)   All those present agreed on the importance of preserving the confidentiality of the constitutional discussions and undertook not to reveal any details to the press and other media.[106]

Smith completely rejected the ANC proposals. A number of reasons contributed to the failure of the Victoria Conference. The major reason for the failure was Ian Smith and his white followers' belief in racism and their unrealistic assessment of their political, economic, and military strength. The second reason was the bitter rivalries within the African leadership that Ian Smith exploited to the fullest degree. The third reason was political turmoil in Angola resulting from the bitter and intense competition for political control of that country by its warring MPLA, UNITA, and FLNA factions.

With the failure of the Victoria Falls Conference, divisions within the fragile ANC multiplied. Joshua Nkomo decided to conduct his own settlement negotiations without the rest of the ANC. The ANC reacted to Nkomo's unilateral overtures to Smith by expelling him from the party. Meanwhile, the Reverend Ndabaningi Sithole issued on May 10, 1975, an order to dissolve his former political party (ZANU), but some ZANU members in control of the war council (DARE) refused to merge with the ANC and chose Robert Mugabe as the new ZANU leader.

Because of the political astuteness of the executive members of the ANC (George Nyandoro, Bishop Abel Muzorewa, James Chikerema, and Eliot Ghabella) Sithole found it difficult to capture the presidency of that organization. Having realized his limitations of becoming the ANC president, Sithole resigned from the ANC and reclaimed his former presidency of ZANU. The former ZANU officials who had chosen Robert Mugabe as the new leader would have nothing to do with Sithole. As these leaders began to compete for recognition by the Frontline states, so did their competition for recruiting Zimbabweans for guerrilla warfare training increase. The independence of Mozambique and Angola, the Angolan civil war, the Cuban assistance to the MPLA, and the declarations of Frontline states that they would provide more fiscal and military assistance to the Zimbabwean liberation movements created further divisions among the Zimbabweans.

Recognizing the Cuban and Soviet involvement in Angolan domestic politics, the United States became convinced that such acts should not be repeated in Zimbabwe. The former U.S. secretary of State, Henry Kissinger, traveled to southern Africa to discuss ways and means to resolve the Rhodesian crisis. While there, the United States, Britain, South Africa, Rhodesia, and the Frontline states agreed (among other issues) on the following:

1.   Rhodesia agrees to majority rule within two years.
2.   Representatives of the Rhodesian Government will meet immediately at a mutually agreed place with African leaders to organize an interim government to function until majority rule is implemented.
3.   The interim government should consist of a Council of State, half of whose members will be black and half white with a white chairman without a special vote. The European and African side would nominate their representatives. Its function will include: Legislation–General supervisory responsibilities; and supervising the process of drafting the constitution.

The interim government should also have a Council of Ministers with a majority of Africans and an African First Minister. For the period of the interim government the Ministers of Defense and of Law and Order would be white. Decisions of the Council of Ministers to be taken by two-thirds majority. Its functions should include: Delegated legislative authority; and executive responsibility.

4. The United Kingdom will enact enabling legislation for the process of majority rule. Upon enactment of that legislation, Rhodesia will also enact such legislation as may be necessary to the process.

5. Upon the establishment of the interim government, sanctions will be lifted and all acts of war, including guerrilla warfare, will cease.

6. Substantial economic support will be made available by the international community to provide assurance to Rhodesians about the economic future of the country. A trust fund will be established outside Rhodesia which will organize and finance a major international effort to respond to the economic opportunities of this country and to the effects of the changes taking place. The fund will, inter-alia, support the internal and external economic circumstances of the country and provide development assistance, guarantees and investment incentives to a wide variety of projects.[107]

Having convinced Ian Smith to agree in principle to the transfer of political power from minority to majority rule, the United Kingdom arranged a conference in Geneva to discuss the mechanism for the transference of the apparatus of government to the African majority. On this basis, the British government appointed Ivor Richard (its representative to the United Nations) as chairman of the Geneva Conference. The conference, which convened on October 28, 1976, was comprised of the following delegations: The ANC led by Bishop Muzorewa; the ANC/ZAPU led by Joshua Nkomo; the Zimbabwe African National Union (ZANU) led by Robert Mugabe; and the Zimbabwe African National Union (ZANU) led by Reverend Ndabaningi Sithole, the Rhodesian government, and the British government. The Frontline states and the United States sent their representatives to Geneva to observe the proceedings leading to the attainment of African majority rule. From the outset, there was no agreement between the African nationalists and the Rhodesian settlers as to what the conference should discuss. The African position was that the conference should discuss the issue of transferring political power from minority to majority rule. The position of Smith's government was that the conference was called to work out mechanisms for the implementation of the Anglo-Rhodesian-American Accord. Smith went on to say that if the African nationalists and Marxists were willing to participate within the specifications of the Anglo-American Accord, he was available; otherwise, he was not interested in the polemics. The governments of the United Kingdom and the United States, he emphasized, had made a solemn agreement with him, and if the Africans and their allies were not prepared to honor the Anglo-American Accord on Rhodesia, he would abandon the Geneva Conference and implement the agreement unilaterally. Because of these differences, the Geneva Conference collapsed.

While the Geneva Conference was taking place, Botswana registered its complaints to the UN Security Council about Rhodesia's violations of its territorial sovereignty. The Rhodesian security forces had on many occasions illegally entered Botswana and harassed and kidnapped Botswana civilians and Zimbabwean refugees. Annoyed by these unwarranted provocations against the people of Botswana, the African group at the United Nations requested the Security Council to take immediate action against Rhodesia. The Security Council on January 14, 1977, unreservedly condemned all acts of provocation and harassment, including military threats, attacks, murder, arson, kidnapping, and destruction of property committed against Botswana by Rhodesia and demanded an immediate cessation of such hostile acts. During the discussions, Botswana, Cuba, Mali, Equatorial Guinea, German Democratic Republic, Kenya, Lesotho, Morocco, Mozambique, Nigeria, Sierra-Leone, Somalia, Togo, Tanzania, Yugoslavia, and Zambia made presentations to the council in support of Botswana.

On January 13, 1977, the Rhodesian government sent a cable to the UN Security Council requesting an invitation to participate in the debate on Botswana's complaints about violations of its borders by Rhodesian military forces. Announcing this move in Salisbury, Smith stated that his action had been taken under the terms of Chapter 5, Article 32 of the United Nations Charter, which provides for the participation in Security Council debates by nonmember states. The message dispatched to the president of the Security Council by Van der Byl noted that the Rhodesian government did not accept Botswana's allegations of aggression and requested adjournment of the Security Council's deliberations to enable Rhodesia to prepare an appropriate response and to arrange for the attendance of a Rhodesian government representative. The Rhodesian memorandum ended with an accusation leveled against Botswana. Rhodesia accused Botswana of harboring Rhodesian black guerrillas who were attacking mostly undefended targets like white farms, stores, and motorists. Through pressure from the members of the General Assembly and the African group at the United Nations, the president of the Security Council denied the Rhodesian request.

The Security Council acted by adopting an eight-power resolution (403) (1977) sponsored in its draft form by Benin, India, Libya, Mauritius, Panama, Pakistan, Romania, and Venezuela, by a vote of thirteen in favor to none against with two abstentions (Britain and the United States). Security Council Resolution 403 of January 14, 1977, noted:

1. *Strongly condemns* all acts of provocation and harassment, including military threats and attacks, murder, arson, kidnapping and destruction of property, committed against Botswana by the illegal regime in Southern Rhodesia;
2. *Condemns* all measures of political repression by the illegal regime that violate fundamental rights and freedoms of the people of Southern Rhodesia and contribute to instability and lack of peace in the region as a whole;
3. *Deplores* all acts of collaboration and collusion which sustain the illegal regime in Southern Rhodesia and encourage defiance with impunity of the resolutions of the Security Council, with adverse consequences for peace and security in the region;
4. *Demands* the immediate and total cessation forthwith of all hostile acts committed against Botswana by the illegal regime in Southern Rhodesia;
5. *Takes cognizance* of the special economic hardship confronting Botswana as a result of the imperative need to divert funds from on-going and planned

development projects to hitherto unplanned and unbudgeted for security needs necessitated by the urgent need to effectively defend itself against attacks and threats by the illegal regime in Southern Rhodesia.

6. *Accepts* the invitation of the Government of Botswana to dispatch a mission to assess the needs of Botswana in carrying out its development projects under the present circumstances, and accordingly requests the Secretary-General, in collaboration with appropriate organizations of the United Nations system, to organize with immediate effect financial and other forms of assistance to Botswana and to report to the Security Council not later than 31 March 1977;

7. *Requests* the United Nations and the organizations and programmes concerned, including the Economic and Social Council, the United Nations Educational, Scientific and Cultural Organization, the World Health Organization, the United Nations Development Programme, the Food and Agriculture Organization and the Fund for Agricultural Development, to assist Botswana to carry out the on-going and planned development projects without interruption as stated in paragraph 5 and envisaged under paragraph 6 of this resolution;

8. *Appeals* to all States to respond positively in providing assistance to Botswana, in the light of the report of the mission of the Secretary-General, in order to enable Botswana to carry out its planned development projects;

9. *Decides* to remain seized of the matter.[108]

In defiance of Security Council Resolution 403, Rhodesia increased its attacks against Botswana, Zambia, and Mozambique.

Following the collapse of the Geneva Conference and the subsequent escalation of guerrilla war in Zimbabwe and the Rhodesian military incursions into Botswana, Zambia, and Mozambique, the special committee on the situation with regard to the Implementation of the Declaration on the granting of Independence to Colonial Countries and Peoples opened its session for 1977 on January 12, after hearing a statement by the secretary-general that the colonial problems of southern Africa, which had long constituted a major concern for the world community, had reached a critical state.

The committee thereafter unanimously reelected as chairman for the sixth year in succession, Salim A. Salim of Tanzania. Salim unequivocally emphasized that the committee must endeavor to seek to achieve extensive publicity and support from the international community for the Zimbabwean people and their liberation movements. Other members elected to serve in the committee with Salim were Frank Owen Abdulah (Trinidad and Tobago), Tom Eric Vraalsen (Norway), and Neytcho Neytchev (Bulgaria), who were unanimously elected the committee's three vice chairmen. Sami Glayel of Syria was unanimously reelected rapporteur of the committee.

In his statement concerning the critical situation in Zimbabwe, Salim declared that the situation in Zimbabwe and Namibia was extremely critical and, if trends continued, must inevitably lead to an escalation of violence, bringing untold suffering to the African populations and threatening the territorial integrity and security of neighboring African states. Salim further noted that in Zimbabwe there was a state of war in existence and that not a week went by without some Africans being brutally killed by the racist soldiers of the illegal Smith regime in Rhodesia.

In the light of those critical developments in Zimbabwe, the international community had a crucial role to play during these trying times. It was necessary, Salim echoed, to mobilize worldwide understanding, sympathy, and support for the African peoples in their struggle; it was equally necessary to try to isolate the racist Rhodesian and South African regimes and to deprive them of the external aid and assistance that enabled them to remain in power. Moral support alone was not adequate: everything possible must be done, he said, to bring about an increase in the flow of material assistance, both bilateral and multilateral, to the African peoples of Zimbabwe and Namibia and their national liberation movements in their present hour of need. [109]

Salim emphasized that one of the first tasks of the committee in organizing its program of work would be to consider measures to be taken in connection with the decision adopted by the holding at Maputo, Mozambique, of an international conference in support of the peoples of Zimbabwe and Namibia in their struggle for majority rule and independence.

Following the collapse of the Geneva Conference, the United Nations increased its support for Zimbabwean liberation. On December 17, 1976, the United Nations General Assembly adopted a resolution requesting the secretary-general in cooperation with the Special Committee of 24 on the issue regarding the Implementation of the Declaration on the Granting of Independence to Colonial Countries and Peoples and the United Nations Council for Namibia, to organize an international Conference in support of the Peoples of Zimbabwe and Namibia at Maputo, Mozambique, in consultation with the Organization of African Unity. The conference was held from May 16 to May 21, 1977. The Conference condemned Rhodesian minority rule and its repression of the African majority and racism, and adopted a comprehensive program of action for the liberation of Zimbabwe and recommended the following:

B. Measures against the illegal Racist Minority Regime in Southern Rhodesia (Zimbabwe)

The Conference calls upon governments to:
(a) refrain from any cooperation or collaboration with the illegal racist minority regime in Southern Rhodesia (Zimbabwe);
(b) observe strictly the arms embargo against the illegal racist minority regime;
(c) enact legislation declaring the recruitment, assembly, financing and training of mercenaries in their territories to be punishable as a criminal act and to do their utmost to discourage and prohibit their nationals from serving as mercenaries;
(d) take measures against corporations and trade interests which operate in or have subsidiaries operating in Southern Rhodesia (Zimbabwe) in violation of sanctions imposed by the United Nations Security Council;
(e) prevent oil companies registered in their territories from supplying oil, directly or indirectly, to the illegal racist minority regime;
(f) take stringent enforcement measures to ensure strict compliance by all individuals, associations and bodies corporate under their jurisdiction with the sanctions imposed by the Security Council and to prohibit any form of collaboration by them with the illegal racist minority regime; [110]

Desperately anxious to find a solution to the Rhodesian problem, the General Assembly in cooperation with the OAU pressured the Security Council to actually involve itself with efforts leading to the procurement of African majority rule. On September 28, 1977, an Anglo-American proposal for the appointment of a special United Nations representative to help in negotiations for African majority rule and also to arrange for a cease-fire was presented to the Security Council. All the Security Council members (except Libya, China, and the USSR) approved the Anglo-American proposal. Following these events, the Security Council and the secretary-general appointed General Prem Chand (of India) as the UN special representative for Rhodesia to work in collaboration with the British Commissioner Designate, Field Marshall, Lord Carver.

The Anglo-American proposals, which were presented to Prime Minister Ian Smith on September 1, 1977, in Salisbury by David Owen, the former British foreign secretary, and Andrew Young, the former American ambassador to the United Nations, outlined the following seven points:

(1) Surrender of power by the illegal (Rhodesia) regime and a return to legality.
(2) An orderly and peaceful transition to independence during 1978.
(3) Free and impartial elections on the basis of universal adult suffrage.
(4) Establishment of a transitional administration by the British government that would conduct elections for the new government.
(5) A U.N. presence during the transition.
(6) A new constitution featuring an elected government, the end of discrimination, protection of individual rights and an independent judiciary.
(7) A development fund to help raise living standards and ease the way for new economic patterns.[111]

This new Anglo-American blueprint for Rhodesia was to require a development fund that would amount to more than US$ 1 billion, over a five-year period for developing the African-run economy. The plan was intended to provide an incentive for making many whites remain in Zimbabwe after its independence. The United States was to contribute about 40 percent and Britain 15 percent of this money for the blueprint to operate. This fund was supposed to have helped finance projects in agriculture and land reform, education, manpower training, and economic infrastructure. Whereas this program was intended to stimulate industrial growth, it was also aimed at achieving the following: To encourage white managerial personnel to contribute to Zimbabwean development; to effect a smooth transition to majority rule; and to redistribute peacefully white controlled lands and public property to the Africans.

After the Frontline states accepted the Anglo-American proposals for settlement in Rhodesia, the United States and Britain submitted it to the United Nations for action. While recognizing the shortcomings of the Anglo-American proposals, both the Security Council and the General Assembly accepted the proposals on the basis that they addressed themselves to the fundamental principles that are an essential prerequisite to a negotiated settlement. More specifically, the Anglo-American proposals provided for the dismantling of the armed forces of the illegal racist minority regime; the formation of a new Zimbabwean army based on the unified ranks of the Zimbabwean people; the preparedness of the British government to assume seriously its responsibility as the colonial power in order to facilitate the decolonization of the territory; and the creation of conditions that would enable the people of Zimbabwe to determine their future government, including the United Nations in the transitional process.

Ian Smith immediately rejected the Anglo-American proposals on the following grounds: That they recommended the replacement of the Rhodesian white-dominated government with a transitional one consisting of the ANC, ZAPU, ZANU, and the Rhodesia Front; that the African nationalist guerrillas be incorporated into the Rhodesian army; and that before there could be any discussion of a settlement, the African nationalist forces must declare a cease-fire and surrender their weapons to the Rhodesian government.

Having rejected the Anglo-American proposals as unacceptable to the Rhodesian government, Smith held negotiations leading to African majority rule with Bishop Abel Muzorewa of the United African National Council, Reverend Ndabaningi Sithole of the African National Council, and Chief Jeremiah Chirau of the Zimbabwe United Peoples Organization. After much bickering and controversy, on March 3, 1978, these negotiators agreed on a formula leading to African independence. The following are some of the provisions of the constitutional agreement:

(1) There will be a Legislative Assembly consisting of one hundred members and the following provisions will apply thereto
(a) there will be a common voters role with all citizens of eighteen years and over being eligible for registration as voters subject to certain recognized disqualifications;
(b) seventy-two of the seats in the Legislative Assembly will be reserved for Blacks who will be elected by voters who are enrolled on the common roll;
(c) twenty-eight of the seats in the Legislative Assembly will be reserved for Whites (i.e., Europeans as defined in the 1969 Constitution)
who will be elected as follows–
(i)twenty will be elected on preferential voting system by White voters who are enrolled on the common roll;
(ii) eight will be elected by voters who are enrolled on the common roll from sixteen candidates who will be nominated, in the case of the first Parliament, by an electoral college composed of the twenty-eight Whites who are members of the Parliament dissolved immediately prior to the general elections;
(d) the reserved seats referred to in (c) above shall be retained for a period of at least ten years or two Parliaments, whichever is the longer, and shall be reviewed at the expiration of that period, at which time a Commission shall be appointed, the chairman of which shall be a judge of the High Court, to undertake this review. If that Commission recommends that the arrangements regarding the said reserve seats should be changed–
(i) an amendment to the Constitution to effect such affirmative votes of not less than fifty-one members;
(ii) the said Bill shall also provide that the seventy-two seats referred to in (b) above shall not be reserved for Blacks;
(e) the members filling the seats referred to in (c) above will be prohibited from forming a coalition with any single minority party for the purpose of forming a Government.[112]

During the transitional period to majority rule, whites were to remain in charge of the entire security of the country, including the administration of its justice department.

The Patriotic Front, headed by Robert Mugabe and Joshua Nkomo, unequivocally denounced the March 3, 1978, Ian Smith internal settlement as unacceptable, and called on the international community to reject it on the basis that it was inimical to the interests of the majority of the Zimbabwean people. While accusing Bishop Abel Muzorewa, Reverend Ndabaningi Sithole, and Chief Jeremiah Chirau as stooges, sellouts, and puppets of Ian Smith, the Frontline states denounced the internal settlement as a device by which the illegal Smith government sought to forestall African majority rule and independence. The OAU Council of Ministers just before the adoption of the Internal Agreement of March 3, passed Resolution 602 (XXX), which rejected and condemned the so-called "internal talks" that were taking place in Salisbury, because those talks were aimed at perpetuating white minority domination in that country. From July 7 to July 19, 1978, the Council of Ministers of the OAU meeting in Khartoum, Sudan, passed Resolution CM/Res. 680 (XXXI). It noted:

> Reaffirming Resolution CM/Res. 602 bis (XXX) which rejected and totally condemned the so-called "internal talks" taking place in Salisbury because these talks were aimed at perpetuating white minority power,
> *Noting* that the Salisbury March 3, 1978, Agreement actually is an attempt to consolidate white minority power and that the unrepresentative elements that were party to the "internal talks" with the racist Ian Smith are now an integral part of the resulting treacherous and illegal Salisbury regime,
> *Recognizing* with appreciation the efforts being deployed by the Frontline States on behalf of the OAU to ensure that a just solution is attained to the problems in that Territory,

1. STRONGLY REJECTS and CONDEMNS the March 3, 1978, Salisbury agreement and the treacherous regime set on those terms
2. CALLS UPON all OAU Member States and the international community not to give recognition to the regime resulting from the March 3rd Salisbury Agreement and never to give any form of encouragement or solace to any of its elements;
3. ENCOURAGES the appreciable prosecution of the armed struggle being waged by the Patriotic Front, the sole Liberation Movement of Zimbabwe;
4. RESOLVES to grant all possible emergency and other requests put forward by the Patriotic Front for the intensification of the armed struggle;
5. CALLS UPON OAU Member States to increase their material and financial aid to the armed struggle being waged by the Patriotic Front;
6. APPRECIATES the role played by the Heads of State, people and governments of the Frontline States who, for the high ideas and principles of the OAU, have committed themselves to the total liquidation of the racist minority regime of Southern Africa.
7. CALLS UPON all OAU Member States to implement resolution AHG/Res. 80 (XII) in support of Frontline States which are constantly subjected to the repeated acts of aggression by the racist colonialist regimes of South Africa and Southern Africa.[113]

At the United Nations, both the General Assembly and the Security Council condemned the Rhodesian Internal Agreement of March 3, 1978. Three days later, the Security Council adopted a resolution declaring "illegal and unacceptable any internal settlement under the auspices of the illegal regime" in Southern Rhodesia, and called upon all states "not to accord any recognition to such a settlement." The Security Council further condemned all attempts and maneuvers by the illegal Smith regime that were aimed at the retention of power by a racist minority and the prevention of the achievement of independence by the African people of Zimbabwe. The speedy termination of the illegal Smith regime and the replacement of its oppressive military and police forces was the first prerequisite for the restoration of legality in Southern Rhodesia so that arrangements could be made for a peaceful transition to genuine majority rule and independence in 1978. Such arrangements, the council observed, "include the holding of free and fair elections on the basis of universal adult suffrage under United Nations supervision."

Within the African Group at the United Nations, there was a general feeling of distrust, resentment, despair, and frustration among African states, who felt that Britain and the United States were going to sanction the Rhodesian Internal Settlement. The frustration of the African Group was vividly portrayed by Ambassador Salim of Tanzania when he observed:

> To our very profound regret and concern we have witnessed over the past few weeks and days, in the wake of the reports of the so-called internal settlement, a kind of resignation on the part of the authors of the Anglo-American plans to the manoeuvres of the Smith regime.
> It is the height of irony that Smith should in fact be allowed to run the show and even be recommended by the very people who in their own proposals had clearly assumed that the rebel leader would never surrender power. We can only observe that if any impression is created that the United Kingdom or the United States, or both, are willing quickly to abandon their own proposals, a legitimate question will arise as how serious they were in the first place in promoting a just settlement.
> At any rate, for our part, in keeping with Africa's clearly declared objective, we shall not fail to promote a genuinely negotiated settlement. In the meantime, in concert with other African States, we shall fulfill our obligation to the liberation struggle in Zimbabwe by unequivocally supporting those who are fighting to bring to an end the oppression and domination of the minority regime.[114]

African states continued to bring to the attention of the United Nations the issue of the unacceptability of the Rhodesian Internal Settlement. The idea behind this strategy was to prevent Britain, the United States, and the Western European countries from striking a secret agreement with Ian Smith. Determined to keep the Rhodesian issue alive at the United Nations, the chairman of the Committee of 24 on Decolonization scheduled a debate on the internal settlement in early August 1978. At the opening of the debate, the committee heard from the representative of Britain, who said that after long years of immobility, the problems of Rhodesia had begun to move in a way which brought a real prospect of seeing power transferred from the white minority to the African majority, and the emergence of an independent Zimbabwe within the near future. In addition, the Patriotic Front representatives also petitioned the Committee of 24, calling for free elections in Zimbabwe that would be supervised by the United Nations. When some of the internal settlement advocates led by Bishop Abel Muzorewa of the ANC petitioned to be heard by the committee, a majority of the OAU countries at the United Nations pressured the Committee of 24, the General Assembly, and the Security Council to deny them a hearing. Instead Bishop Muzorewa held private meetings at the United Nations with the British, American, Canadian, and a few African representatives to the United Nations. While he was in Washington, D.C., Bishop Muzorewa unsuccessfully appealed to President Carter and some leaders of the black American community to use their influence in convincing the United

States not to comply with UN sanctions against Rhodesia. In the U.S. Congress, Senators Jessie Helms of North Carolina and S. I. Hayakawa of California championed Muzorewa's cause.

While representatives of many OAU member states to the UN denounced Bishop Muzorewa as a quisling and stooge of Ian Smith and a sellout, the Committee of 24 unanimously adopted two resolutions. On August 10, 1978, the first resolution of the committee condemned all violations of the mandatory sanctions against Rhodesia imposed by the Security Council, as well as the continued failure of certain member states to enforce those sanctions, and further condemned South Africa for its continued support of the Rhodesian regime in contravention of Security Council resolutions against that oppressive regime.

The first resolution of the committee called upon all governments which had not complied to do so:

(a) to take stringent enforcement measures to ensure strict compliance by all individuals, associations and bodies corporate under their jurisdiction with the sanctions imposed by the Security Council and to prohibit any form of collaboration by them with the illegal regime;
(b) to take effective steps to prevent or discourage the emigration to Southern Rhodesia (Zimbabwe) of any individuals or groups of individuals under their jurisdiction;
(c) to discontinue any action which might confer a semblance of legitimacy on the illegal regime;
(d) to invalidate passports and other documents for travel to the Territory; and
(e) to take all effective measures against international companies and agencies which supplied petroleum products to the illegal regime of Southern Rhodesia.

The committee requested all States to extend financial, technical and material assistance to the Governments of Mozambique and Zambia to enable them to overcome economic difficulties in connection with their application of economic sanctions against the illegal regime and the severe economic loss and destruction of property brought on by the acts of aggression committed by the regime, and requested the Security Council to undertake a periodic review of the question of economic assistance to the two Governments.

It deemed it imperative that the scope of sanctions against the illegal regime must be widened to include all the measures envisaged under Article 41 of the Charter and reiterated its request that the Security Council consider taking the necessary measures in that regard as a matter of urgency.

With respect to the second resolution on Southern Rhodesia, the Committee condemned all manoeuvres of the illegal racist minority regime, including the so-called internal settlement; the continued war of repression against the people of Zimbabwe by the regime of Ian Smith; its repeated acts of repression and threats against Mozambique, Zambia and Botswana; and South Africa for its continued support of the regime in contravention of all the United Nations resolutions and decisions on the question.

To resolve the conflict, the Committee demanded:

(a) The termination forthwith of all repressive measures perpetrated by the illegal minority regime against the people of Zimbabwe, in particular the wanton killings and executions of Africans and their freedom fighters;

(b) The unconditional and immediate release of all political prisoners, detainees and restrictees, the removal of all restrictions on political activity and the establishment of full democratic freedom and equality, as well as restoration to the population of fundamental human rights;

(c) The immediate cessation of all acts of aggression and threats against the neighboring African States; and

(d) to cease the recruitment of mercenaries for Southern Rhodesia.[115]

Within the General Assembly, the Rhodesian Internal Settlement continued to be one of the main subjects of discussion by the African Group and its allies–mainly from Asia, South America, and the Caribbean states. Through pressure from the Third World countries, the Assembly's Fourth Committee (Decolonization) recommended two resolutions that were adopted by the General Assembly as GA Res. (33/38A, and 33/38B). Although it had no power or means to enforce its recommendations, GA Res. 33/38A declared null and void the Rhodesian March 3 Agreement, condemned South Africa and some Western countries for their direct or indirect support of the Rhodesian government, and reaffirmed that there should be no independence before majority rule in Zimbabwe without the full participation of the Patriotic Front. This resolution was adopted by a vote of 130 in favor to none against, with 11 abstentions (Australia, Belgium, Canada, Dominican Republic, El Salvador, France, West Germany, Luxembourg, New Zealand, United Kingdom, and the United States). The countries that abstained were also the ones which were accused of supporting some form of political and commercial ties with Rhodesia and South Africa.

GA Res. 33/38B deplored Britain's continued violations of the Security Council resolutions on economic sanctions against Rhodesia and called on members of the United Nations scrupulously to enforce the sanctions on Rhodesia. This resolution was adopted by 124 in favor to none against, with 15 abstentions (Australia, Belgium, Canada, Dominican Republic, France, Gabon, West Germany, Israel, Italy, Luxembourg, Malawi, Netherlands, New Zealand, United Kingdom, and the United States). Speaking after the vote, Botswana justified its action on the grounds that its economy was extremely dependent on South Africa and Rhodesia, and that any economic boycott on the states would adversely affect the viability of its economy.

Concerning Res. 33/38A, Britain maintained that it was a travesty of the truth to accuse it of complicity in the evasion of the sanctions. In response, Britain argued that in setting up the Bingham Inquiry, it had cleared itself from complicity in the cover-up. As noted previously, the Bingham investigation detailed the activities of some of the British officials in orchestrating British Petroleum and Shell Company plots to evade British and UN sanctions against Rhodesia. In addition, Britain insisted that, in conjunction with the United States, it had continued to advocate for a negotiated settlement in Rhodesia involving all the parties to the conflict. Britain also felt that a majority of the members of the committee had publicly expressed their general support for the Anglo-American proposals as the most desirable framework for a just settlement in Rhodesia. The British representative reiterated that the success of a settlement depended on its impartiality and that the African nationalists inside Zimbabwe led by Bishop Muzorewa, Ndabaningi Sithole, and Senator Chief Chirau must be taken into account in any negotiations or resolutions which accord leadership of the people of Zimbabwe to the Patriotic Front. The British made an outright condemnation of both the present and future internal settlements that could hardly be regarded as impartial. Accordingly, Britain abstained in the vote on Resolution 33/38A.

Concerning GA Res. 33/38B, Britain argued that British South African subsidiaries of its oil companies were no longer supplying or marketing their products in Rhodesia. Thus, the British government considered the assertion in GA Res. 33/38B that British oil companies were "circumventing United Nations sanctions" to be entirely unjustified. Although Britain claimed that its companies were operating within the stipulations of the UN sanctions on Rhodesia, British Petroleum and Shell Company continued to supply oil and petrochemical products to Rhodesia through their South African subsidiaries.

West Germany justified its abstentions on the grounds that no outside authority could decide who are and should be leaders of the people of Zimbabwe. Such a decision should be left to the people of Zimbabwe to make in free, open, and fair elections. West Germany also believed that it was the most honorable task for the United Nations to search for peaceful solutions to all problems even in desperate political periods; UN resolutions should neither sanction nor recommend violence. On the same topic, other UN delegates stated the following:

Italy held that it was inappropriate for the General Assembly to touch on an area which the United Nations Charter restricted to the competence of the Security Council.

New Zealand stated that, while it remained opposed to the illegal Smith regime and to the present internal regime, it was committed to a peaceful settlement, which could only come about through all-party discussions.

Canada could not support the operative paragraph of draft resolution A which strongly condemned South Africa and certain Western and other countries for the direct and indirect support given to the government of Ian Smith. Moreover, it was not prepared to support a resolution of the Assembly recommending action which was properly the responsibility of the Security Council.

The United States, referring to the paragraphs of draft resolution A which condemned the internal settlement in Salisbury, said that the United States did not and would not recognize that settlement. It was not capable of leading Zimbabwe to a free and fair transition to majority rule. However, the United States had abstained in the vote when similar language had been included in Security Council Resolution 423 (1978), because its support for condemnation would impair the ability of the United States Government to deal with the Smith regime and the internal nationalists as it continued to work towards a negotiated, internationally accepted solution in Zimbabwe.

France stated that it had always strictly implemented the sanctions against Southern Rhodesia. Also it was strongly in favor of a negotiated, peaceful solution of the problem of Southern Rhodesia and supported the Anglo-American proposals for an all-party conference. It could not contradict itself by voting in favor of a text which on the one hand stated that the Patriotic Front was the exclusive representative of the people of Zimbabwe, and on the other, implicitly encouraged the use of violence.[116]

Recognizing the hostility of the Patriotic Front, the Frontline states, the OAU, and UN General Assembly to the March 3 Rhodesian Internal Accord, the transitional government of the Rhodesia Front party, the United African National Council, the Zimbabwe African National Union (Sithole), and the Zimbabwean United Peoples Organization (ZUPO) ferociously made limited military attacks against Zimbabwean freedom fighters in Zambia and Mozambique. Although the United Nations condemned the raids, Rhodesia continued them from 1978 to December 1979.

Thousands of Zimbabwean refugees, hundreds of guerrillas, and many Mozambican and Zambian civilians were victims of these raids. Although the OAU passed a resolution that authorized it to set up a military force to assist any African country attacked by Rhodesia or South Africa, no such force was set up specifically to help these countries fight against Rhodesian and South African invaders. While the OAU, the General Assembly, and the Security Council continued to warn Rhodesia of the consequences, its military raids into Botswana, Zambia, and Mozambique, Rhodesia, ignored them with impunity. Rhodesia justified its raids into these countries because they provided sanctuaries for the Patriotic Front guerrillas. Other reasons for these military incursions were aimed at bombing the Patriotic Front forces with the prime objective of reducing their military strength. Bombing them into submission was supposed to encourage the Patriotic Front to sue for a negoitated settlement with the Rhodesian government. Rhodesia also felt that constant military raids had dangerous political destabilizing effects on the governments of Mozambique, Zambia, and Botswana.

For the effective implementation of the March 3, 1978, *Internal Accord*, the transitional Rhodesian government stressed that the agreement must be approved (in a referendum) by a majority of white voters. More than 85 percent of the Rhodesian white electorate voted on January 31, 1979, for the accord. Another requirement for the implementation of the accord was to be an election of seventy-two Africans and twenty-eight whites to the so-called Independence Rhodesian legislature. After the election in April, 1979, Bishop Abel Muzorewa's party (UANC) won fifty-one seats, Rhodesia Front (Ian Smith) twenty-eight, ZANU (Sithole) twelve, Chief Ndiweni (United Federal party) nine, and ZUPO (Chirau), zero. On June 1, 1979, Bishop Abel Muzorewa became the first black prime minister to run the Zimbabwe-Rhodesia government. Zimbabwe-Rhodesia was the name that the transitional government adopted. With pressure from African states within the United Nations and the international community, no country recognized Muzorewa's government. The OAU, the United Nations, and the United Kingdom declared the Muzorewa government illegal. The OAU and the United Nations emphasized that only through a negotiated settlement with Britain and all other parties involved could the Rhodesian government be brought back to legality.

At his appointment as prime minister, Bishop Muzorewa had hoped that the Western countries would ignore UN and OAU calls for withholding recognition of his government. In the United States, former Ambassador Andrew Young, the Congressional Black Caucus, and Trans Africa prevailed upon the Carter administration to deny recognition to Zimbabwe-Rhodesia. Andrew Young had previously warned President Carter and Secretary of State Cyrus Vance that Nigeria, the Frontline states, the OAU, and the United Nations were opposed to the recognition of the Muzorewa government which they considered illegal. Recognizing Zimbabwe-Rhodesia would have jeopardized American political and economic interests in independent African states.

With the Conservative party election victory in the United Kingdom, Muzorewa had hoped that the new Prime Minister, Margaret Thatcher, would soon recognize his government. Unfortunately for him, thirty-four British Commonwealth countries warned Thatcher about the grave consequences that would result should her government recognize Rhodesia. Coupled with pressure from the OAU, Nigeria, the Frontline states, and the United Nations, the British prime minister shied away.

The international community refused to recognize Muzorewa's government because it was created from an illegal base. The internal settlement of March 3, 1979, had not removed the Smith rebellion of November 11, 1965. Furthermore, the much-denounced elections of April 1979, had been conducted in a war atmosphere. Rhodesia was under martial law and the people of Zimbabwe were not free to discuss openly all issues regarding that election. A report by observers on behalf of the British Parliamentary Human Rights Group correctly analyzed the repressive political atmosphere that was prevalent in Zimbabwe-Rhodesia during the time of the election when it noted:

Quite apart from air and ground attacks on targets in neighboring countries, the death toll in Rhodesia is estimated by reliable sources inside the country to be between 100 and 200 a day. Some 90-percent of the country is under martial law. General Walls in a briefing to international observers and press emphasized that martial law "only supplements the ordinary laws of the country" and boasted that "I don't believe you have even realized you've been traveling in martial law areas." A Ministry of Information and Tourism pamphlet, published in December, 1978, and aimed at the black population explained martial law somewhat differently:
"In martial law areas, the security forces can make their own laws to help them find and kill terrorists. They will not have to follow the ordinary laws, because they can take too much time . . . . Here are some of the things the army can do in martial law areas:
1. they can arrest and detain people;
2. they can confiscate or destroy property such as huts and cattle;
3. they can make people work for them.
The security forces can now hold their own courts. These courts will have the power to sentence people to gaol and death."
In addition to the arrest and detention of people under the Emergency Powers legislation (and it must be remembered that Rhodesia has been in a state of emergency since UDI in 1965) who are classed as political detainees and come under the jurisdiction of the Ministry of Law and Order, there are a large number of martial law detainees–often very young people of around 11 and 12 years and old or "mujibas" who are suspected of collaborating with the guerrillas–who come under the jurisdiction of Combined Operations. No one knows precisely how many martial law detainees there are–the International Red Cross does not have access to them, the detainees are held in various centres including prisons and army camps throughout the country. There is also often a "quick turnover" of detainees, their number is not given for security reasons and so on–but reliable sources within the country estimate that there are not less than a thousand. The imposition of curfews, collective fines, the closing of schools, clinics, food stores and grinding mills, the exacting of punishments such as the burning of homes, the killing of cattle, the destruction of crops–from entire communities in reprisals for guerrilla activity have long been commonplace under a whole battery of emergency legislation. Relief and church agencies within the country informed us that such activites had increased since the imposition of martial law in September, 1978. So too had the incidence of beating and killing of civilians as "curfew breakers," "terrorist recruits," "collaborators" and "those running with terrorists."[117]

The British Parliamentary Human Rights Report on Rhodesia reinforced the OAU and UN views that the elections were illegal and that the Muzorewa administ-

ration was an outgrowth of the illegitimate government of Ian Smith. With pressure from the United Nations and African states, the British Conservative government tabled the issue of recognition and moved to finding a basis for holding discussions with the government of Muzorewa and the Patriotic Front concerning the restoration of legality to Rhodesia. After a barrage of vituperative and acrimonious statements about each other, Muzorewa's government and the Patriotic Front of Mugabe and Nkomo agreed to a British proposal for holding a parley leading Rhodesia to legality and African majority rule.

The conference that convened at Lancaster House, London, under the chairmanship of Lord Carrington, the British foreign secretary, met from September to December 1979. The conference ended with an agreement that restored Rhodesia back to legality. Under the Lancaster Rhodesian Agreement, the Muzorewa-Rhodesian government was replaced by that of Lord Soames, the appointed governor general to govern Rhodesia until an elected African majority rule government could take over. British Commonwealth troops from Australia, Kenya, New Zealand, and Fiji were brought in to augment the Rhodesian security forces in maintaining law and order during the transitional period to majority rule. The Lancaster Agreement of a return to legality fulfilled the UN Security Council, General Assembly, and OAU resolutions on the transfer of power from white minority to the African majority. After a British government-administered election, Zimbabwe was granted independence on April 18, 1980.

The African member states of the United Nations should be complimented for their untiring efforts and pressure they exerted on Britain to end the illegal Rhodesian government of Ian Smith. Their activities within the UN system made the Rhodesian issue a subject of discussion from November 11, 1965, to the end of December 1979. Without African contributions in the UN system and other international organizations, it is probable that Britain and the Western nations would have quietly acquiesced to Ian Smith's internal settlement based on the March 3, 1978 agreement.

The Republic of South Africa and the UN System

In a century filled with conflicts among states and races, the struggle against racism and apartheid, as forms of human bondage, has become a central issue of the United Nations system. The Republic of South Africa is the only country in the world community that practices the obnoxious system of apartheid. The OAU and the United Nations Organization and other international agencies have focused their attention on South Africa because of the insistence of its white ruling minority clique on the application of the apartheid principle as a basic method of organizing the economic, political, social, and cultural life of its people. This principle (apartheid) is disputed by almost the whole of the international community. But however much nations and states may differ from one another in respects across the spectrum from extreme right to extreme left, South Africa is unique in building distinctions according to race into the foundations of its political arrangements. It is unique in being the one country in which such discrimination is still openly supported by the government and expressly written into the laws. Painted discrimination and segregation notices can be found on all public amenities–in post offices, railway stations, beaches, parks, buses, taxis, ambulances, hospitals, trains, motels, restaurants, kiosks, and lavatories.

With pressure from the African Group, the General Assembly, the Security Council,and other organs of the UN system have unreservedly condemned South African apartheid policies. Africans in South Africa have suffered every conceivable type of disaster from homicide to humiliation, from expropriation of land to grinding poverty, from savage treatment and brutal imprisonment to relentless persecution. Their family lives have been shattered, careers wrecked, education disrupted, and physical well-being in constant jeopardy, the vast majority of Africans are per-manently maimed in one way or another. Africans are joined by the Asians and Colored people who also encounter disabilities and persecution at every turn of the road. The principal instrument of the pernicious political system of apartheid is the state, which is, more than ever, authoritarian with elaborate surveillance and extreme severity in policing the lives of Africans, Coloreds, and Asians and coercive in watching and monitoring the behavior of these peoples. Because of the unashamed adoption of apartheid laws in South Africa and its gross violations of the fundamental human rights of the African, Colored, and Asian people, the United Nations General Assembly has declared apartheid in South Africa an international crime against humanity. Apartheid is a crime against humanity under the International Conven-tion on the Suppression and Punishment of the Crime of Apartheid adopted by the General Assembly of the United Nations in Resolution 3068 (XXXIII) of November 30, 1973.[118] From the viewpoint of social and political analysis, apartheid is a social malignancy rooted in the obsession of a minority to retain the luxury of privilege through the brutal exercise of force.[119] Not only is apartheid declared a crime, it is also considered politically explosive and likely to threaten international peace and security in the southern Africa region. Apartheid is likely to cause a race war that will eventually engulf the whole world–if it is not destroyed quickly. Based on this rationale the United Nations Special Committee against Apartheid now considers it imperative that the United Nations and the international community take urgent and effective action in view of the present grave situation in South Africa and in southern Africa as a whole, to secure the total eradication of apartheid and assist the South African people to exercise their right to self-determination. The international community must recognize that the South African racist regime, by its practice of the criminal policy of apartheid, continues to pose an ever-increasing grave threat to the people in the area. It must recognize further the legitimacy of the struggle of the oppressed people of South Africa to secure their inalienable rights and must provide all necessary assistance to them in their struggle for liberation. This has now become an urgent responsibility of the international community.[120]

Although South Africa is supposed to be a sovereign state and a founder member of the United Nations, African people and their states have generally excluded South Africa from the list of all sovereign African countries on the grounds that it is in essence a European state colonizing Africans. On this issue, the Malian delegate to the United Nations, Barema Bocoum, called for sanctions against the acts of barbar-ism that are being perpetrated every day against the peaceful and defenseless Africans by white South African rulers.[121]

The white South Africans regard themselves as Europeans and constantly seek closer ties with their fellow Europeans than with Africans. A classical example of the intention of white South Africans to associate themselves with the interests of Europe was clearly enunciated when Nkrumah of Ghana extended his invitation to South Africa to attend a Conference of Independent African States in 1958.

All the Independent African States were invited, even the Union of South Africa. The latter refused to attend unless other "responsible powers" on the African continent, meaning the colonial powers, were invited. The matter was dropped and this was the last time South Africa was invited by other African States to participate in an African Conference at any level.[122]

Another significant act of South Africa's desire to align itself with Europe rather than with African and Arabic states was its decision not to join African and Arabian countries during discussions leading to the formation of the UN Economic Commission for Africa and the Middle East.[123] On this issue Immanuel Wallerstein observed:

> Another factor may have been that the attempt many years earlier to establish a U.N. Economic Commission for the Middle East had been abortive because of the refusal of the Arab States to countenance the membership of Israel; hence, the various North African States were in 1958 affiliated to no regional economic commission. Nor was there any question yet of excluding the colonial powers, although the resolution provided that "states which cease to have any territorial responsibilities in Africa shall cease to be members of the Commission." South Africa was included, but declined to participate "for the present." In its communication to the Secretary-General of the U.N., the South African government raised questions both about the inclusion of North African countries and also the possible overlapping with CCTA.[124]

From the Union Act of 1909, which granted it independence from Britain, South Africa had discriminated, exploited, oppressed, and subjected Africans to all forms of inhumane indignities. Africans are racially brutalized and denied the right to govern themselves and to control and direct their own lives. The South African Nationalist government unashamedly continues to transplant African peasants and workers into Nazi-like concentration camps called *homelands.* In these barren and dry areas, Africans are further denied their fundamental freedoms of movement, association, and assembly.

Although South Africa was one of the founder members of the United Nations, it has been vehemently consistent in its opposition to human rights and African majority rule. African peaceful opposition to apartheid has been met by brutal and savage repression by the South African secret service and police force. The South African government has enacted numerous repressive laws aimed at preventing any form of progression to African majority rule. Not only does South Africa relish its oppression of Africans, it also ignores the international outcries against apartheid.

United Nations concern with racist policies of the apartheid government of South Africa is of long standing. At the request of the government of India, the General Assembly first dealt with complaints of racial discrimination directed against the people of Indian origin in South Africa. (It should be noted that the complaint by

India to the United Nations did not address the problems of Africans and Coloreds.) With the advent of the 1960s, the tenor of the General Assembly's response to the persistent, systematic, and gross violations of human rights by the South African apartheid regime has been phenomenal.

Before 1960 it had not proved possible for the Security Council to deliberate on the issue of apartheid because of the argument that the matter falls within the domestic jurisdiction of a member state (South Africa). Although the permanent members of the Security Council no longer object to such discussion, during the period from 1946 to 1960, many of its members voted against resolutions that stated that the policy of apartheid and the political situation in South Africa were disturbing international peace and security. The General Assembly was content to censure and appeal to the government of South Africa over its policies, notwithstanding South Africa's invocation of Article 2.7 of the Charter of the United Nations concerned with domestic jurisdiction. The first major shift in the international legal order brought out through the Charter was in the field of self-determination and systematic gross violations of human rights. Where these are a matter of state policy, they are automatically lifted from the domestic reserve and regulated by both international law and the United Nations.[125] It is astonishing to note that South Africa's major Western allies (Britain, Canada, France, Netherlands, Sweden, Belgium, Norway, Portugal, and Spain) persisted for a long period to support South Africa's contention that even to discuss its internal policies was a breach of Article 2.7. The change from regarding apartheid as a mere domestic issue of South Africa to something that was international and affecting the nature of international peace and security is a development of paramount importance to all those who support equality and human rights in South Africa.

The turning point in the United Nations Security Council's consideration of the South African apartheid policies came with the notorious Sharpeville Massacre of March 21, 1960. Sixty-seven Africans were shot to death and several hundreds of them were wounded by the apartheid police. During the period, 11,504 people were arrested and detained in connection with the Sharpeville peaceful demonstrations. Because of these cold-blooded murders at Sharpeville, some twenty-nine African and Asian member states at the United Nations requested a meeting of the United Nations Security Council. The Security Council passed Resolution 134 condemning apartheid for the first time in the history of the Council. Security Council Resolution 134 of April 1, 1960 states:

Having considered the complaint of 29 Member States contained in document S/4279 and Add. 1 concerning "the situation arising out of the large-scale killings of unarmed and peaceful demonstrators against racial discrimination and segregation in the Union of South Africa";

Recognizing that such a situation has been brought about by the racial policies of the Government of the Union of South Africa and the continuous disregard by that Government of the resolutions of the General Assembly calling upon it to revise its policies and bring them into conformity with its obligations and responsibilities under the Charter;

Taking into account the strong feelings and grave concern aroused among Governments and peoples of the world by the happenings in the Union of South Africa;

1. *Recognizes* that the situation in the Union of South Africa is one that has led to international friction and if continued might endanger international peace and security;
2. *Deplores* that the recent disturbances in the Union of South Africa should have led to the loss of life of so many Africans and extends to the families of the victims its deepest sympathies;
3. *Deplores* the policies and actions of the Government of the Union of South Africa which have given rise to the present situation;
4. *Calls upon* the Government of the Union of South Africa to initiate measures aimed at bringing about racial harmony based on equality in order to ensure that the present situation does not continue or reoccur and to abandon its policies of apartheid and racial discrimination;
5. *Requests* the Secretary-General, in consultation with the Government of the Union of South Africa, to make such arrangements as would adequately help in and to report to the Security Council whenever necessary and appropriate.
(*Vote*: In Favor: Algeria, Ceylon, China, Ecuador, Italy, Poland, Tunisia, U.S.S.R., United States
    Abstentions: France, United Kingdom)[126]

Security Council Resolution 134, which recognized apartheid as a threat to international peace and security, did not recommend any measures to bring about racial harmony and equality. The change in the tone and content of Resolution 134 of 1960, was originally the result of the admission of eighteen newly independent African states to membership in the United Nations at the fifteenth session of the General Assembly. The membership substantially altered the composition and balance of power in the General Assembly and gave added impetus to the growing demand for a speedy and unconditional end to colonialism, racism, and apartheid. Until 1960, the Western allies of South Africa who were a majority in the United Nations General Assembly stifled any far-reaching initiatives from anticolonialism and antiimperialism minority group of states in that UN chamber.

After the passage of the Security Council Resolution 134 (1960), the objectives of the African states became geared toward persuading the Security Council to continue regarding apartheid as constituting a threat to international peace and security. As a result of African pressure, in November 1962, the General Assembly adopted Resolutions 1761 (XVII) by a vote of sixty-seven to sixteen, with twenty-three abstentions. This resolution requested all United Nations member states, individually or collectively, to apply diplomatic and economic sanctions as well as an arms embargo against South Africa. The Assembly also created a special committee to keep the South African policies under review. Following the creation of the OAU, the African Group at the United Nations requested the Security Council to meet and call on South Africa to abandon its policy of apartheid and to release all its political prisoners. In case South Africa refused to meet these demands, the group suggested that it would recommend that the Security Council proceed to impose an economic, military, and diplomatic embargo on South Africa. The Security Council met and adopted Resolution 181 (1963) of August 7, 1963. The resolution reads:

Having considered the question of race conflict in South Africa resulting from the policies of *apartheid* of the Government of the Republic of South Africa, as submitted by the thirty-two African Member States,

Recalling Security Council Resolution S/4300 of 1 April 1960,

Taking into account that world public opinion has been reflected in General Assembly Resolution 1761 (XVII) and particularly in its paragraphs 4 and 8,

Noting with appreciation the two interim reports of the Special Committee on the Policies of Apartheid of the Government of South Africa contained in documents S/5310 of 9 May 1963 and S/5353 of 17 July 1963,

Regretting that some States are indirectly providing encouragement in various ways to the Government of South Africa to perpetuate, by force, its policy of *apartheid*,

Regretting the failure of the Government of South Africa to accept the invitation of the Security Council to delegate a representative to appear before it,

Being convinced that the situation in South Africa is seriously disturbing international peace and security.

1. *Strongly deprecates* the policies of South Africa in its perpetuation of racial discrimination as being inconsistent with the principles contained in the Charter of the United Nations and contrary to its obligations as a Member State of the United Nations;

2. *Calls upon* the Government of South Africa to abandon the policies of *apartheid* and discrimination as called for in the previous Security Council resolution of 1 April 1960, and to liberate all persons imprisoned, interned or subjected to other restrictions for having opposed the policy of *apartheid*;

3. *Solemnly calls upon* all States to cease forthwith the sale and shipment of arms, ammunition of all types and military vehicles to South Africa; .

4. *Requests* the Secretary-General to keep the situation in South Africa under observation and to report to the Security Council by 30 October 1963.

(Vote: In Favor: Brazil, China, Ghana, Morocco, Norway, Philippines,
             U.S.S.R., United States, Venezuela
             Abstentions: France, United Kingdom)[127]

At the request of thirty-two African and Asian states, the Security Council met again in December 1963. At this conference, the OAU was for the first time, an active participant in the UN deliberations. Representing the OAU were the foreign ministers of Liberia, Madagascar, Tunisia, and Sierra Leone. This session marked a new turn in the history of the UNs' fight against apartheid in the sense that this meeting unanimously adopted Security Council Resolution 182 on December 4, 1963:

Recognizing the need to eliminate discrimination in regard to basic human rights and fundamental freedoms for all individuals within the territory of the Republic of South Africa without distinction as to race, sex, language or religion,

Expressing the firm conviction that the policies of apartheid and racial discrimination as practised by the Government of the Republic of South Africa are abhorrent to the conscience of mankind and that therefore a positive alternative to these policies must be found through peaceful means.

1. *Appeals* to all states to comply with the provisions of Security Council Resolution S/5386 of 7 August 1963;

2. *Urgently requests* the Government of the Republic of South Africa to cease forthwith its continued imposition of discriminatory and repressive measures which are contrary to the principles and purposes of the Charter and which are in violation of its obligations as a Member of the United Nations and of the provisions of the Universal Declaration of Human Rights;

3. *Condemns* the non-compliance by the Government of the Republic of

South Africa with the appeals contained in the above-mentioned resolutions of the General Assembly and the Security Council;

4. *Again calls upon* the Government of South Africa to liberate all persons imprisoned, interned or subjected to other restrictions for having opposed the policy of apartheid;

5. *Solemnly calls upon* all states to cease forthwith the sale and shipment of equipment and materials for the manufacture and maintenance of arms and ammunition in South Africa.

6. *Requests* the Secretary-General to establish under his direction and reporting to him a small group of recognized experts to examine methods of resolving the present situation in South Africa through full, peaceful, and orderly application of human rights and fundamental freedoms to all inhabitants of the territory as a whole, regardless of race, colour or creed, and to consider what part the United Nations might play in the achievement of that end;

7. *Invites* the Government of the Republic of South Africa to avail itself of the assistance of this group in order to bring out such peaceful and orderly transformation;

8. *Requests* the Secretary-General to continue to keep the situation under observation and to report to the Security Council such new developments as may occur, and in any case not later than 1 June 1964, on the implementation of this resolution.[128]

(*Vote*: Unanimous)

The April 20, 1964, expert group established under the auspices of Security Council Resolution 182 recommended the formation of a national convention that would be attended by all South African parties to the conflict. The conference never materialized because of the South African government's unwillingness to cooperate. The Council endorsed the June 1964 main conclusions of the expert group. The June 18, 1964, recommendations as outlined by the Security Resolutions 191 (1964) were:

1. *Condemns the apartheid* policies of the Government of the Republic of South Africa and the legislation supporting these policies, such as the General Law Amendment Act, and in particular its ninety-day detention clause;

2. *Urgently reiterates* its appeal to the Government of the Republic of South Africa to liberate all persons imprisoned, interned or subjected to other restrictions for having opposed the policies of apartheid;

3. *Notes* the recommendations and the conclusions in the Report of the Group of Experts;

4. *Urgently appeals* to the Government of the Republic of South Africa to:
   a. renounce the execution of any persons sentenced to death for their opposition to the policy of *apartheid*.
   b. grant immediate amnesty to all persons detained or on trial, as well as clemency to all persons sentenced for their opposition to the Government's racial policies;
   c. abolish the practice of imprisonment without charges, without access to counsel or without the right of prompt trial;

5. *Endorses* and subscribes in particular to the main conclusion of the Group of Experts that "all the people of South Africa should be brought into consultation and should thus be enabled to decide the future of their country at the national level."

6. *Requests* the Secretary-General to consider what assistance the United Nations may offer to facilitate such consultations among representatives of all elements of the population in South Africa;

7. *Invites* the Government of the Republic of South Africa to accept the main conclusion of the Group of Experts referred to in paragraph 5 above and to cooperate with the Secretary-General and to submit its views to him with respect to such consultations by 30 November 1964;

8. *Decides* to establish an Expert Committee, composed of representatives of each present member of the Security Council, to undertake a technical and practical study, and report to the Security Council as to the feasibility, effectiveness, and implications of measures which could, as appropriate, be taken by the Security Council under the United Nations Charter;

9. *Requests* the Secretary-General to provide to the Expert Committee the Secretariat's material on the subjects to be studied by the Committee, and to cooperate with the Committee as requested by it;

10. *Authorizes* the Expert Committee to request all United Nations Members to cooperate with it and to submit their views on such measures to the Committee no later than 30 November 1964, and the Committee to complete its report not later than three months thereafter;

11. *Invites* the Secretary-General in consultation with appropriate United Nations specialized agencies to establish an educational and training programme for the purpose of arranging for education and training abroad for South Africans;

12. *Reaffirms* its call upon all states to cease forthwith the sale and shipment to South Africa of arms, ammunition of all types, military vehicles, and equipment and materials for the manufacture and maintenance of arms and ammunition in South Africa;

13. *Requests* all Member states to take such steps as they deem appropriate to persuade the Government of the Republic of South Africa to comply with this resolution,

(*Vote*:   In Favor: Bolivia, Brazil, China, Ivory Coast, Morocco, Norway, United
            Kingdom, United States
            Abstentions: Czechoslovakia, France, U.S.S.R.)[129]

In February 1965 the Expert Committee of Council reported that it was unsuccessful in reaching a full agreement. The majority of the committee members comprised of Brazil, Bolivia, the Republic of China, Norway, the United Kingdom, and the United States were of the opinion that whereas South Africa would not be easily susceptible to economic measures, its economy was not immune or insulated from the havoc of economic sanctions. Opposing this reasoning were Ivory Coast, Czechoslovakia, Morocco, and the USSR, which maintained that political and economic sanctions against South Africa would be unquestionably feasible. The Expert Report was never considered by the Security Council because of the committee's failure to recommend common conclusions.

From 1965 on the African group at the United Nations was instrumental in making the General Assembly adopt Resolutions 2054 A (XX) stating that universally applied economic sanctions were indeed the weapons of compelling South African compliance with UN resolutions recommending termination of apartheid. Following this, the General Assembly enlarged the Special Committee against Apartheid from eleven to seventeen specifically to incorporate those states with the responsibility for the maintenance of international peace and security. Also incorporated in this committee were countries with extensive economic relations with South Africa. These countries were unwilling to serve in the new Committee of 17. Apparently frustrated by the lack of support from Western countries, the African states at the United Nations began to adopt more militant and uncompromising stands against

South Africa. An example of this is the General Assembly Resolution 2396 (XXIII) of December 1968, which described apartheid as a "crime against humanity" and called for African majority rule based on adult human suffrage.

The linking of racial equality with decolonization and self-determination, the development of the norm of nondiscrimination, the acceptance of the principle of self-determination as a clear rule of international law, the recognition of apartheid as a crime against humanity (first formulated by the General Assembly in 1965), the recognition of the legitimacy of the use of all possible means of struggle by the oppressed people to overthrow apartheid and racism, and the use of the rules of procedure of the General Assembly to refuse to acknowledge the right of the representatives of the racist regime to represent South Africa are examples of the ways in which the General Assembly and the United Nations have dynamically attempted to isolate South Africa.

In addition to these steps, the General Assembly recommended that the Committee on Apartheid intensify its relentless campaign against apartheid. After the committee was authorized to hold meetings outside New York, the Security Council adopted Resolution 282 of July 23, 1970.

Convinced further that the situation resulting from the continued application of the policies of apartheid and the constant build-up of the South African military and police forces made possible by the continued acquisition of arms, military vehicles and other equipment and of spare parts for military equipment from a number of Member States and by local manufacture of arms and ammunition under licenses granted by some Member States constitutes a potential threat to international peace and security;

Recognizing that the extensive arms build-up of the military forces of South Africa poses a real threat to the security and sovereignty of independent African States opposed to the racial policies of the Government of South Africa, in particular the neighboring States;

1. *Reiterates* its total opposition to the policies of *apartheid* of the Government of the Republic of South Africa;

2. *Reaffirms* its Resolutions 181 (1963), 182 (1963) and 191 (1964);

3. *Condemns* the violations of the arms embargo called for in Resolutions 181 (1963), 182 (1963) and 191 (1964);

4. *Calls upon* all States to strengthen the arms embargo
   (a) by implementing fully the arms embargo against South Africa unconditionally and without reservations whatsoever;
   (b) by withholding supply of all vehicles and equipment for use in the armed forces and paramilitary organizations of South Africa;
   (c) by ceasing supply of spare parts for all vehicles and equipment for use of the armed forces and paramilitary organizations of South Africa;
   (d) by revoking all licenses and military patents granted to the South African Government or to South African companies for the manufacture of arms and ammunition, aircraft and naval craft or other military vehicles and by refraining from further granting such licenses and patents;
   (e) by prohibiting investment in or technical assistance for the manufacture of arms and ammunition, aircraft, naval craft, or other military vehicles;
   (f) by ceasing provision of military training for members of the South African armed forces and all other forms of military cooperation with South Africa.
   (g) by undertaking the appropriate action to give effect to the above measures;

5. *Requests* the Secretary-General to follow closely the implementation of the present resolution and report to the Security Council from time to time.
6. *Calls upon* all States to observe strictly the arms embargo against South Africa and to assist effectively in the implementation of this resolution.
(*Vote*: In Favor: Burundi, China, Colombia, Finland, Nepal, Nicaragua, Poland, Sierra Leone, Spain, Syria, U.S.S.R., Zambia
Abstentions: France, United Kingdom, United States)[130]

The lack of support to the 1970 Security Council Resolution 282 from Britain, France, and the United States was regarded by the African states and the OAU as a major setback against economic sanctions on South Africa. This state of affairs at the United Nations did not dampen the African states' crusade against apartheid. Determined to maintain the antithetical momentum against apartheid at the United Nations, Guinea, Somalia, Sudan, India, and Yugoslavia sponsored an antiapartheid resolution. This resolution was adopted by the Security Council as Resolution 311 of February 4, 1972. Although the Resolution deplored apartheid in general, it specifically noted:

1. *Condemns* the Government of South Africa for continuing its policies of *apartheid* in violation of its obligations under the Charter of the United Nations;
2. *Reiterates* its total opposition to the policies of *apartheid* of the Government of South Africa;
3. *Recognizes* the legitimacy of the struggle of the oppressed people of South Africa in pursuance of their human and political rights, as set forth in the Charter and the Universal Declaration of Human Rights;
4. *Urgently calls upon* the Government of South Africa to release all persons imprisoned, interned or subjected to other restrictions as a result of the policies of *apartheid*;
5. *Calls upon* all States to observe strictly the arms embargo against South Africa.
6. *Urges* Governments and individuals to contribute generously and regularly to the United Nations funds which are used for humanitarian and training purposes to assist the victims of *apartheid;*
7. *Commends* the inter-governmental organizations, nongovernmental organizations and individuals for assisting in the education and training of South Africans and urges those who do not to begin and those who do to expand their efforts in this field;
8. *Decides,* as a matter of urgency, to examine methods of resolving the present situation arising out of the policies of *apartheid* of the Government of South Africa.
(*Vote:* In Favor: Argentina, Belgium, China, Guinea, India, Italy, Japan, Panama, Somalia, Sudan, U.S.S.R., United Kingdom, United States, Yugoslavia
Abstention: France)[131]

Although this was a mild resolution supported by the United Kingdom and the United States, France continued to abstain from voting. France had also not supported any of the Afro-Asian Security Council resolutions condemning apartheid.

With the Portuguese coup of 1974, Angola and Mozambique acquired their independence. With this change in the geopolitical power structure in southern Africa, the former United States Secretary of State, Henry Kissinger, the U.S.

government, and South Africa believed that revolutionary Africans would take over political power in Zimbabwe and establish a socialist government following the patterns set by Guinea-Bissau, Angola, and Mozambique. Another problem for the West was to try and eliminate the possibility of the extension of Soviet influence in Zimbabwe. With these issues (among many others) the United States and South Africa, in collusion with the United Kingdom, pressured Ian Smith to agree to African majority rule in Rhodesia (Zimbabwe).

From the time the Portuguese coup d'etat took place, political unrest on the part of South African students escalated. The students objected to have Afrikaans (South African Dutch) used as a medium of instruction in African schools. Because of the apartheid government's insistence on the use of Afrikaans as a language of instruction, the African students boycotted classes. In response to these developments, the South African government sent its police force into the African townships to break the boycott. The confrontation that ensued ended in a massacre of innocent African children by the South African government.

Africans at the United Nations reacted to these unnecessary cold-blooded killings of the Africans by condemning the racial policies of the South African government. As a result of African requests the United Nations Security Council passed Resolution 392 of June 1976, which declared:

> *Having considered* the letter by the representatives of Benin, the Libyan Arab Republic and the United Republic of Tanzania, on behalf of the African Group at the United Nations, concerning the measures of repression, including wanton killings perpetrated by the *apartheid* regime in South Africa against the African people in Soweto and other areas in South Africa (S/12100),
> *Having considered also* the telegram from the President of the Democratic Republic of Madagascar addressed to the Secretary General (S/12101),
> *Deeply shocked* over large-scale killings and wounding of Africans in South Africa, following the callous shooting of African people including school children and students demonstrating against racial discrimination on 16 June 1976,
> *Convinced* that this situation has been brought about by the continued imposition by the South African Government of *apartheid* and racial discrimination, in defiance of the resolutions of the Security Council and the General Assembly,
> 1. *Strongly condemns* the South African Government for its resort to massive violence against and killings of the African people including school children and students and others opposing racial discrimination;
> 2. *Expresses* its profound sympathy to the victims of this violence;
> 3. *Reaffirms* that the policy of *apartheid* is a crime against the conscience and dignity of mankind and seriously disturbs international peace and security;
> 4. *Recognizes* the legitimacy of the struggle of the South African people for the elimination of *apartheid* and racial discrimination;
> 5. *Calls upon* the South African Government urgently to end violence against the African people, and take urgent steps to eliminate *apartheid* and racial discrimination;
> 6. *Decides* to remain seized of the matter.
> (*Vote:* Adopted by consensus)[132]

The South African government ignored this resolution and continued to oppress the Africans as it had previously done.

Blacks in South Africa are resisting against all forms of oppression perpetrated against them by the government of South Africa. As a result of their determination to free themselves from white subjugation, Africans continued to riot, boycott schools, and refuse to be intimidated. The South African government replied to all the African actions and demands by (1) arbitrarily arresting and detaining Africans without trial; (2) torturing and killing African arrested leaders and followers; (3) imposing curfews in African residential areas; (4) forced exiling of Africans into the so-called homelands; and (5) banning all organizations and newspapers opposed to apartheid. In response to all these repressive acts inflicted on the already dehumanized and suffering Africans, African members of the United Nations and their allies condemned South Africa in the General Assembly and requested the Security Council to pass a resolution that would place an immediate, permanent, and binding embargo on the sale of arms to South Africa.

Initially, the African Group at the United Nations presented three draft resolutions to the Security Council, which they hoped would have imposed both an economic and an arms embargo against South Africa, but France, Britain, and the United States vetoed these resolutions. While the African countries registered their disappointment with the position taken by these nations, they also wanted to avoid creating divisions within the Security Council. As already stated, the council unanimously agreed on an arms embargo against South Africa on November 3, 1977:

Recalling its Resolution 392 (1976) strongly condemning the South African government for its resort to massive violence against and killings of the African people, including school children and students and others opposing racial discrimination, and calling upon that Government urgently to end violence against African people and take urgent steps to eliminate apartheid and racial discrimination.

Recognizing that the military buildup and persistent acts of aggression by South Africa against the neighboring states seriously disturb the security of those states.

Further recognizing that the existing arms embargo must be strengthened and universally applied, without any reservations or qualifications whatsoever, in order to prevent a further aggravation of the grave situation in South Africa.

Taking note of the Lagos Declaration for Action Against Apartheid.

Gravely concerned that South Africa is at the threshold of producing nuclear weapons.

Strongly condemning the South African Government for its acts of repression, its defiant continuance of the system of apartheid and its attacks against neighboring independent states.

Considering that the policies and acts of the South African Government are fraught with danger to international peace and security.

Recalling its Resolution 181 (1963) and other resolutions concerning a voluntary arms embargo against South Africa.

Convinced that a mandatory arms embargo needs to be universally applied against South Africa in the first instance.

Acting, therefore, under Chapter VII of the Charter of the United Nations:

1. Determines, having regard to the policies and acts of the South African Government, that the acquisition by South Africa of arms and related material constitutes a threat to the maintenance of international peace and security;

2. Decides that all states shall prohibit the supply of arms and related material of all types to South Africa including the sale or transfer of weapons and ammunition, military vehicles and equipment, paramilitary police equipment, and spare parts for the aforementioned, and shall cease as well the provision of all types of equipment and supplies, and grants of licensing arrangements for the manufacture or maintenance of the aforementioned;

3. Calls on all states to review, having regard to the objectives of this resolution, all existing contractual arrangements with and licenses granted to South Africa relating to the manufacture and maintenance of arms, ammunition of all types and military equipment and vehicles, with a view to terminating them;

4. Further decided that all states shall refrain from any cooperation with South Africa in the manufacture and development of nuclear weapons;

5. Calls upon all states, including states non-members of the United Nations, to act strictly in accordance with the provisions of this resolution;

6. Requests the Secretary-General to report to the Council on the progress of the implementation of this resolution, the first report to be submitted not later than 1 May 1978;

7. Decides to keep this item on its agenda for further action, as appropriate, in the light of developments.[133]

The effects of this resolution are not substantive but symbolic because in the view of UN experts, the embargo was expected to hit hard at France and to some degree at Israel, which are South Africa's major suppliers of sophisticated weaponry, including jet planes, submarines, and missile-equipped patrol boats. The Security Council resolution on Arms Embargo did not satisfy all the African demands of a total economic and arms embargo against South Africa. However, by passing this resolution, the Security Council had invoked its rarely used powers of placing an arms embargo against a United Nations member state.

The arms embargo against South Africa, now apparently agreed upon by all members of the Security Council, has far-reaching implications on South Africa. The embargo cuts South Africa off from its arms suppliers: Portugal, Italy, Britain, United States, France, Israel, and Jordan. Although South Africa has the ability and technical know-how to produce most of the arms it needs, the cost of producing these arms is very high. If the arms embargo is successfully implemented by all arms-producing countries, South Africa will in the long run be deprived of the new weapons and technology being developed in the Americas and Europe.

Although South Africa's white population is small, it has the most powerful army in all of Africa, excluding Egypt. South Africa's arms arsenals are all obtained from the United States, European countries, and Israel. Between 1971 and 1977, South Africa received its arms from the following countries:

Table 17: Major Identified Arms Agreements 1971-1977

Primary Supplier	Approximate date of Agreement	System	Quantity
France1976		Exocet missile N.A.	
Israel	1976	Reshef fast patrol boats with guided missiles	2
Israel	Feb. 1976	Fast patrol boats with guided missiles	3
France	Feb. 1976	Type A69 frigates	2
France	1975	Agosta class submarines	2
Jordan	Mid. 1974	Tigercat surface-to-air missile	54
Jordan	Mid. 1974	Centurion tanks	41
Britain	Nov. 1971	HS 125 light transport	3
Britain	Nov. 1071	Wasp helicopter	5
France	June 1971	Mirage FLA interceptor	36
France	June 1971	Mirage IIIA fighter	N.A.
Italy	1971	Aermacchi AMBC	40
Portugal	Oct. 1971	Corvettes with surface-to-surface missiles	6

SOURCE: *Financial Times,* November 8, 1976.

Although some of the Western military hardware supplied to South Africa may be old, in terms of Africa, this equipment is relatively modern. More significantly, other equipment, such as the Patton tank has been reconditioned and improved. The Patton tanks are an improved model fitted with the powerful British 105mm gun. Tables 18, 19, and 20 partially illustrate the magnitude of South Africa's military strength.

Table 18:   Deliveries of Weapons Known to Be in Service with the South African Defense Forces (End 1976)

Item	Manufactured/Licensed by	Numbers/Deliveries/IISS	
Mirage III fighter/bomber trainer/recce	France	95+	57
Mirage F-1 all weather multi-purpose fighter	France	48+	16
Aermacchi MB-326M Impala I strike/trainer	S.A./Italy	300	145
Aermacchi MB-326K Impala II strike	S.A./Italy	100	22
Aerospatiale Alouette III armed attack helicopter	France	115+	40
Aerospatiale/Westland 330 Puma assault helicopter	France/U.K.	40+	25
Centurion Mk 7 heavy tank	U.K.	150	141
Daimler Ferret Mk 2 scout car/ antitank armored car	U.K.	450	230
M-3A1 white armored personnel carrier	U.S.	400	N.S.
Saracan FV603 and FV610 armored personnel carrier	U.K.	700	N.S.
T-17 El Staghound armored car	U.S.	450	N.S.

SOURCE: *The Military Balance,* 1976-1977
+ This indicates that additional similar type of weapons will be supplied from the same source.

Table 19:   Deliveries of Weapons Systems Not Generally Known to Be in Service with the South African Defense Forces (End 1976)

Item	Manufactured/Licensed by	Deliveries
Lockheed F-104G Starfighter/ bomber	U,S./ex-Luftwaffe	40
North American F-51D Cavalier counter insurgency strike	U.S.	50
Aerospatiale/Westland 341 Gazelle General purpose helicopter	France/U.K.	2 (?)
Agusta-Bell 205A Iroquois utility/s.r. helicopter	U.S.	25
Lockheed P-2 Neptune antisubmarine patrol	U.S.	12
Centurion Mk 10 heavy tank	U.K.	240
M-47 Patton main battle tank	U.S./Italy	100
M-41 Walker Bulldog light tank	U.S.	100
AMX-13 light tank	France	80
M-113A1 armored personnel carrier	U.S./Italy	(400)
Commando V-150 armored personnel carrier	U.S./Portugal	(300)
Piranha armored personnel carrier	Switzerland	(100)
Shorland Mk3 armored car	U.K.	(200)
Short SB 301 armored personnel carrier	U.K.	(300)
Sexton 25 pdr self-propelled gun	Canada	200
M-7 105mm self-propelled gun	U.S.	200
M-109 155 mm self-propelled gun	U.S./Italy	(50)

Source: Sean Gervasi, testimony to U.S. Congress, House, Committee on International Relations, subcommittee on Africa, July 1977. Also cited in *Military Balance,* 1976-1977, p45.
Figures in brackets indicate orders on which delivery continues. 1. In service with the South African Police.

Table 20: Arms Inventory: South African Defense Forces (End 1976)

	IISS	Gervasi
Combat aircraft	133	625
Helicopters	92	215
Tanks	161	525
Armored Cars	1,050	1,430
Armored Personnel Carriers	250	960
Self-propelled guns	not listed	294
Medium and light artillery	not available	380

Source: Sean Gervasi, "The Breakdown of the Arms embargo against South Africa," testimony to the U.S Congress, House Committee on International Relations, Subcommittee on Africa. July 14, 1977. Also cited in *Military Balance,* 1976-1977 p.45.

These statistics reveal that Western European countries including the United States and Canada have practically been supporting apartheid South Africa, while pretending to condemn it. They have armed South Africa more than the rest of Africa. These arms sold to South Africa are beyond the needs of its internal security. The only conclusion one can draw is that these arms are being stockpiled with the hope that they will be used against African states that support the Pan-Africanist Congress and the African National Congress freedom fighters in their struggle for national liberation. Because of this massive Western military aid, South Africa has built an enormous military capability. In his study of comparative military studies, Sean Gervasi revealed the following:

Table 21: Comparative Strength of Selected Armed Forces (End 1976)

		Iran	Brazil	Egypt	Japan	South Africa[1]
Total Armed Forces	(000s)	281	254	322	236	130
Combat Aircraft		450	190	600	500+	625
Helicopters		125	50+	160	not available	215
Tanks		1,990	350+	1,975	750	525
Armored Cars		not available	120	100	not available	1,430
Armored Personnel Carriers		1,960	500	2,500	460	960
Self-propelled Guns		not specified	not specified	200	660	294

Sources: *Defense and Foreign Affairs Handbook 1976-77*, Washington, D.C., and London, 1977, and various industry sources. 1. Estimate by the author based on South African source material. South Africa can mobilize 200,000 men within two days in an emergency.

Table 22: Major Weapons Systems in Service with the South African Regular Army (Early 1977)

Centurion Mk 10 tank	180	1967-1968
Panhard AML 245 H60 armored car	800	Produced under license
Panhard AML 245 H90 armored car	170	Produced under license
Daimler Ferret Mk 2 with Vigilant ATGW	160	1968-1969
Saracen armored personnel carrier	280	1962-1966
Commando V-150 armored personnel carrier	110	post-1971
Piranha armored personnel carrier	?	delivery beginning 1973-1974
M-113A.1 armored personnel carrier	150	delivery continuing
Sexton 25 pdr self-propelled gun	150	1946
M-109 155mm self-propelled gun	24	1972-1973
Shorland Mk 3 armored car	60	delivery continuing
M-47 Patton tank*	70	1971

Source: *Southern African Perspective:* Africa Fund, New York November 8, 1977,
* Assigned to the Citizen Force, but major equipment.

The United Nations Security Council's arms embargo against South Africa came at a time when American and European countries had significantly strengthened the South African defense system. Although the passage of this Council's resolution is a victory to African diplomacy at the United Nations, it is doubtful whether their desired goals will be achieved. What is unfortunate about this arms embargo resolution is that it does not demand the revocation of existing licensing agreements under which South Africa continues to produce some of its most sophisticated weaponry. American and French military planes, guns, and other NATO weapons continue to be produced in South Africa. The weakness of the resolution is that it only calls for UN member countries to review their existing contracts and licenses granted to South Africa to manufacture specified weapons or spare parts. The weapons being manufactured by South Africa are increasingly strengthening the pernicious apartheid political system that has been condemned and described by the General Assembly and the Security Council as one of the worst crimes against humanity and an abhorrence to the conscience of mankind.

In addition to the regular conventional military weapons the United Kingdom, France, West Germany, the United States, Italy, Canada, and Israel supply to South Africa, these countries also provide the apartheid state with nuclear technological know-how to build nuclear reactors and bombs. Nuclear reactors that are in operation today and atomic bombs both operate on the principle of nuclear fission, the splitting of a large atom to release energy. The fuel most prevalently used in nuclear reactors and bombs is uranium-235 (U^{235}), an isotope of "natural" uranium-238 (U^{238}), and plutonium-239 (Pu^{239}), a by-product of the fissioning of a U^{235} atom. The fission process occurs when the nucleus of a U^{235} or Pu^{239} atom is bombarded by a neutron, a neutrally charged particle, causing the nucleus to split apart, releasing energy in the form of heat, three additional neutrons, and fission by-products. (See equation 1 and 2).

$$\text{eq} \quad 1: \quad U^{235} \quad + \text{neutron} = \text{Heat} + \text{3n's} + \text{fission by-products}$$
$$\text{eq} \quad 2: \quad Pu^{239} \quad + \text{neutron} = \text{Heat} + \text{neutrons} + \text{fission by-products}$$
$$\text{eq} \quad 3: \quad U^{238} \quad + \text{neutron} = Pu^{239}$$

The fission process is sustained by what is called a chain reaction, in which the additional neutrons released in the fission process strike other U^{235} or Pu^{239} atoms, and the process repeats itself. Plutonium is formed when the "liberated" neutrons are absorbed by U^{238} and is converted into Pu^{239}.

Uranium, in order to be used as fuel, must first be mined and processed. Of the two isotopes of uranium that are found naturally in the earth's crust, 99.3 percent is of the isotope U^{238}, whereas the remaining 0.7 percent is U^{235}. Since uranium exists as an ore, the rock bearing the ore must be mined and eventually separated from the uranium. This is accomplished by crushing the ore-bearing rock and subjecting it to a chemical process. The uranium is separated as a yellow powder called *yellowcake*. South Africa's useful uranium deposits amount to 163,000 tons and Namibia, illegally occupied by South Africa, possesses 100,000 tons together amounting to 20 percent of the world's economically recoverable uranium[1]. In 1972, South Africa produced about 4,128 tons of refined uranium[2], and in 1973 it earned $53 million selling uranium[3].

The concentration of 0.7 percent U^{235} found naturally in uranium ore is not sufficient to sustain a chain reaction. In nuclear reactors, a concentration of 3 percent U^{235} is needed, whereas a bomb normally uses 90 percent U^{235} and higher.[134] Thus, the uranium must be enriched; that is, bringing up the concentration of U^{235} in the uranium fuel. This is done by converting the uranium yellowcake into a gas, and through the use of centrifuges or jet nozzles, U^{235} is separated from U^{238} This process is technically complicated, very energy-intensive, and extremely expensive. The process must be repeated several times in order to bring the concentration up to the desired level, as extremely small amounts of U^{235} are separated in one passing. Thus, any country possessing an enrichment facility can manufacture nuclear weapons. South Africa has such a facility at Valindaba, which it acquired by collaborating with West German scientists.

After the uranium is enriched, the gas is reconverted into a solid form, and is manufactured into fuel pellets. The pellets are inserted into long tubes called *fuel rods*, and the fuel rods are packed together in fuel bundles. The fuel bundles are placed into the core of a nuclear reactor where a critical mass is obtained. A critical mass is the necessary amount of fuel to initiate a chain reaction. Once this is achieved, the fission process takes place, releasing heat that converts water into steam, which turns a turbine that produces electricity. South Africa currently operates two small research reactors fueled with weapons-grade uranium (over 90 percent enriched), and is building two 1,000 megawatt (MW) reactors at Koeberg. After a while, the U^{235} in the fuel pellets become depleted. The fuel bundles are removed and temporarily stored, so that some of the radioactive by-products (fission products) can decay into stable elements. Among these radioactive by-products is Pu^{239}, which can be used to manufacture nuclear bombs.

The African group and other Third World countries at the United Nations recognize the military and political significance of South Africa's acquisition of nuclear technology to make bombs. The acquisition of nuclear capability by South Africa will not only make it enforce apartheid efficiently but it will also enable South Africa to threaten militarily any African state that might want to aid South African blacks to achieve majority rule. The acquisition of nuclear weapons capability by South Africa and the collaboration of several technologically advanced Western nations in promoting such nuclear potential have long been of concern to the Special Committee against Apartheid and to the General Assembly. Since 1974, the General Assembly with pressure from the African group has requested all its member states to discontinue all nuclear cooperation with South Africa. In October 1977, the subcommittee on apartheid submitted a draft resolution sponsored by the African group, which would have called on all states to refrain from any cooperation with South Africa in nuclear development, but it was vetoed in the Security Council by Britain, France, and the United States. However, in November 1977, the Security Council, acting under Chapter VII of the United Nations Charter, passed Resolution 418, of which paragraph 4 calls for all states to refrain from any cooperation with South Africa in the manufacture and development of nuclear weapons. Security Council Resolution 418 is totally inadequate, unless the trade in nuclear materials out of which such nuclear weapons are manufactured becomes the central concern. The crucial issue of trade in nuclear materials can only be effectively dealt with until a vigorous program against economic collaboration between South Africa and its major Western supplier states is enforced. In the final analysis, it is the support and cooperation that major nuclear supplier countries lend to South Africa through their multinational corporation and government institutions which are helping to defeat the political aspirations of the African majority in South Africa.

Of all the Western nations that have provided nuclear technology and materials to South Africa, the United States shares the greatest responsibility. The United States was the first country to enter into uranium trade and other nuclear transactions with South Africa. The United States has violated all the Security Council and General Assembly resolutions on arms embargo against South Africa. In August 1957, an agreement governing American and South African relations in the peaceful use of atomic energy came into force. The agreement provided for the free exchange of information, other than restricted information, on peaceful applications of nuclear energy, and the United States agreed for ten years to sell to the government of South Africa uranium enriched up to 20 percent and upon request 90 percent enriched uranium for research purposes. The agreement provided for this sale in amounts not "in excess of the amount of material necessary for the full loading of each defined reactor project . . . plus such additional quantity as . . . is necessary to permit the efficient and continuous operations of such reactors, with a ceiling of 500 kgs."[135]

In 1961, the US Atomic Energy Commission granted an export license to the Allis-Chalmers Manufacturing Company to export a 5 megawatt thermal (as opposed to electric) research reactor to South Africa. This reactor, named Safari-1 was built at South Africa's National Nuclear Research Centre at Pelindaba, near Pretoria, and began operating in 1965. In 1968, the reactor was shut down and enlarged to a 20 megawatt thermal capacity, and reopened in 1969. Most exports transferred under the nuclear cooperation agreement consisted of uranium fuel (93 percent maximum enriched) for the Safari-1 reactor. The United States also exported about 12,000 pounds of heavy water (D_2O) in 1964, and 606 kgs of low enriched uranium in 1966 and 1967 for use in another research reactor, Pelindaba-Zero, which the South Africans built themselves and opened in 1967. This reactor is not covered by IAEA safeguards.[136]

In 1974, South Africa decided to embark upon a nuclear energy program for electrical generation. It ordered two 1,000 megawatt reactors that were to be built at Koeberg. The United States government refused the export request of General Electric to supply enriched uranium to these reactors. Later, the American government agreed to supply the necessary enriched uranium to power South African reactors after it had amended the initial agreement for cooperation. The amendment set forth the framework for the long-term supply of enriched uranium fuel, and extended the agreement to the year 2004. However, when the South Africans decided to buy the two reactors from a French consortium, it also contracted the French government to supply the first several loads of enriched uranium fuel.

Between 1965 and 1975, the United States supplied 104 kgs of highly enriched uranium to South Africa's Safari-1 reactor; "25 kgs have been burned up; through 1974, about 29 kgs have been transferred to the United Kingdom (UK) and 5 kgs in spent fuel to France; 12 kgs in spent fuel have been returned to the U.S. in 1976 and 1977;

approximately 5.5 kgs are in the reactor itself, about 23 kgs are in spent fuel in cooling, and 4.5 kgs are in fresh fuel."[137] There is an export license pending for 26 kgs of more enriched uranium.

In 1976, the United States halted its shipments of weapons-grade uranium to South Africa in an attempt to force it to sign the non proliferation treaty. A year later, the Carter administration considered imposing a ban on all shipments of nuclear fuel to South Africa in order to persuade South Africa to sign the treaty. This ban, however, was never imposed. President Carter sent his special envoy on nuclear nonproliferation in June 1978, to South Africa, presumably to negotiate the terms for South Africa's signing the treaty. To this date, South Africa has still not signed this treaty.

The United States was not alone in continuing to violate General Assembly and Security Council resolutions on arms embargo against South Africa. France, West Germany, and the United Kingdom have also assisted South Africa in developing its nuclear fuel cycle. It has also been alleged that Israel has had some exchange with South Africa in its nuclear research program. These states have, in turn, received the necessary knowledge and technology to develop their own nuclear programs from the United States through the Atoms for Peace Program. Thus, the United States has been at the root of all nuclear development in South Africa.

The French, once they acquired the know-how of nuclear technology, have aggressively pursued nuclear development in their own country, and have tried to become a leading exporter of nuclear technology. When it became apparent that the United States would not allow the export of reactors to South Africa, the French jumped at the opportunity. Through its consortium Framatome (of which Westinghouse, a US corporation owns 15 percent) France sold South Africa two 1,000 megawatt reactors. These reactors will add only about 10 percent to South Africa's electrical generating capacity, while providing the South Africans with another source of plutonium in their nuclear fuel cycle. The reactor itself and the shipments of fuel to it are to be covered by IAEA safeguards.

The West Germans, who also gained their initial knowledge of nuclear technology from the United States, embarked on a similar independent nuclear research program and ultimately devised their own uranium enrichment process. West Germany is currently the second largest exporter of nuclear technology behind the United States. In 1970, the South Africans announced to the world that they were developing their own uranium enrichment process. In 1975, when the South Africans revealed the technology behind their process, it looked surprisingly similar to the West Germans. The African National Congress (ANC) has documented evidence of collaboration between South Africa and the West German Government, and their respective scientists in the development of South Africa's uranium enrichment program. This indicates that this program was a covert attempt on the part of the West Germans to develop nuclear weapons, as they are forbidden by treaty to do so on their own territory. The ANC also revealed information concerning West German collaboration with South Africa in developing a missile system capable of delivering nuclear weapons. In light of this extensive cooperation with South Africa it is interesting to note that West Germany receives about 40 percent of its natural uranium from South Africa.[138]

The British made their major contribution to the South African nuclear fuel cycle by helping South Africa develop a uranium mining industry and by providing enriched uranium for the Safari-1 research reactor. In return, Britain received uranium for its nuclear weapons program. Joined by the French and the Germans, the British helped finance the establishment of the Rossing uranium mines in Namibia. The uranium obtained from these mines is being exported to Western Europe, in defiance of all United Nations resolutions on arms embargo against South Africa. However, it is clear that these nations' nuclear programs not only reinforce the white minority regime's hold over South Africa but also over Namibia in violation of Security Council and General Assembly resolutions. In can, therefore, be argued that the transfer of nuclear materials directly reflects on that particular country's favorable policy toward the country which is acquiring nuclear technology.

American multinational corporations currently dominate the market in nuclear technology. Three firms, Allis-Chalmers, General Electric, and Westinghouse have built 70.8 percent of the world's nuclear electrical generating capacity as of 1974. Each of these firms has contributed to the development of South Africa's nuclear fuel cycle; Allis-Chalmers supplied South Africa with its first research reactor; General Electric almost provided South Africa with its first two large-scale nuclear power plants, and its overseas Capital Corporation owns 12 percent of the German nuclear consortium, Kraftwerk Union, which has been conducting nuclear business with the South Africans.[139] Westinghouse, as a part of the French consortium, Framatome, is building the two nuclear reactors that General Electric was to provide. In other areas of the nuclear fuel cycle, U.S. Nuclear, Inc., of Oak Ridge, Tennessee, has been the major supplier of enriched uranium to South Africa. Additional suppliers of enriched uranium and other nuclear materials to South Africa include Gulf Oil Corporation of San Diego, California; United States Steel Corp.; Texas Nuclear Corp.; and Gulf General Atomic.[140] The Foxboro Corporation sold two computers for use in South Africa's enrichment facility at Valindaba, which are essential to its operation; these computers probably could not have been obtained elsewhere. International Business Machines (IBM) has sold computers to the South African Atomic Energy Board for personnel radiation systems, drawing record systems, and fuel management systems.[141]

French multinational corporations have been involved in developing uranium mining concerns and providing South Africa with two nuclear power plants. The French multinational firm Total owns a 10 percent share of the Rossing uranium mines in Namibia.[142] The French consortium Framatome is building the Koeberg nuclear plants. Until 1977, Westinghouse owned 45 percent of Framatome. However, as a result of pressure from the French government, Westinghouse was forced to reduce its share in Framatome to 15 percent. As compensation for this reduction, Westinghouse was to receive five hundred thousand pounds of uranium to be delivered annually at a price of $18 a pound (uranium now sells for $43 a pound), and Framatome also agreed to market Westinghouse reactors produced in the United States.[143] This illustrates the extent of indirect American involvement in international nuclear technology markets, and the underlying political pressures on decisions made in the United States over the export of nuclear technology.

The major contributions by West German multinational corporations were in the development of uranium mines and the establishment of an enrichment plant. The firms Krupp and BBC also assisted in the construction of the Safari-1 reactor. The West German firm, Urangesellschaft, which is two-thirds controlled by the West German government, has a 15-20 percent share in the Rossing mines.[144] The uranium enrichment project was developed by the state-owned Society for Nuclear Research, the state controlled company STEAG, and the MAN Company. The financing for this plant is expected either to come directly from the West German government or STEAG, or indirectly from parties that may benefit from the plant, including the Brazilians, who have ordered two nuclear plants from the German multinational Kraftwerk Union (KWU). KWU also bidded for the contract to construct the two Keoberg plants.

British multinational corporations have been involved with the South African nuclear fuel cycle since 1952. The African Explosives and Chemical Industries, a subsidiary of the Imperial Chemical Industries, Ltd., "played an important part in the development of the seventeen uranium extraction units and their attendant sulphuric acid plants."[145] The British firm, Rio Tinto Zinc, has a 25 percent share in the Rossing mines.

Some of the most important sources of the international transfers of technology lie in the sharing and discussion of results of scientific research. By attending scientific IAEA conferences in Western countries, the South African scientists gained indispensable Western nuclear knowledge to develop their own nuclear programs. The scientific community is a major force to reckon with in international nuclear politics since it is the most important vehicle through which scientific data is developed, regulated, and disseminated. It also informs its national leaders about strategic and nonstrategic use of its research data.

Scientific exchange programs between the United States and South Africa were a part of the Agreement for Cooperation in nuclear energy development. South Africa had the assistance of more than 150 visiting American scientists, as well as the assignment in the United States of 90 South African nuclear scientists.[146] A more serious consequence of scientific exchange in the nuclear field surfaced in congressional hearings, where it was alleged that the South African government tried to place its scientists in high-level research programs on laser isotope separation, a technology that portends to significantly reduce the cost and technical difficulty of uranium enrichment. Commenting on how South Africa acquired its nuclear technology, Abraham Roux, the president of the South African Atomic Energy Board, enthusiastically stated:

> We can ascribe our degree of advancement today in large measure to the training and assistance so willingly provided by the United States of America during the early years of our nuclear programme when several of the worlds nuclear nations cooperated in initiating our scientists and engineers into nuclear science.[147]

Parenthetically, South Africa gained the ability to develop its pilot enrichment plant at Valindaba by means of similar contacts with West German scientists working on the Becker nozzle enrichment process. While high-level South African scientists were assigned to special training at the West German Nuclear Research Center at

Karlsruhe, West German high-level diplomats were discussing with Abraham Roux about the future basis for nuclear cooperation. For a time in 1970, the German inventor of the Becker nozzle enrichment process worked in South Africa. In 1975, when the South African enrichment process was revealed to the world, it looked remarkably similar to the one developed by Becker. Roux admitted that the basis of the South African process, the vortex tube, was the one developed by Becker.

South Africa became a member of the IAEA in 1957. Some of the IAEA's functions are to foster the exchange of scientific and technical information on the peaceful uses of atomic energy; and to encourage the exchange and training of scientists and experts in the peaceful uses of atomic energy.[148] South Africa was on the board of governors of the IAEA from 1957 to December 1979, when the general conference voted to bar it from further IAEA proceedings. South Africa received $107,800 in technical assistance, until January 1975, from the IAEA for the training of fellows.[149] South Africa was thus able to further the development of its nuclear fuel cycle through its active participation in the IAEA.

The Western supply of nuclear technology as outlined is definitely undermining the African Group and the General Assembly and Security Council resolutions on the imposition of arms embargoes against South Africa. While the major Western suppliers of nuclear technology have all supported the UN Security Council Resolution 418 including its operative paragraph 4 forbidding the sale or sharing of nuclear technology with South Africa, they have, however, acted contrary to the letter and spirit of that resolution. While the West may be accruing short-term economic benefits from supplying new technology and material to South Africa, the long-term effects of these relationships are likely to be adverse within the next decade. With many new nuclear facilities coming into operation in South Africa, the apartheid state will be in a position to join the potential supplier states and the Western nuclear powers will lose much of the leverage derived from trade they currently have. The Western proliferation of nuclear technology into South Africa is definitely inimical to Western trade and also a threat to the maintenance of peace and security in the southern African region.

The United Nations member states and agencies within the UN system that are opposed to apartheid should be extremely concerned with Western nuclear proliferation in South Africa since the arming of that apartheid state undermines the basis of Chapter VII of the United Nations Charter. In the early 1960s, the documentation in the United Nations on apartheid following the Sharpeville massacre of 1960 and the 1963 arms embargo on South Africa revealed that the violation of human rights and the probable eruption of a race war in the region constituted the major reasons upon which oppressive South Africa was adjudged a threat to international peace and security. Today, it should be clear to the world community as repeatedly argued by the African Group that the basis for a threat to international peace and security under Article 39 of the United Nations charter has been actualized by the existence of nuclear weapons in South Africa. It is, therefore, imperative upon the United Nations members including the United States, France, Britain, West Germany, and Israel to join the African Group and the rest of the Third World nations in effectively imposing United Nations General Assembly and Security Council resolutions prohibiting the supply of arms, nuclear weapons, and nuclear technology to South

Africa. The African group, the General Assembly, the Security Council, and other agencies of the United Nations system have condemned apartheid as the worst crime against humanity and an abhorrence to the conscience of mankind.

While frustrations exist over the continued violations by Western UN member states, of Security Council Resolution 418 of November 1977, and its operative paragraph 4 on the ban of supplies of nuclear technology to South Africa, United Nations member states have nevertheless agreed on some measures for action to terminate apartheid in the world community. South African apartheid in sports is one such measure that African states at the United Nations and in the world community have targeted for action. For the first time in the history of the United Nations, on December 2, 1968, the General Assembly adopted Resolution 2396, which requested all United Nations members and organizations to suspend educational, cultural, sport, and other exchanges with the South African government and its institutions or organizations. In subsequent resolutions, the General Assembly went on to declare its support for

> the Olympic principle that no discrimination be permitted on the grounds of race, religion or political affiliation; condemned the actions of the South African Government in enforcing racial discrimination or segregation in sports; and called for the cessation of exchanges with South African sports teams selected in violation of the Olympic principles.[150]

In addition to its condemnation of apartheid in sports, the United Nations has established the Special Committee Against Apartheid, which holds a watching brief and reports to the General Assembly on the progress of the worldwide campaign against apartheid. With pressure from this committee, the African Group then submitted a draft report on the International Declaration Against Apartheid in Sports that was adopted by the General Assembly.[151] The pressure of the African group among UN members has made it possible for many countries to boycott sports against South Africa. Even in Western Europe, the United States, Canada, and some South American countries where South Africa has traditionally competed in sports, many people are now advocating an end to this association with South Africa. Committees to oppose sports against apartheid have mushroomed throughout the world and are exerting pressure on their governments to stop holding sports events with teams from South Africa. The Committee against Apartheid holds seminars, disseminates information against apartheid, and constantly requests all UN member states to boycott sports with South Africa. This committee also pays special attention to those countries that are not implementing the Security Council and General Assembly resolutions against apartheid and apartheid in sports.

The international sports boycott against South Africa has been successful in mobilizing international attention and concern on the issue of apartheid, and in raising the morale of the oppressed Africans by making them aware of international support and solidarity in their struggle for majority rule. Through pressure from Afro-Asian countries and their allies, a majority of the United Nations member states are constantly boycotting sports with South Africa. By 1975, the following few countries were still involved with apartheid in sports: Argentina in rugby; Britain in golf, tennis, croquet, skating, and yachting; Chile in tennis; Denmark in yachting; Canada in trampolining; France in golf, tennis, and yachting; United States in karate, tennis, women's hockey, golf, and yachting; Thailand in golf; El Salvador in polo; and West Germany in golf, skating, gymnastics, and tennis.

The International Olympic Committee (IOC) has championed the campaign against apartheid South African participation in the Olympic Games. Because of African and Asian states' opposition to apartheid and South Africa's continued participation in the Olympic Games, in 1963 the OIC stipulated that before South Africa would be allowed to participate in the Olympics, it should satisfy the following requirements: 1. It must formally declare its acceptance of the spirit of the Olympic Charter and in particular Rules 1 and 24 (the rules relating to nondiscrimination and forbidding government interference); and 2, it must get its government to modify its policy of racial discrimination in sports in South Africa.[152] South Africa made no attempt to satisfy the cited stipulations and this forced the OIC to bar it from participating in most Olympic Games.

While influencing many countries to boycott apartheid in sports, the Special Committee against Apartheid's previous chairperson, and former Ambassador of Guinea to the United Nations, Jeanne-Martin Cisse, also tried to dynamize the activities of her committee through extensive contacts with many supranational organizations:

> On 4 and 5 of February, I held detailed discussions with the leaders of the Organization of African Trade Union Unity (OATUU) aimed at ensuring greater coordination in the struggle against *apartheid.* On behalf of the Committee, I paid a special tribute to OATUU for its efforts to make all African countries observe the boycott of South Africa, for instance with regard to facilities for airlines and ships going to or returning from South Africa. Mr. J.D. Akumu, Secretary-General of OATUU, told me about the Programme of work his organization with respect to the boycott of South Africa, and also informed me that OATUU planned to hold a conference in Dar-es-Salaam, probably in June prior to the OAU summit meeting in Mauritius, and expressed the hope that the Special Committee would be represented at the conference. He suggested that the Special Committee and OATUU should cooperate in the following areas: (a) research (b) the organization of joint meetings to plan actions against South Africa, and (c) the dispatch of joint delegations to certain countries in Europe and Asia in order to discourage investment in South Africa and the recruitment of white workers by the South African regime. I assured Mr. Akumu that the Special Committee would give serious consideration to his suggestions.[153]

After holding discussions on what the Committee against Apartheid could do to increase international support against this pernicious political system, Cisse noted:

> First, in view of the importance of the actual and potential contribution of the Arab States to the struggle against apartheid, I suggest that the Special Committee should invite the League of Arab States to be represented in the Committee by an observer. Secondly, the suggestion had been made during my various consultations that the Special Committee should extend its consultations on the embargo on the sale of oil and petroleum products to South Africa by visiting the headquarters of the Organization of Petroleum-Exporting Countries and also by engaging in direct consultations with other oil-producing States, such as Iran, which provides substantial quantities of oil to South Africa, and countries such as Venezuela,

which South Africa might approach as alternative sources of oil. I suggest that that proposal should be studied by the Working Group prior to discussion in the Special Committee. Thirdly, I wish to put forward the suggestion that the Working Group and the Secretariat should maintain close contact with the Organization of African Trade Union Unity and the Afro-Asian People's Solidarity Organization, especially with regard to conferences they are planning to hold, at which the Special Committee might consider being represented. Fourthly, in the light of my consultations, I think it would be useful for the Director of the Centre against *Apartheid* or the Secretary of the Special Committee to visit Cairo and Accra in due course to work out various practical arrangements concerning cooperation between the Committee and various organizations. In this connection, I wish to suggest that the Working Group be authorized to look into that matter. And fifthly, I think that the Working Group should also be authorized to study the various recommendations made by the organizations I consulted.[154]

In her efforts to maximize the activities of the Special Committee against Apartheid, Ambassador Cisse held discussions with the secretary-general of the Commonwealth countries, Shridath Ramphal, in London on January 28, 1976. After this, Ramphal reiterated that the Commonwealth had agreed with the United Nations on its firm committment to eliminate apartheid. While elaborating on the activities and plans of the Commonwealth Secretariat with respect to the oppressed people of Zimbabwe and Namibia, Ramphal further expressed his appreciation of the vigorous efforts of Ambassador Cisse's committee to promote international action against colonialism.

At the invitation of the Secretary-General (Youssef El Sabai) of the Afro-Asian Peoples' Solidarity Organization (AAPSO), Ambassador Cisse visited the AAPSO headquarters in Cairo, Egypt on January 31, 1976. Although both Cisse and El Sabai expressed satisfaction over the escalating isolation and the ever-increasing condemnation of apartheid South Africa by the international community, they noted that South Africa's trading associates continued to reap huge profits from apartheid, at the expense of the oppressed Africans. They also raised the issue of violations of the United Nations resolutions against apartheid by some of the members of the United Nations. In addition, the AAPSO greatly appreciated the role played by the Special Committee against Apartheid, in its work through the United Nations system and other intergovernmental and nongovernmental organizations and forums.

While she was in Cairo, Ambassador Cisse held meetings with the secretary-general of the League of Arab States on January 31, 1976. During these discussions, Cisse emphasized the following:

Firstly, the necessity of extending the information campaign against the *apartheid* policy adopted by the South African regime and making known the effects and consequences of such an ill favored policy; and secondly, the necessity of strengthening the measures that lead to isolating South Africa, especially in the economic sphere.

She expressed the United Nations Committee's appreciation of the resolution adopted by the Arab League's Council not to establish any diplomatic, economic and trade relations with South Africa. She hailed as well all the efforts exerted by the Arab League and its member states to support the Committee's campaign aiming at the eradication of the *apartheid* policy.

The Arab League Secretary-General reiterated the interest of the Arab States in the eradication of *apartheid* and their solidarity with the African countries in this domain at all the international forums including the United Nations, the Non-aligned Movement, Arab/African cooperation organizations and the Islamic conferences.

He pointed out that the Arab peoples share with the Africans in suffering from the *apartheid* policy, and consider zionism one of its forms.

He further stressed that the Arab States adhere to all the resolutions aimed at achieving the objectives of the United Nations Special Committee against *Apartheid*. [155]

Another delegation of the Special Committee against Apartheid led by Ambassador Cisse paid a visit to the secretary-general (J. D. Akumu) of the Organization of African Trade Union Unity (OATUU) in Accra, Ghana. At the end of these discussions, Cisse commended the OATUU for its efforts to combat racism, racial discrimination, and the policy of apartheid. The two organizations also appealed to the African countries that still provide air and sea facilities to the foreign aircraft and vessels bound for or coming from South Africa to cease these facilities immediately.

Many conferences organized and hosted by the Special Committee have taken place in other countries including Cuba and Nigeria. Apartheid is now universally condemned all over the world, and calls for further political and economic sanctions against South Africa are commonplace.

The Special Committee against Apartheid has also been active on the state of African health in apartheid South Africa. On March 22, 1977, the World Health Organization (WHO) submitted its report on African Mental Health in South Africa to the Special Committee on Apartheid. In summing up its study, the WHO made four allegations about privately provided mental health care for Africans:

(i) The institutions, run by a private enterprise known as Smith, Mitchell & Company, keep in custody an exceedingly large number of Africans, admitted on an involuntary basis through a perfunctory legal and medical procedure.

(ii) The standards of care provided and the living conditions of the patients in these institutions are extremely poor and degrading, not only in comparison with the standards of mental health care ensured for the white population, but also in relation to the most elementary and essential human needs and rights.

(iii) There is a collusion of interest between the private companies and the State, in the sense that the companies are making profit using the Government subsidies, while the Government is spending through this arrangement less than it would have to if mental health care would be provided entirely by the state health services.

(iv) The chain of private institutions for mentally ill black Africans is a tool for human rights oppression and racial discrimination in the field of health care under the apartheid system. [156]

It is not uncommon in South Africa for that government to detain Africans and to declare them mentally ill even though they may not be so. Whites who own private mental institutions in South Africa are generally active in requesting the detention of more and more Africans into their institutions.

Since the private institutions for African patients are operated on a profit-making basis, depending on the number of patients detained, and since the patients are admitted under involuntary provisions (thereby reducing) the burden on the State services, the system is technically open to abuse and is the manifestation of socially harmful policies in the area of health. Such policies, however, are part and parcel of the over all doctrine and practice of apartheid, and racial improvements of the present situation in the mental health services are inconceivable as long as apartheid remains in force.[157]

These African victims of apartheid are the objects of business deals between the repressive government of South Africa and the unscrupulous profit-making white-owned companies that receive government subsidies calculated on a per capita basis. The so-called mental instititutions are more of detention or Hitler-like concentration camps than they are mental institutions. According to the South African government Proclamation on Rehabilitation Institutions in the Bantu Homelands as defined in paragraph 5 of the Proclamation:

> The inmates of an institution shall be detained therein for the purpose of improving their physical, mental and moral condition by:
> (a) training them in habits of industry and work;
> (b) re-orientating them to the traditions, culture, custom and system of government of the national unit to which they belong;
> (c) generally cultivating in them habits of social adaptation in the community and of good citizenship, including the fostering of an awareness in regard to the observance of, and the necessity for, the laws of the country.[158]

This Proclamation implies that any African who does not accept the obnoxious South African apartheid laws is mentally disturbed and in need of compulsory improvement of his or her physical, mental, and moral condition. This deplorable state of human torture and subjugation of the Africans is a great concern to African states, the Special Committee against Apartheid, and the United Nations and its various organs and agencies.

African states have also campaigned extensively at the United Nations against South Africa's continued infringement of the United Nations Universal Declaration of Human Rights. By passing many obnoxious and insulting laws, South Africa ensures that its vigorous crusade to deprive Africans from having any form of human rights and dignity are successful. Africans are subjected to subhuman conditions of living under this iniquitous apartheid government. Discrimination in South Africa is total. Under the Reservation of Separate Amenities Act, no. 49 of 1953, the Motor Transportation Amendment Act, no. 44 of 1953, the State-Aided Institutions Amendment Act, no. 46 of 1957, the General Law Amendment Act, of 1963, the Criminal Law and Procedure Amendment Act, no. 96 of 1965, and Group Areas Act, no. 36 of 1966, all the racial populations in South Africa are forceably kept apart in trains, buses, taxis, parks, museums, zoos, theaters, cinemas, art galleries, hotels, restaurants, post offices, and other public places.

Africans suffer most from the discriminatory laws and other arbitrary regulations that have been imposed on them by the South African president, prime minister, legislature, judiciary, and police force. For example; when the South African president (who acts on the advice of the prime minister and cabinet, which is, in turn, advised by the minister of Bantu administration) in his unfettered discretion finds or considers it fit to issue what he terms a pertinent proclamation, an African who has been required by a court order to leave a certain area must do so, and no court of law may grant an injunction prohibiting such removal, even when it has been established beyond reasonable doubt that the court order was served upon that African in error. A non-African, however, can be granted an injunction, or a stay of the removal order. Because of these abuses, the United Nations General assembly, through pressure from nonaligned states, approved on November 2, 1973, a Program for a Decade of Action to Combat Racism and Racial Discrimination to begin on December 10, 1973, a date which marks the twenty-fifth anniversary of the adoption of the Universal Declaration of Human Rights. While condemning apartheid and denials of freedom to the African majority, the Universal Declaration of Human Rights called upon the world community to use its resources in promoting civil rights in South Africa.

The United Nations and world opinion are against the continued violation of the United Nations Universal Declaration of Human Rights provisions by apartheid South Africa. All over the world, movements and associations in opposition to apartheid have mushroomed. Some of these international nongovernmental organizations are Amnesty International, Association Internationale des Juristes Democrates, International Commission of Jurists, International Defense and Aid Fund, International Union of Socialist Youth, International Union of Students, International University Exchange Fund, International Federation for Human Rights, Friendship World Committee for Consultation, International Council of Social Democratic Women, International Federation of Women Lawyers, Union des Avocates Arabes, World University Service, World Peace Council, World Federation of World Federalists, Women International League for Peace and Freedom, and World Young Women's Christian Association. In addition, numerous national nongovernmental organizations are also intensifying their condemnation of the gross violation of human rights in South Africa. The struggle for the attainment of human rights in South Africa is now a United Nations issue as well as that of the world community.

Efforts by the African Group to force South Africa to change its policies of apartheid have been centered on the diplomatic isolation of that country from the rest of the community of nations. The Organization of African Unity (OAU) has made important contributions. At its establishment, the OAU was committed to the overthrow of the apartheid state and subsequently made an impact on the practice and procedures of the United Nations system. But, even before the creation of the OAU, there were indications in the General Assembly of the United Nations of a changing mood and a shift in the balance of power. In one of the first signs that the African Group and the Third World majority of the world community would no longer tolerate South Africa's open advocacy of apartheid, the General Assembly, in 1961, in one of its rare acts of intolerance censured the foreign minister of South Africa, Eric Louw at its sixteenth session by a vote of sixty-seven to one with twenty abstentions. This was an unprecedented step for the General Assembly to take in trying to isolate South Africa diplomatically. David A. Kay was even more dramatic when he graphically described this unprecedented step in which he blamed South Africa for having "voluntarily placed itself outside the community of nations envisaged in the Charter and, therefore, had no grounds to ask for the normal respect of divergent opinions that usually marked United Nations proceedings."[159]

Activities of the General Assembly in isolating and expelling South Africa from many agencies of the UN system have been important in evolving new rules of international law. After the General Assembly had passed in 1963 its resolution on economic, military, sporting, and cultural sanctions against South Africa, the OAU's African Group and other Third World countries took specific steps to sever their links with South Africa. Although the General Assembly's arms and economic embargo against South Africa was aimed at isolating it politically, economically, and militarily, it also gave a more realistic interpretation of the provisions of the UN Charter in keeping with both changes in the international community and international customary law. These developments in the United Nations and its treaty laws and resolutions have added new dimensions to the apartheid issue. What this implies is that conventional international lawyers and those states that continue to accrue profits from their trade and investments in South Africa can no longer continue to justify their actions as legal.

Concerning the evolution of new norms in international law, Kader Asmal of the Irish Anti-Apartheid movement was convincingly persuasive when he wrote the following:

> Resolutions of the General Assembly, and recommendations of the Security Council not falling under Chapter VII of the Charter, have played a crucial role in the development of new norms of international law. Although resolutions may not directly create legal obligations, they have on occasion had considerable significance for legal questions: they may be cogent evidence of State practice and the *opinio juris sive necessatis,* the conviction that translates practice into custom. But more important, resolutions on a particular subject may provide authoritative interpretation of the Charter of the United Nations, and this could be binding *per se.* This is accepted now even by those who are antagonistic to the "legislative" role of the United Nations or the speedy development of new rules of international law.[160]

Asmal's views are based on Judge Ammoun's legal opinion submitted during the International Court of Justice's advisory opinion of 1971 concerning Namibia. In his report, Judge Ammoun wrote that " ... it would not be correct to assume that, because the General Assembly is in principle vested with recommendatory powers, it is debarred from adopting, in specific areas, within the framework of its competence, resolutions which make determinations or have operative design."[161] It can also be argued that the UN General Assembly Resolution 1514 of 1960 on the Declaration on the Granting of Independence to Colonial Countries and Peoples regarding the principles of self-determination as part of the obligations stemming from the charter is an authoritative and accurate interpretation of the United Nations Charter.

Today, the principle of self-determination has been incorporated in a series of international instruments and associated with the International Convention on the Elimination of All Forms of Racial Discrimination of 1965. International lawyers agree that the principle of self-determination now forms part of the *jus cogens.* This implies that certain overriding principles of imperative norms of international law cannot be set aside by treaty or acquiescence, and specifically by the development of a subsequent norm of contrary effect. While the International Court of Justice was citing examples of these norms that are a part of the *jus cogens,* it described and affirmed these obligations to be part of the international community as a whole. The ICJ further observed that "Such obligations derive, for example, in contemporary international law, from the outlawing of acts of aggression, and of genocide, as also from the principles and rules concerning the basic rights of human person, including the protection from slavery and racial discrimination."[162]

From the foregoing, it is evident that the norm of nondiscrimination forms part of international law and binds all United Nations member states. Although many General Assembly resolutions condemning apartheid and declaring it a crime against humanity have been passed, the Security Council has not used its undoubted legal authority and powers to enforce these treaties and laws. The Western Security Council members (Britain, France, and the United States) have vetoed every resolution that seeks to impose comprehensive military and economic sanctions against apartheid South Africa. Most of the Western countries have strong economic, military, social, political, cultural, and racial links with white South Africans. The African Group and other United Nations members had been responsible for mobilizing world opinion against apartheid with the hope that it would isolate South Africa politically, militarily, economically, socially, and culturally. The passage and adoption of the General Assembly and Security Council resolutions were aimed at fulfilling these objectives. While the Western major powers were busy condemning apartheid within the chambers of the United Nations, they also adopted practices that prevented and obstructed the African Group and other opponents of apartheid from ostracising South Africa from the United Nations and the international community.

Despite the fact that the General Assembly has prohibited the maintenance of diplomatic relations with South Africa, the following countries continue to have embassies in the apartheid nation:

Argentina	Denmark	Ireland	Panama
Australia	Dominican Republic	Israel	Paraguay
Austria	El Salvador	Italy	Peru
Belgium	Finland	Japan	Portugal
Bolivia	France	Luxembourg	Sweden
Brazil	Federal Republic	Malawi	Switzerland
Canada	of Germany	Monaco	Thailand
Chile	Greece	Netherlands	United Kingdom
Colombia	Guatemala	New Zealand	United States
Costa Rica	Iceland	Norway	Uruguay

South Africa belongs to the following international organizations:

United Nations
World Health Organization
International Monetary Fund
International Bank for Reconstruction and Development
International Finance Corporation
International Civil Aviation Organization
Universal Postal Union
International Telecommunication Union
General Agreement on Tariffs and Trade

Although South Africa has been expelled from many associations it still continues to retain membership in several voluntary professional, economic, and technical organizations including the following:

International Airline Navigators Council (IANC)
International Amateur Athletic Federation (IAAF)
International Association for Bridge and Structural Engineering (IABSE)
International Association for the Prevention of Blindness (IAPB)
International Association for the Protection of Industrial Property (IAPIP)
International Association of Biological Oceanography (IABO)
International Association of Physical Education & Sports for Girls & Women
International Association of Universities
International Association of Y's Men's Clubs, Inc.
International Automobile Federation
International Bar Association
International Confederation of Art Dealers
International Council of Women
International Criminal Police Organization (Interpol)
International Federation of Musicians
International Organization of Journalists
International Planned Parenthood Federation
World Federation of Democratic Youth
World Council of Churches
World Chess Federation
World Alliance of Young Men's Christian Association (YMCA)

The Western nations' political, economic, and military support given to South Africa has enabled the apartheid state to continue to strengthen its vicious government. Without Western support, it is extremely unlikely that South Africa would have been able to maintain its policies of apartheid in the face of mounting rebellion by African nationalists. As long as South Africa continues to have access to Western military and industrial technology, it will continue to ignore all General Assembly and Security Council resolutions recommending an end to apartheid and the establishment of a freely elected democratic government.

Although the African Group's efforts to use the UN system as a vehicle to end apartheid in South Africa has been difficult and frustrating, their work has increased the political consciousness of the United Nations and the world about the oppressive nature of the apartheid political system in South Africa. The General Assembly, the Security Council, and all the appropriate political organs of the United Nations condemn apartheid, which they agree is a threat to international peace and security in the world. Prior to the independence of many African countries in 1960, apartheid was hardly discussed in the corridors of the United Nations. It was generally felt by Western countries that any discussion of apartheid in the General Assembly was a contravention of Article 2.7 of the Charter of the United Nations. With a change in the balance of power in the General Assembly as a result of admission into that body of numerous African states in 1960, the issue of human rights violation in South Africa became a concern for the United Nations and the world community.

Persistent efforts by the African Group, Socialist states, and the rest of the Third World countries in focusing the issue of the denial of human rights and decolonization in Africa have greatly transformed the world view of the United Nations. The United Nations is now viewed by many Third World people as an advocate of decolonization, because an overwhelming majority of its membership believes that all colonial subjects have a right to freedom and independence. On this issue, one African scholar, Yassin El-Aouty, has observed:

> The legitimization of African liberation movements by the U.N. system has given rise to a view of the revolutionary organisms in South Africa as legitimate recipients of international aid and as authentic representatives of their population . . . . in terms of international conferences, these quasi-sovereign entities are competitors for international recognition with the "established regimes" in Southern Africa. This is the course of the political revolution which the U.N. system, although based on state membership has undergone since 1945.[163]

The major legitimizing committee on the situation with regard to the implementation of the Declaration on the Granting of Independence to Colonial Countries and Peoples was created in 1961, following the adoption of General Assembly Resolution 1514 of 1960. With an expanded membership, the committee became known as the Committee of 24. Largely under the African group's leadership, the Committee of 24 in the 1960s swept aside all attempts of colonial powers to keep colonial issues under the domestic jurisdiction province of Article 2, Section 7. Some of the Committee of 24's strategies and techniques of legitimization are described by Professor James Mittelman as:

> The Special committee dispatches visiting groups and receives petitions, serves as a channel for communication among global international organization, regional organizations, and liberation movements, gathers information on the economic, social, and political development of non-self-governing territories, monitors the activities of the specialized activities as regards decolonization; and grants oberver status to designated liberation movements.[164]

The legitimization of African liberation movements by the Committee of 24 and by the General Assembly has brought recognition and respectability of these movements within the international community. Various forms of political, economic, social, military, and educational programs have been established to specifically assist the South African ANC, PAC, and the various aspects of the black consciousness movement. United Nations scholarship funds are now available for training black South Africans and Namibians in skills that will enable them to take over the administration of their countries when they attain majority rule and independence. These scholarships used to be available to Africans from the former colonial dependencies of Angola, Cape Verde, Guinea-Bissau, Mozambique, and the British colonial dependency of Rhodesia. In addition to these countries, the legitimization process has been extremely important in the development of numerous nongovernmental organizations, which are useful to the African Group as well as to United Nations committees as resources for information needed to effectively support the antiapartheid movement in South Africa and throughout the world. The antiapartheid movement in collaboration with the African group, the Committee Against Apartheid, and the United Nations Council on Namibia are actively engaged in trying to increase UN support for immediate majority rule in South Africa and Namibia. With direct access into UN committees, and a ready audience, these nongovernmental organizations have become important centers of influence in the UN system. Not only are they becoming centers of influence in the United Nations, they are also becoming powerful interest groups in shaping policy within their national governments with respect to the support for liberation movements and decolonization.

In conclusion, it can be unequivocally stated that the contributions of African states members in trying to influence the United Nations to exert pressure on the colonial powers to hasten the decolonization process have been extremely successful. Their success lies not in the actual attainment of independence, but in educating and persuading the United Nations and the world community to support the principle of decolonization. The General Assembly, the Security Council, and individual United Nations member states are supporting the establishment of freely democratically elected governments based on universal adult human suffrage. While differences still exist between African states and Western major powers friendly to South Africa on the methods that are most appropriate to attain the goals of decolonization, a consensus now exists on apartheid being a threat to international peace and security in the world.

3
The Organization of African Unity (OAU) and the United Nations System

The year 1963 is generally regarded as the year of African unity. In that year, leaders of independent African states formed the Organization of African Unity. The OAU is a comprehensive intergovernmental organization embracing all aspects of inter-state relationships, including political and security questions as well as economic, social, and related matters. African states, with the one-state, one-vote system characteristic of international institutions, cast nearly a third of the ballots in the UN General Assembly. Sometimes Africa votes as a unit in the United Nations, and as a long-term strategy in international politics, the African states aspire to solidarity through the OAU. As a formal entity, the OAU exceeds any other regional organization both in membership and in territorial extent (about one-fourth of the world's land surface). Africa's 400 million people are less than 10 percent of the world population, yet is approximately a third more numerous than the people of the member countries of the Organization of American States (OAS), excluding the United States. Since its formation, the OAU has made a considerable impact on the world community and in the conduct of UN diplomacy. The OAU also contributes extensively to the daily operations of the entire United Nations system. Africans are to be found working in all agencies and organs of the United Nations Organization and contributing to the solution of economic, political, social, and cultural problems of the world community.

During the period preceding the establishment of the OAU, two major trends developed on the political scene: A movement to form and consolidate sovereignty of newly independent African states within the current existing colonial borders; and a Pan-African movement whose purpose was to unite the opposing African regional groupings (Casablanca, Brazzaville, Monrovia, and the Pan-African Movement for East, Central, and Southern Africa). Although these trends seem contradictory, it is generally agreed among African revolutionaries and scholars that African unity and solidarity gives Africa an important voice in the UN system and the international community. However, the question of what form of unity Africa should have was a subject of agonizing controversy for many years. With the outbreak of the Congo crisis in 1960, in which Africa found itself weak, divided, and ineffectual in solving the crisis, Ethiopia called for the creation of a united African regional organization. The importance and need for such an organization was specifically emphasized in a speech made during the sixteenth session of the UN General Assembly by Ethiopia. Ethiopia called upon African states to join in the creation, under Article 52 of the UN Charter, of a regional organization of African states, the basic and fundamental task of which would be to furnish the mechanism whereby problems that arise on the continent and which are of primary interest to the region could, in the first instance, be dealt with by Africans, in an African forum, free from outside influence and pressure.[1]

Disunity and conflicts among African states would result in the control and domination of that continent by foreign powers. Some African states, including Ethiopia, felt that the remedy lay in the creation of an African organization that could be used to exert maximum diplomatic pressure within the UN system, and the world community in areas that affect the political, economic, social, and cultural interests of the peoples of Africa. The founding fathers of the OAU felt strongly that with the establishment of an African regional organization, they would be able to assist effectively in the rapid decolonization of Africa. It was with some of these objectives that the Summit Conference of Independent African States decided to create the OAU in May 1963. After much acrimony, the Charter of the Organization of African Unity was adopted and ratified by a majority of states attending the conference on May 25, 1963.

By adopting and ratifying the OAU Charter, the African independent states had created an African international legal order. (Whether this was one of their intended objectives or not has never been made clear.) At Addis Ababa, African states adopted only those principles of the law of nations directly concerning Africa. These principles have direct bearing in the African continent and are accepted as such by the African states. The principles deal with interstate problems and Africa's relations with the non-African world. These principles are

1. The sovereign equality of all member states;
2. noninterference in the internal affairs of states;
3. respect of the sovereignty and territorial integrity of every state and its inalienable right to an independent existence;
4. the peaceful settlement of disputes, through negotiations, mediation, conciliation, or arbitration;
5. condemnation, without reservation, of political assassinations and subversive activities carried on by neighboring states, or all other states;
6. absolute devotion to the cause of total liberation of African territory not yet independent; and
7. the affirmation of a policy of nonalignment in respect of all political blocks.

There are many weaknesses in the principles and in the charter of the OAU. The enforcement of OAU decisions suffers from a lack of sanctions. A major problem lies in the fact that some OAU resolutions are too verbose or given to political rhetoric hardly conducive to their effective implementation. These decisions or resolutions are usually adopted to satisfy the demands of public opinion or political posturing. Although many problems still are to be solved in the African international legal order, it is still important to seek first elements of a continental African order, to define the specific nature of African regionalism, and even to define African international law outside the traditional Western international law. Despite these problems, the OAU's legal order has the merit of helping to define such specificity: "the principle of the intangibility of the frontiers inherited from the colonial powers, the practices that emerge in the recognition of states, governments, and national liberation movements, the affirmation of the legitimacy of armed struggle against colonial domination."[2] The fact that the signatories of the OAU Charter constitute about a third of the UN membership is important in itself. Because of its size and the role it has played in United Nations and world diplomacy, the OAU has emerged as one of the most effective international organizations in existence.

The relationship between the United Nations and the Organization for African Unity has a comprehensive formal legal base. The OAU Charter mentions the UN Charter specifically as a guide. Not only does the Addis Ababa Charter repeatedly stress compatibility with that of the United Nations, but it evidently considers the United Nations as the center for harmonizing relations between African states and the outside world. Because of this, the UN General Assembly adopted, by acclamation, a resolution on cooperation with the OAU.[3] Despite the adoption of formal resolutions of mutual cooperation between the two organizations, it is a remarkable fact that no precise references were made in the OAU Charter to articles of the UN Charter. The OAU Charter does not contain direct references to the right of self-determination nor does it claim that it is established for collective self-defense under Article 51 of the UN Charter.

One explanation for this failure to give the OAU formal character as a regional arrangement under the UN Charter could be a desire on the part of the African governments to avoid direction by the extra-African Security Council. Another possible explanation for this lacuna may relate to the OAU's nonaligned position. A regional organization under Chapter VII of the UN Charter might be taken as parallel to other organizations that are identified with the cold war East-West protagonists. Whatever the explanation, the situation is not unusual: much of UN practice and most resolutions are related, only vaguely, to specific articles of the UN Charter.

In discussing the issue of conformity of the OAU Charter with the regional arrangements of the UN Charter, as defined in Chapter VII, Articles 52, 53, and 54, it is important to give a short historical background of Africa's political status during the formation of the United Nations Organization. Before the adoption and ratification of the UN Charter, the people of Africa, with the exception of Ethiopia, Egypt, and Liberia, were languishing under Western European colonial subjugation. Excluding these three states, Africans were not involved in shaping the evolution of the UN system and world diplomacy. Of the three independent African states, the government of Egypt was active in shaping the evolution of the UN system insofar as it affected the people of Africa.

The Dumbarton Oaks United Nations proposals submitted to participating countries included a series of provisions dealing with regional organizations closely linked with the UN system and subject to the Security Council. The Arab League and the Organization of American States expressed satisfaction concerning the appropriateness of regional agreements and organs. With respect to Africa, Egypt was a lone voice in submitting amendments to the Dumbarton Oaks Proposals. The Egyptian amendments emphasized the appropriateness of the legal definition of regional organizations. While opposing regional military alliances, the Egyptian government stressed the permanence of interstate association and cooperation, geopolitical proximity of member states, cultural affinity and heritage, and the establishment of common institutions.[4] Egyptian amendments to the Dumbarton Oaks Proposals were later to be of significant impact in the drafting of the charters of the Arab League and the Organization of African Unity.

The OAU attaches great importance to the Charter of the United Nations. This point of view is clearly amplified by the Ethiopian draft that served as the basis for the preparatory work of the OAU. Pertaining to relations between the OAU and the United Nations, nothing in the OAU Charter may be interpreted as violating the rights and duties of member states outlined by the Charter of the United Nations Organization. In addition, the OAU Charter favors Article 3 of the United Nations Charter which calls for international cooperation, based on the Charter of the United Nations and the Universal Declaration of Human Rights. Although they fully support the UN Charter, African states are unequivocally opposed to interference in their domestic affairs by the United Nations or other countries. African states want to settle African problems by themselves and see the UN role as complementing their own. In line with this reasoning, the OAU Charter is viewed as a "Monroe Doctrine" for the African continent, but with one reservation: It is not unilateral; it is a multinational document involving African egalitarian collective diplomacy.[5]

By affirming their adherence to the Charter of the United Nations and the Universal Declaration of Human Rights, the heads of state and government of the OAU countries had expressed their conviction that their organization provides a solid base for peaceful and positive cooperation among states. By incorporating it in the Preamble of the OAU Charter, they made it abundantly clear that they did not want to depart from the principles of the UN Charter. By implication, it may be assumed that, in accordance with Article 103 of the UN Charter, if a conflict arose between the obligations of the OAU and those of the United Nations, the obligations under the UN Charter would take precedence over those of the OAU. This interpretation seems to conform with the spirit and intention of the 1963 Addis Ababa OAU Summit Resolution (CIAS/Plen. 2/Rev. 2c) on *Africa and the United Nations*, which declared;

Believing that the United Nations is an important instrument for the maintenance of peace and security among nations and for the promotion of the economic and social advancement of all peoples,

Reiterating its desire to strengthen and support the United Nations,

Noting with regret that Africa as a region is not equitably represented in the principal organs of the United Nations,

Convinced of the need for closer cooperation and coordination among the African Member States of the United Nations,

1. *Reaffirms* its dedication to the purposes and principles of the United Nations Charter and its acceptance of all obligations contained in the Charter, including financial obligations;

2. *Insists* that Africa as a geographical region should have equitable representation in the principal organs of the United Nations, particularly the Security

Council and the Economic and Social Council and its specialized agencies;
3.   Invites African Governments to instruct their representatives in the United Nations to take all possible steps to achieve a more equitable representation of the African region;
4.   Further invites African Governments to instruct their representatives in the United Nations, without prejudice to their membership in and collaboration with the African Group with a permanent secretariat so as to bring about closer cooperation and better coordination in matters of the common concern.[6]

By adopting this resolution, the OAU heads of state had expressed once again their desire to strengthen and support the United Nations and their conviction that the United Nations is an important instrument for the maintenance of international peace and security among nations.[7]

Another connection between the OAU and the United Nations is provided by Article XXVI of the OAU Charter which states that the "Charter shall, after due ratification, be registered with the Secretariat of the United Nations through the government of Ethiopia in conformity with Article 102 of the Charter of the United Nations. Registration gives any member state of the OAU the right to invoke the Charter of the OAU before the General Assembly, the Security Council, and the International Court of Justice." Although the OAU has registered as a regional organization, it does not imply that the OAU is subservient to the United Nations Organization. The OAU's relationship with the United Nations is that of complementarity in the sense that both organizations have supported each other. For example, when the Congolese civil war was raging, the Security Council adopted a resolution on December 30, 1964, by ten votes and one abstention (France). This resolution referred to the OAU as a regional organization in the meaning of Article 52 and 54 of the UN Charter. The resolution went on to request the OAU to find a political solution to the Congolese civil war in conformity with Article 54 of the UN Charter. Additonally, the Security Council requested the OAU to keep it fully informed of any action it might take in the context of the stated resolution. In the General Assembly, many resolutions calling for closer cooperation with the OAU have been adopted. This was the case when the General Assembly on December 1, 1978, adopted, without a vote, a resolution on cooperation between the United Nations and the Organizations of African Unity (OAU), outlining various areas of common concern to the two organizations. The areas of cooperation covered include the elimination of colonialism, racial discrimination, and apartheid in southern Africa; social and economic development; economic and technical assistance; and assistance to victims of colonialism and apartheid in southern Africa.

In the resolution, the General Assembly commended the continued efforts of the OAU to promote multilateral cooperation among African states and to find solutions to African problems of vital importance to the international community. The General Assembly resolution continued to reaffirm the determination of the United Nations in cooperation with the OAU to intensify its efforts to eliminate colonialism and racial discrimination in southern Africa, and to recognize the importance of promoting African social and economic development. While calling for the reaffirmation of the OAU's role in actualizing the ideas of the New International Economic Order, the General Assembly further requested the secretary-general and the organs within the United Nations system to ensure that adequate facilities continued to be made available for the provision of technical assistance to the OAU General Secretariat as and when required, and requested the secretary-general to continue to take the necessary measures to strengthen cooperation at the political, economic, cultural, and administrative levels between the United Nations and the OAU in accordance with the relevant General Assembly resolutions.[8]

In the same resolution, the General Assembly called upon the United Nations bodies, in particular the Security Council, the Economic and Social Council, the Special Committee against Apartheid, and the United Nations Council for Namibia, to continue to associate closely with the OAU in all their work concerning Africa. The General Assembly also called upon the United Nations Development Program (UNDP) to arrange for a meeting with its governing council and the OAU to discuss relations between the OAU and various organs of the United Nations system. The African Group at the United Nations sponsored the General Assembly resolution on cooperation between the OAU and various organs of the United Nations system. The African Group at the United Nations sponsored the General Assembly resolution on cooperation between the OAU and the United Nations, which was adopted by that body without reference to the main committee of the General Assembly.[9]

While addressing the OAU Assembly of Heads of State and Government in Cairo in July 1964, the late secretary-general of the United Nations, U Thant, saw the relationship of the OAU and the United Nations in this way: The adoption of the United Nations Charter by a resurgent Africa is a welcome support to the United Nations. The growth of regional organizations, in accordance with the principles of the UN Charter, can only strengthen the United Nations. What the secretary-general did not say was how the OAU viewed its relationship with the United Nations Organization. Commenting on the same same topic, the Ghanaian marxist weekly, *The Spark,* on November 5, 1965, noted:

> The Secretary-General's Report revealed that there has been a proliferation of Commissions and Agencies of the OAU which parallel the United Nations Commissions and Agencies almost directly. This has led to the growth of the attitude that the Organization of African Unity exists to be a regional organization of the United Nations. The United Nations agencies are using the OAU as a convenient subordinate organization for their activities and their aims. This situation must be reversed. The OAU is not a regional organization of the United Nations. It is not even a miniature United Nations operating on the African continent. The OAU exists to liberate this continent from imperialism, to eradicate colonialism and to get rid of the monopoly capitalism which still exploits us and directs our economies.[10]

Despite its reservation about the conflicting roles between the OAU and the United Nations, *The Spark* recognized that the two international organizations shared some objectives in common. Some of these shared objectives were international cooperation in solving international problems of an economic, social, and cultural nature; the promoting of respect for human rights; that member states refrain from the threat or use of force against the territorial integrity or political independence of any state; to observe the principle of noninterference in the internal affairs of other member states; and to condemn all forms of political assassination as well as subversive activities in any other states–particularly those of neighboring states. In addition, both organizations support the right to self-determination of all oppressed and colonized people.

One of the major objectives of the OAU has been to increase African activities at the United Nations. At a meeting of the OAU Council of Ministers of the OAU in Dakar, Senegal, August 2-11, 1963, the Council of Ministers proposed Resolution CM/Res. 1 (1) which stated:

Whereas in 1963, Africa has 32 Member States, that is, almost one-third of the total membership of the Organization, and that other African States will shortly increase this proportion,

Considering the absence of any specific representation of Africa in certain United Nations Agencies and Africa's marked under-representation in all the major bodies of the Organization,

Considering the extreme urgency attached by African States to redress this grave injustice committed to the detriment of new Member States in general and African States in particular,

Recalling the stand taken categorically and unanimously by all Heads of State and Governments of Independent African States at the Addis Ababa conference in favor of the just representation of Africa in all organs of the United Nations and their specialized institutions,

Whereas this indispensable redress must take place on the basis of the principles of equality of Member States and equitable geographic distribution enshrined in the Charter of the Organization of the United Nations,

Being of the opinion that this redress, which the African States claim out of considerations of justice, equity and dignity, requires both the amendment of the Charter in accordance with its Article 108 and the redistribution of all existing and future seats,

Noting that the amendment of the Charter requires, in accordance with the provisions of Article 108, the unanimous agreement of all the permanent Members of the Security Council,

1.   Resolves to ask the Members of the African Group at the United Nations to redouble their efforts with a view to achieving, in the best circumstances possible, the just representation of Africa by means of the amendment of the Charter and the redistribution of all existing and future seats;

2.   Appeals with confidence to the Member States at the United Nations, and in the first place to the permanent Members of the Security Council, to facilitate the successful outcome of the just and pressing African claims by not opposing any longer the amendment and the revision of the Charter;

3.   Resolves finally to make all the necessary efforts to bring a successful outcome, at all costs, the justified claims of African States so as to enable them, on the acquisition of their just representation, to participate effectively in the United Nations work for peace, and this during the 18th session of the General Assembly;

4.   Solemnly declares that any impediments placed on the path of the African States by any Member States of the United Nations in the effort of the African States to obtain this objective shall be regarded as an unfriendly act by all Member States of the Organization of African Unity.,[11]

After this, the OAU Council of Ministers requested its group at the United Nations to draft rules and regulations and a budget for the African Group's Permanent

Secretariat at the United Nations headquarters in New York. The group was also further instructed to work cooperatively on all issues affecting the interests of African peoples and states. The objectives of the OAU Secretariat at the United Nations are to obtain benefits in quantity and quality from the United Nations and its specialized agencies for individual African states and to present African views unitedly and effectively. Within the United Nations, the basis of the OAU relationship is the interplay between the demand of the OAU countries for the widest possible support for their objectives. The African Group is primarily an instrument of pressure on the rest of the UN membership in that it helps to mediate between the UN's worldwide concerns and African regional perspectives in the search for solutions common and beneficial to both the UN and the OAU.

Within the chambers of the United Nations, the main diplomatic instruments of pressure as well as coordination are African states who serve in the General Assembly, the Security Council, and other organs and agencies of the UN system. In the Security Council, African states now serve as non-permanent members of that council. The membership of the African Group in the Security Council enables African views on major issues to be aired in that council. The OAU Council of Ministers and the African Group at the United Nations constantly take an active role in nominating African candidates for membership in the Security Council. The participation of African ministers in the nominating process shows the great importance the OAU attaches to the membership of African states nominated by the General Assembly to the Security Council. In their capacity as members of the Security Council, African states are generally expected to combine national, regional (OAU), and international perspectives in dealing with issues that are placed on the agenda of the Security Council. The regional interests are coordinated by the OAU Council of Ministers, which has developed the practice of sending special missions to the United Nations to speak on behalf of its national delegations. The goals of these ministers have been to persuade the Security Council, especially the permanent members, to take positive actions in helping to solve African problems of economic development and decolonization.

The OAU and UN Regional Organizations

Although the UN Charter provides for relations with regional intergovernmental or international nongovernmental organizations, it does not include provisions for non-UN intergovernmental organizations in the economic and social fields. Inside Africa the main problem for the United Nations and the OAU is the existence of competitive regional structures that have entailed the setting up of specialized commissions parallel to the UN Economic Commission for Africa (ECA). Further, the UN transcontinental organs constantly experience problems of effective harmonization of their relations with many African regional organizations and institutions, such as, the African Development Bank, Economic Community of West African States, and the Arab League.

Despite differences between the OAU and the United Nations, it should be noted that the UN Charter envisages universal organizations as coordinators of subordinate regional activities, especially in the political and security fields. Regional organizations received a license to exist and to proliferate under the Charter. This proliferation of regional organizations and the application of the regional principle within the United Nations organizations raises the issue as to whether the UN universalistic regional principle had anything more than a declaratory basis at its creation. The OAU regional organizations now cut across the actual and intended functions of the United Nations organizations and compete with them for a share of attention and resources. Notwithstanding these numerous problems, some of the organs of the UN system have uncomfortably had favorable and impressive relations with some of the OAU's regional organizations. Some of the more significant of these are The United Nations Economic and Social Council (ECOSOC); the United Nations Educational, Scientific and Cultural Organization (UNESCO); the United Nations Food and Agricultural Organization; World Health Organization; the United Nations Economic Commission for Africa (ECA); the United Nations Conference for Trade and Development (UNCTAD); the United Nations High Commission for Refugees (UNHCR); the United Nations Institute for Training and Research (UNITAR); the United Nations Development Program (UNDP); the United Nations Council for Namibia (UNCN); the International Court of Justice (ICJ); the United Nations Trust Fund for South Africa (UNTFSA); the International Bank for Reconstruction and Development (IBRD); the International Monetary Fund (IMF); the Universal Postal Union (UPU); the International Telecommunications Union (ITTU); and the International Civil Aviation Organization (ICAO).

The United Nations General Assembly and the Security Council are actively involved in discussing and making decisions that are supportive of the goals of the OAU. The significance of these relationships lies in the OAU's desire for effective participation in the proceedings and deliberations of the various bodies of the UN system. This was accomplished through the activities of the African Group and its Secretariat at the United Nations headquarters in New York City.

The OAU actively tries to make the United Nations Organization responsive to African interests by requesting it to pay particular attention to specific issues. It was in this spirit that the OAU Council of Ministers passed Resolution 56 (iv), which expressed the hope that the Negotiations Committee to be appointed by the president of the United Nations General Assembly would take into serious account African interests in seeking a solution to the problems entailed by peacekeeping operations.[12] In addition to making the United Nations address the interests of Africa, the OAU intends to increase its cooperation with this organization. By cooperating with the United Nations, the OAU can benefit tremendously from the economic and technological resources of the United Nations. The OAU's recognition of the usefulness of the United Nations made the OAU Council of Ministers pass Resolution 65 (v) in October 1965. While praising the growing relations between the OAU and the United Nations system, Resolution 65 (v) of October, 1965 stated:

> Requests the Administrative Secretary-General to invite the Secretary-General of the United Nations to follow the work of the OAU Assembly of Heads of State and Government and Council of Ministers as well as that of all the OAU Specialized Commissions;

Welcomes with satisfaction the establishment of relations of cooperation between the UNO and OAU and requests the OAU Administrative Secretary-General to do his utmost in order that this cooperation be as close as possible and cover all fields that interest both organizations. [13]

The OAU constantly encourages African countries to increase their membership in numerous United Nations agencies. Because of the OAU's pressures on its members, the United Nations now devotes many of its discussions to issues that affect African economic and political development. African countries are represented in all organs and agencies of the UN system. Of all these countries, Egypt and Nigeria have the largest representation of African countries in the UN agencies. Nigeria has membership in the following U.N. bodies and agencies:

Committee on the Peaceful Uses of Outer Space

Committee of the World Disarmament Conference

Special Committee on Peacekeeping Operations

United Nations Trust Fund for South Africa

United Nations Council for Namibia

United Nations Special Fund

International Civil Service Commission

Ad Hoc Group of Experts on Nuclear Weapon Free Zones

Commission on Human Rights

Subcommission on Prevention of Discrimination and Protection of Minorities

Committee on Natural Resources

Committee on Review and Appraisal

United Nations Industrial Development Organization

Special Committee on the Charter of the United Nations and on Strengthening of the Role of the Organization

International Court of Justice

Ad Hoc Committee on the Restructuring of the Economic and Social Sectors of the United Nations System

United Nations Commission on International Trade Law

Committee on the Elimination of Racial Discrimination

Committee on Crime Prevention and Control

United Nations Research Institute for Social Development

International Labor Organization

International Monetary Fund

United Nations Educational Scientific and Cultural Organization

Universal Postal Union

World Health Organization

Food and Agriculture Organization

United Nations Conference on Trade and Development

International Telecommunications Union

Executive Secretary of the Economic Commission for Africa

Intergovernmental Maritime Consultative Organization

International Bank for Reconstruction and Development

International Finance Corporation

General Agreement on Tariffs and Trade

International Atomic Energy Agency

World Intellectual Property

International Civil Aviation Organization

World Meteorological Organization

African Development Bank

Group of Experts on the Draft Convention on Territorial Asylum

Committee on Conferences

Economic and Social Council

Commission on Transnational Corporations

Committee for Development Planning

Other OAU member states are enlisted in numerous UN agencies, councils and committees. As can be expected, the OAU is actively involved through its represent-ation by member countries in the daily decision-making process and operations of the United Nations Organization.

The general structure and framework governing the OAU and its relations with the United Nations Organization are provided for by the OAU African Heads of Government Resolution 33 (II) and that of the UN General Assembly Resolution 2011 (XX). The resolutions of these two international organizations provide for mutual and reciprocal representation at the meetings and conferences held either at the OAU or at the United Nations. Since 1965 many United Nations agencies have held many of their meetings in OAU member countries. The United Nations ECA operates in Africa, and the United Nations Security Council has held at least one of its meetings in Africa. From May 16-21, 1977, the OAU jointly organized with the United Nations a conference in support of the peoples of Zimbabwe and Namibia in Maputo, Mozambique. Ninety-two United Nations member states including OAU representatives and OAU member states attended this historic conference.

Cooperation between the OAU and the United Nations has increased on eco-nomic-related matters. The Economic and Social Commission (ESC) of the OAU held its first meeting six months after the formation of this organization in Niamey, the capital city of Niger. Prior to this convocation, the African heads of state and government had met in Addis Ababa and urged all African states to conduct negotiations in concert with the hope of obtaining from the industrialized consumer countries "real price stabilization and guaranteed outlets on the World Market so that the developing countries may derive considerable greater revenue from international trade."[14] This statement was made partially in support of the United Nations Conference on Trade and Development (UNCTAD) and also the joint declaration of the developing countries on international trade that was later adopted as Resolution 963 (XXXVI) of the United Nations Economic and Social Council (ESC). The UNCTAD Conference was later held in Geneva in April 1964. The OAU-ESC Niamey Resolution noted inter alia:

1. Expresses its conviction that the main objective of the United Nations Conference on Trade and Development should be to define the elements of a better policy in the field of international economic cooperation so as to secure for the developing countries an optimum rate of economic growth.
2. Recommends to Member States of the Organization of African Unity to pursue jointly the following common positions:
    (i) Support all measures aimed at enabling the foreign exchange resources of developing countries to increase at a rate proportionate to the needs of their development.
    (ii) Urge the acceptance of the principle that the developed countries should, in any programme they adopt for reducing the barriers to trade, give priority to the trade needs of the developing countries. The developed countries should further accept the non-implementation of the principle of reciprocity in their trade with developing countries as well as adjustment of the most-favored nation clause.
    (iii) Urge further the acceptance by the developed countries the principle that the developing countries should be accorded preferential treatment, particularly in the protection of infant industries based on the recognition that even with a complete liberalization of trade the developing countries would not be in a position to compete on even terms with industrialized countries.
    (iv) Appeal to the developed countries to take measures which would lead to the maximum utilization of primary commodities and obviate the harmful effects that may arise from the increased use of synthetic products.
    (v) Request the developed countries, jointly or separately, to have as an objective, the abolition of all discrimination applicable to their imports from the developing countries.
    (vi) Recommend that the developing countries should liberalize and strengthen their trade and monetary relationships amongst themselves, with a view to setting up mutually beneficial trade agencies within the framework of integrated and coordinated programs of action or development schemes.
    (vii) Recommend the coordination of plans for the development of transport and communications aimed at expanding continental and inter-continental trade.
    (viii) Urge in particular that the Conference should take concrete measures for the improvements of the terms of trade of the developing countries and the maintenance at equitable and remunerative levels of the relationships between prices of primary commodities and industrial goods.
    (ix) Consider the establishment of multi-commodity schemes for the stabilization of prices of primary commodities so that international arrangements for any given commodity not only take into account existing levels of production but also the potentialities and the alternative means of production over a wider spectrum of commodities.
    (x) Request that the existing institutional machineries in the field of international trade be reviewed and revised in order to create an international trade organization adjusted to meet the needs of the developing countries.

(xi) Further request that the economic groupings formed by the industrialized countries should avoid taking any actions which might have an adverse effect on the economies of the developing countries.

(xii) Support the setting up of an international machinery for the financing of the flow of trade of developing countries not only for their short-term requirements, but also for the requirements of their long-term development schemes. [15]

At its creation, the OAU-ESC was charged with these responsibilities:

1. The creation of a free trade area among the African countries, and of developing trade among them.
2. The establishment of a common external tariff and a common fund for raw material price stabilization.
3. The restructuring of international trade.
4. The setting up of an African payments and clearing union and a Pan-African monetary zone, following the progressive freeing of national currencies from all non-technical external attachments.
5. The harmonization of existing and future national development plans.
6. The raising of social standards and the strengthening of inter-African cooperation through the exchange of social and labor legislation, the organization of vocational training courses for African workers, the establishment of an African Trade Union, and African youth organization, an African scouts union and annual African sports. [16]

The rationale behind the OAU-ESC Niamey Resolution was the assumption that the OAU countries would accrue more economic benefits by coordinating their economic policies in their conduct of international trade. While pursuing the expressed objective, African states also intended to extricate their countries from the continued economic dependence that characterizes their relations with the OECD. African states continue to serve European, Canadian, Japanese, and American economic developmental needs more than those of Africa.

Aware that economic development is necessary for the attainment of African social and political sovereignty, Africans are now calling for radical economic changes between them and the developed countries. This call for a new world economic order is aimed at making African states as well as other Third World less developed countries (LDCs) realize maximum economic benefits from their sale of raw materials to the developed countries (OECD). Presently, the OECD continues to have favorable balance of trade surplus in its commerce with the Third World states that are not members of OPEC. The developmental gap between the OECD and the LDCs continues to widen. It was this economic realization that forced the African group to use the UN system as a forum for persuading the OECD countries to reevaluate their economic relations with the Third World countries. Concerned about the African group's desire to promote social progress and economic development for Third World peoples, the United Nations General Assembly passed Resolution 1710 (xvi) of December 19, 1961, on the Development Decade. The following are the highlights of Resolution 1710 (svi):

1. During the tenure of the United Nations Development Decade Member States and their peoples shall intensify their efforts to mobilize and to sustain

support for the measures required on the part of both developed and developing countries to accelerate progress towards self-sustaining growth of their economies. Each developing country should set its own target, taking as the objective a minimum annual rate of growth of aggregate national income of 5-percent at the end of the Decade;

    2. Calls upon Member States of the United Nations and its specialized agencies to:

    Pursue policies designed to enable the LDC's and those dependent on the export of a small range of primary commodities to sell more of their products at stable and remunerative prices in expanding markets, and to ensure them an equitable share of earnings from the extraction and marketing of their natural resources by foreign capital, in accordance with the generally accepted reasonable earnings on invested capital;

    3. That the heads of international agencies with responsibilities in the financial, economic and social fields, the Managing Director of the Special Fund, the Executive Chairman of the Technical Assistance Board, and the regional economic commissions, shall develop proposals for the intensification of action in the fields of economic and social development by the United Nations system of organizations with particular reference to economic development, increased productivity, and the elimination of hunger, disease and illiteracy;

    4. The Economic and Social Council must accelerate its examination of, and decision on, principles of international economic cooperation directed towards the improvement of world economic relations and the stimulation of international cooperation;

    5. The Secretary-General must submit the recommendation of the Economic and Social Council together with its views and its report on actions undertaken to States Members of the United Nations, specialized agencies, and to the General Assembly at its seventeenth session.[17]

The resolution designated the development decade also requested the UN Secretary-General, U Thant, to develop proposals for the decade. In the introduction setting out these proposals, U Thant provided a rationale for the global strategy of development. In his remarks, U Thant observed that in the presence of so much affluence, poverty continued to exist among the majority of the peoples of the world. He called on the rich and affluent nations to take special efforts in assisting the LDCs to eliminate poverty, hunger, and starvation throughout the world.

After the African group's discovery that their use of the United Nations system for obtaining economic benefits from the OECD was realized by other LDCs, it became imperative for African states to work closely with the rest of the developing countries. Following the adoption of the resolution of the development decade, the United Nations Economic and Social Council (ESC) convened a UN conference on Trade and Development (UNCTAD) to discuss the problems of underdevelopment. Prior to the conference, seventy-five nations of the LDCs welcomed the idea of such a conference and outlined the major areas on which it wished the ESC to concentrate in its deliberations. Some of the areas of concern were (1) that UNCTAD should represent a special event in international cooperation conducive to the development of the LDCs' economies and to the integrated growth of the world economy as a whole; (2) that international trade may become a more powerful instrument and a vehicle of economic development not only the widening of traditional exports of the developed countries but also through the development of markets for their new products and a general increase in their share of world resources and exports under new improved terms of trade; (3) that the existing principles and patterns of trade which favor the industrialized countries should be reversed; (4) that a new dynamic international trade policy which recognizes the need to provide special assistance and protection of the economies of the LDCs; and (5) that the LDCs and the developed countries work cooperatively on the basis of a new international trade and development policy.

After the preparatory sessions of the committee on UNCTAD, the General Assembly at the urging of the LDCs passed Resolution 1785 (XVII) of December 8, 1962. This resolution expected to achieve, inter alia, the following:

(a)   Creation of conditions for the expansion of trade between countries at a similar level of development, at different stages of development, or having different systems of social and economic organization;

(b)   Progressive reduction and early elimination of all barriers and restrictions impeding the exports of the developing countries, without reciprocal concessions on their part;

(c)   Increase in the volume of exports of the developing countries in primary products, both raw and processed, to the industrialized countries, and stabilization of prices at fair and remunerative levels;

(d)   Expansion of the markets for exports of manufactured and semi-manufactured goods from the developing countries;

(e)   Provision of more adequate financial resources at favorable terms so as to enable the developing countries to increase their imports of capital goods and industrial raw materials essential for their economic development, and better coordination of trade and aid policies;

(f)   Improvement of the invisible trade of the developing countries, particularly by reducing their payments for freight and insurance and the burden of their debt charges;

(g)   Improvement of institutional arangements; including, if necessary, the establishment of new machinery and methods for implementing the decisions of the conference.[18]

With the passage of Resolution 1785 (XVII), the African Group was convinced that UNCTAD would greatly contribute to the acceleration of the development of their economies. The African group as well as the rest of the LDCs expected fuller economic cooperation of the developed countries in the attainment of UN collective economic security. They also hoped that increased economic cooperation would strongly guarantee world peace and security as specified in the UN Charter. The belief that the United Nations can effectively contribute to African development is based on the assumption that aid from the UN system is least likely to impair their independence.

When the OAU was formed on May 25, 1963, the United Nations Economic Commission (ECA) had been in existence since 1958. The history of the ECA can be traced to 1946, when the United Nations was preoccupied with the reconstruction of Europe following the end of World War II. The UN Economic and Social Council (ESC) resolution of June 21, 1946, created a Temporary Subcommission on Economic Reconstruction of devastated areas (TSER). The TSER was divided into two working divisions, one for Europe and North Africa, and a second for Asia and the Far East. In March 1947, the ESC established the Economic Commission for Latin America (ECLA) and the Economic Commission for Asia and the Far East (ECAFE). The ESC's efforts to create the Economic Commission for North Africa and Ethiopia failed in 1947, 1950, 1951, and 1956. It was only after the November 1957 General Assembly's Second Committee's request that the ESC gave a prompt and favorable consideration to the establishment of a UN Economic Commission for Africa (ECA). As a result, the ESC in its resolution of April 20, 1958, created the ECA based on the provisions of Article 8 of its charter. On the basis of this article, the General Assembly and UNESC, in a resolution, charged ECA with the following:

(a) Initiate and participate in measures for facilitating concerted action for the economic and social development of Africa, including its social aspects . . .
(b) Make or sponsor studies of economic and technological problems and developments within . . . Africa . . . and disseminate the results . . .
(c) Undertake or sponsor the collection, evaluation and dissemination of economic, technological and statistical information . . .
(d) Perform . . . advisory services to the countries and territories of Africa . . .
(e) Assist the (Economic and Social) Council at its functions (in Africa) in connection with any economical problems, including problems in the field of technical assistance; and
(f) Assist in the formulation and development of coordinated policies as a basis for practical action in promoting economic and technological development in the region . . . .[19]

Addis Ababa was selected as the site for the ECA headquarters.

The ECA discharges its functions in a dual capacity. Although it operates as an integral part of the UN system, it also serves the special economic and other developmental needs of Africa. The ECA has been a major force for regional cooperation and economic integration of the African economies since 1958. An example of how the ECA operates in its dual capacity was its work with African states in preparation for the UNCTAD I held in Geneva in the spring of 1964. The ECA made its experts available to OAU countries that needed them.

While reiterating the importance of UNCTAD I as marking the beginning of a new epoch in the evolution of international cooperation in the field of trade and development, the ECA in concert with the OAU states and the whole group of seventy-five developing countries stated that such cooperation must serve as a decisive instrument for ending the division of the world into the areas of affluence and those of suffering and intolerable poverty. Among other issues, UNCTAD I resolutions adopted included some of the following:

The Conference has considered the general targets on which the international community might focus in dealing with the problems of development through trade and international cooperation. A number of principles and criteria aimed at providing constructive guidelines for policies in the various areas of international financial and technical cooperation, have been formulated. The major questions identified are as follows:
(a) The need for higher growth rates for developing countries; measures to be taken by developed and developing countries including measures to increase foreign exchange availabilities.

(b) Guidelines for international financial and technical cooperation; terms and conditions of aid, and the relation of trade and aid to maintain the continuity of sound development plans or programmes.
(c) External debt problems.
(d) The need and means for increasing the flow of financial resources to the developing countries.
(e) Compensatory finance; supplementary financial measures.
(f) Aspects of shipping and all other invisible items.
(g) The need for periodic reviews.

There is wide recognition of the importance and gravity of the problem posed by the financing of development, in all its many complex aspects, and this recognition should form the basis for continuing reviews and action in this field.

There is also recognition of the need for greater and more systematic efforts by all parties involved, with a fair division of responsibilities among developed and developing countries, in order to engender the necessary cooperative efforts at the national, regional, and international levels.

More specifically, there is wide agreement in some key areas which, though necessarily limited in scope, constituted forward steps. These areas include measures for accelerated growth in developing countries and increase in foreign exchange availabilities; guidelines for international financial and technical cooperation, compensatory financing and supplementary financial measures, and for dealing with external debt problems; and some aspects of shipping in relation to the trade of developing countries.

Finally, in some other areas, there is also agreement that specific measures, which have been proposed, should be given further consideration or should be studied by the appropriate international organizations.[20]

The major achievements of UNCTAD I were in the political realm. The very fact that the ECA could work closely with all OAU states in trying to solve African economic problems was in itself an important accomplishment. Although major issues were raised and discussed, no solutions were ever agreed on or devised. Instead, these economic issues were assigned to a committee for further study and consideration.

In October 1967, the ECA and the OAU-ESC jointly held a strategy meeting with the Council of Ministers of the OAU in preparation for the UNCTAD II, which was held in 1968 in New Delhi, India. The reason for the Algiers meeting was for the OAU and ECA countries to agree on specific proposals that they would jointly support at UNCTAD II. At the end of the conference, the ECA and the OAU agreed on what is now referred to as the African Declaration of Algiers. This declaration on the need for a reform of the international commodity trade system in favor of the exports of the LDCs called for the (a) elimination of excessive price fluctuations; (b) maintenance and increase of the purchasing power of the products exported by developing countries in relation to their imports; (c) international support for the execution of viable diversification programs in developing countries, especially coordinated programs within a subregional or regional framework; (d) an undertaking by developed countries to abstain from harming the interests of LDCs by pressing production of commodities produced principally by developing countries and, in that regard, the encouragement by the developed countries of industries processing primary commodities produced by them.[21]

On the subject of the accessibility of products of LDCs to the markets of the

OECD, the ECA-OAU Algiers Declaration recommended that the examination of commodity problems might usefully be carried out by classifying the latter in this manner: (1) commodities produced wholly or mainly in LDCs and which do not face serious competition from substitutes; (2) commodities produced in LDCs subject to competition from substitutes, especially by synthetic materials; (3) commodities produced in substantial amounts by both LDCs and the OECD; and (4) the abolition of economic preferences.[22] The abolition of preferences should have as a prerequisite special arrangements whenever it is likely to create serious disruptions in the trade flows of the developing countries. The compensation for the removal of existing preferences should correspond to equivalent benefits as called for in the recommendation of the first UNCTAD.

The Algiers Declaration was aimed at creating a strong lobby for the LDCs to bargain with the OECD. By operating as a strong lobby, the OAU and ECA would easily convince the rest of the Third World LDCs to team up with them in restructuring the world economic order. African states felt strongly that as long as the LDCs remain unorganized, their economies would remain extremely dependent on the OECD. This dependency does not allow for the real political and economic independence of the LDCs. The OECD countries own and control the multinational corporations that are in part responsible for the continued and prolongation of the underdevelopment of the LDCs. The recognition that this economic dependency on the OECD leads to neocolonialism and the usurpation of real independence of the LDCs was an important factor in the OAU's objective to work cooperatively with other developing countries in restructuring the economic order. UNCTAD was seen by the OAU and the ECA as the most important organ through which the LDCs could influence the OECD to pay fair prices for the raw materials they procure from them. The OAU and the LDCs had the objective to rectify the shortcomings of this system in mind when they held the UNCTAD I and the Algiers joint OAU and ECA conference.

The Western developed countries (OECD) were opposed to UNCTAD. Although the OECD attended the Geneva UNCTAD I, they were definitely opposed to the creation of a U.N. machinery (controlled by the LDCs) which threatened significantly to alter the economic status quo. UNCTAD I was held against the will of the OECD. The position of the OECD at Geneva was that no existing institution could cope with all the issues of commerce and economic development in a rational order. Despite the fact that the OECD nations became contracting parties to the General Agreement on Tariffs and Trade (GATT), these countries felt that even GATT was not in a position to provide remedies to the problems of underdevelopment or of exploitation. At UNCTAD I, the OECD did not want to disturb the status quo nor to establish any distinct UN international trade organization. Their objective was to preserve GATT, which had not produced any tangible results of economic consequence to the LDCs. In addition, the OECD was of the view that any meaningful changes to the world economic order must be done outside the United Nations system. GATT was considered the appropriate instrument through which such problems could be discussed and resolved. Other OECD-dominated organizations and institutions, such as the International Bank of Reconstruction and Development (IBRD), the International Monetary Fund (IMF), and the International Development Association (IDA), were more desirable to them than UNCTAD.

While recognizing the existence of conflicting interests between the OECD and the LDCs, both parties made efforts to work cooperatively. The OAU-ECA, the Committee on Latin American Coordination (CECLA)), the Western contracting parties of GATT, and the ASEAN Group of the Group of 77 all held discussions to minimize their differences with respect to UNCTAD. It was under this political atmosphere that UNCTAD II was held in Delhi, India, from February to March 1968. Many issues discussed at UNCTAD II were extremely complex. The areas of discussion centered on the following: (1) trends and problems in trade and development; (2) commodity problems and policies; (3) expansion and diversification of exports of manufactures and semimanufactures of developing countries; (4) growth, development finance, and aid (synchronization of international and national policies); (5) problems of developing countries in regard to invisibles including shipping; (6) trade expansion and economic integration among developing countries, measures to be taken by developing and developed countries–including regional, subregional, and interregional arrangements; and (7) special measures to be taken in favor of the least developed among the developing countries aimed at expanding their trade and improving their economic and social development.

Table 23:   Negative Votes and Abstentions of Major Developed Countries on Special Principles in UNCTAD
(Negative vote indicated by "V"; abstention indicated by "A")

Country	\multicolumn{12}{c}{Special Principles*}	Total V	Total A
	1	2	4	5	6	7	8	9	10	11	12	13	V	A
United States	V	-	A	A	-	V	V	A	--	A	V	A	4	5
United Kingdom	A	-	-	-	-	V	A	--	A	V	--		2	4
Canada	V	-	-	A	-	V	A	A	--	A	A	A	2	6
Australia	A	-	-	A	-	V	A	A	--	A	--	A	1	6
South Africa	A	-	-	A	-	V	A	A	--	A	--	--	1	5
France	-	-	-	A	-	A	A	-	--	A	A	--	0	5
Italy	-	-	-	A	-	A	-	-	--	A	A	--	0	4
Belgium	-	-	-	A	-	A	-	--	A	A	--		0	4
Netherlands	A	-	-	A	-	A	-	-	--	A	A	--	0	5
Germany (Federal Republic)	A	-	-	A	-	V	-	-	--	A	V	--	2	3
Sweden	A	-	-	A	-	A	A	A	--	A	V	--	1	6
Norway	A	-	-	A	-	V	-	A	--	A	V	--	2	4
Denmark	A	-	-	A	-	V	A	--	A	V	--		2	4
Japan	A	-	-	A	-	V	-	-	--	A	A	A	1	5
Soviet Union	-	-	-	-	-	A	-	-	--	--	--		0	1

* Key to Special Principles
1. Setting targets for trade expansion.
2. Need for industrialization, modernization of agriculture.
3. Preferences (no action taken)
4. Right to protect infant industries.
5. Domestic support prices should not stimulate uneconomic production.
6. Developed countries help less developed re-substitution for their commodities.
7. Compensatory financing of worsening terms of trade.
8. Surplus disposal by international rules.
9. No dumping.
10. Technical assistance.
11. Assistance: more multilaterial aid; easier terms; repayment in local currency or commodities.
12. Action to promote invisible earnings.
13. Multilateral trade and payments arrangements among less developed countries.

Source: Final Act of the United Nations Conference on Trade and Development (United Nations, E/Conf. 46/L. 28, June 6, 1964).

Although the African Group has pressed very hard for the success of UNCTAD II, the outcome of the conference was a failure from their point of view. UNCTAD II did not sufficiently deal with subjects of great importance to Africa. A significant case was the great concentration on the proposed systems of general preferences as against the superficial treatment of the problems of primary commodities that are of concern to Africa. The problems of the least developed countries and the landlocked countries were hardly discussed. Despite the adoption of many resolutions UNCTAD II also failed to establish a machinery to implement them. The OECD governments that had been opposed to UNCTAD were generally interested in working outside its framework. Their lack of support for UNCTAD can be dramatized vividly by the results of OECD voting records on issues affecting the interests of Africa and the LDCs.

Table 24: *Negative Votes and Abstentions of Major Developed Countries on General Principles in UNCTAD*
(Negative vote indicated by "V"; abstention indicated by "A")

Country	1	2	3	4	5	6	7	8	9	10	11	12	13	14	15	Total V	Total A
United States	V	V	V	V	A	V	V	V	-	--	V	V	--	A	--	9	2
United Kingdom	A	A	V	A	A	-	V	V	-	--	V	A	--	V	--	5	5
Canada	-	V	V	A	A	-	V	V	-	--	A	A	--	A	A	4	6
Australia	-	A	V	A	A	-	V	V	-	--	V	A	--	V	--	5	4
South Africa	-	A	A	A	A	-	V	V	-	--	V	A	--	A	--	3	6
New Zealand	-	-	A	-	-	-	A	A	-	--	--	--	--	A	--	0	4
France	-	-	A	A	A	-	A	A	A	--	A	--	--	--	A	0	8
Italy	-	-	A	A	A	-	A	A	A	--	A	A	--	A	--	0	9
Belgium	-	-	A	A	A	-	A	A	A	--	A	A	--	A	--	0	9
Netherlands	-	A	A	A	A	-	A	A	A	--	A	A	--	A	--	0	10
Germany (Federal Republic)	-	V	A	A	A	-	A	A	A	--	V	A	--	A	--	2	8
Sweden	-	A	-	-	-	-	A	V	-	--	A	A	--	A	--	1	5
Norway	-	A	-	-	-	-	A	V	-	--	A	A	--	A	--	1	5
Denmark	-	A	-	-	-	-	V	A	-	--	A	A	--	A	--	1	5
Japan	-	-	A	A	A	-	A	A	-	A	A	--	--	--	A	0	8
Soviet Union	-	-	-	-	-	-	-	-	-	--	--	A	--	--	--	0	1

*Key to General Principles:
  1. Sovereign equality of nations.
  2. Against discrimination by socio-economic system.
  3. Freedom to trade and dispose of natural resources.
  4. Acceleration of growth, narrowing of income gap.
  5. International division of labor; developed countries help less developed.
  6. Increase export earnings of less developed, regardless of system.
  7. International arrangements for market access, remunerative prices of primary products.
  8. Preferences and nonreciprocity.
  9. Regional groupings should not harm outsiders.
  10. Encouragement of regional groupings and integration.
  11. Increasing aid without political or military strings.
  12. Disarmament-freed resources to be used for development.
  13. Transit trade of land-locked countries.
  14. Complete decolonization necessary.
  15. Recognition of differences in stages of development.

Source: Final Act of the United Nations Conference on Trade and Development (United Nations, E/Conf, 46/L. 28, June 6, 1964).

The African Group and their Third World allies had placed their hopes of restructuring the world economic order through UNCTAD. However, it became clear after UNCTAD II that LDCs would have to do much to achieve their own development. The voting pattern of OECD on issues and problems affecting LDCs further convinced the LDCs to do more for their own development. In line with this philosophy, the OAU in conjunction with some ECA members participated in the Third Conference of Heads of States or Government of Non-Aligned Countries held in Lusaka, Zambia on September 10, 1970. The conference called on the LDCs to intensify and unite efforts between themselves and the OECD to carry out urgent structural changes in the world economy and establish such international cooperation as will reduce the gap of economic development between their respective groups, and also pledged their countries to the following:

(i) to cultivate the spirit of self-reliance and to this end to adopt a firm policy of organizing their own socio-economic progress and to raise it to the level of a priority action programme;
(ii) to exercise fully their right and fulfill their duty so as to secure optimal utilization of the natural resources in their territories and in adjacent seas for the development and welfare of their Peoples;
(iii) to develop their technology and scientific capability to maximize production and improve productivity;
(iv) to promote social changes, to provide increasing opportunity to each individual for developing his worth, maintaining his dignity, making his contribution to the process of growth and for sharing fully in its fruits;
(v) to promote social justice and efficiency of production, to raise the level of employment and to expand and improve facilities for education, health, nutrition, housing and social welfare;
(vi) to ensure that external components of the developmental process further national objectives and conform to national needs; and in particular to adopt so far as practicable a common approach to problems and possibilities of investment of private capital in developing countries;
(vii) to broaden and diversify economic relationships with other nations so as to promote true inter-dependence;[23]

Having made these pledges, the declaration then urged the United Nations:

(i) to fulfill the objectives enshrined in the Charter to promote social progress and better standards of life in larger freedom;
(ii) to employ international machinery to bring about a rapid transformation of the world economic system, particularly in the field of trade, finance, and technology so that economic domination yields to economic cooperation and economic strength is used for the benefit of the world community;
(iii) to view the developmental process in a global contact and to adopt a programme of international action for utilization of world resources in men and materials, science and technology, benefiting developed and developing countries alike;
(iv) to adopt at the forthcoming Commemorative Session a Declaration on an international economic strategy.[24]

While calling for the adoption of a new economic strategy, the attendees at the conference also declared their determination,

(a) to undertake sustained and continuous endeavours within the United Nations system to secure faithful implementation of international development policies and programmes;

(b) to further the unity and solidarity of the Group of seventy-seven at all levels including the convening of a ministerial meeting to prepare for the United Nations Conference on Trade and Development (UNCTAD) III;

(c) to review and appraise periodically, the progress of mutual cooperation in the field of development in pursuance of the programme of action;

(d) to seek ways and means for strengthening the capabilities of the United Nations system, to fulfill its commitments to social and economic progress.[25]

The realization by the OAU and the ECA that the African states had to rely more on their own resources for development did not imply that they would cease to pressure the OECD for capital and technological aid for their development. With support from the ECA, the African group teamed up with the rest of the Group of 77 in making the twenty-fifth Session of the General Assembly, September 1970 adopt the Second Development Decade and Social Progress. The African states argued that the Second United Nations Development Decade could make a universal and substantial contribution to the cause of social and economic development if decisive measures and realistic programs were adopted. They further reminded members of the General Assembly that economic growth did not in all cases automatically lead to an improvement of social and economic status of all members of society. Determined to redress this problem, the African Group reiterated that the results of economic development envisaged in the Second United Nations Development Decade should be designed to solve social problems and improve substantially the economic position of workers and peasants in the LDCs. They also called for the adoption of the following:

Practical experience shows that neither national plans nor any development programmes prepared under United Nations auspices can guarantee real progress in the field of social and economic development, unless their execution is accompanied by decisive and consistent implementation of genuinely practical measures, such as:

–the implementation of radical social and economic reforms designed to eliminate obstacles hampering the development of productive forces, and to guarantee the consolidation of national sovereignty and the protection of natural resources in the interests of national development;

–the perfection of budget and tax legislation in order to bring about a radical change in the system for the distribution of the national wealth, as an important factor in the mobilization of efforts in the interests of development;

–the creation and consolidation of the State and cooperative sectors of the economy, the introduction of a planned basis for economic management, the exercise of effective pressure on the private sector and the subordination of that sector to the national interests;

–the creation of vitally important sectors of national industry as a reliable source for the accumulation of resources, the provision of mass consumption goods for the population, and the production for export of a certain part of the country's output;

–the adoption of effective legislation regulating the activities of foreign private capital and subordinating it to the objectives fixed in national development plans;

–the adoption of measures to prevent effectively any capital drain;

–the annulment of all inequitable economic treaties, agreements and individual commitments which restrict national sovereignty, particularly sovereignty over natural resources;

–the creation of conditions for the training of national highly skilled personnel, and the implementation of measures to stop the brain drain;

–the introduction of State-wide planning in the economic and social fields, which–as is clear from the example of an ever-increasing number of States–is demonstrating its possibilities as a reliable instrument of development, although the extent to which these possibilities can be utilized differs considerably, depending on the socio-economic structure and particular characteristics of individual countries.[26]

The objectives and goals of the Second United Nations Development Decade were welcomed by the LDCs. With the hopes of improving on UNCTAD II and the Second United Nations Development Decade, the OAU ministers of state jointly held an UNCTAD III preparatory meeting with the representatives of the UN Economic Commission for Africa in Addis Ababa on October 4, 1971. Their proposals became an integral part of the First Lima Declaration and Program of Action that was subsequently adopted by the Second Ministerial Conference of the Group of 77 on November 7, 1971.

Like the Delhi UNCTAD II, a lack of consensus between the LDCs and the OECD, the Santiago, Chile UNCTAD III was also a failure. Most of the OECD states either abstained or voted against a majority of the resolutions adopted by the participants. Although the LDCs did not get all that they wanted, UNCTAD III recommended greater trade expansion, economic cooperation, and regional integration among the developing nations. In addition, the OECD countries agreed to expand their trade, financial, and technological support for the industrialization of the LDCs.

Having recognized the slow rate of industrialization in Africa during the first two years of the Second United Nations Development Decade in comparison with the target set by the United Nations Strategy, the OAU ministers of industry met in Cairo on December 23, 1973, and adopted a Declaration on Industrialization in Africa: Principles and Guidelines for Co-operation and Development. The Declaration, among other issues, went on to:

(1) Urge the developed countries to assume their responsibility and to ensure a net transfer of financial resources to the African countries in conformity with the targets set by the United Nations International Development Strategy particularly to enable the African countries to develop their economies by increasing the share of the industry sector in their gross national product;

(2) That the basic principles and guidelines set out in this Declaration constitute the African stand in international negotiations particularly during the Second General Conference of UNIDO to be held in Lima, Peru in March, 1975;

(3) That the effectiveness and efficiency of national planning and industrial development policies determine the rate and direction of industrialization and the need to foster the fastest development of the skills, institutions and financial resources required for accelerated industrialization;

(4) That African countries would need to formulate export policies and pursue deliberate actions to increase and diversify their sources for foreign exchange earnings;

(5) That the basic prevailing feature of industrialization in Africa is the prevalence of small-scale, high-cost industries which have succeeded neither in bringing about the desired transformation of economic structures nor in securing higher incomes and employment needs to be changed;

(6) That foreign investment and especially the transfer of managerial and technological skills will be crucial to industrialization in Africa;

(7) That intra-African economic and technical cooperation must be expanded throughout the continent;

(8) That sustained meaningful industrialization can only occur if the present state of African economic dependence and exploitation is eliminated.[27]

In addition to the Cairo Declaration of 1973, the OAU Algiers summit, hosted and in many ways directed by the Algerian government, was a dramatic development of great importance to UNCTAD. The Algiers Conference called for closer cooperation of all the LDCs in their bargaining with the OECD. By the time the conference adjourned, it had adopted an Economic Declaration and an Action Programme for Economic Cooperation calling for the establishment of a New International Economic Order. Some aspects of the Algerian OAU summit declaration were adopted by the General Assembly's Ad Hoc Committee of the Sixth Special Session. A summary of this report reads:

1. In order that the developing countries may exercise effectively their sovereign right, which has been recognized, of disposing freely of their natural resources and of really benefiting from these resources, the United Nations should:

Assist those developing countries which decide to nationalize their means of production and development of their natural resources;

Explicitly condemn any interference with this right and particularly with the right of nationalization;

Assist in the improved development of the primary commodities of the developing countries and in particular encourage any measures for protecting the prices of these commodities.

2. In order that the developing countries may use the fruits of their natural wealth for development purposes, the United Nations and the developed countries should provide their aid and support for the local transformation of this wealth, particularly through technical assistance and the opening of the developed markets to products manufactured by the developing countries. This support would be over and above the individual efforts which are incumbent on each of the developing countries.

3. Development aid must be based on an exhaustive evaluation of the priority needs of countries requiring it. It should be mobilized within the framework of a vast movement of international solidarity and should be based essentially on the financial, technological and commercial contributions of the rich and developed countries.

4. The developed countries should lighten the burden weighing upon the developing countries, in particular by cancelling or rescheduling their debts.

5. As an immediate solution to the urgent and serious problems facing the most deprived countries, the international community should launch at once a special programme, of specific duration, whose objectives would be:

To provide these countries with capital goods and services which will be financed with contributions from the developed countries and from developing countries having surplus resources.[28]

The adoption of these views was definitely an affirmation of the UNCTAD declarations on the new International economic Order by the LDCs and non-OECD countries. The LDCs had hoped that the OECD would support their call for the recognition of the fact that all nations of the world have a claim and an undisputed right to exercise total control over their national resources. The representatives of the OECD as expected, vigorously opposed the call for a restructure of the OECD economic order.

An issue of great importance to UNCTAD is the rapidly growing external debt of the African States and other LDCs. UNCTAD IV and V addressed this issue of chronic deficits and unfavorable terms of trade. The total external debt of seventy-five nonoil-exporting LDCs rose from $66.8 billion in 1973 to $128.8 billion by January 1977. If undisbursed debt were included, the increased debt would have risen from $43 to $171.1 billion. From 1973 to 1977 the ability of the LDCs to service their undisbursed debt deteriorated considerably. For the OAU countries, which form the largest group with the LDCs, their external debt rose from $6.8 billion in 1973 to $12.7 billion in 1977 (disbursed). If we include the undisbursed contracted debt, it rose within the same period from $9.6 to $20.9 billion.

The ever growing debt of the OAU states and the LDCs severely weakens the economic viability of these governments. Money that would have been used for developmental projects is being diverted to service these mushrooming external debts. The problem of servicing external debts has been elevated to a position of eminence both within UNCTAD and for North-South dialogues of the LDCs and OECD. The Conferences of International Economic Co-operation (CIEC) and various groups of UNCTAD IV and V have dealt with the problems of the escalating debts. The CIEC reviewed this serious problem during its 1976 meeting in Paris. At this meeting the Group of 77 called for a moratorium in the repayment of external debts and advanced the idea of a loan consortium as a means of replacing creditors clubs. The idea of a loan consortium was generally supported by the Group of 77 because it thought that it would produce developmental programs that were liekly to be of benefit to the LDCs. No formal binding agreement at this conference was concluded.

Although there was no agreement reached at the 1977 CIEC meeting in Paris, this subject was later brought to the attention of UNCTAD's Trade and Development Board (TDB) during its March 1978 meeting in Geneva. Although the meeting did not make a decision on the loan consortium proposal, it did agree to increase aid to the least developed countries, that aid would be granted on a case-by-case approach, and that a conference of a group of experts would be convened to reexamine the problems of debt servicing. UNCTAD IV and V have not provided solutions to the problems of debt servicing. Not only has the OECD refused to soften its position on debt servicing, but it has also been antagonistic to the call for the adoption of a new international economic order.

Apparently frustrated by the CIEC, TDB, and OECD's continued reluctance to place a moratorium on debt servicing and to support the declaration on the new international economic order, UNCTAD IV and V recommended the establishment of an intergovernmental committee that would mobilize the international community and organizations to help the LDCs to increase cooperation among themselves. The importance of UNCTAD's role in assisting in this cooperation was later reiterated by Gamarir Corea, the secretary-general of UNCTAD, when he stated that:

> We also look forward to continuing and strengthening the contribution that we have made to the concept of cooperation itself, both in its specific and in its overall dimension, and to being of assistance to the developing countries in giving real meaning to the idea of collective self-reliance. As this idea evolves and becomes a major part of the global strategy for development, so also will it play an increasing role amidst the preoccupations of UNCTAD and of its secretariat.[29]

Although the OAU and other LDCs want closer economic cooperation, there is now a realization for the need for national self-reliance and dependence. The ECA, the OAU, and the Economic Community for West African States (EOWAS) have joined the call for Africa to rely more on its own resources for development than on the resources of developed countries and international organizations. This approach to African development was enthusiastically endorsed by the joint OAU, UNESCO, and ECA Dakar Declaration of January 30, 1974.

> Africa must rely, first and foremost on its own strength. It has, then, to reconsider the ties of dependence that have been imposed on it and fashion links of a new type which will be radically different from those of the past.
> It is particularly urgent for Africa to tighten the links between its universities and its research organizations and to find the most suitable personnel for scientific and technical exchanges.
> The role of the Organization of African Unity is vital in this connection. The Conference thus advocates the development of the activities of the African Science Council and the organizations that come under it.
> It urges countries in the continent to hold an increasing number of regional and inter-regional meetings and to set up rapidly at these two levels appropriate machinery for exchanging experience and information in regard to science and technology and for pooling, with a view to their more rational utilization, the resources that Africa posesses.
> It advocates the tightening of scientific links between the Third World Countries and, more particularly, between African and Arab countries, within the framework of Arab-African solidarity.[30]

Prior to this, the United Nations Economic Commission had developed an African Regional Plan for the Application of Science and Technology to Development. The objective of this plan is to provide a framework for the United Nations Organization and its organs and agencies to collaborate with and to provide assistance to African developing countries for the conception and implementation of action program, in a number of selected sectors of these countries' economies. These programs are to be directed toward creating or reinforcing the basic infrastructure essential for the proper application of science and technology to development in Africa and the rest of the developing world.[31] This United Nations African Plan of Action stressed the following areas of concern and cooperation: general development of scientific and technological capacity; natural resources development; food and agriculture; industrial design; research and development; health and sanitation; science and

Table 25: *United Nations Offices in West Africa*

	UNDP	UNFPA	UNICEF	UNHOR	UNIDO	REC. EC. COM.	UN FAO WTP	INF. CTN.	ILO	FAO	UNESCO	WHO	IBRD	ICAO	Other	Total
Benin	RR						FS			SAA/		WR				4
Cape Verde	SUB															1
Gambia	RR						FS									2
Ghana	RR		LO		IDFA		FS	IC		RO SAA/ FO		WR	RM			9
Guinea	RR									SAA/ FO		WR				3
Guinea-Bissau	RR						FS									3
Ivory Coast	RR			CM			FS					WR	RCM			6
Liberia	RR				IDFA		FS	IC		SAA/ FO		WR				4
Mali	RR						FS			SAA/ FO						3
Mauritania	RR						FS			SAA/ FO						3
Niger	RR					SUB	FS			SAA/ FO		WR				5
Nigeria	RR	FC	AO RO		IDFA		FS	IC	AO	SAA/ FO	CM	WR	RM			12
Senegal	RR	FC	AO	RO	IDFA		FS	IC	AO	SAA/ FO	RO	WR		RO	IDEP	13
Sierra Leone	RR						FS			SAA/ FO						3
Togo	RR						FS					WR				4
Upper Volta	RR		LO		IDFA		FS	IC		SAA/ FO	RCM	WR	RM			9
TOTAL																84

Source: Adopted from U.N. Regional and Branch Offices Informational Circular (Coordination/R.1169, 1976).

Key: AO = Area Office
CM = Chief of Mission
FC = Field Coordinator
FO = Field Office
FS = Field Staff
IC = Information Center

IDEP = Institute for Economic Development & Planning
IDFA = Industrial Development Field Office
LO = Liaison Office
RCM = Regional Chief of Mission
RM = Resident Mission
RO = Regional Office

RR = Office of UNDP Resident Representative
SAA = Senior Agricultural Advisor
SUB = Suboffice of Regional Office
WR = WHO Representative

UN development Program.

technology education; demography; and the issue of the transfer of technology. This African Regional Plan is supposed to be financed by the UNDP, the World Bank, and ECOSOC at the approval and advice of the Advisory Panel on Program Policy of the UNDP.

The OAU also maintains beneficial relations with the UNDP that provides for:

1. technical assistance for strengthening the OAU Secretariat–involving training, provision of fellowships and equipment with a financial ceiling of $50,000 a year.
2. financial and technical assistance of persons for major projects arising from OAU decisions involving intercountry, sub-regional or regional cooperation;
3. assistance for the education of persons displaced from African Territories under colonial rule or subject to racial discrimination; and
4. cooperation in the form of reciprocal representation at meetings (including those of the OAU Assembly and Council of Ministers as well as the Governing Council of UNDP), mutual consultations and exchange of information.[32]

Whereas the UNDP maintains offices in African countries and provides much assistance to the OAU member states through their individual governments, it also channels aid to these states through its agencies. The UNDP works in close collaboration with the ECA, UNCTAD, the U.N. Statistical Office, UNICEF, FAO, UNHCR, UNESCO, NGOs, and the OAU. (See Table 25). Although most of West African states have at least a UNDP resident representative office, they do not have UNDP offices in the region to deal with projects and programs set by this UN organ. The Regional Bureau for Africa at the UNDP headquarters at the United Nations in New York is responsible for these programs and projects. When contrasted to other organs and agencies of the UN system, the UNDP's arrangements are rather unique. The World Health Organization (WHO) has ten representatives in West Africa, who individually cover from one to several countries. WHO officials come under an African regional office based in Congo, Brazzaville. This office has direct responsibility for thirty-three African states located in Africa south of the Sahara. In the ECOWAS area, UNICEF has three regional offices, which are liaison officers. Only in Accra and Ouagadougou are these liaison officers attached to the UNDP resident representative office. FAO regional offices for Africa are located in Ghana. UNESCO's arrangement is also different; it has regional offices in Dakar, Lagos, and Ouagadougou. UNIDO's staff is attached to the UNDP resident resrepresentative's office.

The way the organs of the UN system are structured and operated in Africa make it cumbersome for African governments to maintain continuous liaison between them and the United Nations. As the UN activities have increased in Africa, a need for coordinating the activities of these organizations is now imperative. The United Nations system has attempted to deal with these problems by designating the UN representative in each African country as the lead of all other UN officials, Leadership was entrusted to UNDP officials because UNDP resources overshadow those of other organs of the UN system in Africa. In quantitative terms, aid provided by the United Nations system to ECOWAS is less than that of bilateral providers.

Official Development Assistance (ODA) to ECOWAS received from bilateral sources has been significantly greater than what is donated by UNDP and other UN agencies. Table 26 is a statistical breakdown of the aid given to ECOWAS by the UN, UNDP bilateral, and multilateral doners (ODA).

Table 26: Bi- and Multilateral Aid Flows to ECOWAS, 1976 (US $ 000)

	U.N.[I]	UNDP[II]	Total[III]	Bilateral ODA[IV]
Benin	811	2,987	3,798	27,490
Cape Verde	191	1,143	1,334	6,820
Gambia	202	878	1,080	5,410
Ghana	2,905	4,634	7,539	34,040
Guinea	1,783	3,301	5,084	4,390
Guinea-Bissau	997	1,618	2,615	11,810
Ivory Coast	828	3,675	4,503	75,630
Liberia	874	1,578	2,452	21,190
Mali	3,281	2,857	6,138	53,260
Mauritania	2,450	1,474	3,924	17,810
Niger	3,403	2,430	5,833	80,050
Nigeria	2,621	2,530	5,151	26,170
Senegal	1,492	1,709	3,201	81,630
Sierra Leone	2,490	2,210	4,706	7,480
Togo	579	1,449	2,028	20,490
Upper Volta	3,757	4,022	7,779	60,080
Total	28,670	38,495	67,165	533,750

SOURCES: I. "Information on the Regular and Extra-Budgetary Programmes of Technical Cooperation in 1976 of the Organizations in the United Nations System" (DP/265, 1977).
II. "Report of the Administrator for 1976," *Statistical Annex* (DP/255/Annex 1, 1977).
III. Does not include capital assistance from World Bank Group.
IV. *Development Cooperation; Efforts and Policies of the Members of the Development Assistance Committee; 1976* Review (Paris: OECD, 1976).

Multilateral and bilateral aid is usually provided by donor countries for the purpose of neocolonizing the recipient nations. The recipient states do not have a free hand in determining how the bilateral aid should be utilized. Bilateral or multilateral aid definitely furthers the foreign policy interests and objectives of the donor countries.

Although bilateral and multilateral aid to Africa is in quantitative terms larger than that of the UN system, UN aid does not have neocolonial political interests tied with it. The UN system aid is generally preferred because it focuses on important developmental projects. Outside the ECA, most of the regional or multinational cooperative projects of the UN system are funded by the UNDP. Between 1972 and 1982, the UN system in collaboration with the UNDP funded some of the following projects in Africa:

Table 27: Some of the Relevant UNDP Projects in Africa 1972-1982

Name of Project	Countries Covered	Executing Agency
Flood Control and Warning System on the River Niger basin (Phase 2)	Guinea Mali, Niger	WMO
Hydrological Forecasting System for the Middle and Lower Basins of the Niger River	Benin, Cameroon, Mali, Niger, Nigeria, Upper Volta	WMO
Programme for the Strengthening of Agromateorological and Hydrological Services of the Sahelian Countries: Training Center for Agrometeorology and Applied Agrology	Chad, Gambia, Mali, Mauritania, Niger, Senegal, Upper Volta	WMO
Onchocerciasis Control Program in the Volta River Basin Area: Applied Research (Epidemiology and Chemotherapy) and Training	Benin, Ghana, Ivory Coast, Mali, Niger, Togo, Upper Volta	WHO
Applied Research on Trypanosomiasis Epidemiology and Control	Ivory Coast, Niger, Nigeria, Upper Volta	WHO
Regional Center for Postal Training, Abidjan	Ivory Coast, Mali, Mauritania, Niger, Senegal Upper Volta, Togo	UPU
Multinational School for Medium Level Telecommunications Personnel, Rufisque	Benin, Ivory Coast, Mali, Mauritania, Niger, Senegal, Upper Volta	ITU
Agricultural Equipment Improvement	Kenya	FAO
Pilot Asparagus Industry	Lesotho	UNCDF/FAO
Artisan Development	Madagascar	ILO
National Oilseed Development Program	Zambia	FAO
Youth Training Centers	Sudan	ILO/UNICEF
Introduction to Jojoba Cultivation	Sudan	FAO
Beef and Milk Production	Seychelles	FAO
Strengthening of Applied Nutrition Programs	Rwanda	FAO
Construction and Start-up of a Pyrethrum Refinery	Rwanda	UNIDO
Self-help Housing	Mozambique	UNDP

Name of Project	Countries Covered	Executing Agency
Research on the Swamp and Dryland Soils of the Okavango	Botswana	FAO
Training of Instructors for Secondary School Teachers	Angola	UNESCO
Research and Development in Water Pumping Technology for Rural Areas	Ethiopia, Zaire	UNIDO
Mass Education Prgram	Ethiopia, Zaire	UNESCO/UNICEF
Mineral Surveys	Burundi	UNOTC
Support for Fishing Development	Cape Verde, Central African Republic	FAO
Assistance to the Rural Access Roads Program	Kenya	ILO
Irrigation and Arid Regions	Kenya	FAO
Telecommunications Link between Gambia and Senegal	Gambia, Senegal	ITU
Water Resources in the Lake Chad Basin (LCBC)	Cameroon, Chad, Niger, Nigeria	FAO
Livestock Development in Assale-Servewel (LCBC)	Cameroon, Chad, Niger, Nigeria	FAO
Development of the Fisheries in Lake Chad	Cameroon, Chad, Niger, Nigeria	FAO
Research on Desert Locust (OCLALAV)	Benin, Cameroon, Chad, Ivory Coast, Mali, Mauritania, Niger, Nigeria, Senegal, Somalia, Upper Volta	FAO
Control of Grain-eating Birds (Phase 2)	Benin, Cameroon, Chad, Ivory Coast, Mali, Mauritania, Niger, Nigeria, Senegal, Somalia Upper Volta	FAO
Agricultural Development in the Senegal River Basin (Phase 2) (OMVS)	Mali, Mauritania, Senegal	FAO
Hydraulic Development of Pastoral Areas (LCBC)	Cameroon, Chad, Niger, Nigeria	FAO
Applied Research on Tsetse Control in Dry Savanna Zones	Ivory Coast, Niger, Nigeria, Upper Volta	FAO

Name of Project	Countries Covered	Executing Agency
West Africa Rice Development Association (Phases 1 & 2)	Benin, Gambia, Ghana, Ivory Coast, Liberia, Mali, Mauritania, Niger, Nigeria, Senegal, Sierra Leone, Tot, Upper Volta	FAO
West African Clearing House Agreement	Benin, Cameroon, Ghana, Ivory Coast, Liberia Mali, Mauritania, Niger, Nigeria, Senegal, Sierra Leone, Togo Upper Volta	ECA/UNCTAD
Mano River Union Assistance to the Secretariat	Liberia, Sierra Leone	UNCTAD
Adviser in Sales Promotion Assigned to Africa Groundnut Council	Gambia, Mali, Niger, Nigeria, Senegal, Sudan	UNCTAD
Sahel Groundwater Assistance	Chad, Mali, Mauritania, Niger, Senegal, Upper Volta	UNOTC
Study of Hydroelectric and Irrigation Potentials in the Mano River Basin	Liberia, Sierra Leone	UNOTC
Hydrological and Topographical Study of the Gambia River Basin	Gambia, Senegal	UNOTC
Indicative Development Plan for the Niger River	Benin, Ivory Coast, Niger Cameroon, Chad, Guinea, Mali, Upper Volta, Nigeria	ECA
Assistance to Banque ouest-Africaine de development	Benin, Ivory Coast, Niger, Senegal, Togo, Upper Volta	IBRID

SOURCE: Compiled from "UNDP Regional Programme for Africa 1972-1982." The Projects listed in this table are illustrative rather than exhaustive.

From March 1976 to March 1977 the ECA developed a program of work and priorities for 1978 and 1979 to be utilized by the OAU countries. In its' report, the ECA identified and targeted the following as priorities for African development: agriculture; development planning, projections and policies; promotion of economic cooperation and integration; education and training; human settlements; industrial development; international trade; manpower; natural resources; mineral resources development; water resources development; energy; cartography; human environment; population; public administration management and finance; fiscal, monetary, and financial policies and institutions; science and technology; social development;

statistics; transport; communications and tourism; special program in integrated rural development; special program for least developed countries and a special program for the Sahel. This program of work is based on the assumptions that there is need for an increasing measure of economic self-reliance; the development of individual, regional, or collective planning directed toward the attainment of the objectives of socio-economic policies; that there should be accelerated and diversified growth to meet the needs of the populace; the widespread development capabilities for generating and retaining real income; and the need for effective programs to reduce unemployment and to bridge the gap between rural and urban growth. To achieve the stated goals of economic development, the ECA developed the following:

> ... strategy on which the programme is based places emphasis on the development of industry, the transformation of agriculture and the promotion of the accelerated development of the rural sector in such a way as to engineer positive growth promoting and diversifying inter-actions among these actors. The sub-sectors of the industrial sector are concerned as structurally and dynamically related to each other, not as a casual and miscellaneous aggregation of industrial enterprises, activities and products. The development of industry is seen as a chain running from multinational basic and strategic industries (Section 332) to national industries and rural industries, tied together, where necessary, by complementation agreements and subcontracting arrangements (project 334.04, 334.27 and 332.05). The instrumentation for industry includes African multinational corporations supported by (project 551.06, 551.05 and Section 552) and the adoption on a regional basis, of common technical design standards for key products. The African multinational corporation would include among its functions technological development, management techniques and general support to industries in its particular sector. It would negotiate joint enterprises and technology contracts as well as promote extra-African exports of manufactures.[33]

Although the ECA program of action as supported by the OAU places emphasis on the transformation of agriculture partly through improved policy and partly through an improved food distribution system, there are also stresses on regional planning, urbanization, development of infrastructure, and an accelerated rate of construction of industries. The UNDP is also involved with organizing seminars for economic development in transportation and communications, postal organizations, agriculture, education, and industrial and technological development. The UNDP together with the ECA also actively contributes and supports the welfare of African refugees from both dependent as well as independent African states.

Apart from its phenomenal contributions to the cause for African social and economic development, the ECA has had numerous problems. One such problem is related to the vastness of the African continent and the numerous number of states the ECA has to deal with. No other UN regional organization has as many states to deal with as the ECA. Aware of this enormous amount of territory it had to deal with, the ECA has set up four administrative subregional offices: one in Zaire to serve central Africa; one in Zambia to serve eastern Africa; one in Tangiers, Morocco, to serve northern Africa; and one in Niger to serve western Africa. In addition to working cooperatively with the ECA, these administrative regional offices were expected to coordinate their activies with all UN agencies operating in their regions.

Because of inadequate staff, bureaucratic weaknesses, and conflicting economic philosophies of African states, these regional offices were a complete failure. They were unable to devise or coordinate programs that could have lessened the work of the ECA or those of other UN agencies.

Recognizing the ineffectiveness of the regional offices, the General Assembly at the inception of the Second United Nations Developmental Decade created the Mutlidisciplinary Development Advisory Teams (UNDATs) or Multinational Programming and Operational Centers (MULPOCs) as they were renamed in 1977, to help the LDCs plan their economic programs and to coordinate UN regional economic and social organizations. Of the seven UNDATs set up, three were established in Africa, operating from Lusaka, Niamey, and Yaounde. The UNDATs were to supplement the work of the ECA and other UN agencies operating in Africa, and were expected to identify the need for local products and the possibility of selecting those projects that could be multinationalized. While avoiding involvement with projects of a national nature, they were to concentrate on fostering multinational cooperation in fields dealing with transportation, trade, and industry. Drawing from the teams of specialists on their staff, and the ECA, the UNDATs was expected to recommend sound solutions to African problems.

The selection of leaders for the African UNDATs were to be made jointly by the UN Department of Economic and Social Affairs in New York and the ECA. Although the financing of the UNDATs was partly through its regular budget and partly out of funds in-trust deposited under bilateral agreements with interested governments, the daily operations of the UNDATs are entrusted to the ECA. The UNDATs' reports are sent to the ECA, the UNDP resident representative, the host governements, and the UN Department of Economic and Social Affairs. The UNDATs, like their predecessors the regional administrative offices, remain directly under the supervision of the ECA. In case of problems, the UNDATs are supposed to appeal to the ECA for help.

Although the UNDATs have had fruitful relations with ILO, UNCTAD, the Economic Community for West African States (ECOWAS), UNICEF, and the OAU, their problems have been immense. In creating the UNDATs, the United Nations, the ECA, and the OAU did not create long-term financing arrangements for them. Initially, funds for the UNDATs programs came from the United Nations, and voluntary donations from the Netherlands, Sweden, Denmark, and the United States. The UNDP also provided funds to the UNDATs in 1976 as it was being evaluated by the ECA. The ECA has not been able to sustain its financial contributions to the UNDATs. The budget of the ECA is also small and insufficient to carry out all of the projects the ECA would want to implement. The ECA budget is shown in Table 28.

More funds are needed for the ECA to expand its programs and to recruit more skilled specialists to operate its technologically advanced schemes. Because of its financial problems, the ECA is no help in solving the financial problems of the UNDATs. The lack of funds has seriously affected the quality of specialists the UNDATs can afford to hire. This in turn has substantially lowered the quality of work the UNDATs are presently doing.

Table 28:   ECA Operational Program 1979-1981 Sectorial Distribution (United States Dollars)

		Total	1979	1980	1981
1.	Socioeconomic research and planning	98,132	98,132	--	--
2.	Agriculture	1,189,990	273,202	477,988	429,800
3.	Industry	1,053,075	593,177	344,098	115,800
4.	International trade and finance	2,067,088	077,171	699,917	390,000
5.	Social development	3,110,882	1,584,318	797,310	729,254
6.	Natural resources	3,741,568	1,725,980	1,187,588	828,000
7.	Transport communications and tourism	819,780	593,990	142,790	83,000
8.	Public administration	5,075,885	1,724,885	1,631,250	1,719,750
9.	Statistics	2,145,700	880,700	608,000	657,000
10.	Population	2,116,900	748,900	615,000	753,000
11.	Economic cooperation	2,965,432	1,045,132	945,000	966,300
	Subtotal	24,375,432	10,245,587	7,457,941	6,671,904
	Program support costs	3,111,029	1,339,640	944,581	826,808
	Total	27,486,461	11,585,277	8,402,522	7,498,712
	Support services	3,349,350	1,032,350	1,114,400	1,202,600
	Grand Total	30,835,811	12,617,577	9,516,922	8,701,312

SOURCE: UN ECA Program Budget, 1979-1981 E/CN. 14/709 p.s.

As demonstrated, the cooperation between the United Nations system and the OAU is increasing. One area of importance where closer relations are developing is the United Nations International Labor Organization (ILO), which was established at the end of World War I as part of the League of Nations. In 1946, the ILO was incorporated as a special agency of the United Nations system. Its purpose is to contribute to the establishment of lasting peace by promoting social justice and to improve, through international action, labor conditions, living standards, and the promotion of economic and social stability. In order to achieve the cited purposes,

> ILO brings together Government, labor and management to recommend international minimum standards and to draft international labor Conventions on such subjects as wages, hours of work, minimum ages for employment, conditions of work for various classes of workers, workmen's compensation, social insurance, vacation with pay, industrial safety, employment services, labor inspection and freedom of association. The Organization carries on extensive technical assistance to Governments.[34]

The ILO currently has numerous management training, manpower planning, and trade union organization projects throughout Africa. ILO management training is supported by the productivity centers or management institutes that contribute to management research, training, and consultation for private and public business. Aware of how its member states could benefit from the ILO resources, the OAU passed Resolution CM/129 (IX) which noted the following:

Recommends to the Member States of the Organization of African Unity that they choose African nationals to represent their governments, employers and workers within their delegations to the International Labor Conference;

Draws the attention of Member States to the necessity for the African representatives of the International Labor Organization (governments, employers and workers) to present a united front with a view to defending African interests at the International Labor Conference;

Urgently calls upon the Administrative Secretary-General of the Organization of African Unity to continue his activities aimed at organizing, before 30 April 1968, a meeting for the unification of the African trade union movement;

Appeals to the governments of the Member States to lend their assistance in the preparation as well as in the holding of this meeting.[35]

With encouragement and pressure from the OAU, African countries are now active participating members of the ILO. Their association with the ILO benefits them from the specialized technical knowledge, and the organizational and managerial skills of the ILO. These benefits are made easily available to OAU members through ILO offices in Africa. An ILO regional office for Africa is located in Addis Ababa. Under this regional office are area offices covering one or more countries throughout Africa. Of great importance to Africa and the LDCs is that the main areas of activity of the ILO are employment promotion, vocational guidance, social security, safety and health, labor laws, labor relations, labor administration, workers education, cooperatives, rural, and a host of other related institutions. Because of the broad issues with which the ILO concerns itself, its work overlaps with other agencies of the UN system like FAO, UNDP, UNESCO, WHO, UNIDO, ECA, and others. The ILO relationships with other UN system agencies makes it an extremely important organization for the OAU to develop a closer and an amicable relation.

Areas in which the OAU member states have a poor record of performance deal with the ILO labor standards and the ratification and implementation of international labor conventions in Africa. These ILO labor conventions relate to employment policy, forced labor, social policy, and labor inspection. ILO labor inspection, evaluation of employment policies and practices, and the ratification of international labor conventions by the UN member states are matters of concern to it. On these issues it has been stated that:

a conviction of the importance of ILO standards and a desire to see them accepted and applied as widely as possible as a contribution to the economic and social development of countries and a means of achieving social justice and peace; awareness that their application is accompanied by difficulties of all kinds; a desire to identify the difficulties and to consider measures which both the Organization and governments could take, with the cooperation of the national employers' and workers' organizations, to overcome them so that national action can be brought into line with ILO standards; and a desire to deal with them at regional meetings where the problems common to countries in the region can be discussed less formally than at sessions of the General Conference.[36]

In this connection, the Nairobi Fourth African Regional Conference held between

November and December 1973, after discussing the Director-General's Report on the position of African countries with respect to the international labor standards, adopted a Resolution concerning the Ratification and Implementation of International Labor Standards in Africa. The resolution outlined the following:

1. Calls upon all African States Members of the International Labor Organization to make arrangements for the regular and systematic examination of the situation of national law and practice in regard to matters dealt within international labor Conventions and Recommendations with a view to advising the government on the further measures which might be taken for the purpose of implementing the standards laid down in these instruments and on the ratification of Conventions.

2. Calls upon the States concerned to examine, within the framework of such tripartite consultative arrangements, analysis of the position regarding the ratification and implementation of selected Conventions prepared for ILO regional meetings in Africa and any conclusions thereon reached by such meetings.

3. In relation to the selected Conventions considered by the African Advisory Committee at its Fifth Session (Addis Ababa, 1972), draws the attention of the governments concerned to the following considerations:
   (a) the importance of the ratification of the Employment Policy Convention, 1964 (No. 122), as the basis of policy for the implementation at the national level of the Jobs and Skills Programme for Africa aimed at the creation of productive jobs and the development of manpower skills;
   (b) the need to ensure the strict observance of ILO Conventions relating to forced labor, in law and in practice, as means of protecting the freedom and dignity in Africa whose populations are still being subjected to this form of exploitation;
   (c) the special relevance to the problems and policies of African countries of the Social Policy (Basic Aims and Standards) Convention, 1962 (No. 117), which was adopted in response to a resolution of the First African Regional Conference (Lagos, 1960);
   (d) the importance of strengthening labor inspection services as a means of ensuring the effectiveness of labor legislation and social policy.

4. Reiterates the special importance attached to the ratification and strict application of Conventions relating to the protection of certain fundamental human rights (freedom of association, elimination of discrimination in employment and occupation, abolition of forced labor and of penal sanctions for breach of contracts of employment), which the First African Regional Conference (Lagos, 1960) declared to be a question of honor and prestige for all African States.

5. Invites African States encountering difficulties in the implementation of ILO standards to have recourse to the procedure of direct contacts with the International Labor Organization and, where appropriate, to have recourse also to technical cooperation as a means of overcoming such difficulties.

6. Calls upon governments to associate representatives of workers and employers in the preparation, implementation and evaluation of technical cooperation programmes, with a view to ensuring that these programmes are directed to the realization of social policy and in particular, to the progressive implementation of international labor Conventions and Recommendations.

7. Invites the International Labor Office to intensify its action to assist African countries to draw fully on ILO standards in developing their social policies and legislation, by action such as:
(a) the assignment to the Regional Office for Africa of an official with special responsibility for advising governments, employers and workers on questions concerning Conventions and Recommendations and their implementation;
(b) the further organization of regional study courses on international labor standards and assistance to workers' education programmes at the national level in this field.

8. Invites the Governing Body of the International Labor office to ensure that the examination of the ratification and implementation of ILO instruments is pursued as a regular feature of the regional activities of the International Labor Organization.[37]

In conformity with the recommendation of this resolution, in December 1975, a discussion took place at the Sixth Session of the African Advisory Committee held in Lomé, Togo. While discussing problems encountered by OAU states in implementing and adopting ILO labor conventions, several members of the committee emphasized in particular that international labor standards remain the keystone of ILO activities and that they can be of assistance to the OAU states in taking measures conducive to parallel social and economic development. At the conclusion of the session, the advisory committee submitted a report to all African states that were members of ILO and to representative organizations of employers and workers. Comments were received from nine OAU member states and three employers organizations. The governments of Morocco and Senegal had no comments to make. These governments of the Central Africa Republic, Chad, and Kenya provided information on issues that had been the subject of comments by the Committee of Experts on the Application of Conventions and Recommendation. The government of Gabon made comments about the importance of the ratification of conventions by African states, the difficulties, inherent in respecting the obligations regarding ILO standards, and ways of eliminating these difficulties. The government of Mali emphasized the influence of international labor standards on the development of national legislation and in the negotiation of collective agreements. The government of Sudan announced that a study of international labor conventions was being conducted with a view to increasing the number of ratifications by OAU states. The government of Rwanda appreciated the role played by the direct contacts procedure and exchanges of views between governments concerned and representatives of the director-general of the ILO in solving problems concerned with the ratification of labor conventions.[38]

Pertaining to the responses of the organization of employers and workers, the Federation of Swaziland Employers stated that the Labor Advisory Board was being reorganized in accordance with specifications of ILO Conventions and Recommendations. The Zambian Federation of Employers and the Employer's Consultative Association of Malawi responded by saying that they had no comments to make. The rest of the African states and employers and workers associations did not bother to respond to the reports of the director-general and that of the African Advisory

Committee. Although African states have stated on numerous occasions that they attach great importance to the ratification of the ILO conventions, their records of ratification of these conventions have not been praiseworthy. Africa accounts for about 24 percent of all ratifications. The average number of ILO conventions ratified by African states is 26 percent, for Europeans is 51 percent, for Asian countries it is 18 percent, and for North and South American countries it is 37 percent. Another problem accounting for this low percentage of ratification by African states lies in the variations in the number of ratifications from one African state to another. For instance, seventeen OAU member states have ratified thirty or more conventions and seven have ratified fewer than seven.

A number of factors account for the low percentage of ILO ratification of its conventions and the implementation of labor standards in Africa by African members of the United Nations. Many African United Nations member states are not members of the ILO. Those that have ratified the ILO conventions have been members of this organization for the last two decades. Moreover, most of the ILO conventions were formulated and adopted before the independence of all African states with the exception of Egypt, Ethiopia, Liberia, and South Africa. As a result of this, some African UN members are not in favor of the ILO conventions because they are of the opinion that they are not relevant to the social and economic levels of African development. Even if they wanted to ratify them, many African states do not have the requisite expertise to implement the conventions and the ILO labor standards. The ILO in conjunction with other UN system agencies like the ECA, FAO, UNDP, WHO, UNIDO, UNESCO, and others are still setting up manpower development as well as labor union training projects throughout Africa. Not until most ILO conventions are amended to reflect the social and economic levels of development of their societies will a majority of the African states ratify the ILO conventions.

Despite these problems, the ILO has had a healthy relationship with the OAU states. Every year witnesses an increase of African membership in the ILO. African states are increasingly becoming active members of the various organs of the ILO. By being active in the ILO, the OAU states will be able to influence this UN organ to formulate, adopt, and ratify labor conventions that will not only benefit the LDCs but OECD members of the UN system. The ILO as a part of the UN system is actively involved in helping Africa and the LDCs improve the standard of living of their workers by educating and training them in trade union schools. Educating workers enables them to enter into employers and workers associations or representative councils charged with the responsibility of improving relations between labor and management.

Cooperation between OAU states and the UN has not only increased through the activities of the ECA, UNCTAD, UNDP, FAO, WHO, ILO, UNITAR, UNIDO, UNICEF, and UNESCO but also those of the United Nations High Commissioner for Refugees (UNHCR). The question of African refugees has created social, economic, and political problems to many OAU countries. The OAU and the UNHCR have cooperated in their efforts to help alleviate the plight of African refugees. According to the 1951 Convention and also the Statute of the UNHCR, a refugee is an individual who, owing to well-founded fear of being persecuted for reasons of race, religion, nationality, membership of a particular social group or political opinion, is outside the country of his nationality and is unable or, owing to such fear, is unwilling to avail himself of the protection of that country; or who, not having a nationality and being outside the country of his former habitual residence as a result of such events, is unable or, owing to such fear, is unwilling to return to it.[39]

While it adopted the 1951 UN Convention on Refugees, the OAU Council of Ministers also passed Resolution CM/Resolution 88 (VIII), which called upon states that have not adhered to the Convention to apply their humanitarian principles and recommended that "the signatory States continue their consideration of various recommendations and of the provisions of the said draft convention and, taking into account the above considerations, convey their comments and observations, in writing, to the OAU Secretariat, with a view to the transmission of a final draft to the next session of the Council of Ministers."[40]

Whereas African states are contributing money and manpower in the social rehabilitation of the uprooted African refugees, the UNHCR in conjunction with the OAU are creating better living facilities for them. Also aiding these two organizations are the ILO, UNESCO, and the ECA. The Bureau for Placement and Education of African Refugees cooperates with these agencies and advises them on issues affecting resettlement, education, medical care, social well-being, and any other problems that the refugees may confront. In pursuance of these objectives, the council of ministers of the OAU at their twenty-ninth Ordinary Session in Libreville, Gabon, adopted Resolution CM/Res. 547 (XXIX), which stipulated the following:

1.   Reiterates its gratitude to the host countries of the region and urges them to generously grant to refugees the hospitality and assistance they need irrespective of their political affiliations;

2.   Expresses its gratitude to other Member States which are taking action to provide assistance for these refugees and encourage them to continue their efforts and increase their valuable assistance;

3.   Congratulates the Commission of Ten and the BPEAR on the interest they are showing in this matter and on their successful initiative in this regard;

4.   Further notes with satisfaction the concrete proposals made by the U.N. Mission of Experts on Refugee Students in Botswana, Lesotho and Swaziland;

5.   Strongly supports the appeal made by the United Nations High Commissioner for Refugees for increased assistance to refugees and recommends that Member States generously consider the requests for assistance made to them, and especially recommends that they make more vacancies, bursaries and scholarships available to these refugees in their educational institutions;

6.   Invites Member States to inform the BPEAR at the latest by 31 August 1977 the number of these young refugee students whom they can receive in their countries or grant scholarships;

7.   Decides to set up a special fund for aid, similar to the Liberation Committee Fund for Southern African refugees to be funded from extra budgetary contributions and administered by BPEAR;

8.   Appeals once again to the international community and particularly to the international organizations of humanitarian interest to continue to give an assistance;

9.   Calls on the Secretary-General to convene urgently a meeting of Committee of Experts set up under Resolution CM/536 (XXVIII), follow-up developments of

the situation in this region and assist in finding a solution to this problem in consultation with Member States, Liberation Movements and the UNHCR, and report to the Council of Ministers at its Thirtieth Ordinary Session;
10.   Expresses satisfaction with the harmonious cooperation between the United Nations High Commission, the Coordinating Committee and BPEAR and urges them to continue their efforts in order to find suitable solutions to the problem of refugees.[41]

The Bureau for Placement and Education of African Refugees (BPEAR), established in Addis Ababa in 1967 by the OAU has as its task to promote the resettlement and the employment of African refugees and to collect and provide information concerning education, training, and employment opportunities in Africa.[42] The OAU-BPEAR is the only organ of OAU that deals with the social and political welfare of the African refugees. BPEAR raises many political, social, educational, and economic issues concerning refugees with African governments and other international agencies. The following diagrammatic structure illustrates BPEAR's linkages with the international agencies involved with the plight of African refugees.

OAU-BPEAR
Administrative Level

Resettlement Section of UNHCR	WCC, IUEFF, and other voluntary agencies	All African Conference of Churches Offices

Operational Level

UNHCR representatives	Joint Refugee Services	Christian Councils and other Refugee Offices

Through the collaboration of the OAU and the various United Nations organs, African refugees are receiving shelter, food, and clothing from African states, churches, various UN agencies, and many other international and transnational organizations. Scholarship funds are now available from the OAU member states and the United Nations for providing African refugees with some form of technical skills. Although the aid provided to these refugees is not enough, it is a great contribution in the amelioration of their dreaded condition of habitation.

Other major issues of discussions that affect the relations of the OAU, the United Nations, and the developing as well as the developed countries are the Law of the Seas Conferences. These conferences deal with such issues as navigation, telecommunications, pollution, disposal of wastes, the seas as sources of food, minerals, fuel, and energy. Although the oceans and seas provide many desirable resources to mankind, many problems have to be solved. For example, there are no marked boundaries in the seas and no one nation owns the seas and oceans resources. Some questions that arise are: How far out to sea or ocean do the states' sovereignty extend? What are the rights of commercial business to the resources of the oceans? Who owns these resources? Do landlocked countries have any rights in exploiting these seabed resources? Should there be some form of international control over the exploitation of these aquatic resources that are outside national jurisdiction? How can we save the seas and oceans from being polluted by business developers? Because of the importance of these issues, the United Nations has arrogated to itself special responsibilities regarding the distribution of the aquatic natural resources. Specialized agencies such as the FAO and the Intergovernmental Maritime Consultative Organization were active in promoting the 1958 Geneva Conventions on the law of the seas.

The 1958 Geneva Conventions on the Laws of the Seas are a product of centuries of gradual developments among the Europeans and other developed countries. These conventions have been ratified by less than 50 percent of the United Nations member countries and rejected by the OAU. Although the Afro-Asian countries recognize the necessity of these conventions, they also believe that these laws of the seas should be revised. In reinforcing their uncompromising opposition to the 1958 Geneva Conventions, the Afro-Asian countries reiterated that these 1958 conventions reflected the imperialists and colonial interests of the major maritime powers whose voices were overrepresented at this conference. The conventions did not address the interests of the developing Afro-Asian countries.

The first United Nations Conference of the Law of the Seas of 1958 and the second conference in 1960 and the various conventions they adopted left the issues on the breadth of the territorial sea and a host of other issues unresolved. Meanwhile, from 1960 to the present, new factors have emerged: Continental African representation has increased from twenty to fifty-one; the attainment of independence by some Asian and Caribbean countries that had no voice in the drafting of the early conventions on the law of the seas; the accelerating progress in drilling and mining at much greater depths because of technological breakthroughs in the pertinent industries; the increased pressure and recognition by many states on the economic importance of their coastal and offshore resources; disputes among countries over fishing and drilling rights; and the increased awareness of the dangers of pollution and the dumping of potentially harmful nuclear wastes in oceans. These and many other factors have convinced many UN member states that something must be done in the way of drawing a code of acceptable guidelines of conventions to regulate the conduct of nations in the exploitation of the resources of the seas and oceans.

Many Afro-Asian and Caribbean countries are of the position that the militarization of the seas by the industrialized states and their intense competition in exploiting the resources of the seas are matters of international concern. Because of these concerns, the Afro-Asian states were instrumental in having the United Nations General Assembly adopt Resolution 2750C (XXV) on December 17, 1970, to convene the Third Conference on the Laws of the Seas in 1973. Having enlarged the Committee on the Peaceful Uses of the Sea-Bed to reflect world geographical interests represented in the General Assembly, Resolution 2750C (XXV) further instructed the enlarged Committee on the Peaceful Uses of the Sea-Bed and the Ocean Floor beyond the Limits of National Jurisdiction to hold two sessions in Geneva in March and in July-August 1971, in order to prepare draft treaty articles for the Conference on the Law of the Sea. The draft treaty included an international machinery to govern the resources of the seabed and the ocean floor and the subsoil thereof, beyond the limits of national jurisdiction, taking into account the equitable sharing by all states in the benefits to be derived therefrom, bearing in mind the special interests and needs of developing countries, whether coastal or landlocked, on the basis of the Declaration of Principles Governing the Sea-Bed and the Ocean Floor. The committee was instructed to invite the United Nations Educational, Scientific and Cultural Organization and its Intergovernmental Oceanographic Commission, the Food and Agriculture Organization of the United Nations and its Committee on Fisheries, the World Health Organization, the Intergovernmental Maritime Consultative Organization, the World Meteorological Organization, the International Atomic Energy Agency, and other specialized agencies to participate in its meetings on the peaceful uses of the seabed and the ocean floor.[43]

As the OAU countries were active in passing the General Assembly Resolution 2750V (SSV), their convictions were also reinforced by the fact that 20 percent of the world's current output of petroleum is obtained from offshore areas. By 1980 this production was increased to 33 percent and is likely to increase five times as much by the end of the twentieth century. The catch in ocean fisheries is also likely to have a fourfold increase from the 1970 base of 62 million tons. Further, the greatest volume of the known marine mineral resources (excluding petroleum) is located in the deep seas. Many geological and geochemical studies confirm the presence of vast quantities of copper, cobalt, nickel, manganese, and molybdenum. Because many countries of the world have great interest in utilizing these and other marine resources, on December 17, 1970, the General Assembly in its Declaration of Principles Governing the Sea-Bed and Ocean Floor forbade any claims of ownership of oceans and seas by individuals, business companies, and states.

After the adoption of the General Assembly Resolutions 2749 and 2750, the OAU countries intensified their participation in the proceedings of all discussions and conferences dealing with the exploitation of resources of the oceans and seas. While these discussions were taking place, disagreements emerged within the ranks of the OAU with respect to the coastal landlocked countries' perception on the control and exploitation of marine resources. The major area of disagreement was removed after the OAU countries held many discussions among themselves. The rationale behind these discussions was that the OAU should agree on how the world's aquatic resources should be exploited and distributed. Unity within the OAU would be an important factor in enhancing its position within the nonaligned countries and also in bargaining with the highly technologically developed and industralized countries. The desire on the part of the OAU to influence the rest of the world community on this subject is clearly demonstrated by its adoption of Resolution CM/Res. 570 (XXIX). While acknowledging the lack of progress made by the United Nations and its agencies, Resolution CM/Res. 570 (XXIX) recommended to the African group at the Law of the Seas Conference to work in concert so that some of the ideas of the New International Economic Order would be actualized.

At the May 1977, New York Conference on the Law of the Seas there was greater cohesion among the OAU and the nonaligned group of 77. Although there was a unanimous agreement on all issues concerning the Law of the Seas, it is now evident that the former European and U.S. conventions are no longer accepted without question as the basis for regulating the conduct of the new states. In addition, the fact that the world community is able to address the issues of control, exploitation, and distribution of the wealth of the oceans and seas are positive steps toward a complete agreement and cooperation in utilizing these resources.

The United Nations and Conflicts Among African States

One of the areas of cooperation between the OAU and the United Nations is the resolution of conflicts among African states. Since the founding of the OAU, many boundary conflicts have occurred among African states. The most serious of these conflicts are the Algerian-Moroccan dispute and the Mauritanian and Moroccan conflict with the Polisario over the Arab Democratic Republic. The main areas of conflict that involve only OAU states are of two types: territorial disputes among adjacent African states; and particular situations within each African country resulting from political, religious, and ethnic conflicts and inequitable distribution of national wealth which create domestic or intrastate wars.

Like the United Nations, the OAU supports peaceful resolution of conflicts within African states and the international community. With respect to its intention of settling all African conflicts peacefully, the OAU's Article XIX notes:

> Member States pledge to settle all disputes among themselves by peaceful means and, to this end, decide to establish a Commission of Mediation, Conciliation and Arbitration, the composition of which and conditions of service shall be defined by a separate Protocol to be approved by the Assembly of Heads of State and Government. Said Protocol shall be regarded as forming an integral part of the present Charter.[44]

The Algerian-Moroccan boundary dispute was one of the first conflicts that the United Nations and the OAU seriously tried to resolve. Morocco claimed the Algerian Sahara on the grounds that it was its integral territory prior to the colonization of the area by France. When oil and other mineral resources were discovered in the Algerian Sahara, Morocco intensified its demands for annexure. Before Algeria became independent, the Moroccan government had concluded a secret agreement with the provisional government of Algeria that recognized this as a territorial problem created by French imperialism and colonialism which had to be resolved when Algeria attained its independence.[45] After its independence, Algeria repudiated Moroccan claims to its state and would not entertain any negotiations leading to the cessation of Algerian territory to any other state. The refusal by Algeria to surrender part of its territory to Morocco led to the eruption of a full-scale war between the two countries on October 14, 1963. As the war raged, Algeria insisted that Morocco abide by Article III of the OAU Charter, which states the following:

The Member States in pursuit of the purposes stated in Article II, solemnly affirm and declare their adherences to the following principles:
1. the sovereign equality of all Member States;
2. non-interference in the internal affairs of States;
3. respect for the sovereignty and territorial integrity of each State and for its inalienable right to independent existence;
4. peaceful settlement of disputes by negotiation, mediation, conciliation or arbitration;

5. unreserved condemnation, in all its forms, of political assassination as well as of subversive activities on the part of neighboring States of any other States;
6. absolute dedication to the total emancipation of the African territories which are still dependent;
7. affirmation of a policy of non-alignment with regard to all blocs.[46]

While the newly independent Algerian Republic sought OAU mediation in the resolution of the conflict with Morocco, the kingdom of Morocco felt that the issue would be better resolved by the United Nations Security Council. Morocco was not optimistic about the role the OAU would play in the arbitration of the conflict since its charter emphasized the principle of sovereignty and territorial integrity of African states and the preservation of the existing de facto colonial boundaries. Thinking that the OAU position would be favorably disposed toward Algeria, Morocco sent a letter to the secretary-general of the United Nations informing him about its conflict with Algeria. Recognizing the Moroccan attempts to internationalize the conflict, the OAU exerted pressure on Morocco to stop bringing the issue up at the Security Council before the matter was considered by the OAU.

On behalf of the OAU, the then emperor of Ethiopia and the former president of Mali, Mobido Keita, succeeded in persuading the former Algerian president (Ahmed Ben Bella) and the king of Morocco to meet with them on October 29, 1963, at Bamako, Mali to resolve the conflict. The agreement between the king of Morocco and President Ben Bella outlined the following:

i)   to effect a cease-fire from midnight on 1 November 1963;
ii)   to establish a commission of Algerian, Moroccan, Ethiopian and Malian officers to determine a demilitarized zone;
iii) to invite Ethiopian and Malian observers to supervise the cease-fire and watch over security and military neutrality in the demilitarized zone;
iv)   to request an extraordinary meeting of the OAU Council of Ministers in order to set up a commission that would determine responsibility for the outbreak of hostilities, study the frontier question and make proposals for a settleement of the dispute;
v)   to request Algeria and Morocco to cease all public and press attacks on each other as from 1 November and to observe strictly the principles of non-interference in each other's affairs and of settlement of all disputes between African States by means of negotiations.[47]

Fighting between the two countries did not end after the signing of the Bamako agreement. Because of this, Morocco held meetings with France and the United States about the possibility of the UN's role in mediating in the conflict. The two countries advised Morocco to have the matter resolved through the OAU because this would eliminate the possibility of great and superpower rivalry and conflict on the subject. With pressure from both the United Nations and the OAU, the two countries agreed to arbitration. The OAU Extraordinary Council of Ministers supported the Bamako Agreement and advised Morocco to abide by the stipulations of the OAU Charter, particularly with respect to border disputes.

The efforts of the OAU to resolve the Moroccan-Algerian conflicts within its framework had been successful. With the encouragement of the OAU Council of Ministers, relations between these two warring countries were greatly improved. In May 1970 the two nations signed an agreement to recognize the OAU position on the de facto recognition of the colonial boundaries being the basis for accepting territorial delimitations. The success of the OAU arbitration in this conflict was largely the result of the Security Council's recommendation that the crisis be resolved at the OAU regional level. Also to be commended for the successful acts of the OAU in resolving the dispute are the two concerned African members of the United Nations that were willing to provide a favorable environment for the OAU to mediate.

The OAU's peaceful resolution of the Algerian-Moroccan border dispute created a precedent that African conflicts can be resolved by the good offices of the OAU. When Kenya became independent in December 1963, and hostilities broke out between it and Somalia over the future of the Somali-speaking people who lived in the northeast of Kenya and eastern Ethiopia as well as 50 percent of the new Republic of Djibouti on grounds that these territorial areas were once integral parts of Somalia before the advent of British, French, and Italian colonialism in the Horn of Africa. Somalia contended that the right to self-determination of the Somali people residing in the Ogaden and Haud regions of Ethiopia, Southern Djibouti, and the Northeastern Frontier District of Kenya was enshrined in the UN Charter. In addition, the General Assembly has passed and adopted numerous resolutions in support of colonized peoples' right to self-determination. Somalia's claims that these UN resolutions also applied to the case of dismembering the three countries ran counter to the OAU and UN charters that upheld the sanctity of the national sovereignty of states and the noninterference in the internal affairs of members of the OAU and the United Nations.

On February 9, 1964, Somalia urgently requested the UN Security Council to convene and consider its complaints against Ethiopian acts of aggression that infringed upon the sovereignty and security of its territory. The Security Council, the United States, the USSR and the great powers opted for an OAU regional solution rather than UN mediation. Meanwhile, Ethiopia, and at a later date, Somalia, requested the OAU to resolve these border conflicts. As the negotiations were progressing, Somalia constantly informed the UN Security Council president on the developments of its complaints to the OAU. In its 1964 mediation meeting in Dar es Salaam, the OAU Council of Ministers, as later ratified by all the heads of African governments (excluding Morocco and Somalia), upheld the observance of Article III of the OAU Charter which states that the respect for sovereignty and territorial integrity of member states should be respected by the conflict and that they should resolve their differences peacefully. At the end of 1977, Somalia invaded Ethiopia again with the hope that it would wrestle the Ogaden and Haud regions from it. With Russian military hardware and support from Cuban government troops, Ethiopia won a resounding victory against the Somalian aggressors. Although the OAU and the United Nations deplored the outbreak of the war they supported Ethiopian, Kenyan, and Djiboutian sovereignties over their states which Somalia was aggressively seeking to annex.

An ongoing conflict which the OAU and the United Nations have not yet resolved is the issue of the Spanish Sahara that became independent in 1976, but was divided between Morocco and Mauritania. After intense political conflicts, Mauritania gave up its occupation of the southern part of the Spanish Sahara. Immediately following Mauritanian renunciation of its political claims to the Spanish Sahara, Morocco proceeded to annex the whole territory. While refusing to be incorporated into Morocco and Mauritania, the people of the Spanish Sahara declared themselves independent and renamed their country the Sahara Arab Democratic Republic (SADR).

Prior to the 1976 annexation of the Spanish Sahara by Morocco and Mauritania, the African Group at the United Nations had raised on numerous occasions the issue of the attainment of independence of the people of the Spanish Sahara. Both the United Nations and the OAU have persistently passed resolutions calling on Spain to grant independence to the people of the Spanish Sahara through their party known as the Populaire pour la libération de Saguia el Hamara et Rio de Oro (Polisario) Front. Although the OAU and the United Nations General Assembly did not publicly and openly denounce Moroccan and Mauritanian annexure of the SADR, they continued to exert pressure on the two countries to change their expansionistic policies. Constant threats by Mauritania and Morocco to quit the OAU if its demands were not met had initially and severely undermined the capability and willingness of the OAU to adopt a position contrary to Morocco and Mauritania. However, constant pressure by Algeria kept the issue alive. Just how problematic this issue has been is clearly and vividly illustrated by the events surrounding the adoption of the Resolution of the OAU Council of Ministers meeting in its twenty-seventh Ordinary Session at Port Louis, Mauritius, from June 24 to July 3, 1976. The resolution noted:

Having examined in depth the report of the Committee of Coordination for the Liberation of Africa and, in particular, paragraphs 73-74 and 75 relating to the question of the Western Sahara (Doc. CM/755)-(XXVII);

Gravely concerned by the aggravation of the situation prevailing in the Western Sahara;

Recalling the principles and objectives of the OAU Charter and that of the United Nations,

Recalling Resolution 15-15 (XXV) of the United Nations dated December 15, 1960, relating to self-determination and the independence of lands and peoples under foreign domination;

Recalling the resolutions of the OAU relating to the decolonization of the Western Sahara:

1.   Reaffirms the inalienable right of the people of the Western Sahara to self-determination and to national independence in accordance with the Charters of the OAU and the UNO;

2.   Requests the U.N. Secretary-General to pursue his mission so as to allow the Sahrawi people freely to exercise its right to self-determination;

3.   Gives its unconditional support to the just struggle of the Sahrawi people to recover its national rights;

4.   Demands the immediate withdrawal of all foreign occupying forces and the respect of both the territorial integrity of the Western Sahara and the Sovereignty of the Sahrawi people;

5.   Exhorts all parties to the conflict in the Western Sahara to take urgent steps to implement all measures necessary to arrive at a solution acceptable to all

parties and, in particular, to the people of the Western Sahara, in the context of African unity and in the interest of peace, friendship and good neighborliness in the region;
6. Requests the Administrative Secretary-General of the OAU to report at the next session of the OAU Council of Ministers upon the implementation of this present resolution.[48]

This resolution was first discussed and proposed at a ministerial conference in Benin and later at Addis Ababa in 1976. Although the resolution had been supported by a majority of the OAU states, threats by Morocco and Mauritania to quit the OAU if it was adopted effectively blocked its passage. When the Council of Ministers voted to discuss the Port Louis Resolution, Moroccan and Mauritanian delegations walked out of the conference while threatening to quit the OAU if it recognized the SADR. Without specifically recognizing the SADR, the Port Louis Resolution was adopted by twenty-nine votes in favor, two against, ten abstentions, and six absent. The Moroccan and the Mauritanian delegations subsequently left Mauritius in protest. In an attempt to resolve this conflict, on July 5, 1976, Nigeria presented a resolution to the OAU summit calling for an extraordinary summit on the question of the SADR. Mauritanian and Moroccan opposition thwarted every effort to hold such a conference.

Political instability, which led to the overthrow of President Ould Daddah of Mauritania, led to a reversal of policy with respect to the SADR. In 1979, Mauritania officially renounced its claims on the SADR. On being informed of the Mauritanian change of policy over the SADR, Morocco annexed the rest of the SADR. In July 1979, Mauritania joined the African heads of state and government of the OAU meeting in Monrovia in adopting the following resolution:

Having heard the introductory remarks by the outgoing Chairman and the Chairman of the *Ad Hoc* Committee of Heads of State on Western Sahara on the Committee's report on the Question of Western Sahara,
Having discussed the Question of Western Sahara,
Having exhaustively considered the report of its *Ad Hoc* Committee contained in Doc. AHB/93/XVI which included reports of the Subcommittee of the *Ad Hoc* Committee on its mission to Algeria, Mauritania and Morocco and that of the OAU Secretary-General to Spain in the company of the Ambassadors of Mali and Nigeria to Spain,
Considering the fact that all the parties concerned except Morocco agree that the right of self-determination for the people of Sahara has not been fulfilled.
Also considering that the tripartite agreement between Spain, Morocco and Mauritania transferred only administration of the territory to Morocco and Mauritania and not sovereignty,
Aware of the fact that Morocco maintains that the right to self-determination has been exercised by the Sahraouis through the Assembly known as the Djemaa,
Decides the following:
1. The preparation of a proper atmosphere for peace in the area through a general and immediate cease-fire.
2. The exercise of the right of self-determination by the people of Western Sahara in a general and free referendum which will enable them to choose one of the following options:
   a) Total independence
   b) Maintenance of the *Status quo*

3. The convening of a meeting of all the parties concerned including the representative of Western Sahara to request their cooperation for the implementation of this decision;

4. The establishment of a special committee of six OAU Member States composed of Guinea, Liberia, Mali, Nigeria, Sudan and Tanzania, to work out the modalities and to supervise the organization of a referendum with the cooperation of the U.N. on the basis of one person one vote. The special committee shall be chaired by Liberia, the current Chairman of the Organization of African Unity.[49]

With both the OAU and United Nations calling for the recognition of the right of independence of the Sahrawi people, many Africans are now in the process of recognizing the SADR as an independent sovereign African state.

This resolution ignored Morocco's protests and called on the government of Morocco to allow the people of the SADR to determine their own political future. The position of the OAU was later reinforced by the United Nations Committee on Decolonization when in November 1979 it adopted a resolution reaffirming the inalienable right of the people of the SADR to self-determination and independence. The General Assembly adopted this resolution by a vote of eighty-three in favor, five against, and forty-three abstentions. For the first time the Committee on Decolonization recognized Morocco as an expansionistic colonial power and called upon the government of Morocco to end its occupation of the SADR.

Some of the major conflicts that brought United Nations and OAU involvement have been interstate tensions arising from internal conflicts in Rwanda, Burundi, the Democratic Republic of Congo (now Zaire), and Nigeria. The intra- and interstate conflicts in Rwanda and Burundi were characterized by a revolt in 1963 against the Rwandan government by the Batutsi. This was followed by reprisals from the Bahutu majority on the Batutsi people in Rwanda, and in neighboring Burundi, the Bahutu majority overthrew the Batutsi supremacist monarchy which they accused of collaboration in the Bahutu murders in Rwanda. As the civil wars raged between the Bahutu and the Batutsi, the Burundi government requested the secretary-generals of the OAU and the United Nations to mediate in its conflict with Rwanda. After a careful investigation of these conflicts, the United Nations concluded that it was its duty to be as helpful as possible in situations of this kind. Following this development, the UN secretary-general sent his special representative to Rwanda and Burundi and the UNHCR and other pertinent UN agencies to provide emergency assistance to the victims of this conflict. The OAU and the UN diplomatic activities in the two countries contributed to the reduction of the hostilities.

In 1966 the OAU appointed President Mobutu of Zaire to mediate on the Rwanda and Burundi crisis because he had previously signed Joint Agreements on Mutual Security, Trade, and Cultural Affairs (The Kinshasa Agreements). By 1967, President Mobutu had managed to make the two antagonistic governments agree to put an end to their constant plots against each other. At this point, the UN activities became concerned with the work of the UNHCR in Rwanda and Burundi.

After a year of its existence, the OAU became actively involved in the Congo Crisis, which brought into discussion the issue of what roles were the OAU and the United Nations to play in the resolution of the conflict. Also making the situation more difficult to resolve were the presence of European and American mercenaries in the Congo; the intervention of non-African States in Congolese internal affairs; the economic interests of non-African States in Congolese mineral resources; the conflicting ideologies of Congolese leaders and the East-West cold war confrontations; and the appointment of the late Katangan seccessionist leader Moise Tshombe as prime minister of the Congo.

The civil war that had broken out in 1960 had not completely resolved all the bitterness which had developed among the Congolese. When the United Nations pulled its troops out of the Congo in June 1964, fighting erupted again in the Katanga, Kivu, Kwilu, and Orientale provinces. Being unable to cope with the situation, Prime Minister C. Adoula resigned and was succeeded by Moise Tshombe, who claimed that he was the only Congolese leader with the ability to unify the country. African countries were very distressed to see the man they identified with the imperialist and neocolonial interests assume the prime ministership of the Congo. Because of their dislike for Tshombe, some African leaders tried to have him barred from attending the OAU Heads of State Summit Conference in Cairo, Egypt, in July 1964.

Tshombe's recruitment of white mercenaries to fight against his opponents in the Congo escalated their resentment. Apparently frustrated by the activities of the mercenaries in the Congo, the OAU passed Resolution E CM/Res. 7 (IV) on December 21, 1964, which declared:

Deeply concerned by the deteriorating situation in the Democratic Republic of the Congo,

Convinced that the Congo problem would find its best solution within the framework of the OAU,

Conscious of the gravity of the recent Belgo-United States military intervention in the Democratic Republic of the Congo,

1. Takes note of the interim report of the ad hoc Commission;

2. Expresses gratitude and appreciation to the ad hoc Commission; and in particular to its Chairman, His Excellency Mr. Jomo Kenyatta, for their efforts in bringing about national reconciliation in the Democratic Republic of the Congo;

3. Reaffirms in full resolution ECM/Res. 5 (III) of 10 September 1964, and reiterates in particular paragraphs 1, 2, 3, 4, 7, and 8 of said resolution;

4. Requests the ad hoc Commission to continue its mandate in accordance with paragraph 5 of the said resolution, and to ensure that all the measures recommended by the Council for the settlement of the Congolese problem are carried out;

5. Appeals to all Powers who are interfering in the internal affairs of the Democratic Republic of the Congo to cease such interferences in order to enable the Organization of African Unity to work for the achievement of national reconciliation;

6. Appeals to all Member States, especially to the Democratic Republic of the Congo, the Republic of Congo Brazzaville, and the Kingdom of Burundi to cooperate with the ad hoc commission for the successful implementation of its mandate;

7. Requests the ad hoc commission to submit reports as appropriate;

8. Disapproves of the recent foreign military intervention in the Democratic Republic of the Congo, which is disturbing the peace and security of the African continent;

9. Requests the Administrative Secretary-General to continue to provide the Commission with all the necessary assistance to accomplish its mission;

10. Calls upon the Security Council:
   a) to condemn the recent foreign military interventions which have compromised the efforts being made by OAU to secure national reconciliation in the Congo;
   b) to recommend an African solution to the Congo problem;
   c) to recommend to all the Powers concerned that they cooperate with OAU in order to facilitate the solution of the Congolese problem.[50]

Although it was critical of Tshombe, the OAU tried to help in the resolution of the Congo crisis by requesting the Congolese government to stop further recruitment of mercenaries and also to expel those mercenaries who were already in the country. After this, the OAU mediating committee headed by President Jomo Kenyatta held meetings with the parties to the conflict with the hope that the antagonists would be reconciled. Having been unable to resolve the conflict, the OAU committee brought the issue before the United Nations. Meanwhile, the British, the Belgian, and the United States governments invaded the Congo on the pretext that they were rescuing their besieged nationals in the Congolese city of Stanleyville. Immediately after this, the Congolese government requested the UN Security Council to examine what it described as a flagrant interference in its internal affairs by the governments of Ghana, Egypt, the USSR, and the People's Republic of China.[51] As the Security Council responded by condemning all interferences in the domestic affairs of member countries, the OAU and the Tshombe crisis came to an end when the Congolese president (Joseph Kasavubu), expelled Prime Minister Tshombe from office. Not long after this, General Sese Seku Mobutu assumed the presidency of the Congo through a military coup d'etat, and promised to expel all the mercenaries as had previously been stated by the ousted Kasavubu.

As more mercenaries entered the Congo to fight with the dissident groups and bandits, the OAU assembly meeting in Kinshasa, September 11-14 1967, condemned aggression by mercenaries and demanded their immediate departure from the Congo, if necessary with the help of the competent international bodies. Should these mercenaries refuse to be evacuated, the OAU promised help to the Congolese government in its efforts to expel them.[52] Upon the request of President Mobutu the International Committee of the Red Cross commenced to arrange for peaceful evacuation of the mercenaries from the Congo, but they refused to leave. As more mercenaries entered the Congo from Angola, Mobutu requested the Security Council to help. The Security Council only responded by condemning Portugal for allowing its colony of Angola to be used as a springboard for Congolese invasion. Through aid from some of the OAU countries, the mercenaries were bombarded into surrender and immediately thereafter the International Red Cross arranged for the peaceful evacuation of the mercenaries through Rwanda.

Another problem requiring OAU and UN contacts was the Nigerian civil war, which was a result of a bloody military coup d'etat on January 15, 1966. A group of army junior officers (most of them Ibos) waged the coup in which the federal prime minister, Sir Abubakar Tafawa Balewa, was killed. Some of the people killed included the northern region premier, western region premier, the federal minister of finance, and many prominent northern officers and politicians. Following this, Major-General Johnson Aguiyi-Ironsi, an Ibo, took control of the apparatus of government, abolished the federal constitution, declared Nigeria a unitary state, and appointed a majority of Ibos as his advisers. Meanwhile, the disgruntled northern and western Nigerians who regarded the army's overthrow of the legally constituted government as an Ibo attempt to dominate the Nigerian government, retaliated by their own coup d'etat on July 29, 1966, and placed Lieutenant Colonel, later General Yakubu Gowon, a northerner as head of the Nigerian army and government. Attempts to reconcile the Ibos at Aburi, Ghana, failed. The new Ibo leader, Lieutenant Colonel Odumegwu Ojukwu, governor of the eastern region seceded from Nigeria on May 31, 1967, and his region became known as the Republic of Biafra. As a result of this secession, the federal government declared war on the breakaway eastern region (Biafra).

Whereas many of the OAU members wanted the Nigerian civil war resolved within the OAU framework, Nigeria insisted that this could not be possible because it would have been an interference in its (Nigerian) domestic affairs. After much discussion Nigeria finally agreed to let the OAU discuss its civil war. Following its deliberations, the OAU adopted a resolution that condemned secession in any member state and recognized the Nigerian conflict as an internal affair which had to be solved by the Nigerian people.

As the Nigerian crisis could not be discussed at the United Nations without Nigeria's consent, the United Nations authorized its various organs to provide humanitarian services to the victims of the war. With the concurrence of the federal government on August 1, 1968, the United Nations secretary-general appointed his representative to help in the relief and humanitarian services. Such organizations as UNICEF, WFP, UNHCR, and the International Committee of the Red Cross were actively involved in many humanitarian programs. Following the complete decimation of the Biafran army and Ojukwu's escape to the Ivory Coast, the United Nations secretary-general appealed to the Nigerian government to show mercy and kindness to many Ibo secessionists. As observed, the United Nations never had an occasion to discuss the internal affairs of the Nigerian civil war as it had done in the Congo. The OAU support for Nigerian unity contributed to this.

Outside of these major conflicts, the OAU and the United Nations had other incidences to discuss on African states' conflicts. The Ghanaian coup d'etat was one such conflict. After the overthrow of President Kwame Nkrumah by the Ghanaian army, President Sékou Touré of the Republic of Guinea appointed Nkrumah as a copresident of his country. Having done that, President Touré announced that his fifty thousand-man army augmented by additional twenty thousand ex-servicemen would be dispatched to Ghana to assist the people of that country to overthrow the military regime that had deposed Nkrumah's Convention Peoples Party government.[53] In reaction to Touré's statements, the government of Ghana notified the United Nations Security Council of the purported intentions of Guinea to invade Ghana.

While they were en route to the seventh session of the OAU Council of Ministers, the Ghanaian government detained all the members of the Guinean delegation after its plane made an unscheduled landing in Accra. The Ghanaian government explained that its drastic action has been precipitated by the government of Guinea's arrest of Ghana's embassy staff in Conakry, Guinea. Prior to the arrest of the

Guinean delegation, the Ghanaian military junta had demanded the repatriation of Kwame Nkrumah by Guinea. The secretary-general of the United Nations reacted to the Ghana-Guinea conflict by appealing to Ghana to release the Guinean delegation and also by requesting Guinea to allow the International Committee of the Red Cross or any other international organization to investigate whether Ghanaian diplomats in Guinea were indeed political prisoners. Neither Ghana nor Guinea responded affirmatively to the secretary-general's efforts to mediate.

Following the UN's efforts to resolve the conflict the OAU Council of Ministers sent a delegation to Accra and Conakry to mediate and secure the release of all the people detained in either Ghana or Guinea. This negotiating committee of three members from Sierra Leone, Kenya, and the Congo failed to secure the release of the imprisoned, but no evidence was reported that the Ghanaians in Guinea were being kept in that country against their will.[54] It was only after the OAU heads of state met that the emperor of Ethiopia and the presidents of Mali, Liberia, Tanzania, and Egypt exerted pressure on Major-General Joseph Ankrah to release the Guinean delegation.

The OAU and the United Nations also became involved in the Guinea-Ivory Coast conflict of 1966-67, the mysterious invasion of Benin, the South African invasion of Angola, and the Rhodesian military attacks on Zambia and Mozambique. In addition, the United Nations and the OAU have been powerless to resolve numerous other African conflicts, including the Chad-Libya border dispute, the Sudanese-Anya-Nya spearheaded conflict, the Ugandan-Tanzanian war that ended in April, 1979, the 1977 and 1978 civil wars in Zaire, the Libyan-Egyptian miniwar, the 1978 Ethiopian-Somalian war, and the Ethiopian-Eritrean secessionist war.

In evaluating the OAU and its relationship with the United Nations, it is clearly evident that the United Nations had adopted the principle which Berhanykun Andemicael terms as "Try OAU First." This principle is based on Article 52 (2) of the United Nations Charter, which states that "the members of the United Nations entering into such arrangements or constituting such agencies shall make every effort to achieve pacific settlement of local disputes through such regional arrangements or by such regional agencies before referring them to the Security Council."[55] The support for a try OAU first principle is that it eliminates superpower rivalry in the solution of African problems, cold-war confrontation in Africa, and the competition for the establishment of superpowers and great powers clientele states in Africa. By letting the OAU mediate and solve African conflicts, the United Nations is relieved of these responsibilities and can spend more time on other issues.

With respect to the United Nations preference for the OAU to first mediate and try to resolve African conflicts, it can be argued that this approach greatly enhances the stature of the OAU within Africa, the nonaligned states, and in world politics as a whole. Whereas many African states may prefer a United Nations solution to their conflicts, it is becoming clear that the role of the OAU has signficantly increased. It is now common for African countries to talk of an African solution to African problems. Once the OAU takes a stand on particular issues of conflict, these issues are now generally not debated by the General Assembly. Examples of these are OAU support of the Nigerian federal government against secessionist Biafra, OAU support for the Ethiopian war against the Somalian invasion of the Ogaden, OAU support for Ethiopia against Eritrean secession, and the OAU support for the Sudan during the period in which the Anya-Nya movement was engaged in a secessionist war against what it termed Arab domination and oppression of the non-Muslim Africans of the South.

Although there may be rivalry and differences in approaches and styles between the OAU and the United Nations system, but greater cooperation has emerged between these two international organizations in social, political, economic, technical, health, and agricultural solutions of numerous problems and conflicts. Both organizations have tremendous influence on each other; OAU countries are also members of the United Nations. In their role as UN members, the OAU states operate cooperatively with other UN members in fulfilling the objectives of the United Nations. The OAU states are fulfilling the objectives of the UN Charter by participating actively in the Security Council, the General Assembly and its committees, ECOSOC and its specialized agencies, and in the coordination of the entire UN system through the work of the ACC and the office of the secretary-general.

The relationship between the OAU and the UN system has a complicated and a comprehensive formal legal basis. The OAU Charter not only subscribes to the UN Charter but also stresses the necessity of working cooperatively with the United Nations in the pacific settlements of international conflicts. In response to the OAU's adoption of the UN Charter, the United Nations General Assembly adopted by acclamation a resolution on cooperation with the OAU in 1964. The OAU and the UN's legal framework has enabled an easy, mutual, and reciprocal collaboration among the agencies of the two international organizations. The ECA, UNDP, FAO, WHO, UNHCR, ILO, UNICEF, UNITAR, UNCTAD, UNESCO, UNIDO, and other UN specialized agencies work closely with the OAU states and agencies.

The legal framework of relationships between the OAU and the UN system can be taken as an indication that the overlapping members of the two world organizations plan to coordinate their activities and programs. This cooperation will hopefully offer ample opportunities for mutual and reciprocal exchange of ideas and information. Assuming that the OAU and the United Nations will continue to exist side by side, both organizations will have to learn to accept each other's differences and to cooperate more in those areas of mutual interest.

4
Conclusion

The analysis undertaken in the preceding chapters of Africa in the UN system reveals that African states are increasingly extending their participatory roles throughout all the structures, organs, committees, units, and specialized agencies of the UN system. Africans are to be found working in most of the positions in the UN civil service. They work in the General Assembly, ECOSOC and its bodies dealing with coordination, for example, CPC, CDP, ACAST, the governing council of UNDP and ECPC, and the Office of Secretary-General of the United Nations. Under the secretary-general, the office for Inter-Agency Affairs and ECOSOC, the Administrative Committee on Coordination (ACC) is charged with the responsibility of arranging and harmonizing the relationships of the specialized agencies such as the ILO, FAO, UNESCO, WHO, IAEA, ICAO, UPU, ITU, WMO, IMCO, IMF, IBRD or IDA, and IFC. Africans are on the staff of these specialized agencies and participate in all their deliberations.

By participating in the proceedings of the UN organs, committees, and specialized agencies, Africans are now part and parcel of the whole UN system. Africans now share in both the successes and failures of the United Nations. Instead of asking the United Nations to do something for Africa, Africans now initiate programs and pilot passage of resolutions in the appropriate organs and agencies of the UN system with the hope of solving particular African problems. Because of its numerical preponderance in the General Assembly, the OAU caucusing bloc easily marshals enough votes to pass resolutions that are of special interest to Africa. Africa finds it easy to get votes in the General Assembly because of its traditional support from its allies among the LDCs. Support for Africa from its Third World allies usually hovers around problems of decolonization, racism, imperialism, neocolonialism, and underdevelopment.

The work of ECOSOC and some of the specialized agencies of the UN system, such as the WHO, FAO, UNHCR, UNICEF, UNRWA, UNECA, UNESCO, ILO, and UNDP, is normative or ethical. The normative aspect of the work of these agencies is geared toward the elimination of social and economic plight of the LDCs. Commenting on the ethical aspects of the specialized agencies of the UN system,

René Maheu of UNESCO reiterated that in a world that is marked by profound differences–unequal levels of development, diverse cultures, and ideological divergencies–it is the task of these organizations to initiate, foster, and nurture with the lessons of their own experience the frame of mind to conceive, and the determination to organize, international relations in accordance with methods, standards, and ideas which are acceptable to the whole community of man. While constantly referring to concrete situations and questions, which are all rooted in a particular sociohistorical context, the work of these organizations is aimed at promoting a universal way of thinking and strengthening the primacy of such thinking in the minds of men throughout the world by constantly defining the road that lies ahead and their aspirations.[1] Many treaties that seek to improve the socioeconomic conditions have been signed through the initiative of numerous UN specialized agencies. These include treaties on human rights, refugees, narcotics, health, the status of women, slavery, labor conventions, international trade, navigation, transportation and communication, and laws of the seas. As a regulator of the international system, the United Nations and its agencies are trying to establish internationally acceptable norms and standards of harmonizing interstate conduct and cooperation.[2]

Because of their experiences of oppression and racial subjugation, Africans are trying to make the United Nations live up to its obligations of attaining human equality. Africans have constantly reminded fellow UN members that the Charter of the United Nations accords a prominent place in its preamble to fundamental human rights . . . the dignity and worth of a human being . . . social progress, and better standards of life in a world of freedom. Freedom in a broader context is associated with human social welfare. In paragraph 3 of Article 1, of the United Nations Charter, the purpose of general welfare is expected to achieve international cooperation in solving international problems of an economic, social, cultural, or humanitarian character, and in promoting and encouraging respect for human rights and for fundamental freedoms for all without distinction as to race, color, sex, creed, language, or ethnic origin.

The concept of general welfare is subdivided into two main areas: the normative activities concerning human rights, colonization, and racial discrimination, which is of universal application; and the new technical assistance and preinvestment programs to aid the African and other LDCs through the specialized agencies of the UN system. On issues of human rights, decolonization, and racial discrimination, African states have been successful in making the United Nations and its agencies champion the cause for African struggles for national liberation. The General Assembly, the Security Council, specialized agencies of ECOSOC, the intergovernmental organizations and nongovernmental organizations (NGOs), and numerous UN committees have come out in support of human rights and majority rule. By supporting African liberation and recognizing SWAPO, ANC, and PAC, the United Nations has given legitimacy to the ideas of national liberation. In addition to legitimizing African liberation in southern Africa within the international community, the UN agencies, through pressure from their African members, are providing humanitarian, social, economic, technical, and educational aid to the colonized southern Africans.

The activities of the African states in the General Assembly pressured that body to adopt General Assembly Resolution 1541 (XV) of 1960 concerning the Declaration of the Granting of Independence to Colonial Countries and Peoples. For the first time in the existence of the United Nations, a resolution condemning colonialism and calling for decolonization in Africa had become a cardinal principle and an immortalized phrase in the vocabulary of the history of African decolonization. Through the General Assembly and its committees, African states have been able to influence the United Nations system to declare apartheid an international crime against humanity, to condemn racism and colonialism, to impose an economic embargo against Rhodesia, to impose a military embargo against Portugal and South Africa, and to withdraw South Africa's mandate over Namibia. As a result of these African pressures on the UN system, the Western European countries (Britain, Canada, France, United States, and West Germany) prevailed on South Africa to hold discussions leading to majority rule in Namibia. Britain, the United States, and South Africa pressured rebel Prime Minister Ian Smith to agree to African majority rule in Rhodesia, which has since attained independence as Zimbabwe.

African influence in the UN system has not been welcomed by some of th OECD members, many of which have reacted to the African and LDCs' majority in the United Nations by calling it a crisis of confidence. Lord Home (former secretary of state for Foreign Affairs of Britain and later its prime minister) was unusually hostile and critical to the anticolonial stance of the Afro-Asian states:

> Why then, if there is such a universal urge for peace and the machinery to achieve it is ready to hand, is there a crisis of confidence in the United Nations? . . .
> Many of us had foreseen this crisis of confidence. For years the Russians had been frustrating the proper working of the United Nations, but lately a new and dangerous practice had begun to prevail.
> Resolutions have been persistently passed by the Assembly, in particular on colonialism, which could only be described as reckless and careless of peace and security. Everyone has seen the chaos in the Congo and everyone knows that it derives from a premature grant of independence to a country whose people were totally unprepared for their new responsibilities. Yet many Delegates were instructed by their Governments to sponsor and vote for resolutions which could only multiply and magnify chaos in other places.[3]

Lord Home went on to criticize the Third World countries for being against colonialism. To him, Soviet expansionism in Eastern Europe and the worldwide spread of communism were more important than the colonial subjugation of Africans in South Africa, Namibia, Rhodesia, and the Portuguese colonial dependencies in Africa and Asia. It was not only Britain (through the activities of Lord Douglas Home) that was appalled by the anticolonial activities of the African delegates at the United Nations, but the Western colonial powers as well.

Although Britain, France, Portugal, South Africa, and to a lesser extent, the United States, West Germany, and Canada were in most cases antagonistic to the anticolonial activities of African states in the General Assembly, ECOSOC, and its specialized agencies, when it came to protecting their economic and political interests throughout the world, these Western nations had no reservation in requesting African support. When Rhodesia declared its independence from Britain on November 11, 1965, and it appeared as if there was a likelihood of military intervention on behalf of ZANU and ZAPU by the OAU, socialist countries, and their sympathizers, Britain with the support of its allies appealed to OAU states as well as other LDCs to support UN sanctions against Rhodesia as an alternative to a military option. The Western world viewed the objectives of the African revolutionaries and socialists as being directed toward the destabilization of their economic and political strategic interests in southern Africa, the Indian Ocean, and the oil route around Cape Town. The Western antisocialist strategy was invoked in southern Africa after the Portuguese government was overthrown by its army in April 1974. With Marxist MPLA and FRELIMO in power in Angola and Mozambique, the Western capitalist world, concerned over the likelihood of communists winning power through military means in Zimbabwe and Namibia, decided to launch alternative nonrevolutionary approaches to end colonialism in the two territories. Britain, the United States, West Germany, France, and Canada appealed to OAU states to support the objectives of the Geneva Conference in 1976 and the Lancaster Conferences of 1979 aimed at granting majority rule in Zimbabwe through peaceful and constitutional means.

With the increase of African membership in the United Nations, their anticolonial activities at the General Assembly and at meetings of the ECOSOC specialized agencies, and the intensification of guerrilla warfare throughout the 1960s and 1970s, and NGOs and the international community are now actively denouncing colonialism. African embassies, African liberation movements, representatives of Third World countries, socialist parties throughout the world, and NGOs have successfully lobbied against colonialism in Western Europe and in the United States and Canada. Their crusades for human equality, freedom, national liberation, and democracy have successfully convinced Western European countries, including the United States and Canada to support African anticolonial objectives within the UN system. Western nations are presently supporting decolonization in southern Africa not only because they believe in liberty, freedom, democracy, and majority rule, but to reduce the current levels of activities of the USSR within the region and to safeguard their political and strategic interests. For entirely different reasons, the capitalist world, the socialist world, African states, and their Third World allies are now using the UN system to hasten the decolonization process in Namibia and the abrogation of the pernicious apartheid political system of South Africa.

The additional normative aspects of the concept of the welfare of African nations is involved within the entire UN system and concerns both economic and technical assistance to LDCs. The objective of this assistance is to help African states as well as other LDCs raise their standard of living. In quantitative terms, UN aid to Africa is extremely small. Although this may be the case, UN aid to Africa is qualitatively meeting some of the Africans' most basic and elementary social and economic needs. Aid from the UN system to Africa is through programs established to achieve specific developmental objectives. UN committees, organs, and ECOSOC specialized agencies are now established throughout Africa.

Attempts to ameliorate the socioeconomic problems of Africa are prime objectives of the ECA, UNDP, ILO, UNICEF, WHO, FAO, UNICR, UNIDO, UNCTAD, and other agencies. Some of the major objectives of the United Nations and its specialized agencies are geared toward economic development and the redistribution of world resources. The activities of UNCTAD and the ideas of the First and the Second Development Decades address themselves to the problems of economic disparities between the LDCs and the OECD. African states in the United Nations are now reiterating that:

> It is no longer a case of looking at economic development in a narrow sense of the term, or, to put it differently, of becoming oblivious of social factors, political cross-currents, cultural changes and so on. The (strategy) document clearly recognizes that the process of development is a complex whole . . . it looks at the underlying issues from the viewpoint of the world community as a whole. It highlights development as a process in which all members of the world community must play their respective parts.[4]

Recognizing the necessity to narrow the developmental gap between the LDCs and the OECD, the African states began to argue at UNCTAD conferences that additional aid was not adequate. International development means a willingness to look to the total economic relations between the LDCs and OECD. The developmental economic gap between the developing and the developed countries continues to widen. African LDCs continue to be suppliers of raw materials to the OECD. The balance of payment deficits of these countries continue to escalate. The future prospects of improvement in the state of the economics of these countries remain bleak.

Being frustrated about the adverse economic relations between the LDCs and the OECD, the African states, through their participation in UNCTAD III, IV, V and VI, began to call for a New International Economic Order. Throughout the 1960s and 1970s the OAU Council of Ministers and UNECA worked collaboratively in developing economic proposals that were submitted to UNCTAD conferences. The New International Economic Order proposals have been endorsed by the OAU, the Group of 77, and all LDCs. Some of the proposals call for LDCs to exercise effectively their sovereign control over their natural resources, the condemnation of all forms of interference in the right of LDCs to nationalize their industries and natural resources, and development based on the priority needs of nations requiring it. The proposals also called for the OECD to provide developmental aid to LDCs who needed it, and for the African states and other LDCs to cooperate economically more than they were presently doing.

Since African states are part of the UN system, their activities in all United Nations General Assembly committees, ECOSOC and its specialized agencies, and the Secretariat are nothing exceptional. As members of the United Nations, it is the obligation of the African states to participate in the daily operation and maintenance of the UN system. Unlike the Western capitalist and Eastern socialist states, the African states including other LDCs need to participate most in the administration of the United Nations system. African states are, by and large, small powers with minimal influence in world affairs. Their influence as OAU and UN members is maximized within the international community if they work as members of these international organizations. They also look at the United Nations as an international organization that can protect their sovereignty and national interests.

To the African states, the United Nations is an important organization that has political, economic, and technological importance to them. In times of conflict with the superpowers, African states appeal to the United Nations for help. The United Nations also provides a mechanism for African states (minipowers or small states) to participate in the solution of world conflicts and international diplomacy. Not only do small states involve themselves in the preservation of peace and international security, they also engage themselves in reducing and neutralizing hostilities between powerful and small states. Without the United Nations, the major conflicts and issues of the day could be resolved by the superpowers and the great powers over the heads of ministates, which may be affected by the outcome. Without the influence of the international organizations, small African states would increasingly look at themselves as pawns and puppets dependent on the whims and caprices of the great powers and superpowers. As long as African states remain members of the United Nations and continue to operate within the UN system, their role in the preservation of international peace and security will continue to be of great importance to the world community.

The UN system has provided an opportunity for African states to participate in the settlement of international disputes. Africans are involved in settling international disputes through the United Nations Organization as third parties. As third parties, African states have involved themselves in the diplomatic solution of the Israeli-Arab conflict, the Vietnamese war, the Iranian crisis, the Indo-Chinese border conflicts, and others. The approach to the settlement of international disputes, as it has taken shape within the UN system, rests on the principle of conciliation through diplomatic means. Third-party settlement of international disputes in which African states are participating can be analyzed through diplomatic, regulatory, cognitive, legal, and institutional approaches. The table showing the complementary structures of third-party involvement in the settlement of international disputes developed by Vratislav Pechota is illustrative of the roles played by African states. (See Table 29.) The participation of African states in third-party conflicts offers these countries an opportunity to solve world problems. Not only do they solve world problems through diplomatic means but they also reinforce the UN principle of consent. According to the specifications of international law and those of the United Nations,

> "international disputes shall be settled on the basis of the sovereign equaliy and in accordance with the principle of free choice of means" together with its corollary that "the parties shall agree upon such peaceful means as may be appropriate to the circumstances and nature of the dispute" only emphasizes the centrality of this proposition.[5]

Without consenting to international diplomatic mediation or conciliation of a dispute, the roles of third-party states in the peaceful resolution of international conflicts are greatly minimized. Some of the cases in which the United Nations was not successful in mediating area include the Nigerian civil war, the Tanzanian invasion of Uganda, and the recent Iranian and U.S. dispute over American hostages.

The effectiveness of African states in making the United Nations respond to their needs depends on their capability and ability to influence other members of the

Table 29: *Complementary Structures of Third-Party Involvement in the Settlement of Disputes*

Approach	Diplomatic	Regulatory	Cognative	Legal
Role of third party	Compromise seeking	Protective and integrative	Evaluative and prognostic	Interpretive, law-standard-building and quasi-adjudicative
Sources of authority	Political and moral influence	Preponderance of power and influence of the international organ concerned	Objectivity of judgment	Persuasive force of legal norms
Promoting communications and changing perceptions	Contacts to ensure an uninterrupted flow of information and to judge differences in outlook	Diffusion of information using the channels of international organizations; correcting distortions through debate and other means	Promoting debate and assisting the parties in making correct images of reality	Providing common language that signals relevant norms of conduct and indicates procedures to be followed
Means and instruments available	Negotiating skills and techniques	Institutional and procedural facilities of international organs	Methods and techniques of analysis and prediction	Legal techniques, rules, and institutions
Properties of settlement	Acceptability to the parties	Recognition by the international community, including guarantees	Relevance to prevailing and future conditions	Equity and binding nature
Cumulative effect on the outcome of settlement		Effectiveness, durability and rationality		

SOURCE: Vratislav, Pechota, *Complementary Structure of Third Party Settlement of International Disputes: A UNITAR Study* (New York; United Nations Institute for Training and Research, 1971), p. 11.

United Nations to support their positions on a multitude of issues and causes. An authority that depends on influence rather than power has to use that influence with extreme caution. If African states and other LDCs constantly take positions that antagonize and destabilize the interests of the OECD, the result would be a great weakening of the influence of the LDCs within the UN system. The OECD could well react by reducing financial, managerial, and technological contributions to the United Nations and its specialized agencies; resorting to solving international disputes outside the framework of the UN system; and disregarding the United Nations norms of the noninterference in the domestic affairs of sovereign states. If this were to occur, minipowers would have no acceptable international organization to appeal to in case of conflict with either great powers or superpowers. In general, governments favor international action when it promotes their own interests. They resist or ignore pressures from international organizations whose positions and policies are antithetical to their own.[6] Taking this into consideration, African states and other minipowers have to exercise extreme caution in their desire to maintain their present level of influence throughout the United Nations system. The United Nations has no instruments of coercion to enforce its decisions and the United Nations cannot, in most cases, impose settlements on the basis of a majority vote in the General Assembly on unwilling members, whether they are minipowers, great powers, or superpowers.

Although African states are working within the UN system to improve the socioeconomic, medical, and nutritional needs of Africans, they are also concerned with maintaining international peace and security; enacting, codifying, and implementing international treaties and laws; working as UN civil servants in ECOSOC and its specialized agencies, the Office of the Secretary-General, and other various organs; serving in the General Assembly and its various committees; and in resolving international conflicts through mediation. African states are also involved in disarmament, nonproliferation of nuclear weapons, and in trying to lessen the level of economic development gaps between the OECD and LDCs through either the North/South diaglogues or the UNCTAD conferences. These UNCTAD, UNECLA, UNECA, OAU, UNESCAP, and the Group of 77 Conferences, led to the adoption of the New International Economic Order whose objectives were, to narrow the gap of development between the OECD and LDCs, to raise the standard of living of the poverty-stricken masses of the Third World, and to establish a fair exchange value of raw materials between the producers and the industrialists.

Despite the immense contributions African states have made in the daily operation and coordination of the UN system, the need for changes in the structure of the UN system still remains. Although Africans are now members of every organ and agency in the UN system and are making decisions that affect the future of this system, no OAU member nation has a veto in the Security Council. To this extent, African interests are represented by nonpermanent members of the Council. Since Africa has the largest number of states that are UN members Africa should have been given at least a veto in the Security Council. The present Security Council permanent members do not adequately reflect the interests of Africa and South America, the only regions of the world without permanent membership in the Security Council. The fact that the Western world and the OECD are overrepresented in the Security Council accounts for the reason why this Council has vetoed every resolution by the OAU-UN States to expel South Africa from the United Nations. These countries have also vetoed Security Council resolutions to impose total economic sanctions against South Africa despite General Assembly calls for the adoption of such resolutions. If African interests are to be given important considerations in the Security Council, Africa should be allowed to appoint its own representative to the Security Council based on a rotation system as is already being done with respect to the selection of the chairperson of the OAU.

On the whole, whereas the relations between the OAU states and the U.N. system are mutually beneficial to each other, Africa will continue to need assistance from the UN system in decolonization, economic development, modern and sophisticated technical know-how, arbitration and mediation of conflicts among and within African states, the elimination of various forms of deadly and contagious diseases, the redistribution of the wealth of the world under an internationally agreed formula, world disarmament, the peaceful uses of atomic and nuclear energy, and the development of an international control guideline to monitor the disposal of potentially harmful chemical, industrial, and nuclear wastes. The UN system also needs African states for its efficient operation, coordination, and stabilization.

Notes

Chapter 1

1. *"Bandung Conference Communiqué,"* cited by Robert A. Goldwin, Ralph Lerner, and Gerald Sourzh, *Readings in World Politics* (New York: Oxford University Press, 1959), p. 539.
2. Sydney D. Bailey, *The General Assembly of the United Nations: A Study of Procedure and Practice* (New York: Frederick A. Praeger, Publishers, 1966), p. 251.
3. Ibid., p. 142.
4. United Nations, *Basic Facts About the United Nations* (New York: United Nations, 1972), p. 6.
5. Ibid., pp. 7-8.
6. Evan Luard, *The United Nations: How It Works and What It Does* (London: Macmillan & Co., 1979), p. 95.
7. David A. Kay, *The New Nations in the United Nations: 1960-1967* (New York: Columbia University Press, 1970), p. 1.
8. David Horowitz, *From Yalta to Vietnam: American Foreign Policy in the Cold War* (Harmondsworth, Middlesex, England: Penguin Books, 1967), p. 68.
9. Jesse D. Clarkson, *A History of Russia* (New York: Random House, 1969), p. 695.
10. Thomas Hovet, Jr., *Africa in the United Nations* (Evanston, Ill.: Northwestern University Press, 1963), p. 8.
11. G. E. Taylor and B. Cashman, *The New United Nations: A Reappraisal of the United States Policies* (Washington, D.C.: American Enterprise Institute for Public Policy, June 1965), p. 7.
12. Norman A. Graham and Robert S. Jordan, *The International Civil Service: Changing Role and Concepts* (Elmsford, N.Y.: Pergamon Press, 1980), p. 10.
13. Ibid.
14. United Nations General Assembly 1559 (XV) of 1960.
15. United Nations General Assembly Resolution 1852 (XVII) of 1962.
16. Ibid.
17. United Nations General Assembly Resolution 31/26 of 1976.
18. *Summary Records,* October 7, 1977, Meeting of the Fifth Committee (A/C-5/32/SR.11).
19. Y. A. Tandon, *Readings in African International Relations,* vol. 2 (Nairobi: East African Literature Bureau, 1974). See Richard Gardner's analysis of UNCTAD on this point: "The United Nations Conference on Trade and Development," in *The Global Partnership: International Agencies and Economic Development* ed. Richard N. Gardner and Max F. Millikan (New York: Frederick A. Praeger, Publishers, 1968), pp. 99-130. See also Hill, *The United Nations System* (London: Cambridge University Press, 1978).
20. Thomas Hovet, Jr., *Bloc Politics in the United Nations* (Cambridge, Mass.: Harvard University Press, 1960).
21. *United Nations Chronicle,* vol. 2, no. 10 (New York: United Nations, January, 1965), pp. 17-18.
22. Address by His Excellency Mwalimu Julius K. Nyerere, president of the United Republic of Tanzania, to the Fourth Ministerial Meeting of the Group of 77, Arusha, February 12-16, 1979 (Mimeographed by the Ministry of External Affairs of the United Republic of Tanzania).
23. Kwame Nkrumah, *Revolutionary Path* (New York: International Publishers, 1973), p. 126.
24. *The African Voice,* 2 no. 3 (Accra: African Affairs Center, May 1958): 12.

25. *The Ghanaian Times,* December 5, 1960.
26. *The African Voice, 3 no. 4 (Accra: African Affairs Center, September 1964): 10.*
27. *Ibid., p. 11.*

Chapter 2

1. *United Nations, A Trust Betrayed: Namibia* (New York: United Nations, 1974), p.4.
2. Ibid.
3. Permanent Mandates Commission, Minutes III, 325; Session IV OJ V 1412.
4. *League of Nations Official Journal,* twenty-first Assembly, 32-33 (Plenary, 1946).
5. Department of Foreign Affairs, Republic of South Africa, *South West Africa Advisory Opinion, 1971: A Study in International Adjudication* (Cape Town: Transvaal Printers Ltd., 1972), p. 14.
6. League of Nations, Document 1947, p. 20.
7. GAOR, First session (2nd part) Fourth Committee, Part I (Doc. A/123-1), pp. 200-201.
8. *United Nations, A Trust Betrayed: Namibia* (New York: United Nations 1974), p. 4.
9. Ibid., p. 6.
10. General Assembly Resolution 65 (1) December 14, 1946.
11. *United Nations, A Trust Betrayed: Namibia* (New York: United Nations, 1974), p. 6.
12. GAOR Fourth Committee, Annex to the Summary Records of Meetings 1949, (Doc. A/929), pp. 7-8.
13. House of Assembly Debates, vol. 66, col. 1275 (February 1949)
14. GAOR Fourth Committee Annex to the Summary Records of Meetings, pp. 11-12.
15. *United Nations, A Trust Betrayed: Namibia,* p. 9-10.
16. Ibid., pp. 10-11.
17. Ibid., p. 13.
18. Ibid., p. 14.
19. Ibid., pp. 19-20.
20. Report of the Committee on South West Africa Concerning the Implementation of General Assembly Resolutions 1568 XV and 1596 XV, GAOR, Sixteenth Session, Suppl. No, 12A (A/4926), pp. 18-19.
21. Ibid., p. 22.
22. GAOR Sixteenth Session, Fourth Committee, 1, November 2, 1961, Resolution 1702 (XVI).
23. *United Nations, A Trust Betrayed: Namibia,* pp. 25-26.
24. Richard Gibson, *African Liberation Movements: Contemporary Struggles Against White Minority Rule* (London: Oxford University Press, 1972), p. 112.
25. General Assembly Resolutions 2145 (XXI) of October 27, 1966.
26. General Assembly Resolution 2248 (S-V) of May 19, 1967.
27. United Nations: *The United Nations and Decolonization: Highlights of Thirty Years of United Natons Efforts on Behalf of Colonial Countries and Peoples* (New York: United Nations, 1977), p. 24.
28. Security Council Resolution 269 of August 12, 1969.
29. Security Council Resolution 283 of July 29, 1970.
30. Security Council Resolution 301 of October 20, 1971.
31. *United Nations Objective Justice,* vol. 7 no. 2, April/May/June, 1975, p. 30.
32. *Report of the United Nations Council of Namibia,* 1976, vol. 1, p. 67.
33. *Objective Justice,* vol. 7, no. 1, January/February/March, 1975, p. 44.
34. General Assembly/Security Council Document A/31/181-5/12185, August 23, 1976.
35. United Nations Report on the Conference in Support of Peoples of Zimbabwe and Namibia, Mozambique, May 16-21, 1977, p. 6.
36. Report on the Wingspread Conference on Namibia Convened by the Lutheran Council in the U.S.A. and the Johnson Foundation, May 1976, pp. 9-10.
37. *Africa: News and Comment: News Digest and Comment on African Affairs,* 3, no. 5 (October 1977): 7.
38. *Decolonization: Issue on Namibia,* A Publication of the United Nations Department of Political Affairs, Trusteeship and Decolonization, no. 9 (New York: United Nations December, 1977), pp. 66-69.

39. Report of the United Nations Council on Namibia, *General Assembly Official Records:* Ninth Special Session Supplement no. 1 (A/S-9/4) United Nations.

40. Justin Ellis, *Elections in Namibia?* (Nottingham: British Council of Churches and Catholic Institute for International Relations, Russell Press Limited, May 1979), p. 11.

41. Letter dated April 10, 1978, from the representatives of Canada, France, Germany, Federal Republic of Germany, the United Kingdom of Great Britain, and Northern Ireland and United States of America addressed to the president of the Security Council.

42. Security Council Resolution 431, July 27, 1978.

43. United Nations Security Council S/12827, August 29, 1978.

44. Ellis, *Elections in Namibia?*, p. 14.

45. United Nations Security Council, S/128699, September 28, 1978.

46. *United Nations Chronicle,* August-September, 1978, vol. XV, no. 8, p. 20.

47. *United Nations Chronicle,* December 1978, vol. XV, no. 11, pp. 6-7.

48. Ibid., p. 16.

49. Ibid., p. 9.

50. United Nations: *Principle in Torment: The United Nations and Portuguese Administered Territories* (New York: United Nations, 1970), p. 7.

51. Ibid., p. 10.

52. United Nations, *United Nations and Decolonization,* p. 13.

53. General Assembly Resolution 1514 (XV), December 15, 1960.

54. United Nations: *Principle in Torment,* pp. 13-14.

55. United Nations, *United Nations and Decolonization,* p. 21.

56. United Nations Report of Subcommittee I, 1965.

57. Wellington Winter Nyangoni, *United States Foreign Policy and South Africa* (New York: Society for Common Insights Press, 1981), pp. 46-48.

58. Ferreira E. deSousa, *Portuguese Colonialism from South Africa to Europe* (Freiburg, West Germany: Druckerei Horst Ahlbrect, 1972), p. 107.

59. *Financial Mail,* South Africa, August 15, 1969.

60. "Assistance to the Victims of Colonialism and Apartheid in Southern Africa" (United Nations Secretariat for the International Conference of Experts for the Support of Victims of Colonialism and Apartheid in Southern Africa, Oslo, 1973).

61. Wellington Winter Nyangoni, *Ambiguity of National Security Symbols in U.S. Foreign Policy Formulation* (Waltham, Mass.: AAAS Department, Brandeis University, 1979), p. 44.

62. Quoted from the transcript of a speech "With the Honest Intention of Serving the Portuguese People in the Best Way," The Secretaria de Estado da Informacao e Turismo (SNI), Lisbon, 1968, pp. 7-8.

63. M. El-Khawas and B. Cohen, *National Security Study Memorandum 39, Kissinger Study of Southern Africa* (Westport, Conn.: Lawrence Hill and Co., 1976), p. 24.

64. Nyangoni, *United States Foreign Policy and the Republic of South Africa,* p. 36.

65. Ibid., pp. 100-110.

66. *Objective Justice* 6 no. 2 (April/May/June, 1976): 12.

67. United Nations, *United Nations and Decolonization,* p. 29.

68. United Nations Department of Political and Security Affairs, *The Struggle Against Colonialism in Southern Africa* (New York: United Nations, March, 1974), p. 27-28.

69. *Objective Justice,* (October/November/December, 1973): 47.

70. Ibid., p. 31.

71. Wellington Winter Nyangoni, *African Nationalism in Zimbabwe (Rhodesia)* (Washington, D.C.: University Press of America, 1977), p. 73.

72. Ibid., p. 31.

73. United Nations, *United Nations and Decolonization,* p. 18.

74. *African Voice* 3 no. 4 (December 1965): 14.

75. Harold Wilson, *A Personal Record: The Labour Government 1964-1970* (New York: The Atlantic Monthly Press, 1971), p. 25.

76. *OAU, Assembly of Heads of State and Government,* Accra, Ghana (AHG Res. 26 11), October 1965, pp. 40-41.

77. Prime Minister Harold Wilson's speech to the House of Commons on November 11, 1965 (mimeographed).
78. Ibid.
79. OAU-ECM Res. 14 (vi), 15 (vi), and 16 (vi). Addis Ababa, Ethiopia, December 3-5, 1965, pp. 91-92.
80. Wilson, *A Personal Record: The Labour Government, 1964-1970*, pp. 185-86.
81. Ibid., p. 91.
82. Ibid., p. 91.
83. OAU ECM/S, pp. 100-101.
84. United Nations, *United Nations and Decolonization*, p. 21.
85. Nyangoni, *African Nationalism in Zimbabwe*, p. 84-85.
86. T. H. Bingham, Q. C. and S. M. Gray, F.C.A. *Report on the Supply of Petroleum Products to Rhodesia, Foreign and Commonwealth Office* (London: Her Majesty's Stationery Office, 1978), pp. 24-25.
87. *Objective Justice* 5 no. 4 (October/November/December 1973).
88. *News of the World*, September 10, 1978.
89. Bingham, and Gray, *Report on the Supply of Petroleum Products to Rhodesia* p. 3.
90. Martin Bailey, *Oilgate: The Sanctions Scandal* (London: Coronet Books, Hodder and Stoughton, 1979), p. 136.
91. Bingham, and Gray, *Report on the Supply of Petroleum Products to Rhodesia*, pp. 69-70.
92. Ibid., p. 67.
93. Ibid., pp. 79-80.
94. Bailey, *Oilgate: The Sanctions Scandal*, p. 65,
95. Ibid., p. 66.
96. Ibid., p. 67.
97. Bingham, and Gray, *Report on the Supply of Petroleum Products to Rhodesia*, p. iii.
98. U.N. Security Council Official Records, pp. 11-12.
99. Ibid., pp. 12-14.
100. Ibid., pp. 15-17.
101. Nyangoni, *African Nationalism in Zimbabwe*, p. 88.
102. *United Nations and Decolonization*, p. 30.
103. Nyangoni, *African Nationalism in Zimbabwe*, pp. 111-12.
104. *OAU Council of Ministers, Bulletin I*, Dar-es-Salaam, January 8, 1975, p. 2.
105. Pretoria Agreement, Press Release by the governments of the Republic of South Africa and Rhodesia, August 12, 1975 (mimeographed).
106. ANC-Press Release, Lusaka, August 26, 1975 (mimeographed).
107. The Radio and Television Broadcast made by Prime Minister Ian Smith, Salisbury, Rhodesia, September 24, 1976 (mimeographed).
108. *U.N. Chronicle* 15, no. 2 (February 1977): 11.
109. Ibid., p. 19.
110. *OAU Bulletin*, vol. 10, 1977 (New York Office).
111. "U.S., Britain Unveils Plan on Rhodesia," The Sun, *AF Clips U.S. State Department*, p. 1.
112. Rhodesian Constitutional Agreement, March 3, 1978, Salisbury, Rhodesia.
113. OAU-CM Res. 680 (XXX) July 7-18, 1978, Khartoum, Sudan.
114. *Objective Justice*, United Nations Office of Public Information 10, no. 1 (Spring 1978): 8.
115. *U.N. Chronicle* 15, no. 8, (August/September/November, 1978): 22-23.
116. *U.N. Chronicle*, January, 1979, p. 36.
117. Free and Fair? The 1979 Rhodesian Election: A report by observers on behalf of the British Parliamentary Human Rights Group (London: House of Commons, May 1979), p. 19.
118. Julian R. Friedman, "Basic Facts on the Republic of South Africa and the Policy of Apartheid," *Notes and Documents, Centre Against Apartheid: Department of Political and Security Council Affairs* (New York: United Nations, April 1972), p. 1.
119. Ibid., p. 1.

120.   Special Reports of the Special Committee Against Apartheid, *General Assembly Official Records: Thirty-first Session Supplement* no. 22A (A/31/22/Add. 1 to 3) (New York: United Nations, 1977), p. 11.

121.   Thomas Hovet, Jr., *Africa in the United Nations* (Evanston, Northwestern University Press, 1963), p. 20.

122.   Immanuel Wallerstein, *Africa: The Politics of Unity* (New York: Random House, Vintage Books, 1967), p. 26.

123.   Ibid., p. 30.

124.   Kader Asmal, "International Law and the Liquidation of Apartheid," *Notes and Documents Centre Against Apartheid: Department of Political and Security Affairs* (New York: United Nations, 1978), p. 2.

125.   For details read Rosalyn Higgins, *The Development of International Law Through the Political Organs of the United Nations* (London: Oxford University Press, 1963).

126.   Asmal, "International Law and the Liquidation of Apartheid," p. 2.

127.   Robert Kashta, "General Assembly and Security Council Resolutions Against Apartheid," *United Nations, Centre Against Apartheid: Department of Political and Security Council Affairs* (New York: United Nations No. 13/76, 76-13608 June 1976), pp. 3-4.

128.   Ibid., p. 6.

129.   Ibid., pp. 8-10.

130.   Ibid., pp. 11-12.

131.   Ibid., p. 15.

132.   Ibid., p. 15.

133.   U.N. Security Council Resolution 392, June 1976 (mimeographed).

134.   *U.N. News Bulletin:* Text of Security Council Arms Embargo Resolution (New York: United Nations, November 4, 1977).

135.   African National Congress, "The Nuclear Axis," *Sechaba* 9 no. 11/12 (November/December, 1975): 12.

136.   Ibid., p. 65.

137.   Committee on International Relations, House of Representatives, *United States-South Africa Reltions: Nuclear Cooperation,* Hearings, June 30 and July 12, 1977, Washington, D.C., 1978, p. 26.

138.   Ann Seidman and Neva Makgelta, "Activities of Transnational Corporations in the Republic of South Africa," U.N. *Centre Against Apartheid,* May, 1978, p. 1.

139.   *United States-South African Relations: Nuclear Cooperation Hearings,* 1976, p. 78.

140.   Ibid., p. 31.

141.   Western Massachusetts Association of Concerned African Scholars, *U.S. Military Involvement in Southern Africa,* Boston: 1978, p. 189.

142.   African National Congress, *Sechaba,* p. 12.

143.   *United States-South African Relations: Nuclear Cooperation Hearings,* 1976, p. 72.

144.   African National Congress, *Sechaba,* p. 23-24.

145.   Christian Concern for Southern Africa, *ICI in South Africa* (London: 1977), p. 18.

146.   UN Notes and Documents, *Center Against Apartheid, Department of Political and Security Affairs* (New York: United Nations, October 1973), p. 1.

147.   Ibid., p. 14.

148.   Committee on International Relations, House of Representatives and Committee on Governmental Affairs, U.S. Senate, *Nuclear Proliferation Factbook,* Washington, D.C., 1977, p. 43.

149.   *United States-South African Relations: Nuclear Cooperation Hearings,* 1976, p. 237.

150.   United Nations, *Centre Against Apartheid: Department of Political and Security Council Affairs,* August 1976, p. 3.

151.   Report of the Ad Hoc Committee on the drafting of an International Convention Against Apartheid in Sports. General Assembly Official Records: Thirty-second Session Supplement no. 36 (A/32/36) (New York: United Nations, 1977), p. 1.

152.   Ibid., p. 6.

153.   *United Nations Center Against Apartheid,* April 1976, p. 7.

154.   Ibid., p. 9.

155.   Ibid., p. 17.

156. *Objective Justice* 9, no. 1 (Spring 1977): 37-38.
157. Ibid., p. 45.
158. *Objective Justice* no. 4 (October/November/December, 1973): 21-22.
159. David A. Kay, *The New Nations at the United Nations* (New York: Columbia University Press, 1970), p. 67.
160. Asmal, "International Law and the Liquidation of Apartheid," p. 11.
161. Judge Ammoun in the Namibia Opinion, *ICJ Reports*, 1971, p. 50.
162. *The Barcelona Traction Case* (Second Phase), ICJ Reports, 1970, p. 3.
163. Yassin El-Ayouty, "Legitimization of National Liberation: The United Nations and Southern Africa" (Issue No. 4, 1972), p. 43.
164. James Mittelman, "Collective Decolonization and the U.N. Committee of 24," unpublished paper for the International Studies Association, February 19-22, 1975, p. 9.

Chapter 3

1. General Assembly, Official Records (GAOR) Sixteenth Session 1020th Plenary Meeting, October 2, 1961, p. 177 (A/PV. 1020).
2. Romain Yakemtchouk, "The OAU and International Law," *The Organization of African Unity After Ten Years: Comparative Perspectives,* (ed.) El-Ayouty, Yassin, (New York: Praeger Publishers, 1975), pp. 84-85.
3. *United Nations Chronicle* (New York: United Nations, January 1965), pp. 17-18.
4. Yakemtchouk, "The OAU and International Law," p. 86.
5. Ibid., p. 86.
6. *Organization of African Unity, Assembly of Heads of State Resolutions and Declarations of Ordinary and Extra-Ordinary Sessions* (Resolution CIAS/Plen. 2/Rev. 2 C Addis Ababa, Ethiopia, May 1963), p. 10.
7. Zdenek Cervenka, *The Organization of African Unity* (New York: Frederick A. Praeger Publishers, 1969), p. 102.
8. *Charter of the Organization of African Unity,* Article XXVI, Addis Ababa, Ethiopia, May 1963.
9. *United Nations Chronicle,* January 1979, p. 27.
10. *The Spark* (Bureau of African Affairs, Accra, Ghana) November 5, 1965.
11. *Organization of African Unity: Council of Ministers Resolutions of Ordinary and Extra-Ordinary Sessions* (The General Secretariat of the Organization of African Unity, Addis Ababa, 1969), p. 7.
12. Ibid., p. 65.
13. Ibid., p. 81.
14. UNITAR Document Service no. 1, *A New International Economic Order,* Selected Documents, 1974-1975, vol. 1, p. 20.
15. Ibid., pp. 20-21.
16. OAU-ECOS Resolution, ECOS/16/Res. 2 (I), December 13, 1963.
17. General Assembly Resolution 1710 (XVI). *The United Nations Development Decade: A Programme for International Economic-Cooperation,* vol. 1 (New York: United Nations, December 19, 1961).
18. General Assembly Resolution 1785 (XVII) of December 8, 1962.
19. General Assembly Resolution 1155 (XXII) of November 26, 1957, and ECO SOC Resolution 67 IA (XXV), April 29, 1958.
20. UNCTAD I Geneva. Final Act and Recommendations Adopted by the Conference at Its Thirty-fifth Plenary Meeting (Geneva, June 15, 1964), p. 9.
21. Report of the Preparatory Meeting, Algiers, October 7-15, 1967 (U.N. Doc. E/CN. 14/UNCTAD II/PM/2/Rev. 2, November 20, 1967), Annex III and Appendix to Annex III. Circulated as Group of 77 Doc. mm. 77/I/Misc. 9.
22. Ibid., p. 2.
23. Lusaka Declaration on Peace, Independence Development, Cooperation and Democratization of Internal Relations on the Non-Aligned Conference of the Heads of States, September 10, 1970, pp. 3-8.

24. Lusaka Declarations on Non-Alignment and Economic Progress Adopted by the Third Conference of Heads of States or Governments of Non-Aligned Countries, Lusaka 10, 1970, pp. 84-85.

25. Ibid., p. 86.

26. UN GAOR, 25th Session, Annexes vol. 1, Agenda Item 42, Doc. A/8074, pp. 2-3.

27. For details, see the Declaration on Industrialization in Africa, 1973, Adopted by the Second Conference of African Ministers of Industry, Cairo, December 23, 1973, pp. 1-11.

28. Summary of the Algerian Proposal on Raw Materials and Development at the Sixth Special Session of the UN General Assembly, 1974, New York, April 10, 1974.

29. Statement made by Gamarir Corea, secretary-general of UNCTAD at the Second Plenary Meeting of the Conference of Economic Cooperation Among Developing Countries (CECADC). "Annex VI in Report of the UNCECADC" (A/C-2/31/7 Add I, 1976), Annex VI, p. 8.

30. UNESCO: Conference of Ministers of African Member States Responsible for the Application of Science and Technology to Development, Dakar, 1974. Final Report (UNESCO) 1970; Doc. SC/MD40, p. 10.

31. United Nations, World Plan of Action, African Regional Plan for the Application of Science and Technology to Development, United Nations Economic Commission for Africa, E/CN. 14/579, 1973, p. 1.

32. UN Document, DP/L.241, December 10, 1971.

33. Economic Commission for Africa, Annual Report vol. 2, Programme of Work and Priorities for 1978 and 1979. Supplement 740.7, United Nations, New York, 1977, p. 3.

34. Office of Public Information: Basic Facts about the United Nations (New York: United Nations Document 72-13869, October 1972), p. 74.

35. Organization of African Unity, Council of Ministers, Resolutions of Ordinary and Extra-Ordinary Sessions, Kinshasa, Congo, 1967, p. 130.

36. Fifth African Regional Conference Report of the Director General: Position of African Countries regarding the ratification of International Labor Standards. Abidjan, September-October 1977.

37. Ibid., pp. 35-36.

38. Ibid., p. 2.

39. Article I, A(2) of the United Nations' Convention Relating to the Status of Refugees and Paragraph 6 of the Statute UNHCR.

40. Organization of African Unity, Council of Ministers Resolutions, pp. 107-8.

41. OAU Council of Ministers Resolution CM/Res. 547-593 (XXIX), Libreville, Gabon, June 23-July 3, 1977.

42. Final Report on Conference on the Legal, Economic, and Social Aspects of the African Refugee Problems, Sponsored UNECA, the OAU and the Dag Hammerskjold Foundation, December 1968.

43. United Nations General Assembly Resolution 2750 (XXV), 17, December 1970.

44. CM/Res. (XXIX) Resolution on the Law of the Sea. The Council of Ministers of the Organization of African Unity meeting in its Twenty-ninth Ordinary Session in Libreville, Gabon, June 23-July 3, 1977, pp. 1-2.

45. Organization of African Unity, Charter of the Organization, p. 17.

46. Le Monde, October 1963.

47. Organization of African Unity. Charter of the Organization, pp. 10-11.

48. The Council of Ministers of the Organization of African Unity Meeting in its Twenty-seventh Ordinary Session at Port-Louis, Mauritius, June 24-July 3, 1976.

49. OAU Summit Conference of the Heads of State and Government Resolution AHG/Doc. 114 (XVI) Monrovia, Liberia, July 17-20, 1979, pp. 1-2.

50. U.N. Press Release SG/SM/5, February 7, 1964.

51. Organization of African Unity, Council of Ministers Resolutions p. 55.

52. Official Records of Security Council, Nineteenth Year Supplement, October/December 1964, Document B/6096, December 9, 1964, pp. 217-18.

53. OAU Assembly Resolution AHG/49 (IV), September 11-14, 1967.

54. Kessing's Contemporary Archives, vol. 15, 1965-1966 (March 12-19, 1966): 21738.

55. Ibid., vol. 15, 1965-1966, November 26, 1966 and December 3, 1966, p. 21738.

Chapter 4

1. René Maheu, *The United Nations System and UNESCO in the Grand Larousse* (Paris: Encyclopedique, 1970), Article 13, paragraph I.

2. Madhi Elmandjra, *The United Nations System: An Analysis* (London: Faber and Faber, 1973), p. 287.

3. Lord Home, "The United Nations: The Crisis of Confidence," *Emerging Africa in World Affairs*, (ed.) David K. Marvin (San Francisco: Chandler Publishing Company, 1965), p. 252.

4. Quoted from a statement made by Talwar, Omprakash, a senior economist in the U.N. Secretariat, New York, November 18, 1970.

5. See Declaration on Principles of International Law Concerning Friendly Relations and Cooperation among States in accordance with the Charter of the United Nations General Assembly Resolution 2625 (XXV) of October 24, 1960.

6. Evan Luard, *The United Nations: How It Works and What It Does* (London: Macmillan & Co., 1979), p. 257.

Bibliography

Books

Adam, H. *Modernizing Racial Domination: The Dynamics of South African Politics.* Berkeley: University of California Press, 1971.

Andemicael, Berhanykum. *The OAU and the UN: Relations Between the Organization of African Unity and the United Nations.* New York: Africana Publishing Company, 1976.

Anstee, Margaret J. *The Administration of International Development Aid.* Syracuse, N.Y.: Syracuse Unitersity Press: The Maxwell School of Citizenship and Public Affairs, 1969.

Arnold, Guy. *Sanctions Against Rhodesia, 1965 to 1972.* London: The African Bureau, 1972.

——and Baldwin, Alan. *Rhodesia: Token Sanctions or Economic Warfare.* London: The Africa Bureau, 1972.

Arrighi, Giovanni. *The Political Economy of Rhodesia.* The Hague: Mouton, 1967.

The Atlantic Council Working Group on the United Nations. *The Future of the United Nations: A Strategy for Likeminded Nations.* Boulder, Colo.: Westview Press, 1977.

Aufricht, Hans. *The International Monetary Fund: Legal, Bases, Structure Functions.* London: Stevens and Sons 1964.

Ayouty, Yassin (Ed.), *The Organization of African Unity After Ten Years: Comparative Perspectives* (New York: Praeger Publishers, 1975) pp. 84-85.

Bailey, Martin. *Oilgate: The Sanctions Scandal.* London: Coronet Books, Hodder and Stoughton, 1979.

Bailey, Sydney, D. *The General Assembly of the United Nations: A Study of Procedure and Practice.* New York: Frederick A. Prager Publishers, 1966.

——*The Secretariat of the United Nations.* New York: Frederick A. Praeger, 1964.

Barber, James. *South Africa's Foreign Policy, 1945-1970.* London: Oxford University Press, 1973.

Barros, James. *Betrayal from Within.* New Haven: Yale University Press, 1970.

——*The United Nations: Past, Present and Future.* New York: The Free Press, 1972.

Battacharya, A. K. *Foreign Trade and International Development* Lexington, Mass.: Lexington Books, 1976.

Bennett A. LeRoy. *International Organizations, Principles and Issues.* Englewood Cliffs, N.J.: Prentice-Hall, 1977.

Bhagwati, J. H., ed. *The New International Economic Order: The North-South Debate.* Cambridge: M.I.T. Press, 1977.

264

Bingham T.H., Q.C., and Gray, S.M.F.C.A. *Report on the Supply of Petroleum Products to Rhodesia.* London: *Foreign and Commonwealth Office.* London: Her Majesty's Stationery Office, 1978.

Brooks, H. C., and El-Youty, Y., eds. *Refugees of the Sahara: An African Dilemma.* Westport, Conn.: Negro University Press, 1970.

Bull, Theodore. *Rhodesia: Crisis of Color.* Chicago: Quadrangle Books, 1968.

Carter, A. M., and O'Meara, eds. *Southern Africa: The Continuing Crisis.* Bloomington: Indiana University Press, 1979.

Cervenka, Zdenek. *The Organization of African Unity.* New York: Frederick A. Praeger Publishers, 1969.

Clarkson, Jesse D. *A History of Russia.* New York: Random House, 1969.

Clements, Frank. *Rhodesia: A Study of the Deterioration of a White Society.* New York: Frederick A. Praeger Publishers, 1969.

Cline, W. R., *International Monetary Reform and the Developing Countries.* Washington, D.C.: The Brookings Institution, 1977.

Cockran, Gail-Maryse. *Vorster's Foreign Policy.* Pretoria: Academica, 1970.

Cox, Robert W., ed. *International Organization: World Politics.* London: Macmillan & Co., 1969.

——ed. *The Politics of International Organizations: Studies in Multilateral Social and Economic Agencies.* New York: Praeger Publishers, 1969.

——, and Jacobson, Harold, eds. *The Anatomy of Influence: Decision Making in International Organization.* New Haven: Yale University Press, 1973.

Coyle, David Cushman. *The United Nations and How It Works.* New York: Columbia University Press, 1969.

Cronje S.; Ling, M.; and Cronje, G. *Lonrho: Portrait of a Multinational.* Harmondsworth, Middlesex, England: Penguin Books Ltd., 1976.

Curtin, T.R.C., and Murray, David. *Economic Sanctions and Rhodesia.* London: Institute of Inernational Affairs, 1967.

Dam, Kenneth W. *The GATT: Law and International Economic Organization.* Chicago: University of Chicago Press, 1970.

deSousa, Ferreira E. *Portuguese Colonialism from South Africa to Europe.* Freiburg, West Germany: Druckerei Horst Albrecht, 1972.

Dolman, A. J. and Eltinger, J. V., eds. *Partners in Tomorrow: Strategies for a New International Economic Order.* New York: Sunrise Books, E.P. Dutton, 1978.

Doob, L., ed. *Resolving Conflict in Africa: The Fermeda Workshop.* New Haven and London: Yale University Press, 1970.

Doxey, Margaret P. *Economic Sanctions and International Enforcement.* New York: Oxford University Press, 1971.

Drysdale, J. *The Somali Dispute.* London: Pall Mall Press, 1964.

Dugard, John. *Human Rights and the South African Legal Order.* Princeton: Princeton University Press, 1978.

——. *The South West Africa/Namibia Dispute: Documents and Scholarly Writings on the Controversy Between South Africa and the United Nations.* Berkeley: California University Press, 1973.

El-Ayouty, Y. *The United Nations and Decolonization: The Role of Afro-Asia.* The Hague: Martinus Nijhoff, 1971.

——, and Brooks, H. C. *Africa and International Organizations.* The Hague: Martinus Nijhoff, 1973.

——. *The Organization of African Unity After Ten Years: Comparative Persepctives.* New York: Praeger Publishers, 1975.

El-Khawas, M., and Cohen, B. *National Security Study Memorandum 39, Kissinger Study of Southern Africa.* Westport, Conn.: Lawrence Hill and Co., 1976.

Ellis, Justin. *Elections in Namibia?* Nottingham: British Council of Churches and Catholic Institute for International Relations, Russell Press Limited, 1979.

Elmandjra, Mahdi. *The United Nations System: An Analysis.* London: Faber and Faber Limited, 1973.

Etzioni, Minerva M, *The Majority of One: Towards a Theory of Regional Compatibility.* Beverly Hills, Calif.: Sage Publications, 1970.

Falk, R.A. *A Study of Future Worlds.* New York: The Free Press, 1975.

——, and Black, C. E., eds. *The Future of the International Legal Order,* Vol, 1. Princeton, N.J.: Princeton Unversity Press, 1969.

First, R.; Steel, J.; and Gurney, C. *The South African Connection: Western Investments in Apartheid.* London: Temple Smith, 1972.

Fisher, Roger. *International Conflict for Beginners.* New York: Harper & Row, 1969.

Foot, Wilder, ed. *Servants of Peace: A Selection of the Speeches and Statements* of Dag Hammarskjold. New York: Harper & Row, 1963.

Fosdick, Raymond. *Letters on the League of Nations.* Princeton: Princeton University Press 1966.

Freeman J., ed. *World Future: The Great Debate.* Sussex: University of Sussex, 1977.

Friedman, Julian R. "Basic Facts on the Republic of South Africa," *Notes and Documents, Centre Against Apartheid: Department of Political and Security Affairs* New York: United Nations, April, 1972.

Gardner, Richard, ed. *The Future of the United Nations Secretariat.* New York: United Nations Institute for Training and Research and the Institute on Man and Science, 1972.

——, and Millikan, Max, F., eds. *The Global Partnership: International Agencies and Economic Development.* New York: Frederick A. Praeger Publishers, 1968.

Gibson, Richard. *African Liberation Movements.* New York: Oxford University Press, 1972.

Goldwin, Robert A., Lerner, Ralph; and Sourzh, Gerald. *Readings in World Politics.* New York: Oxford University Press, 1959.

Good, Robert C. *U.D.I.: The International Politics of the Rhodesian Rebellion.* Princeton: Princeton University Press, 1973.

Goodrich, Leyland M. *The United Nations in a Changing World.* New York: Columbia University Pres, 1974.

——, Hambro E., and Simons A. *A Charter of the United Nations: Commentary and Documents, Third and Revised Edition.* New York and London: Columbia University Press, 1969.

——, and Kay, David A., eds. *International Organization: Politics and Process.* Madison: University of Wisconsin Press, 1973.

Goodspeed, Stephen S. *The Nature and Function of International Organization.* New York: Oxford University Press, 1959.

Goodwin G. *Race Relations and the United Nations.* London: Pall Mall Press Limited, 1966.

Gordenker, Leon, ed. *The United Nations in International Politics.* Princeton, N.J.: Princeton University Press, 1971.

——. *The United Nations Secretary General and the Maintenance of Peace*. New York: Columbia University Press, 1967.

Gosovic, Branislav. *UNCTAD: Conflict and Compromise*. Leiden, Holland: A. W. Sythoff, 1972.

Graham, Norman A., and Jordan, Robert S. *The International Civil Service: Changing Role and Concepts*. Elmsford, N.Y.: Pergamon Press, 1980.

Gregg, Robert W., and Barkun, Michael. *The United Nations System and Its Functions: Selected Readings*. Princeton, N.J.: Van Nostrand Company, 1968.

Grundy, Kenneth W. *Confrontation and Accommodation in Southern Africa: The Limits of Independence*. Berkeley, Calif.: University of California Press, 1973.

——. *Guerrilla Struggle in Africa: An Analysis and Preview*. New York: Grossman Publishers, 1971.

Haas, E. B.; Butterworth, R. L.; and Nye, J. S. *Conflict Management by International Organizatons*. Morristown, N.J.: General Learning Press, 1972.

Hammarskjold, Dag. *The International Civil Servant in Law and in Fact, A Lecture Delivered to the Congress on 30 May 1961*. Oxford: The Clarendon Press, 1961.

Hance, William, Kuper, Leo, McKay, Vernon and Murger, Edwin. *Southern Africa and the Unied States*. New York and London: Columbia University Press, 1968.

Hansen, Roger D. *Beyond the North-South Stalemate*. New York: McGraw-Hill Book Company, 1979.

Hargas, Kamal. *U.N. Conference on Trade and Development: A Case in U.N. Diplomacy*. New York: Praeger Publishers, 1965.

Hawden, J. A., and Kaufmann, J. *How United Nations Decisions are Made*. New York: Oceana Publishers, 1962.

Hazlewood, Arthur, ed. *African Integration: Economic Integration: The East African Experiene*. London: Heinemann, 1975.

——, ed. *African Integration and Disintegration: Case Studies in Economic and Political Union*. London: Oxford University Press, 1967.

Hazzard, Shirley. *Defeat of an Ideal: A Study of the Self-Destruction of the United Nations*. Boston: Atlantic Monthly Press, 1973.

Higgins, Rosalyn. *The Development of International Law Through the Political Organs of the United Nations*. London: Oxford University Press, 1963.

Hill, Martin. *The United Nations System: Coordinating Its Economic and Social Work: A Study Prepared Under the Auspices of the United Nations Institute for Training and Research (UNITAR)*. London: Cambridge University Press, 1978.

Hoagland, J. *Civilizations in Conflict*. Boston: Houghton, Mifflin Company, 1972.

Hoole, Francis W. *Politics and Budgeting in the World Health Organization*. Bloomington: Indiana University Press, 1976.

Hopkins E., and Krorten A. *Equality of Opportunity and Treatment for Women in the ILO: A Study Sponsored by ILO Staff Union*. Geneva, 1976.

Horowitz, David. *From Yalta to Vietnam: American Foreign Policy in the Cold War*. (Harmondsworth, Middlesex, England: Penguin Books, 1967.

Hovet, Jr., Thomas. *Africa in the United Nations*. Evanston, Illinois: Northwestern University Press, 1963.

——. *Bloc Politics in the United Nations*. Cambridge, Mass.: Harvard University Press, 1960.

Howard, Ellis C. *The Origin, Structure and Working of the League of Nations*. London: Allen and Unwin, 1928.

Jacobson, H. K. *The USSR and the UN's Economic and Social Activities*. Indiana: University of Notre Dame Press, 1963.

Jansen, G. H. *Nonalignment and the Afro-Asian States.* New York: Praeger Publishers, 1966.

Jeffries, Sir James J. *The Colonial Empire and Its Civil Service.* Cambirdge: Cambridge University Press, 1938.

Jenks, C. Wilfred. *The World Beyond the Charter.* London: Allen and Unwin, 1969.

Johnson, H. *Economic Policies Towards Less Developed Countries.* New York: Praeger Publishers, 1975.

Jordan, Robert S., ed. *International Administration: Its Evolution and Contemporary Applications.* New York: Oxford University Press, 1971.

——. *Multintational Cooperation: Economic, Social and Scientific Development.* New York: Oxford University Press, 1972.

——. *The NATO International Staff/Secretariat, 1952-1957: A Study in International Administration.* London: Oxford University Press, 1967.

Kader, Asmal, "International Law and the Liquidation of Apartheid," *Notes and Documents Centre Against Apartheid: Department of Political and Security Affairs* (New York: United Nations, 1978).

Kapungu, L. T. *Rhodesia: The Struggle for Freedom.* Maryknoll, New York: Orbis Books, 1974.

——, *The United Nations and Economic Sanctions Against Rhodesia.* Lexington, Mass. D. C. Heath and Company, 1973.

Robert Kashta. "General Assembly and Security Council Resolutions Against Apartheid." *United Nations, Centre Against Apartheid: Department of Political and Consular Affairs* New York: United Nations, no, 13/76, 76-13608 June 1976, pp.3-4

Kay, David A. *The New Nations in the United Nations: 1960-1967.* New York: Columbia Univesity Press, 1970.

Keenleyside, Hughs L. *International Aid: A Summary with Special Reference to Programmes of the United Nations.* Toronto: McClelland and Stewart, 1966.

Kimche, David. *The Afro-Asian Movement: Ideology and Foreign Policy of the Third World.* New York: Halsted Press, 1976.

Lake, Anthony. *The Tar Baby Option: American Policy Toward Southern Rhodesia.* New York: Columbia University Press, 1976.

Langrod, Georges. *The International Civil Service.* Dobbs Ferry, N.Y.: Macmillan Press, 1954.

Laslo E., Baker Jr.; R., Eisenberg E.; and Raman V. *The Objectives of the New International Economic Order.* New York: Pergamon Press, 1979.

——; Lozoya J.; Bhattacharya, A. K.; Estevez J.; Green R., and Raman V. *The Obstacles to the New International Economic Order.* New York: Pergamon Press, 1980.

Laves, Walter H. C., and Thompson, Charles A. *UNESCO: Purpose, Progress, Prospects* Bloomington: Indiana University Press, 1957.

Legum, Colin. *After Angola: The War Over Southern Africa.* New York: Africana Publishing Company, 1975.

——. *Pan-Africanism: A Short Political Guide.* New York: Frederick A. Praeger, 1965.

——. *Southern Africa: The Secret Diplomacy of Détente.* New York: Africana Publishing Company, 1975.

Leiss, A. C., ed. *Apartheid and United Nations Collective Measures.* New York: Carnegie Endowment for International Peace, 1965.

Lemarchand, R. *Rwanda and Burundi.* New York: Praeger Publishers, 1970.

Lewis, Arthur W. *The Evolution of the International Economic Order.* Princeton, N.J.: Princeton University Press, 1977.

Lie, Trygve. *In the Cause of Peace* (New York: Macmillan Press, 1954).

Lozoya, Jorge and Cuadra, Hector. *Africa, The Middle East and the New International Economic Order.* New York: Pergamon Press, 1980.

Luard, Evan, ed. *Conflict and Peace in the Modern International System.* Boston: Little Brown, 1968.

— ed. *The Evolution of International Organizations.* London: Thames and Hudson, 1966.

—. *International Agencies: The Emerging Framework of Interdependence.* Dobbs Ferry, New York: Oceana Publications, 1977.

—. *The United Nations: How It Works and What It Does.* London: Macmillan & Co., 1979.

Maheu, René. *The United Nations System and UNESCO in the Grand Larousse.* Paris: Encyclopedique, 1970.

Mangone, Gerard J. *A Short History of International Organization.* New York: McGraw-Hill 1954.

—, ed. *United Nations Administration of Economic and Social Programs.* New York: Columbia University Press, 1966.

Marcum, John. *The Angolan Revolution Volume I 1950-1962.* Cambridge, Mass.: M.I.T. Press, 1978.

Marshall, Charles B. *Crisis Over Rhodesia: A Skeptical View.* Baltimore: The John Hopkins University Press, 1967.

Marvin, David K., ed. *Emerging Africa in World Affairs.* San Francisco: Chandler Publishing Company, 1965.

Mazrui, A. A. *Africa's International Relations: The Diplomacy of Dependency and Change.* Boulder, Colorado: Westview Press, 1979.

—. *On Heroes and Uhuru-Worship: Essays on Independent Africa.* London: Longman Group Limited, 1967.

—. *Towards a Pax Africana: A Study of Ideology and Ambition.* Chicago: University of Chicago Press, 1967.

—, and Patel, Hasu H. *Africa in World Affairs* New York: The Third Press, 1973.

Meadows, D., and Meadows, H. *The Limits of Growth.* London: Universe Books, 1972.

Mellor, John W. *The New Economics of Growth.* Ithaca, N.Y.: Cornell University Press, 1976.

Mennes, L.B.M. *Planning Economic Integration Among Developing Countries.* Rotterdam: University Press, 1973.

Meron, Theodor. *The United Nations Secretariat: The Rules and the Practice.* Lexington, Mass.: Lexington Books, 1977.

Metrowich, F. R. *Rhodesia: The Birth of a Nation.* Pretoria: Africa Institute of South Africa, 1969.

Mezerik, A. G., ed. *Rhodesia and the United Nations.* New York: International Review Service, 1966.

Minter, W. *Portuguese Africa and the West.* London: Penguin Books, 1972.

Mitrany, David, ed. *A Working Peace System.* Chicago: Quadrangle Books, 1966.

Moats, Helen M. *The Secretariat of the League of Nations: International Civil Service or Diplomatic Conference.* Chicago: University of Chicago Press, 1939.

Morse, Edward L. *Modernization and the Transportation of International Relations.* New York: The Free Press, 1976.

Mortimer, Robert A. *The Third World Coalition in International Politics.* New York: Praeger Publishers, 1980.

Mtshali, B. V. *Rhodesia: Background to Conflict.* London: Leslie Frewin, 1968.

Mutharika, B. W. T. *Toward Multinational Economic Corporation in Africa.* New York: Frederick A. Praeger Publishers, 1972.

Nicholas, Herbert. *The United Nations As a Political Institution* (5th Edition). London: Oxford University Press, 1975.

Nicol, Davidson, and Croke, Margaret, eds. *The United Nations and Decision-Making: The Role of Women,* Volumes I and II. New York: UNITAR, 1978.

Nkrumah, Kwame. *Consciencism: Philosophy and Ideology for Decolonization.* New York: Monthly Review Press, 1964.

——. *Dark Days in Ghana.* New York: International Publishers, 1968.

——. *Neocolonialism: The Last Stage of Imperialism.* New York: International Publishers, 1965.

——. *Revolutionary Path.* New York: International Publishers, 1973.

Nolutshungu, Sam C. *South Africa: A Study in Ideology and Foreign Policy.* New York: Africana Publishers, 1975.

Nyangoni, Wellington W. *African Nationalism in Zimbabwe (Rhodesia).* Washington, D.C.: University Press of America, 1977.

——. *Ambiguities of National Security Symbols in U.S. Foreign Policy Formulation.* Waltham, Mass.: AAAS Department, Brandeis University, 1979.

——. *The O.E.C.D. and Western Mining Multinational Corporations in the Republic of South Africa.* Washington, D.C.: University Press of America, 1982.

——. *United States Foreign Policy and South Africa.* New York: The New World Research Committee of the Society for Common Insights Inc., S.C.I. Press and The African Institute for the Study of Human Values, Accra, Ghana, 1981.

Packenham, R. A. *Liberal America and the Third World.* Princeton University Press, 1973.

Padelford, Norman J., and Goodrich, Leyland M., eds. *The United Nations in the Balance.* New York: Praeger Publishers, 1955.

Panshofen-Wertheimer, Egon F. *The International Secretariat.* Washington, D.C.: Carnegie Endowment for International Peace, 1945.

Park, Y. S. *Oil Money and the World Economy.* Chicago: Wilton House, 1975.

Potholm, C.P., and Dale R., eds. *Southern Africa in Perspective: Essays in Regional Politics.* New York: The Free Press, 1972.

Rathore, N. A. *In Defense of the International Civil Service: Statements and Submissions.* New York: United Nations (Litho), 1973.

Renninger, John P. *Multinational Cooperation for Development in West Africa.* Elmsford, N.Y.: Pergamon Press, 1979.

Rosenthal, Albert H. *Administration in the Establishment of UNESCO.* Washington, D.C.: U.S. Department of State, 1948.

Roskill, Stephen. *Hankey, Man of Secrets.* London: Collins, 1970.

Rothstein, R., *Planning Prediction and Policy-Making in Foreign Affairs.* Boston: Little Brown, 1972.

Sachs, Moshe Y., ed. *The United Nations: A Handbook on the United Nations. Its Structure, History, Purposes, Activities and Agencies.* New York: John Wiley & Sons, Worldmark Press, Ltd., 1977.

Sampson, A. *The Arms Bazaar.* Baltimore: Penguin Books, 1978.

Sauvant, Karl P., ed. *Changing Priorities on the International Agenda: The New International Economic Order.* Elmsford, N.Y.: Pergamon Press, 1980.

——. *The Group of 77: Evolution, Structure, Organization.* New York: Oceana Publications, Inc., 1981.

——, and Hasenpflug, H., eds. *The New International Economic Order: Confrontation or Cooperation Between North and South.* Boulder, Colorado: Westview Press, 1978.

Sharp, Walter R. *Field Administration in the United Nations System.* New York: Frederick A. Praeger Publishers, 1961.

Spence, J. E. *Republic Under Pressure: A Study of South African Policy.* London: Oxford University Press, 1965.

Stoessinger, J. *Financing the United Nations.* Washington, D.C.: Brookings Institutuion, 1964.

Strack, Harry R. *Sanctions: The Case of Rhodesia.* Syracuse, N.Y.: Syracuse University Press, 1978.

Sutcliffe, Robert B. *Sanctions Against Rhodesia.* London: Africa Bureau, 1966.

Szalai, Alexander. *The Situation of Women in the United Nations.* New York: UNITAR, 1973.

Tandon, Y. A. *Readings in African International Relations,* vol. 1. Nairobi: East African Literature Bureau, 1972.

——. *Readings in African International Relations,* vol. 2. Nairobi: East African Literature Bureau, 1974.

Taylor, G. E., and Cashman, B. *The New United Nations: A Reappraisal of the United States Policies.* Washington, D.C.: American Enterprise Institute for Public Policy, June 1965.

Thant, U. *Toward World Peace.* New York: Yoseloff Publishers, 1964.

Touval, S. *The Boundary Politics of Independent Africa.* Cambridge, Mass.: Harvard University Press, 1972.

Townley, Ralph. *The U.N.: A View from Within.* New York: Charles Scribner's Sons, 1968.

Wallerstein, I. *Africa: The Politics of Unity.* New York: Random House, Vintage Books, 1967.

Western Massachusetts Association of Concerned African Scholars, *U.S. Military Involvement in Southern Africa.* Boston: South End Press, 1978.

Wilson, Harold. *A Personal Record: The Labour Government 1964-1970.* Boston: Little Brown, 1971.

Woronoff, J. *Organizing African Unity.* Metuchen, N.J.: The Scarecrow Press, 1970.

Wriggins, Howard, and Bock, Edwin A. *The Status of the United Nations Secretariat.* New York: Woodrow Wilson Foundation, 1954.

Zartman, William I. *International Relations in Africa.* Englewood Cliffs, N.J.: Prentice-Hall, 1966.

Public Documents

1. Organization of African Unity: *Charter of the Organization of African Unity: Protocol of the Commission of Mediation, Conciliation and Arbitration.* (Con.1-73), Addis Ababa, May 1963.

2. United Nations Economic and Social Council: Commission on Transnational Corporations Intergovernmental Working Group of the -- on the Code of Conduct (First Session); *Transnational Corporations: Material Relevant to the Formulation of Conduct* (76-27398) A report of the Secretariat, United Nations, New York, January 10-14, 1977.

3. United Nations Economic Commission for Africa. *Industrial Development in Africa* (ID/CONF.1/RBP/1) United Nations Publications, New York, 1967.

4.   United Nations Department of Economic and Special Affairs: *Multinational Corporations in World Development* (ST/ECA/190), United Nations Publications, New York, 1973.

5.   United Nations Economic and Social Council: *Report of the Secretariat on Transnational Corporations: Activities of Transnational Corporations in Southern Africa: Impact on Financial and Social Structures* (78-05257), United Nations, New York, March 16, 1978.

6.   Security Council Official Records: *Eleventh Report of the Security Council Committee Established in Pursuance of Resolution 253 (1968) Concerning the Question of Southern Rhodesia:* Thirty-fourth Year, Special Supplement 1 no. 2, (S/13000), United Nations, New York, January 11, 1979.

7.   United Nations Centre on Transnational Corporations: *Survey of Research on Transnational Corporations* (ST/CTC/3), United Nations Publication, New York, 1977.

8.   Office of the U.N. Secretary General. *United Nations Cocoa Conference, 1975* (TD/COCOA.4/10), United Nations, New York, 1976.

9.   General Assembly Official Records: *Report of the Security Council: Thirty First Session,* Supplement no. 2 (A/31/2), United Nations, New York, June 6,-June 15, 1976.

10.   General Assembly Official Records. *Report of the Committee on Relations with the Host Country, Thirtieth Session,* Supplement no. 26 (A/10026), United Nations, New York, 1975.

11.   United Nations Economic and Social Council. *Transnational Corporations in World Development: A Re-examination* (78-05492). United Nations Commission on Transnational Corporations, Fourth Session, New York, May 15-26, 1978.

12.   United Nations Centre on Transnational Corporations: *The Activities of Transnational Coporations in the Industrial, Mining and Military Sectors of Southern Africa* (ST/CTC/12), United Nations Publications, New York, 1980.

13.   United Nations Department of Economic and Social Affairs. *Petroleum Co-operation Among Developing Countries:* Proceedings of the United Nations Meeting on Cooperation Among Developing Countries, Geneva, November 10-20, 1975 (ST/ESA/57), United Nations Publications, New York, 1977.

14.   *National Treatment for Foreign Controlled Enterprises Established in O.E.C.D. Countries* (O.E.C.D., Paris Cedex, 1978).

15.   United Nations Economic Commission for Africa, *Annual Report* (E/CN.14/683/Add.1), United Nations Publications, New York; 1977.

16.   United Nations Office of Public Information. *The United Nations and Decolonization: Highlights of Thirty Years of United Nations Efforts on Behalf of Colonial Countries and Peoples* (OP1/573-76-36167), United Nations Publications, New York, January 1977.

17.   Report on the Wingspread Conference on Namibia, Convened by the Lutheran Council in the U.S.A. and the Johnson Foundation, May 1976. Report prepared by Edward C. May, Director, Office on World Community, Lutheran Council in the U.S.A.

18.   Government of the Republic of South Africa. *Commission of Enquiry Into South West African Affairs, 1962-63.* Odendaal Report, Pretoria, 1964.

19.   Permanent Mission of Nigeria to the United Nations, *Nigeria in the United Nations, 1976,* United Nations, New York, 1977.

20.   United Nations Department of Political and Security Council Affairs, Unit on Apartheid. *Foreign Investment in the Republic of South Africa* (ST/PSCA/SER.A/6), United Nations, New York, 1968.

21.   United Nations Economic Commission for Africa/FAO: *Agricultural Economics Bulletin for Africa* (E/CN.14/AGREB/13), United Nations Publication, New York, 1971.

22.   United Nations Department of Political and Security Council Affairs, Unit on Apartheid: *Foreign Investment in the Republic of South Africa* (ST/PSCA/SER. A/11), United Nations Publications, New York, 1970.

23.   United Nations Department of Economic and Social Affairs. *The Acquisition of Technology from Multinational Corporations by Developing Countries* (ST/ESA/12), United Nations Publications, New York, 1974.

24.   United Nations, Department of Political and Security Council Affairs, Centre Against Apartheid: *The Campaign Against Bank Loans for Apartheid:* A Statement made before the Special Committee on Apartheid on June 6, 1979.

25.   United Nations Department of Political and Security Council Affairs, Centre Against Apartheid. *Life and Labor in Transnational Enterprises in South Africa* (Information No. 25/80) A paper presented by John Gaetsewe, secretary-general of the South African Congress of Trade Unions (SACTU) to the United Nation's Symposium on Transnational Corporations in South Africa and Namibia held in London from November 6 to 7, 1980.

26.   United Nations Department of Political and Security Council Affairs, Centre Against Apartheid. *International Seminar on the Role of Transnational Corporations in South Africa* (Sem.2/79) A paper presented by Vella Dillay, member of the Executive of the British Anti-Apartheid Movement and Chairman of its International Unit at the request of the Special Committee Against Apartheid in London on November 2-4, 1979.

27.   United Nations Department of Political and Security Affairs, Centre Against Apartheid. *Role of Transnational Mining Corporations in the Plunder of South Africa's Mineral Resources* (Sem. 3/79) A paper presented by Greg Lanning to the International Seminar on the Role of Transnational Corporations in South Africa held in London from November 2 to 4, 1979.

28.   United Nations Department of Political and Security Council Affairs, Centre Against Apartheid. *Secret Collaboration of the West with South Africa* (no. 32/78). A statement made by Mr. Sean MacBride on May 30, 1978, at a seminar on South Africa's Military Buildup and Nuclear Plans held under the auspices of the Special Committee Against Apartheid.

29.   United Nations Department of Political and Security Council Affairs, Centre Against Apartheid: *Acts of Aggression Perpetrated by South Africa Against the People's Republic of Angola* (2/81). A report of the International Mission of Inquiry published at the request of the Special Committee Against Apartheid, New York, January 1981.

30.   United Nations Department of Political and Security Council Affairs, Centre Against Apartheid: *Activities of Transnational Corporations in South Africa* (9/78): A paper prepared by Dr. Ann W. Seidman and Mrs. Neva Makgetla and published at the request of the Special Committee Against Apartheid, New York, May 1978.

31.   United Nations Economic and Social Council. *Decade for Action to Combat Racism and Racial Discrimination* (81-02374). A report of the secretary-general prepared for the First Regular Session of the General Assembly, 1981.

32.   United Nations Department of Political and Security Council Affairs, Special Committee Against Apartheid: *Report of the World Conference for Action Against Apartheid*, Lagos, 22-26 August, 1977. (A/CONF. 91/9 (Vol. II), United Nations Publications, New York, 1977.

33.   United Nations Economic and Social Council. *Activities of Transnational Corporations in Southern Africa: Impact on Financial and Social Structures* (E/C.10/39). A report of the Secretariat, New York, March 16, 1978.

34.   United Nations Department of Political and Security Council Affairs, Unit on Apartheid. *Military and Police Forces in the Republic of South Africa* (ST/PSCA/SER. A/3), United Nations, New York, 1967.

35.   United Nations Security Council: Letter dated 27 January 1976 from the permanent representative of South Africa to the United Nations Addressed to the secretary-general (S/11948/Add. I), United Nations, New York, 1976.

36.   United Nations Office of Public Information. *A Principle in Torment: The United Nations and Southern Rhodesia,* United Nations, New York, 1969.

37.   United Nations General Assembly: *Provisional Verbatim Record of the Thirty-first Meeting* (77-72183/A), United Nations, New York, October 12, 1977.

38.   United Nations General Assembly: *Provisional Verbatim Record of the Twenty-second Meeting* (77-72189/A), United Nations, New York, October 13, 1977.

39.   United Nations General Assembly: *Provisional Verbatim Record of the Twenty-seventh Meeting* (77-72159/A), United Nations, New York, October 10, 1977.

40.   United Nations General Assembly: *Provisional Verbatim Record of the Thirtieth Meeting* (77-72177/A), United Nations, New York, October 12, 1977.

41.   United Nations General Assembly: *Provisional Verbatim Record of the Thirteenth Meeting* (77-72075/A), United Nations, New York, September 29, 1977.

42.   United Nations General Assembly: *Provisional Verbatim Record of the Twenty-first Meetng* (77-72123/A), United Nations, New York, October 5, 1977.

43.   United Nations General Assembly: *Provisional Verbatim Record of the Twenty-third Meeting* (77-72135/A), United Nations, New York, October 6, 1977.

44.   United Nations General Assembly: *Provisional Verbatim Record of the Eighteenth Meeting* (76-70105/A), United Nations, New York, October 5, 1976.

45.   United Nations General Assembly: *Provisional Verbatim Record of the Fifteenth Meeting* (76-70087/A), United Nations, New York, October 4, 1976.

46.   United Nations Security Council: *Provisional Verbatim Record of the Nine Hundred and Forty-fourth Meeting* (76-81371/A), United Nations, New York, July 27, 1976.

47.   United Nations Security Council: *Provisional Verbatim Record of the Nine Hundred and Fourth Meeting* (76-81171/A), United Nations, New York, March 30, 1976.

48.   General Assembly Official Records: Thirty-third Session. Supplement No. 29 (A/33/29): *Report of the Adhoc Committee on the Indian Ocean,* United Nations, New York, 1978.

49.   United Nations Department of Political and Security Council Affairs-Centre Against Apartheid: *Basic Facts on the Republic of South Africa and the Policy of Apartheid* (ST/DSCA/SER.A/14), United Nations, New York, 1978.

50.   United Nations Conference on Trade and Development: *Dominant Positions of Market Power of Transnational Corporations: Use of the Transfer Pricing Mechanism* (ID/B/C.2/167, United Nations, New York, 1978.

51.   *Another Blanket: Report on an Investigation into the Migrant Situation,* June 1976. The Agency for Industrial Mission, Morija and Roma, Lesotho, June 1976.

52.   *The Namibians of South West Africa: Report Number 19: Minority Rights Group.* Prepared by Peter Fraenkel, Benjamin Franklin House, Carver Street, London.

53.   United Nations Food and Agricultural Organization: *An Analysis of an FAO Survey of Post Harvest Food Losses in Developing Countries* (AGPP: MISC/27), United Nations, Rome, 1977.

54.   Official Records of the United Nations: *Third United Nations Conference on the Law of the Sea, Volume III:* Informal Negotiating Text (Documents A/CONF.62/WP.10 AND ADD 1), United Nations, New York, May 23-July 15, 1977.

55.   United Nations Department of Political and Security Council Affairs, Unit on Apartheid: *Industrialization, Foreign Capital and Forced Labor in South Africa* (ST.PSCA/SER. A/10), United Nations, New York, 1970.

56.   United Nations International Labor Organization: Report of the Director-General, Parts I and II: *Position of African Countries Regarding the Ratification and Implementation of International Labor Standards:* Fifth African Regional Conference, Abidjan, September-October 1977. ILO Office, Geneva, 1977.

Resolutions

1.   Organization of African Unity, Council of Ministers: Resolutions and Declarations of the Seventh Ordinary Session (CM/Res. 241 (XVII), CM/Res. 258 (XVII), CM/St.5 (XVII) and CM/St. 6 (XVII)), Addis Ababa, June 15-19, 1971.

2.   Organization of African Unity, Council of Ministers: Resolutions of the Eighteenth Ordinary Session (CM/Res. 259 (VIII) and CM/Res. 265 (XVIII)), Addis Ababa, February 14-19, 1972.

3.   Organization of African Unity, Council of Ministers: Resolutions of the Nineteenth Ordinary Session (CM/Res. 266 (XIX) and CM/Res. 291 (XIX)), Rabat, June 12-15, 1972.

4.   Organization of African Unity, Council of Ministers: Resolutions and Statement of the Twentieth Ordinary Session (CM/Res. 290 (XX), CM/Res. 297 (XX) and CM/St. 8 (XX)), Addis Ababa, February 5-9, 1973.

5.   Organization of African Unity, Council of Ministers: Resolutions and Statements of the Twenty-first Ordinary Session (CM/Res. 298 (XXI), CM/Res. 316 (XXI) CM/St. 9 (XXI) and CM/St. 11 (XXI)), Addis Ababa, May 17-24, 1973.

6.   Organization of African Unity, Assembly of Heads of State and Government: Resolutions and Declarations of Ordinary and Extra-Ordinary Sessions, 1963-1969.

7.   Organization of African Unity, Council of Ministers: Resolutions of Ordinary and Extra Ordinary Sessions, 1963 to 1969.

8.   Organization of African Unity, Council of Ministers: Resolutions and Declarations of the Fourteenth Ordinary Sessions (CM/Res. 20 (XIV) CM/Res. 218 (XIV) and CM/St. 3 (XIV)), Addis Ababa, February/March 1970.

9.   Organization of African Unity, Council of Ministers: Resolutions and Declaration of the Fifteenth Ordinary Session (CM/Res. 219 (XV), CM/Res. 237 (XV) and CM/St. 4 (XV)), Addis Ababa, August 1970.

10.   Organization of African Unity, Council of Ministers: Resolutions of the Sixteenth Ordinary Session (CM/Res. 238 (XVI) and CM/Res. 240 (XVI)), Addis Ababa, February/June 1971.

11.   Organization of African Unity, Council of Ministers: Resolutions of the Twenty-third Ordinary Session (CM/Res. 332 (XXIII), CM/Res. 336 (XXIII) CM/Res. 339 (XXIII), CM/Res. 340 (XXIII), CM/Res. 341 (XXIII), CM/Res. 342 (XXIII) CM/Res. 344 (XXIII), CM/Res. 347 (XXIII), CM/Res. 348 (XXIII), CM/Res. 349 (XXIII), CM/Res. 350 (XXIII), CM/Res. 351 (XXIII), CM/Res. 352 (XXIII), CM/Res. 354 (XXIII), CM/Res. 363 (XXIII), CM/Res. 364 (XXIII), CM/St. 13 (XXIII)), Mogadishu, Somalia, June 6-15, 1974.

12.   Organization of African Unity, Council of Ministers: Resolutions of the Twenty-second Ordinary Session (CM/Res. 317 (XXII) and CM/Res. 331 (XXII)), Kampala, Uganda, April 1-4, 1974.

13.   Organization of African Unity, Assembly of Heads of State and Government: Resolutions and Declarations of the Eighth Extra-Ordinary Session (A.H.S.G./Res. 19-21/Rev. 1 (VIII) and A.H.S.G./St. 1 (VIII)), Mogadishu, June 12-15, 1974.

14.   Organization of African Unity, Council of Ministers: Resolutions of the Twenty-fourth Ordinary Session (CM/Res. 389 (XXIV), CM/Res. 390 (XXIV), CM/Res. 391 (XXIV), CM/Res. 392 (XXIV), CM/Res. 393 (XXIV), CM/Res. 395 (XXIV), CM/Res. 398 (XXIV), CM/Res. 399 (XXIV), CM/Res. 403 (XXIV), CM/Res. 412 (XXIV), CM/Res. 413 (XXIV), CM/Res. 416 (XXIV)), Addis Ababa, February 13-21, 1975.

15.   Organization of African Unity, Council of Ministers: Resolutions of the Twenty-fifth Ordinary Session (CM/Res. 419 (XXV), CM/Res. 420 (XXV), CM/Res. 421 (XXV), CM/Res. 422 (XXV), CM/Res. 428 (XXV), CM/Res. 429 (XXV), CM/Res. 430 (XXV), CM/Res. 433 (XXV), and CM/Res. 435 (XXV)).

16.   Organization of African Unity, Council of Ministers: Resolutions of the Twenty-seventh Ordinary Session (CM/Res. 473-525 (XXVII)), Port Louis, Mauritius, June 24-July 3, 1976.

17.   Organization of African Unity, Assembly of Heads of State and Government: Resolutions of the Thirteenth Ordinary Session (A.H.S.A./Res. 79-83 (XIII)), Port Louis, Mauritius, July 2-6, 1976.

18.   Organization of African Unity, Council of Ministers: Resolutions of the Twenty-ninth Ordinary Session (CM/Res. 547-593 (XXIX)), Libreville, Gabon. June 23-July 3, 1977.

19.   Organization of African Unity, Council of Ministers: Resolutions of the Twenty-eighth Session (CM/Res. 525-543 (XXVIII)), Lomé, Togo, February 21-28, 1977.

20.   Organization of African Unity, Assembly of Heads of State and Government: Declarations and Resolutions of the Sixteenth Ordinary Session (AHG/St. 3 (XVI), AHG/St. 4 (XVI), AHG/Res. 96-98 (XVI)), Monrovia, Liberia, July 17-21, 1979.

21.   Organization of African Unity, Assembly of Heads of State and Government: Decisions of the Sixteenth Ordinary Session (AHG/Dec. 111-AHG/Dec. 117 (XVI)), Monrovia, Liberia, July 17-20, 1979.

22.   Organization of African Unity, Council of Ministers: Resolution of the Thirty-third Ordinary Session (CM/Res. 717-765 (XXXIII)), Monrovia, Liberia, July 6-20, 1979.

23.   Organization of African Unity, Council of Ministers: Resolutions of the Thirty-first Ordinary Session (CM/Res. 620-680 (XXXI)), Khartoum, Democratic Republic of the Sudan, July 7-18, 1978.

24.   United Nations Office of Information: *The United Nations and Decolonization: Highlights of Thirty Years of United Nations Efforts on Behalf of Colonial Countries and Peoples*, United Nations, New York, 1977.

Journals, Magazines, and Periodicals

American Economic Review, 1980-1982
International Organization, 1976-1982
IOSA Bulletin, 1980-1981
The Middle East, 1978-1982
African Mirror, 1980-1982
New African, 1980-1982
African Business, 1980-1981
Africa Now, 1980-1981
South: The Third World Magazine, 1981-1982
The Courier: The European Community—Africa, Caribbean, Pacific, 1975-1981
Objective: Justice, 1970-1982
Issue, 1970-1981
South Africa/Namibia Update, 1977-1980
Black Scholar, 1972-1980
Africa: The International Business, Economic and Political Magazine, 1973-1981
Africa Woman, 1979-1981
Southern Africa, 1972-1981
United Nations Chronicle, 1970-1982
The New African Observer, 1982
Third World Diplomacy, 1982
Africa Confidential, 1972-1978
Pan-African Notes, 1972-1976
Africa Report, 1969-1981
To the Point International, 1971-1978
UNITAR News, 1975-1982

Foreign Affairs, April 1976
International Review of Administrative Sciences 1959-1980
League of Nations Official Journal, 1946
The African Communist, 1976-1980
United Nations News Bulletins, 1976-1981
Review of African Political Economy, 1975-1981
Sechaba, 1975-1981
Africa Today, 1970-1981
Counter Spy, 1981-1982
West Africa, 1965-1981
Monthly Review, 1974-1981
UFAHAMU, 1973-1981

Index

278